Siberia and the Soviet Far East

Siberia and the Soviet Far East
Strategic Dimensions in
Multinational Perspective

Edited by RODGER SWEARINGEN

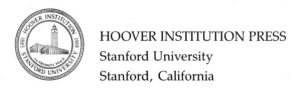

HOOVER INSTITUTION PRESS
Stanford University
Stanford, California

Hoover Press Publication 336

First printing, 1987
Manufactured in the United States of America
91 90 89 88 87   9 8 7 6 5 4 3 2 1

Library of Congress Cataloging in Publication Data
Siberia and the Soviet Far East.

    Includes bibliographies and index.
    1. Siberia (R.S.F.S.R.)—Economic conditions.
2. Soviet Far East (R.S.F.S.R.)—Economic conditions.
3. Siberia (R.S.F.S.R.)—Foreign economic relations.
4. Soviet Far East (R.S.F.S.R.)—Foreign economic
relations.   I. Swearingen, Rodger, 1923–
HC337.R852S5269   1987   330.957'085   86-21388
ISBN 0-8179-8361-9
ISBN 0-8179-8362-7 (pbk.)

Design by Elizabeth F. Gehman

to Darlene

Contents

RODGER SWEARINGEN
Foreword

The striking development in so many arenas—communications, economy, energy, commerce, and military—of that vast Soviet region east of the Urals, largely during the past decade and a half, serves to dramatize the Soviet Union's metamorphosis from a European to a world power. Still, except for the gas pipeline controversy, a few romantic stories centered on the legendary Trans-Siberian and the new BAM railways, and such shocking incidents as the Soviet shootdown of Korean Air Lines passenger flight 007, the Siberian story rarely finds its way into the Western press. Indeed, for every book or major article on Siberia published in the West during the past ten years, perhaps fifty have appeared on China, Japan, and Korea. To most Americans, the region of Siberia and the Soviet Far East remains a vast, frozen wasteland—remote in miles, distant in relevance, and inhospitable to vacation travel, academic research and field work, or normal business pursuits.

To be sure, Khabarovsk is not Paris; nor Nakhodka, London or Tokyo. Yet for a certain group of Western scholars, research specialists, dogged business types, and adventurous travelers, the region has a curious appeal, a vitality and fascination all its own. Moreover, beyond the often exaggerated Soviet claims and systemic economic shortcomings—or perhaps because of them—serious Western analysts (as well as a number of Soviet authors) see the area as the key to the economic and strategic future of the Soviet Union.

Among the several significant volumes on the subject published during the past decade, two may be characterized as emerging contemporary classics. They are *Siberia Today and Tomorrow* (1975) by Violet Conolly, formerly of the British Foreign Office and the "dean" of Western specialists on the subject, and *Gateway to Siberian Resources: BAM* (1977) by Theodore Shabad and Victor Mote, both geographers and university professors. *The Kuril Islands: Russo-Japanese Frontiers in the Pacific* (1974) by John J. Stephan remains the best study of that important dimension of the subject. Four other substantial recent titles in English also merit special attention: *Siberian Development and East*

Asia (1981), by Allen Whiting; *Regional Studies for Planning and Projecting: The Siberian Experience* (Novosibirsk, 1981), edited by A. B. Aganbegian, with contributions by some twenty Soviet specialists, each treating a particular dimension (contemporary Soviet work on the subject is reviewed in some detail by Patricia Polansky in her bibliographic profile at the end of this volume); *The Soviet Economy in the 1980s: Problems and Prospects* (2 vols., 1982), edited by John Hardt of the Library of Congress; and *Soviet Natural Resources and the World Economy* (1983), edited by Robert G. Jensen, Theodore Shabad, and Arthur Wright.

A further comment on the "state of the research art" emerges from the data developed in my own analysis of two series of computer printouts covering the period from March 1950 to March 1983: 14 databases, 1,800 entries, and 470 pages. While there was some inevitable overlap, the following pattern reflecting the nature of Western specialization on the region emerged (to the extent, that is, that disciplines could be identified):

Geographers	27
Geologists	25
Journalists	22
Oceanographers/ Fisheries specialists	18
Economists (economic development)	16
Historians	12
Geophysicists	12
Engineers/ Petroleum engineers	10
Biologists/ Ecologists	7
Military analysts	7
Political scientists	
(International Relations)	7
Anthropologists	6

After five visits to the Soviet Union (the most recent during the summer of 1986) and a number of years of intensive research and consultation in Moscow, Siberia, and the Soviet Far East, and at research centers and with academic and governmental specialists in Europe and East Asia, I became increasingly convinced that the kind of research and analysis appropriate to the broad-gauged international and security problems of the mid-1980s ranged beyond the capabilities of a single author. The research-analysis frame of reference employed in this volume is thus multilingual, interdisciplinary (or at least multidisciplinary), and multinational. This eclectic, representative approach may also be seen in the political spectrum of the authors' viewpoints: from moderate to tough-line to somewhere in between. Moreover, the perspectives developed from long professional association with government and industry, also demanded inclusion of such author-contributors if the volume were to achieve the desired scope, depth, and practical relevance.

Finally, our splendid British, Canadian, German, Japanese, and American multinational, multidisciplinary, and multiprofessional team would clearly have preferred to have had a Soviet colleague, perhaps from the Novosibirsk center. However, despite my persistent efforts and correspondence, that did not prove feasible. This volume is, nonetheless, replete with substantial documentation, translations, and quotations from Soviet sources. Accordingly, the various Soviet perspectives of Moscow, Novosibirsk, and elsewhere on many of these critical issues are carefully and appropriately reflected and analyzed.

Acknowledgments

To Ross Berkes, good friend and long-term, former director of the School of International Relations at USC—without whose kindness, support, and confidence this book would not have been written—I owe a special debt of gratitude. The good offices of Claude Buss, Richard Staar, and Ramon Myers of the Hoover Institution and Robert Scalapino of Berkeley have also been professionally invaluable. Richard Burress and John Moore of the Hoover Institution were most encouraging and instrumental in the final decision to publish this volume.

Support for the research, travel, and conference process essential to the production of the manuscript came, over the years, from a number of quarters: Deans John Schutz and Paul Bohannan of USC provided encouragement, funds, and timely sabbatical leaves for research and field work in Siberia, Europe, and the Far East. Michael Fry, director of our School of International Relations, has throughout the planning, research, and editing process, been most generous with his time and resources. The East Asian Studies Center at USC also provided supplementary support for a trip to Japan.

Earlier support for travel and a month of research in the Soviet Union came from the International Research and Exchanges Board (IREX) in New York (with special appreciation to its associate director, Daniel Matuszewski) and provided background and incentive for this book. In this respect, Soviet colleagues mentioned in my earlier work on Soviet-Japanese relations should be again acknowledged for their contribution to my perspectives on Soviet policies in Asia and the Siberian scene. I am grateful for the time and interest, given me during earlier visits to the Soviet Union, of Dimitri Petrov of the Far Eastern Institute, Boris Zanegin of the Institute of the USA and Canada, Boris Slavinsky of the Far Eastern Center in Vladivostok (who introduced me to Siberia), and Leonid N. Kutakov and Serge L. Tikhvinskii, well-known Far Eastern specialists and consultants to the Soviet Ministry of Foreign Affairs. The pioneering contributions in the area of Siberian development made by Academician A. G. Aganbegian,

xiv   *Acknowledgments*

whose research and writings I have followed for some years, should also be acknowledged.

I should also like to express my appreciation for the generous assistance of a number of other institutions, foundations, governments, and individuals: the Yoshida International Education Foundation and its directors, Yasusuke Katsuno and Masaru Ogawa; the Japanese Foreign Ministry and Japan Defense Agency; the Republic of Korea, especially the Institute of Foreign Affairs and National Security and its helpful successive directors; the Slavic Research Institute in Hokkaido and its director, Hiroshi Kimura; and the U.S. International Communications Agency.

Among the many friends and colleagues in Japan whose time and expertise, so generously given, have contributed to my understanding of the complicated issues approached in the book, I would especially like to thank Shinsaku Hogen ("dean" of Japan's specialists on the Soviet Union); Kinya Niiseki (former ambassador to Moscow, now director of the Japan Institute of International Affairs); Minoru Tanba, Kazuhiko Togo, and Toshiyuki Takano of the Foreign Ministry; Koichi Arai and Kiyoshi Furukawa of the Defense Agency; and Masamichi Inoki, director of the Research Institute for Peace and Security. The bibliographical assistance of Konosuke Hayashi of the National Diet Library in Tokyo is also greatly appreciated.

I am likewise indebted to colleagues in the foreign offices of London, Bonn, and Paris for their helpful suggestions, especially during my visit to Europe in the summer of 1983.

U.S. government representatives in Washington, Hawaii (CINCPAC), Europe, Japan, and Korea have been most generous with their guidance and documentation. I especially wish to thank ambassadors Mike Mansfield in Tokyo, Richard Walker in Seoul, and Arthur Hartman in Moscow for taking time from busy schedules to share thoughts and offer suggestions. Admiral R. E. Kirksey and members of his staff at CINCPAC, likewise, were most generous in providing briefings and available documentation relative to Pacific security matters. Other former U.S. military officials were also most helpful, especially Admiral Robert J. Hanks (ret.), member, Institute for Foreign Policy Analysis, Washington, D.C.; and Admiral Lloyd R. Vasey (ret.), director of the Pacific Forum, Honolulu. Except where attributed, the views and conclusions are, of course, my own.

In addition to several readers engaged by the Hoover Institution Press, whose collective comments and suggestions on the overall manuscript proved most valuable, a number of other colleagues read my chapter on strategic issues and offered helpful suggestions and guidance. In this respect, I am endebted to Peter Berton, Hammond Rolph, Robert Friedheim, William Van Cleave, and William Tow of USC; Harry Gelman of the Rand Corporation; Cdr. James Tritten of the Defense Department; Jan Breemer, a specialist on the Soviet navy; and Stephan Young of the U.S. Embassy in Moscow.

Lynn Sipe and Janice Hanks of our von Kleinsmid Library provided invaluable bibliographic and resource assistance. Likewise, several of my graduate students were helpful in various ways in the research and documentation process: Jerry Gideon, Brian Dailey, Dario Moreno, Keh-Ming Lin, Walter Fischer, Tony Poplawsky, and Glen Tait.

Most of all, of course, this volume owes its existence to my fellow colleagues and contributors, whose substantial commitment in time and effort are gratefully acknowledged. Together, they provide the multinational, multidisciplinary character of the book as well as what I trust will be perceived as a high degree of professionalism and timeliness throughout its pages.

Contributors

Michael J. Bradshaw is a doctoral candidate in the geography department at the University of British Columbia. His research interests include Soviet northern development, industrial location policy, and technology transfer. He is currently recipient of an Izaak Walton Killam Memorial Predoctoral Fellowship and a British Council Postgraduate Fellowship to the Soviet Union which he visited in 1985. He has a B.Sc. in geography from the University of Birmingham and an M.A. from the University of Calgary, Alberta.

Violet Conolly is a leading British authority on Siberia and Soviet Central Asia. She worked for years in the British Foreign Office as head of the research department's Soviet section. Earlier, as a Rockefeller Traveling Fellow, she traveled widely in the Middle East. She was also awarded a Hayter Research Fellowship of London University (1965–1967), enabling her to travel in Siberia and Soviet Central Asia. In recent years she has frequently visited the Soviet Union, returning to Siberia, Soviet Central Asia, and areas of interest in European Russia. In 1968 Dr. Conolly was awarded the Sykes Medal of the Royal Society for Asian Affairs for her work on Soviet Asia. Her publications include *Soviet Tempo* (Sheed & Ward, 1937), *Beyond the Urals* (Oxford University Press, 1967), *Siberia Today and Tomorrow* (Collins, 1976). She also contributes articles on Siberian problems to journals in Great Britain and Europe.

Wilfried Czerniejewicz is vice-president, governmental and international affairs, Ruhrgas AG, West Germany. Earlier he was principal administrator with the Ministry of Economics, Energy Division, Bonn (1975–1978) and with the Organization for Economic Cooperation and Development (OECD), Environment and Energy Directorate, Paris (1972–1974). He is a member of the East Committee of the German Industry Association. He received his undergraduate education and doctorate in economics and energy policy at the University of Cologne.

xviii   *Contributors*

Harry Gelman is a senior staff member of the political science department of the Rand Corporation, and a former assistant national intelligence officer for the Soviet Union and Eastern Europe. He retired from the CIA in 1979 after many years' involvement in political and strategic analysis of Soviet affairs. He is the author of numerous books, reports, and articles, including *The Soviet Far East Buildup and Soviet Risk-Taking Against China* (Rand Corporation, 1982) and *The Brezhnev Politburo and the Decline of Detente* (Cornell University Press, 1984). He was educated at Cornell University, Brooklyn College, and the School of Slavonic and Eastern European Studies of London University.

Thane Gustafson is director of the Soviet Studies Program, Center for Strategic and International Studies, Georgetown University. Prior to that he was a political scientist with the Rand Corporation and associate professor of government at Harvard University. He is the author of *Reform in Soviet Politics* (Cambridge University Press, 1981), *Selling the Russians the Rope* (Rand Corporation, 1981), and a forthcoming study on the politics of Soviet energy.

John Hardt is associate director for senior specialists and senior specialist in Soviet economics at the Congressional Research Service. He is also adjunct professor in economics at both George Washington and Georgetown universities. Dr. Hardt is a frequent traveler to the Soviet Union and Eastern Europe, often with Congressional delegations such as the trade mission of the Ways and Means Committee to Eastern Europe in December 1983 and the economic study delegation to the People's Republic of China (PRC) in November–December 1984. He has edited, coordinated, and contributed to many volumes on the economics of the Soviet Union, East Europe, and the PRC for the U.S. Congress.

Victor L. Mote is an associate professor of geography and Russian studies in the department of political science of the University of Houston. He is a former president of the Soviet and East European Interest Group of the Association of American Geographers. An ex-Marine captain and Vietnam veteran, he is coauthor of *Gateway to Siberian Resources: BAM* (Washington, D.C.: V. H. Winston and Sons, 1977) and a contributor to *Soviet Natural Resources and the World Economy,* edited by R. G. Jensen, T. Shabad, and A. J. Wright (Chicago: University of Chicago Press, 1983). During March 1985, he visited the central and western sections of BAM and became the first American to ride on a BAM train. He graduated Phi Beta Kappa from the University of Denver and the University of Washington.

Kazuo Ogawa is director of the department of economic studies of the Japan Association for Trade with the Soviet Union and Socialist Countries of Europe in Tokyo, and editor of the *Monthly Bulletin on Trade with the USSR and East Eu-*

rope published by the association. He is also a professor at Niigata University and a lecturer at Tokyo University. His professional affiliations have included service in the statistical division of the Tokyo municipal government as well as work for the Japan External Trade Organization (JETRO). He is the author of some ten books in the field, including *Soren no Taigai boski to Nippon* [Soviet foreign trade and Japan] (Tokyo: Jiji Tsushin Sha, 1983). He was educated at the Tokyo University of Foreign Studies.

Patricia Polansky is a Russian bibliographer at the Hamilton Library, University of Hawaii at Manoa, Honolulu. A leading specialist on the bibliography of Siberia and the Soviet Far East, as well as on Asia, the Pacific, and Russian America, she has published numerous articles in professional journals.

Rodger Swearingen is professor of international relations, School of International Relations, University of Southern California. A consultant to the Department of State, the Rand Corporation (fourteen years), the Ford Foundation, and to business and industry, he has made numerous research and conference visits to the Soviet Union (including Siberia and the Soviet Far East) and to East Asia. He is the author or editor of eight books, including *Red Flag in Japan* with Paul Langer (Harvard University Press, 1952), *The World of Communism* (Houghton Mifflin, 1962), *Soviet and Chinese Communist Power in the World Today* (Basic Books, 1966), *Leaders of the Communist World* (Free Press, Macmillan, 1971), and *The Soviet Union and Postwar Japan* (Hoover Institution Press, 1978). He received his Ph.D. from Harvard University.

JOHN HARDT

Introduction
Soviet Siberia: A Power-to-Be?

The vast material resources and geographical location of Siberia and the Far East offer the Soviets the possibility of strengthening their newly established position as a Pacific power, both economically and militarily. Siberia—West, East, and the Soviet Far East—is endowed with the broadest and richest range of natural resources in the world. These resources could contribute to economic growth throughout the USSR and Western Europe as well as throughout the Pacific community of nations. West and East Siberia have quite different orientations: the western portions of Siberia are keyed to domestic growth and trade with Europe; East Siberia and the Far East are keyed to potential Pacific trade.

West Siberia has become the major source of Soviet energy supplies for both domestic usage and foreign trade; more than three-fourths of the nation's total oil, gas, and coal are produced in this region. Oil and gas exports, largely from West Siberian reserves, accounted for 80 percent of Soviet convertible currency (hard currency) trade in 1983. East Siberia has a range of exportable materials: timber and wood products, marine products, oil, steam and coking coal, and asbestos are among the short-term prospects; natural gas, copper, iron, graphite, phosphates, sulfur, gold, and possibly aluminum are longer-term prospects.

Soviet exploitation of the resources of East Siberia and the Far East might result in an upsurge in Soviet trade development with the other nations of the Pacific community. The "natural fit"—the abundant resources of East Siberia and the material deficiencies of the other areas of the Pacific region, especially Northeast Asia—would allow for balanced, productive trade. Siberia could become a prime area of future economic growth for the USSR, as well as a major trading partner of Japan, South Korea, northeast China, and other Pacific areas. While Japan and South Korea could provide the technology, capital, and infrastructure needed for Siberian development, the People's Republic of China (PRC) could relieve Siberian food deficits.

East Siberia and the Far East have actually provided the USSR with a base for projecting its military power in the northern and western Pacific region. Although their Asian neighbors, who have generally de-emphasized military development, present the Soviets with a very limited military challenge, Soviet efforts to build up the East Siberian and Far Eastern military have run apace with general military expansion, second only to the defense buildup facing NATO. Compare Soviet Far Eastern militarization of the Sea of Okhotsk and the Kamchatka Peninsula with the Kola Peninsula and the Soviet buildup in northern Europe; compare the garrisoning of the China border with the expansion of Warsaw Pact forces in Central Europe; compare the naval buildup in the North Pacific with the North Atlantic naval expansion. Despite the relative weakness of the military forces of the People's Republic of China and Japan compared to NATO forces, the modest U.S. Pacific buildup, and the distance of those forces from vital Soviet political centers, the buildup of Soviet Pacific forces has been substantial.

The most puzzling aspect of the Soviet Siberian development strategy is: why "guns" over "growth" in East Asia and the Far East? Why have Soviet leaders invested so heavily in the expansion of military assets in East Asia instead of exploiting its vast economic resources, when the economic and defense growth rates were equal in West Siberia? From 1976 to 1983 overall Soviet defense spending was reduced and the resource claims of such priority projects as West Siberian energy development were met, along with those of the defense sector. In fact, energy development, especially in West Siberia, has been the leading claimant of industrial investment. Evidently, in the Pacific region, the perceived political benefits from more guns have thus far outweighed the economic benefits anticipated from expanded trade.

The various authors of the chapters that follow deal with the many facets of this guns versus growth question. Rodger Swearingen, focusing on Soviet security forces, sees the possibility of a changed military balance in Asia as a result of this substantial expansion of Soviet power in the Pacific region—unless the United States is prepared to pay relatively more strategic attention to the Asian-Pacific region than it has to date.

ECONOMIC POWER OF SIBERIA

Siberia's Place in the Soviet National Economy

In order to integrate the various regions of the USSR effectively, an improved planning process is needed. Capital stock and infrastructure, labor, and natural resources—the three factors necessary for expanded production—are dispersed: capital stock and infrastructure are concentrated in the traditional European economic centers; labor growth is in the southern republics; and natural resources are in Siberia. Each area is thus experiencing critical shortages in two of these three essential factors. Better management of the distribution of resources would undoubtedly influence future economic performance, and the current emphasis on transportation via expanded national pipeline networks, electric power grids, and improved rail, road, and water connections may improve this situation.

Indeed, recent plans to bring these national networks, including West Siberia, into operation as a unified system are expected to overcome imbalances and bottlenecks in the existing interregional system and, subsequently, to reduce the locational constraints on economic development. Although the spatial incongruity of resource availability in West Siberia may be ameliorated in the near term by expanding the national infrastructure, East Siberia is still beyond the integrating-transit networks being developed in the other areas of the USSR. The potential for integrating East Siberian and Far Eastern resources into a balanced economic process lies in trade with the capital-rich, developed economies of northern Asia.

The wealth of natural resources in East Siberia and the Soviet Far East provides a potential basis for satisfying many of the country's long-term domestic and export needs. Violet Conolly in her chapter on "Siberia: Yesterday, Today, and Tomorrow" seems to capture the eternal, often frustrating promise of Siberian development. The Soviets may be able to exploit rich energy resources as well as an untold amount of nonenergy material reserves. But, like Tantalus in Greek mythology, who was consigned by the gods to a fate of reaching for sustenance to find it forever removed from his grasp, the Soviets may be doomed in the near term to having these material gifts in East Siberia and the Far East denied to them by the cost of access. Oil, gas, and coal output in West Siberia might meet future domestic and export needs if Soviet leaders continue the "energy campaign," according to Thane Gustafson in his chapter on "The Energy Scene." While progress has been made in developing the oil and gas riches of Tyumen in West Siberia, the delayed opening of new resource and industrial bases in East Siberia—even with the completion of the Baikal-Amur Mainline (BAM) railroad—limits future development and trade prospects with the Pacific region.

Human and labor-force problems throughout the Soviet Union also have a regional character, with East Siberia and the Far East as extreme cases. Declining fertility and health are of particular concern in the traditional Slavic and Baltic regions of the Soviet Union, with their developed economic infrastructures and political bases of power, but they are even more serious problems for Siberia. Labor-force deficiency reinforces the negative effect of absence of capital and infrastructure. Although most developing countries have wrestled with the question of human resource dispersion by increasing labor mobility, in the USSR material incentives have thus far been insufficient to attract a new, stable emigrant labor base to East Siberia and the Far East. The estimated half-million new workers required for developing the BAM region will be difficult to attract from the civilian labor force. "Military builders" who completed the eastern section of the BAM may fill part of the needs. In a regional context of Siberian resource development, East Siberia is the key to open economic relations between Soviet Siberia and the Pacific region, especially Japan, whereas West Siberia is the major source for meeting oil, natural gas, and coal requirements, for both Soviet domestic and West European use. The regional development of oil and gas in West Siberia has received almost military priority, leading all industrial claimants on investment. The environmental hostilities that continue to inhibit resource development in East Siberia and the Soviet Far East are referred to as "anti-resource" by Victor Mote (see his chapter on "The Communications Infrastructure"). "Anti-resource" especially refers to the absence of capital and infrastructure necessary for natural resource development. The "natural fit" thesis finds Japan relieving this deficiency of capital and infrastructure (the anti-resource constraint), while East Siberia and the Soviet Far East expand from their natural-resource base to material-deficient Japan.

East Siberia as an Export Base
for the Pacific

Regional development of East Siberia and the Far East, keyed to the Pacific region, has been deferred. In capital and infrastructure, in working-age population, and in resources, significant gaps exist between what is needed and what is available. The opening of the BAM to traffic will provide access to the material riches of at least a 600,000-square-mile region in East Siberia. But metal, energy, and timber resources cannot be exported until an extraction and infrastructure base has been developed. The BAM was conceived as a two-part development project: the railroad and the region. The railroad opens the door to the Siberian "treasure house." The development project would exploit that potential.

The energy base in East Siberia is extensive: rich steam and coking coal, abundant natural gas, enormous hydro potential, possible oil prospects. The Yakutsk gas reserves compare with those of Urengoi in northwest Siberia, the major source of Soviet gas exported to Europe. These Yakutsk gas reserves were to be the East Siberian leg of the proposed U.S.–USSR natural gas projects of the early 1970s, a part of the Nixon-Brezhnev economic détente. The exploration of Yakutsk gas reserves, however, stopped before production, when cooperative U.S., Japanese, and Soviet exploration found resources in commercial quantities. Agreement on pipeline construction and terms of trade for gas exports was not reached. The production of Yakutsk natural gas is not imminent. By contrast, the development of the West Siberian Urengoi reserves has proceeded, with the assistance of West European capital and technology and increased Western demand for energy, in spite of the pipeline dispute of 1981–1982 in which the

United States sought to block the project. In his chapter on "Trade and High Technology," Michael Bradshaw presents evidence that Soviet planners key trade to the structure of Soviet regional development; for example, the orientation of Soviet East Asian trade to the Pacific region.

The mammoth Sayansk hydro project is another contribution to the energy balance, via the East Siberian hydroelectric power grid. Although some industrial development in aluminum processing goes forward, the new electric power capacity appears to be running well ahead of demand, due in part to lack of interconnection with the developed European regions of the USSR. This current imbalance has some historical parallels. When the earlier East Siberian hydro giants, Bratsk and Krasnoyarsk, were being debated in 1959, critics in the Soviet Union referred to their installation of unused capacity ahead of demand as "frozen assets." The processing of materials such as copper and aluminum in East Siberia might eventually produce attractive, energy-embodied exports for energy-deficient northern Asia.

Japan, with its dynamic, technologically advanced, industrial economy, had seriously negotiated with the Soviets for an economic partnership in the development of Soviet Siberia. As described by Kazuo Ogawa in his chapter "Economic Relations with Japan," the Soviet-Japanese agreements from 1966 to 1975 seemed to lay out a process of mutually beneficial, expanding trade relations. Discussions on the joint development of Siberia began early in 1966. The Joint Japan-Soviet Economic Committee, consisting of Japanese businessmen and Soviet commercial representatives, was created to exchange ideas on future cooperation. Among the projects discussed were the development of West Siberian oil and gas reserves and pipelines; exploration for oil, gas, and other mineral reserves on the continental shelf off Sakhalin Island; development of Siberian copper deposits; construction of port facilities in the Soviet Far East; and development of Siberian timber and pulp resources.

But several of those projects showed only limited progress and agreement, for several economic reasons: first, it was difficult to determine the feasibility of various projects; second, world prices for oil and gas were rapidly rising; third, and finally, the Soviets required very large and preferential credits. Two massive projects were discussed and negotiated by leaders of the two nations; they were shelved by the mid-1970s. One was to pursue joint development of the Tyumen oil field in West Siberia. Another was to combine Soviet industry and U.S. and Japanese companies in joint exploitation of natural gas reserves in the northern Yakutsk area of East Siberia. Negotiations also took place on joint development of the oil and natural gas reserves of Sakhalin, including offshore deposits. The Sakhalin development was the only bilateral hydrocarbon project that went forward. Japanese and Soviet negotiators also agreed in 1975 on joint development of northern Yakutsk coking and steam coal; Japan extended a credit of about $450 million, to be repaid in the form of 104 million tons of coal, delivered between

1979 and 1998. The Japanese loan was to be used to buy Japanese rails and other equipment needed to develop and transport the coal. The Soviets' commitment was to build a 400-kilometer railroad linking the coal mines to the Trans-Siberian Railroad.

With the decline of U.S.-Soviet détente in the mid-1970s, the Afghanistan invasion in 1979, and the Korean Air Lines incident in 1983, Soviet relations with Japan have been continuously on the downslide. A number of important political issues continue to impede bilateral Soviet-Japanese commercial relations developments: the resolution of political disputes over the Northern Territories, continued fishing disputes, uneasiness of PRC and some Japanese leaders about the military implications of the projects, and the problem of Japan becoming too dependent on a potential adversary for essential raw materials.

Still, Japan remains the natural market for resource exports from East Siberia and the Far East, which would provide the Soviets with additional hard-currency earnings. Moreover, Japan is a natural source of capital, technology, and industrial products for the USSR. Soviet trade with Japan and the other Pacific countries was an "empty box" in the commercial plans with the West for the Eleventh Five-Year Plan (1981–1985); the five-year directives included no reference to Pacific trade although that had always been implicit in the development of the BAM. Although bilateral economic relations are potentially the most beneficial aspect of Soviet-Japanese relationships, the future of trade relations is uncertain at best, according to Kazuo Ogawa.

MILITARY POWER IN SIBERIA

During the Brezhnev era the Soviets militarized East Siberia and the Far East, presumably to counterbalance an increasingly hostile China and to project Soviet military power in the North and West Pacific from bases in the Soviet Far East. This military expansion occurred in spite of the moderate military augmentation of other Pacific powers: The PRC held down military expenditures to the point that the military became the fourth (lowest) priority in modernization; Japan retained its low defense priority, symbolized by the 1 percent GNP ceiling on defense outlays, and continued its "nuclear allergy"; and the United States, caught in the so-called Vietnam syndrome, reduced its commitment to northern Asia and the West Pacific. When the major U.S. defense buildup began in 1980, the West Pacific did not rival the European priority in strengthened U.S. security forces. The Soviet buildup in the Far East continues unabated, albeit secondary to its European military expansion.

Whether the Soviets have benefited from their tremendous investments in building up their military power in East Asia is questionable. The use of force against the Chinese on the Ussuri in 1969, Soviet military support of Vietnam against China in 1978–1979, and the shooting down of the Korean Air Lines plane (KAL 007) in 1983 were not effective uses of military means as diplomatic tools. Indeed, the lack of success of these incidents may have demonstrated poor combat readiness as much as the inadequacy of Soviet weapons. Still, combat-ready forces and expensive weaponry alone may not be appropriate or effective means for managing future political-military crises in the North or West Pacific. The problem for the Soviets may be in the imbalance of their military, political, and economic investments of power in the Pacific.

In addition, even with their increased military buildup, the Soviets have yet to change the Pacific balance of power in their favor. In fact, Soviet buildup and use of force from North Asia to Afghanistan have been factors in military recommitment by the United States, Japan, and the PRC in Northeast and Southeast Asia.

Arming the Border with China

After the political split between the communist giants in 1969, the isolation, encirclement, and containment of China became an imperative of Soviet policy in Asia. This policy was implemented by several means: tripling of Soviet deployments along the Chinese border, up to 50 Soviet divisions (the major increase in Soviet military manpower under Brezhnev and his successors); the establishment of a Soviet base in Vietnam; the attempt to make Afghanistan a secure Soviet ally; and the further wooing of India to a Soviet-oriented position.

The initial military buildup along the Sino-Soviet frontier and the use of force in the border skirmishes were apparently direct Soviet responses to China's new position as a global communist leader, a sovereign Asian state, and a potential great power. The ideologically and politically independent People's Republic of China was acting as a "second Rome" within the communist world, challenging Soviet dominance. At the same time, China was emphasizing its sovereignty by raising historical border questions. Although the Chinese may have seen a parallel between Soviet actions in Czechoslovakia in 1968 and on the China border a year later, the outcomes of those events were almost preordained to be different. The PRC was not Czechoslovakia, and so the Soviet use of military power did not have the unilateral result of reversing Chinese moves toward independence and challenge to Soviet hegemony in Asia.

A broader reason for the Soviets' military buildup in the Far East, as Harry Gelman explains in his chapter on the Sino–Soviet–U.S. triangle, may have been "their decision to take steps to offset the worst-case possibility of eventual Sino–U.S.–Japanese military coalition against them." Gelman also credits opportunism as a motive for the buildup: "their perception of the heightened importance of their strength in the Far East as a result of changes in Submarine Launched Ballistic Missile (SLBM) technology and the new opportunities for power projection from the Far East that have emerged in Southeast Asia and beyond." This concern over a PRC equipped with modern U.S. and Japanese military technology and support, plus the opportunity for unsettling the Pacific power balance by a unilateral buildup at a time when the PRC, Japan, and the United States were passive in Pacific military affairs, were probably both principal reasons for the Soviet militarization of the Far East. Top-ranking Soviet military officials may also have pressured Brezhnev to reverse the Khrushchev policies of holding down the incremental military manpower burden, thereby permitting the manning of the China border.

Militarization of the Soviet Far East

The Brezhnev strategy for the Soviet Far East was an unparalleled, across-the-board military buildup. The trend has continued in the post-Brezhnev period. In the Transbaikal and Far Eastern Military Districts, increases of naval, missile, aircraft, and modernized ground forces transformed the region into the most formidable military garrison in Asia. The Sea of Okhotsk, the Kamchatka Peninsula, and the contested Northern Territories have all become well-developed Soviet military bases.

Whereas the economic base for projecting Siberian resource power to Pacific markets was only partially developed and decades away from full economic take-off, the military buildup proceeded more rapidly in an integrated fashion toward an effective basis for projecting Soviet military power to the Pacific region. Historically, weak logistical and support constraints have limited the full effectiveness of Soviet military outreach, but the trend continues toward an increasingly effective, balanced Soviet force in the Pacific region. Despite known logistical constraints, the projection of Soviet power and influence in Asia and the West Pacific continues through both direct and indirect means: direct, as in Afghanistan, and indirect, as in India, where power-in-being is employed for political purposes. Other regions in the Pacific rim may feel either the indirect or direct use of Soviet power in the future, although the indirect use appears more likely.

THE SOVIET UNION AS A PACIFIC POWER: COMITY OR CONFLICT?

"Guns Versus Growth" Tradeoff

The Brezhnev leadership was clearly committed to military over economic development in East Asia—"guns over growth." This equation could change in the post-Brezhnev period, though there is little evidence of reversal yet. In the long term, Soviet leadership may find continued military augmentation in Siberia and the Far East an onerous economic burden that yields too few political, strategic benefits. They may see the development of the East Siberian region, especially the Baikal area, as sufficiently important in potential economic gains from trade to place a new emphasis on regional development of the BAM in the Twelfth Five-Year Plan (1986–1990) and thereafter. This would require a shift in resources from the military to the civilian economy. Were such a shift to occur, manpower utilization—like the extensive use of military builders on civilian projects such as the Udokan copper project—would be an early indicator. In the short run, manpower is the most mobile resource in the USSR. Moreover, the eastern sector of the BAM had been the responsibility of the military builders. Greater civilian use of military manpower would alleviate labor problems and thereby upgrade economic prospects in East Siberia and the Far East.

Politics Still Dominate Trade in the USSR

For the Soviets to change their economic development policy in East Siberia and the Far East, an upsurge of economic cooperation with Japan and the United States would probably be necessary, requiring a reduction of tensions and a new political basis of cooperation. However, industrial cooperation and increased Pacific trade may still be viewed by the Soviet Union, Japan, and the United States as sources of potentially unacceptable dependency and vulnerability.

This fear of dependency and vulnerability stands in striking contrast to a Soviet–West European trade that focuses on "gas for pipe" cooperation. To be sure, a "mini-détente" between Europe and the USSR continues to provide a political umbrella for economic cooperation. The West Europeans insist that they have not accepted undue dependency or vulnerability. The energy-technology trade between the Soviet Union and the Federal Republic of Germany, according to Wilfried Czerniejewicz in his chapter, "Linkage with Europe," was based on four Western criteria: no dependence on energy imports from the Soviet Union, no increase in the foreign exchange income of the USSR, no transfer of sensitive technology, and equitable contractual arrangements. It was also based on a continued adherence to a European "mini-détente" policy.

The "natural fit" between the Soviet Pacific regions and Asian countries such as Japan is not enough to overcome the mutual political and security concerns. Some new political basis for cooperation would be needed to assuage these concerns. If a new period of great power accommodation should emerge, bringing with it expanded and mutually beneficial East-West economic relations, it could provide the context within which Pacific-power conflicts with the USSR might be assuaged and the Soviet Union might become an important economic force in the Pacific region.

In the trade-oriented, economically dynamic Pacific region, the military and political threat of the Soviet Union is destabilizing in the short run and disorienting in the long term. As Rodger Swearingen notes, until the Soviet Union makes fundamental changes in its assumptions, objectives, policy, and practice toward the Asian region, the Pacific countries must face an ongoing dilemma of accommodation with the USSR and increasing concern about the growing Soviet threat to their security.

Siberia: Yesterday, Today, and Tomorrow

In tsarist days, many learned expeditions into Siberia, either undertaken by private initiative or sponsored by the Imperial Geographical Society, unearthed a considerable amount of miscellaneous information about this area, including the location of some of its natural resources. While agriculture flourished in West Siberia on well-run Russian farms, the scientific study of the natural features and peoples of Siberia was progressing rapidly in the last century of tsarist Russia. On the whole, however, little was done to develop Siberia's great wealth of mineral reserves before the Russian Revolution.

This picture changed with the emergence of Soviet power in 1917. It became a matter of strategic importance to the Kremlin to develop and further investigate Siberian mineral resources, as a means of reducing imports of various raw materials. This policy was actively pursued in a series of five-year plans starting in the 1930s. And as the result of wide geological research in the 1950s, many valuable resources, previously unknown, were discovered, such as the great north Tyumen oil and gas fields.

In the following pages, the Siberian economy, particularly the contribution to Soviet economic power of Siberia's natural resources, including agriculture, are considered. Research is hampered by the restrictions on Soviet statistical information, as well as secrecy about production of all nonferrous metals, in which Siberia is very rich.

Siberian economic development has also been accompanied by serious problems of population, labor shortages, poor living conditions, and "narrow departmentalism." On these problems the Soviet press now offers a wealth of acute comment not sparing, where necessary, party and other officials.

THE ENVIRONMENT

The geographical and environmental features of Siberia have inevitably exercised a decisive influence on its economic development. Area, climate, and topography are almost uniformly unfavorable and go far to explain Siberia's late emergence in the modern industrial world, in spite of its extremely rich resource endowment. Across the Atlantic, the more favorable geographical situation of the United States has facilitated the much more rapid modernization of North America.

Siberia, in the traditional sense of the lands lying between the Urals and the Pacific, covers 12.4 million square kilometers—larger than the People's Republic of China or the United States and more than twice the size of European Russia.

For economic planning purposes, Siberia is now divided into three economic regions: West Siberia, East Siberia, and the Soviet Far East. It is therefore convenient to discuss the Siberian environment—which varies considerably from region to region—on this basis. All three regions are very large by European standards; the largest, the Far East, is five times the size of France and larger even than the entire continent of Australia.

Administratively, the three regions are subdivided as appropriate into a framework of oblasts, krais, Autonomous Soviet Socialist Republics (ASSRs), Autonomous Oblasts (AOs), and Autonomous (formerly National) Okrugs (autonomous districts). There are no separate Soviet republics in this area, which forms part of the Russian Soviet Federated Socialist Republic (RSFSR).

There are many climatic variations within the three Siberian regions. All have relatively hot summers and extremely rigorous winters with varying degrees of frost, and an annual mean temperature of 0 degrees Celsius. The Siberian climate thus presents some surprising anomalies. In Verkhoyansk, within the Arctic Circle, for example, one of the coldest places in the world, there are wide differences between the hottest and the coldest days. The summer can be as hot as the south of France or Italy, but the mean for the coldest month is −50 degrees Celsius.

The permafrost (permanently frozen ground), one of the characteristic features of Siberia, extends from the arctic and subarctic zones of West Siberia, mostly east of the Ob River, with varying degrees of depth to almost the whole of Yakutia and the northern Siberian extremity of Chukotka. In East Siberia only small patches of ground are free of it.

The existence of this frozen subsoil creates many technical problems for the construction of engineering or industrial projects, such as pipelines or hydroelectric power stations in the arctic and subarctic regions. As a result of much careful scientific research, especially in the Permafrost Institute in Yakutsk, modern buildings can now be constructed on piles driven deep into the frozen ground, which provide rocklike foundations. Good examples of such constructions are to be found in Yakutsk and Norilsk and hydropower stations at Khantayka and Ust Ilimsk, which are built in the permafrost.

Throughout the permafrost areas of northern Siberia, only moss and lichen can grow in the tundra (areas of lakes and bogs and patchy vegetation of grasses and shrubs) and survive the ferocious winds and frosts. This is the summer home of the reindeer, whose natural fodder is this moss and lichen. But even the reindeer move south to the cover of the taiga (coniferous forest) in winter. These chilly territories are very thinly populated, mostly by small settlements of native fishermen and hunters.

Where oil and natural gas or minerals have been found, as at Norilsk, new towns and settlements have grown up. So, in spite of all the difficulties of establishing civilized life there, it can be done. But there are still many unsolved problems arising from this environment.

Valuable oil and natural gas deposits have been found in the swampy wastes of West Siberia, but the unstable nature of the marshy terrain has greatly complicated their exploitation. It has been graphically described by Dr. James Gregory: "Between the confluences of the Irtysh and Vasiugan rivers, a wide expanse of lowland extends westward across the Irtysh to the Tavda River. The western and northern parts constitute an immense, virtually uninhabited wilderness, where water and forest are inextricably mingled in a complex of streams and countless lakes. South of the Ob, the Vasiuganye swamp includes large tracts of bog and moss-covered land with few trees."[1] This formerly desolate Vasiuganye swamp is now being activated by all the mechanical implements of a modern oil industry working under great difficulties.

The southern areas of West Siberia, where there are large expanses of wooded and true steppe, contrast sharply with the frozen northern scene. There is little wind and often blue sky. The best agricultural land in Siberia is to be found here, and the famous "black earth" (chernozem soils) produce high-quality grain crops. Harvests in this area are, however, constantly threatened by endemic, sultry winds and droughts and the danger of flooding from the local rivers such as the Ob and the Irtysh.

East Siberia lacks the favorable basis for agricultural development that West Siberia has. It is traversed by many mountain ranges, permafrost is widespread throughout the region, and the climate is more continental than in West Siberia. The best agricultural lands are in the eastern hinterland of Irkutsk and the southern mild zone around Minusinsk. Agriculture is well developed there, and livestock thrives in the hills and valleys of the Khakass AO. The soil and climate of the highlands and prairielike country of eastern Transbaikalia also favor livestock breeding, notably in the Buryat ASSR. East Siberia has a great wealth of timber in its taiga, but the important regional timber industry has been hampered by inefficient lumbering practices and other obstacles to production.

Siberia is traversed by many of Russia's greatest rivers: the Ob, the Irtysh, the Yenisei, the Angara, the Lena, the Amur, the Yana, and the Kolyma. They are powerful sources of hydroelectric power and useful means of transport. To date, only the hydro potential of the Yenisei, the Ob (at Novosibirsk), the Zeya, Bureya, Kolyma, and the Angara is being developed.

A great deal has been done to take advantage of the short navigation periods before the lower courses of the northern Siberian rivers are frozen solid in winter. In these brief periods, local raw materials such as minerals or timber are collected at the river ports, to distribute supplies downstream and to promote the northern sea route farther east. The Lena River, which is an essential communications link between the rail transhipment point of Ust Kut and Yakutsk, is exceptional: its lower reaches and enormous delta are not navigable.

A scheme to divert some of the immense volume of water annually discharged into the Arctic Ocean by the Siberian rivers and to fructify certain arid deserts of Central Asia, has been under consideration for some years, but is opposed by some Siberian scientists on ecological and environmental grounds.

Since the 1930s, the Soviet government has expended much money and scientific effort on the development of the northern sea route between Russian ports in northern Europe and the Soviet Far East. The aim has been to ensure safe passage through the perilous Arctic waters for oceangoing ships by better ice forecasting, ice breakers, and improved navigation aids and port facilities. The northern sea route is much shorter than either the Suez or Black Sea routes. From Arkhangelsk to Vladivostok it is 7,000 sea miles via the Bering Strait, while it is 10,800 sea miles from Odessa and 14,700 from Leningrad via the Suez Canal. Soviet ships now annually pass through, aided by powerful ice breakers, during the short navigation season. In this way, much-needed supplies can reach the coastal settlements and be sent upstream by barge and other river craft to many of the new mining settlements in the north. It now seems that year-round operations on this route are in sight.

Because it extends over such a vast area from north to south and east to west, it is not surprising that the Soviet Far East has a wide range of climates and soils within its boundaries. The permafrost area reaches far south from the arctic and subarctic zones, with temperatures and soils that preclude any substantial development of agriculture. With careful husbandry, livestock can be raised, in conjunction with fur farming, even in the region of Verkhoyansk—though Verkhoyansk and Oimyakon contend for the honor of being the "cold pole" of the northern region. The abundant fish in the Far Eastern and Siberian rivers are a main source of food both in this region and throughout European Russia; large quantities of fish are also processed and exported abroad.

The high and difficult Cherskogo and Verkhoyanskiy mountains in northeast Yakutia were long an insuperable barrier to exploration of the hinterland. A rich belt of gold and tin is now being developed there; this "Golden Arc" extends to the northeastern massif of the Chukot district, also very rich in gold and tin. The nature of the terrain changes to the south in the Kolyma River basin. The area here is low-lying, often little above sea level, with large swamps and many shallow lakes. This is gold-mining territory, where the reindeer play an essential part, supplying meat for the miners and transport and other commodities for the native inhabitants.

In the Soviet Far East, agriculture can be practiced with any degree of success in only three areas: (1) the upper Amur-Bureya-Zeya district adjoining the southern Sino-Soviet border; (2) the Olekminsk district of central Yakutia, which produces good crops of wheat and potatoes in a grain-deficient land; (3) the Lake Khanka district and the Ussuri valley, specializing in sugar beets, soybeans, and rice. Great efforts are being made to extend dairy farming and the cultivation of vegetables and other crops in the vicinity of Yakutsk. But there the possibilities are limited owing to the northern climate and permafrost soil.

More temperate zones are found in the Amur basin, the Ussuri valley and the Primorski coastal region, where semitropical humid conditions are found. These areas of the Soviet Far East would lend themselves, under more efficient management, to more intensive agricultural development and better all-around farm production. The soil and climate are relatively propitious, though the prevalence of monsoons and flooding is a disadvantage.

The lands of the extreme Soviet Far East—Kamchatka, the island of Sakhalin, and the Kuril Islands—suffer from serious natural handicaps. Kamchatka has many active volcanoes on the east coast, and there are frequent earthquakes and tremors in this volcanic soil. Kamchatka's seas and rivers abound in fine seafood (including salmon and crab, for which Kamchatka is world-famous), but otherwise most of its food must be imported. Sakhalin and the Kuril Islands are also afflicted by earthquakes, dense fogs, and very severe winters with ferocious winds and blinding snowstorms. Nevertheless, agricultural production, though small, has expanded in recent years in Sakhalin.

The problems of the environment—pollution and conservation—have become of increasing importance with the expanding development of Siberian natural resources. General attention to these problems was first triggered by the outcry in the 1960s about the pollution threat to Lake Baikal by effluent from pulp mills on its shores. Subsequently many official decrees were passed to protect the environment. Nevertheless, the establishment of large hydroelectric power stations with huge dams, construction of chemical plants without the necessary environmental safeguards, the extension of mining operations, and the often ruthless felling of trees over wide stretches of taiga, all pose potential threats to the Siberian environment. Economic expediency, bureaucratic inefficiency or indifference, and overtly lenient official attitudes continue to obstruct the strict enforcement of the antipollution and conservation laws.[2]

Accounts of Siberian wildlife and its environment being ravaged by unscrupulous and extremely ingenious poachers frequently appear in Soviet sources. The sable is now threatened by these intruders in some of its best natural habitats, while valuable fish like the salmon suffer from ruthless overfishing. To protect wildlife and preserve threatened animal species, the government has established some large reservations in Siberia and the Soviet Far East.

POPULATION AND LABOR

An adequate labor force is an essential factor for success in industry and agriculture, and the problems of population and labor supply play a major role in the economic development of Siberia. Since the inception of Soviet industrialization under Stalin's five-year plans in the 1930s, the population of the vast territory (12.4 million square kilometers) of Siberia and the Soviet Far East has been increasingly unable to fill the demands of the expanding economy. During the Stalinist period, labor for the new mining and timber industries, located to a large extent in the rigorous climate of northern East Siberia and the Soviet Far East, was supplied by the inmates of local concentration camps. This forced labor built the town and the nickel and platinum mines of Norilsk and worked many of the valuable gold deposits in the region.

The abolition of this forced labor in the late 1950s after Stalin's death coincided with the launching of a series of planned projects to promote the development of Siberian natural resources. This in turn required large inputs of labor. These resources were either located in the traditional homelands of a number of small native peoples of the north, strung out within Siberia's arctic zone from the Urals to the Pacific coast, or in uninhabited areas of Siberia. These northern peoples might therefore seem to offer a conveniently situated source of labor for some of the industries arising in their midst. But in fact they have never participated to any extent in these activities; they are primitive nomadic peoples with no aptitude or training for industrial life but extremely skilled in their traditional occupations of reindeer breeding, trapping, and fishing, to which they mostly remain attached.

According to the 1979 Soviet census, these northern peoples numbered only 156,000. However, this figure excluded the largest of them—the Yakuts (327,000)—and many of the smallest groups as well, although the Yukagirs, amounting to only about 800, were included. Smaller groups ignored by the census officials could thus be on the way to extinction unknown to the outside world. Though numerically insignificant in the millions-strong multinational Soviet population, this northern group is unique in its peculiar social-cultural traditions and individual languages. It is therefore of considerable interest to ethnographers.

Historically, these northern peoples suffered great losses in numbers and status during three centuries of tsarist rule. It brought them in contact with decimating diseases hitherto unknown—smallpox, syphilis, and leprosy—and with unscrupulous officials whose extortions ruined many tribal chiefs. Tsarist officialdom, though it did not interfere with the "internal autonomy" of these peoples, also left them bereft of modern medicine or education. The fate of the Yukagirs may be taken as typical of the results of tsarist rule. Originally a leading northern tribe, they are competently estimated to have fallen from 5,000 to about 500 during this period.[3]

Under the Soviet system of government, these northern peoples may be said to have both gained and lost, socially and culturally. Education and public health measures have been widely introduced, and even though these measures have not produced significant increases in their numbers, some individuals have availed themselves of the opportunities of a higher Soviet education to become doctors, teachers, or writers. For the most part, however, they have rejected official pressures to adopt a permanent, settled form of life, which they find unsuitable for reindeer breeding. Their reindeer meat provides useful food for the thousands of Slav migrant industrial workers now living in their homelands as well as extra money for the deer breeders.

An administrative framework of Soviet territorial units (mostly in the form of autonomous okrugs) containing Soviet and party institutions has been established among the northern peoples, while their old tribal religious customs have been officially derided and undermined. The Marxist-Leninist policy of *sblizhenie* or assimilation of peoples has tended to Russify these traditional peoples and weaken their sense of separate ethnic identity. Moreover, in the 1979 census an increasing number of them (varying greatly from 72 percent of the 800-strong Nganasany to 10 percent of the 500 Aleuts) stated that they "command freely" the Russian language. Whether this is an indication of a gradual process of Russification, or merely an appreciation of the undoubted value of the Russian language in opening a wider world of opportunity and culture, is of course debatable.

The 1979 census showed some slight increases in certain northern peoples, while others remained stationary or decreased. These census statistics throw no light on the extent to which smaller groups have been absorbed by the larger nationalities, such as the Yakuts or Chukchi, among whom they live. On the whole, the future of the smaller groups of northern peoples as national units within the Soviet Union does not seem promising.

Problems of population and labor have become more urgent and important in Siberia and the Soviet Far East with the development of their natural resources. In the 1979 census these areas had a population of 27.9 million, about 10 percent of the population of the Soviet Union, a number grossly disparate with the huge territories they occupy—about 58 percent of the entire country. The largest of these Siberian areas, the Soviet Far East (enlarged by post–World War II acquisitions such as Sakhalin), is the most thinly populated, with only 6.8 million

TABLE 1.1
Population of the USSR, Siberia, and the Soviet Far East (in millions)

	1939	1959	1970	1979
USSR	170.5	208.8	241.7	262.4
Siberia and				
the Far East	16.6	21.7	25.2	27.9
West Siberia	8.9	11.2	12.0	12.9
East Siberia	5.3	6.7	7.4	8.1
Far East	2.3	3.6	5.7	6.8

SOURCE: 1979 Soviet census.
NOTE: The figures in the source contain some statistical discrepancies that have not been altered. They are not very significant.

people or approximately 1 person per kilometer in an area of 6.2 million square kilometers (Table 1.1).

The demographic position in Siberia, with its low birthrate and a dwindling natural increase, is unsatisfactory in line with official statistics of all-Union trends. Siberian families tend to be small and limited by housing accommodations and other domestic difficulties on some construction sites and in new towns. As a result, the Siberian population as a whole is rising only slowly, and certainly not in relation to labor demands or government expectations. The current large demands for extra labor for Siberian industries and mines cannot be met from local sources. Nor can European Russia be relied on (as formerly) to fill Siberia's labor gaps, for there is also a labor shortage in European Russia. There is a surplus of labor in Soviet Central Asia, but Central Asians are unwilling to move northward permanently from the South.

The Siberian labor problem is relatively new. Since the early years of industrialization, a flow of workers, mainly from Russia and the Ukraine, has filled the Siberian work sites. These one-time migrant Slav workers, now permanent residents, have entirely swamped the native inhabitants of the autonomous republics and okrugs of Siberia and the Soviet Far East. According to the 1979 census, 72 percent of the population of the Buryat ASSR was Russian, for example, and in the Khakass AO the figure was 79 percent. Only in the Tuva ASSR is there still a predominance of native people over the Russians. (See Table 1.2.)

Another change in the Siberian population is that it is now heavily concentrated in the towns rather than as formerly in the countryside. Rural people have been drawn to the towns by the better living conditions and job opportunities there, thus diminishing the rural communities and the agricultural work force.

The Soviet statistics for 1984 (compared with the previous decade) show that the populations in the new and older towns have been constantly rising. Thus, in

1984, Surgut had a population of 188,000 and Bratsk 236,000; both have risen from insignificant hamlets in a few decades. Meanwhile, older industrial centers like Novosibirsk and Omsk grew to 1,384,000 and 1,094,000, respectively. Even though their populations are rising, labor shortages are not unknown in Novosibirsk and Omsk.

The Soviet government's concern about the economic effects of labor shortages and the "flight of labor" on Siberian construction sites has been reflected in its various recruitment measures. Since the 1960s, incentives in the form of higher wages, extra leave, paid holiday fares, and living accommodations have been offered to attract labor to the more arduous north Siberian sites. Thousands of workers from European Russia have gone to work there, but many have also thrown off their jobs, disillusioned with living and domestic-social conditions, when their contracts expired. These departing workers cost the state considerable financial losses, for the cost of establishing them in northern Siberia is high: about 20,000 rubles per worker (1971 estimate).[4] Patriotic appeals are frequently addressed to the Komsomols to "volunteer" for major construction projects such as the BAM or the north Tyumen oil-gas developments and thus assist the "native land" and the "people." As a result of these appeals, thousands of young people have built the great Siberian hydroelectric stations beginning at Bratsk and now labor on the BAM, and a big mix of Soviet nationalities is engaged in the north Tyumen oil and gas industry where "labor brigades" of young people are constructing the European-Urengoi pipelines.

Notwithstanding these activities and a number of high-powered Soviet measures to improve general living conditions, the Siberian labor problem has not been solved nor have living conditions yet improved to a noticeable extent. At the twenty-sixth party congress in 1981, Brezhnev stressed the links between good living conditions and normal work and insisted that living conditions should be improved. This line was later followed in a number of party resolutions, notably the 1983 decree of the Communist Party of the Soviet Union (CPSU) on housing and living conditions with special reference to Siberia and the Soviet Far East.[5]

The causes and results in the economy of the Siberian "flight of labor," long deplored in the Soviet press, have now also been frankly discussed in detail by Academician Abel Aganbegian and other members of the Siberian branch of the Soviet Academy of Sciences. Aganbegian, writing in 1981–1982, asserted that the flight of labor depends on how "comfortable the living accommodation is, how well organized the supply of food products and the cultural-domestic services are, and how possible it is to educate children and to widen one's outlook." He blamed the "constructors" for not providing living space and amenities where the inflow of workers is highest. "Systematically," he continued, "plans for the erection of housing and domestic-cultural institutions are not fulfilled." The result is that thousands of specialists coming temporarily to work in Siberia might wish to stay but frequently cannot do so, for lack of accommodation. Formerly,

TABLE 1.2
National Composition of Siberia (1979 census)

Ethnic Groups by Region	Population
Buryat ASSR	899,398
Buryats	206,860
Russians	647,785
Ukrainians	15,290
Tatars	10,291
Peoples of the North	1,634
Evenki	1,543
Tuva ASSR	267,599
Tuvinians	161,888
Russians	96,793
Khakass	2,193
Ukrainians	1,729
Yakutsk ASSR	851,847
Yakuts	313,917
Russians	429,588
Ukrainians	46,326
Peoples of the North	18,445
Evenki	11,584
Eveny	5,763
Yukagiry	560
Tatars	10,980
Adygei Autonomous Oblast	404,390
Adyge	86,388
Russians	285,626
Ukrainians	12,078
Armenians	6,359
Jewish Autonomous Oblast	188,710
Jews	10,166
Russians	158,765
Ukrainians	11,870
Gorno-Altai Autonomous Oblast	172,040
Altais	50,203
Russians	108,795
Kazakhs	8,677
Khakass Autonomous Oblast	498,384
Khakass	57,281
Russians	395,953
Nentsy	11,130
Ukrainians	10,398
Agin-Buryat National Okrug[a]	69,035
Buryats	35,868
Russians	29,098
Taimyr National Okrug	44,953
Dolgany	4,388
Nentsy	2,345
Nganasany	746
Russians	30,642
Ukrainians	3,075

TABLE 1.2
(*continued*)

Ethnic Groups by Region	Population
Ust-Ordynsky Buryat National Okrug	132,153
Buryats	45,436
Russians	76,731
Tatars	4,782
Khanty-Mansi National Okrug	570,763
Khanty	11,219
Mansi	6,156
Nentsy	1,003
Russians	423,702
Ukrainians	45,484
Tatars	36,899
Chukot National Okrug	139,944
Chukchi	11,292
Eskimos	1,278
Russians	96,424
Belorussians	2,448
Tatars	1,995
Evenki National Okrug	15,968
Evenki	3,239
Russians	10,400
Yakuts	822
Ukrainians	472
Yamalo-Nenets National Okrug	158,844
Nentsy	17,404
Khanty	6,466
Selkupy	1,611
Russians	93,750
Ukrainians	15,721
Tatars	8,556
Komi	5,642
Belorussians	2,121

SOURCE: Central Statistical Administration, *Numbers and Composition of the Population of the USSR; According to the Data of the All-Union Census of Population of 1979* (Moscow: Finances and Statistics, 1984).

NOTE: The most numerous nationalities are listed for Siberia's autonomous republics (ASSRs), autonomous oblasts, and national (autonomous) okrugs; nonautonomous krais and oblasts are not included.

a Although *Webster's New Geographical Dictionary* (Springfield, Mass.: Merriam-Webster, 1984) refers to these districts as "national okrugs," they are better known in the literature as autonomous okrugs (AOs).

more left than stayed, but now more stay than leave—but not in sufficient numbers to satisfy the demand for labor on Siberian sites. Aganbegian found that the lowest provision of housing in recent years existed on the territory of the major West Siberian oil and gas complex.[6] This surprising fact confirms the inefficiency and slackness of the central construction ministries and their subdepartments, which are so frequently criticized in other Soviet sources and which "have no thought as to how people will live."[7]

Apart from the poor state of housing and living conditions on Siberian construction sites, important though they are for the retention of labor, the shortcomings and delinquencies of the labor force itself cannot be ignored in considering the Siberian labor problem. These failings are frequently criticized in Soviet sources and most recently were graphically stressed in the pre-election speeches of both K. U. Chernenko and Marshal D. F. Ustinov. Chernenko hit out at the loafers, rolling stones, and drunkards who under the exalted name of "worker" try to conceal their idleness and slackness.[8] Marshal Ustinov for his part insisted that there must be an end to the stoppages and losses of working time, the unrhythmical pace of work and technological discipline, and substandard fulfillment of plans.[9]

Drunkenness is likely to be at the root of many of these breaches of labor discipline deplored by the Soviet leadership and often common in a predominantly Russian-Slav work force. However, Soviet measures against heavy drinking have so far had little effect. The problem can even arise among workers not normally prone to drinking, on the bleak northern construction sites with intolerably bad living conditions and little or no entertainment.

The so-called flight of labor and absenteeism, though different phenomena, both create production difficulties in Siberian plants. Workers in the "flight of labor" group voluntarily abandon their jobs because of lack of social-cultural amenities. In these respects, things were so bad in 1983 at the large Shimanovski industrial complex serving the new Baikal-Amur Mainline railway (BAM) that it was losing a third of its workers and engineering staff annually. Because of the labor shortage, it then employed anyone regardless of qualifications, with often nefarious results to equipment, according to *Pravda*.[10]

In the case of absenteeism, workers do not voluntarily abandon their jobs but may be dismissed for this offense. Apparently, dismissal does not seem to have much effect on the delinquent worker; he knows that when hard pressed, the overseer (master) will re-employ him—a rather hopeless situation as long as shortages of labor continue. Time-consuming practices, not subject to absentee penalties, such as long "smoke breaks" or extended leave, tolerated by too-lenient managers, could, however, be curtailed by tighter administrative controls.[11]

The gravity of the continuing labor shortage problem in Siberia (and elsewhere in the Soviet Union) is reflected in the current high-powered Soviet drive for more rapid installation of robots and modern technology in industry to reduce the need for the unreliable human element as far as possible. The Soviet press also reported that a "robot dread disease" had appeared in some enterprises, including the Siberian Altai tractor plant and the Krasnoyarsk park of harvesting machines.[12] Whether this "dread" arose from inertia or from a conservative attitude to a novelty was not explained, nor was it stated if in fact robots were eventually installed in these reluctant enterprises.

THE SIBERIAN ECONOMY

Other chapters in this book discuss major sections of the Siberian economy—energy, transport, agriculture, mining, and metallurgy. The following comments view this comprehensive subject in much more general terms.

The great natural resource base characteristic of Siberia and the Soviet Far East is marked by the disparity between the rich mineral reserves and huge forest cover, and the relatively meager extent of land suitable for agriculture. The geological research of postwar years has greatly increased our knowledge of these reserves. Some of the most valuable—gold, oil, and natural gas—are located where terrain and climate are extremely harsh, and construction therefore difficult.

Very large capital investments and inflows of labor are required to develop these reserves, but these investments are quickly recouped. The foreign capital and labor that have played an important role in developing the economic resources of the United States, Canada, and Australia have not been used by the Soviets to develop Siberian reserves. Contingents of East European workers were, however, employed on construction sites such as the Ust-Ilimsk hydroelectric power station (HES). Also, U.S. and West European technology has been used, when available, to supplement less advanced Soviet equipment, notably in the well-advertised recent case of the Urengoi gas pipeline to Western Europe.

The first phase of Soviet interest in the Siberian economy was reflected in Stalin's decision to construct a second metallurgical base in the Kuznetsk Basin (Kuzbas) (as formulated in the early five-year plans of the 1930s), far from the Leningrad-Ukrainian bases vulnerable to a German attack. Using Urals iron and Kuzbas coal, a powerful metallurgical industry was built up at Novokuznetsk, reinforced with a labor force evacuated from the Ukraine. Later, some gold and other mining industries were exploited, mostly in incredibly harsh conditions with forced labor.

After Stalin's death, renewed interest in Siberia's economic possibilities was expressed by Khrushchev at the twentieth and twenty-first party congresses and decisions were made to develop Siberian natural resources more actively. Long starved of investment, Siberia was allotted useful funds destined mainly for the energy-extraction and engineering industries, housing, and domestic facilities.

Relatively little attention was paid to the light industries. The Siberian economy continued to expand, backed by further investment, under the rule of Brezhnev and Andropov. The position of some light industries, including the manufacture of boots, shoes, and knitted garments, considerably improved, although Siberia continues to be largely dependent on European Russia for many domestic supplies.

As a result of these policies, both industry and population have expanded in older Siberian towns like Omsk (population 1,094,000 in 1984), Novosibirsk (population 1,384,000), and Krasnoyarsk (population 859,000). Moreover, entirely new towns have been established in the virtually uninhabited Siberian tundra and taiga to serve the hydropower and oil and gas industries. For example Bratsk now contains 236,000 people, Surgut 188,000, and Nizhnevartovsk 178,000.

Since the 1950s, the growth of productive forces east of the Urals has considerably altered the economic relation between European Russia and the eastern territories of Siberia and the Soviet Far East. Academician Aganbegian estimates that Siberia is developing faster than other Soviet regions, with about a tenth of the country's industrial and agricultural production. At the present time more than half a billion tons of fuel a year (in standard terms) are sent from Siberia and the Far East to the European part of the country, along with more than half the increased production of the timber and chemical industries. The contribution of Siberia to the solution of the food industry is also considerable, in his view.[13]

As the important subject of energy is discussed in a separate chapter, only a few general pointers to its significance in the Soviet economy will be given here. The largest oil and natural gas reserves in the Soviet Union are now being worked in the north Tyumen oblast of West Siberia, making the Soviet Union a leading world producer of these resources. High production targets were set for both oil and gas in 1985; some foreign experts considered them unrealistically high in view of unfavorable accounts in the Soviet press in 1984 of production volumes of the oil industry.[14] This oil and gas are now reaching European Russia by several pipelines; the natural gas arrived in France from Urengoi via the West European pipeline in 1984. The prospects of oil and gas development in East Siberia are now considered good by Soviet geologists and, if exploited, these resources should be a boon to the eastern regions and further boost the Soviet Union's already high place in this field of energy.

The development of the great hydraulic potential of the Angara and Yenisei rivers in East Siberia since the 1950s has been phenomenal. On this power basis, industrial centers have been built at Shelekhov, Bratsk, Ust Ilimsk, and Dvinogorsk (Krasnoyarsk), while the many-sided industrial complex of Sayanogorsk, based on the Sayan HES, the most powerful in the USSR, is nearing completion. The chief products manufactured at these plants are aluminum, cellulose, paper, and other wood products. Siberian aluminum is of major importance to the Soviet defense industries, and all aspects of the industry are surrounded with great secrecy. Visitors to Bratsk, for example, may look around the cellulose plant but are forbidden to enter the aluminum center. No statistics of aluminum output are published. Native Soviet bauxite is scarce, so the Siberian aluminum industry has to rely on either imported bauxite or alumina and nephelite ore, mostly from the Urals and Achinsk. Aluminum plants are widely distributed throughout the Soviet Union, which is now the second largest world producer of this metal.

In the Soviet Far East, the power of the great Lena and Amur rivers has not yet been exploited. The Zeya HES in the Amur oblast and the Vilyui HES in Yakutia provide invaluable power locally. Another HES is under construction at the Bureya River, and a number of small thermal power stations serve the domestic requirements of the southern areas of the Far East. In the extreme northern zone, the Kolyma HES has been under construction since 1970 (under very difficult conditions), and the atomic power station at Bilibino serves gold and tin mines in the Chukot okrug.

The hard coal reserves of the Kuzbas mines now rival and may soon surpass in production the older Donbas (Donets Basin) fields. This high-quality coal is exported in large quantities to European Russia. On the basis of this coal and the regional iron supplies, a major metallurgical industry operates at Novokuznetsk (which will be described in more detail later in the Metallurgy-Engineering section). Farther east a start has been made in developing the immense Kansk-Achinsk brown coal mines. This fuel is to be used in a number of unusually large thermal power stations. Its high friability makes it economically impossible to transport by rail or road, though transport is possible by a slurry pipeline.

Notwithstanding the rich Soviet energy base (Siberian hydro power alone supplies the cheapest electricity in the world), the need for greater conservation of energy and all raw materials is strongly stressed today in an effort to reduce waste by industrial workers.[15] In his speech at the November 1982 plenum of the Central Committee of the CPSU, Andropov declared that it was "very important economically to use coal, natural gas, oil, oil products, thermal and electrical energy." However, cases of wasteful misuse of most of them, including fuel oil by motorists, are frequently mentioned in the Soviet press. The underlying implication of this campaign is that however rich, these energy resources are not inexhaustible and if wasted cannot be replaced. Soviet scientists' interest in this subject was expressed in their draft regulations for the conservation of mineral resources, formulated in 1983.[16]

The economic importance of efficient management and direction of industry, now at last recognized in the Soviet Union, raises points of special interest to Siberia. Individual subdepartments of the centralized construction ministries in Moscow have imposed excessive controls on construction sites of Siberian new towns and industries. They have created costly and largely unnecessary infrastructures to further their own interest in the more profitable industrial construction, while often neglecting less advantageous construction of housing and social-cultural amenities. This departmental indifference to workers' living conditions, which caused many workers to leave Siberia, has been sharply and frequently criticized in the Soviet press.[17]

These problems have long demanded solution. It is far from clear how the "territorial approach, an organic interdependence of departmental interests with the interests of the economic and social development of one or another region," proposed by Academician Aganbegian, would work out in practice and "overcome narrow departmentalism" and "create comfortable conditions of life for the people."[18]

"The effective use of labor forces" with good labor discipline, suggested by Aganbegian, remains another unsolved problem of the Soviet economy. The situation in the industrially important Tyumen oblast and the Novosibirsk krai was well illustrated at the local party conferences in 1984 by their respective representatives. According to the Tyumen delegate, mismanagement and waste was rife in the north Tyumen oil and gas industry. In 1983 the oil plan was not fulfilled for the first time, and for much more discreditable reasons than the weather. Serious defects in storage and use of pipes and in the construction of wells and gas pipelines were tolerated, he stated. Every fifth enterprise in the Tyumen oblast failed to fulfill production volume targets, and many contractual obligations were broken. The work of even cadres and party members was found to be unsatisfactory, and some of them were even accused of attempting to lower plan targets.[19]

Much the same criticism of waste and mismanagement was made by the Krasnoyarsk delegate. In his krai, he said, many of the production collectives failed to fulfill labor productivity obligations while half of the enterprises broke their contractual supply obligations. The poor organization of robots was held partly responsible for this state of affairs and the amount of manual labor employed was still too high. The volume of unfinished production and the abnormal level of uninstalled equipment showed the need for improvement by construction agencies.[20]

Other delegates noted the serious defects tolerated in the management of capital construction work in the Khakass oblast, Sayanogorsk, and Minusinsk towns—all big industrial development areas. Lack of discipline among some workers was so bad at an Omsk broiler factory that other workers were "fed up" with their "unruliness, slipshod work, coverup of all kinds of dodging and drunkenness" while widespread absenteeism left thousands of fowls unfed and injured the plant's production in many ways, according to *Pravda*'s report.[21] The prevalence of this kind of labor indiscipline and slackness in the Soviet economic system at all levels inspired Yuri Andropov's determined drive for labor discipline before he died.

In Siberia, labor problems are probably best viewed in the perspective of the great industrial projects brought to fruition since World War II, even though construction was beset with most frustrating problems of labor and inefficiency. The volume of expenditure by Moscow on these major developments is not exactly known. In view of the high costs of labor and equipment and the formidable terrain of many of the construction sites, notably that of the north Tyumen oil and gas industry, investment must have been of a very large order.

Today the emphasis is rather on completing the many lagging enterprises in Siberia and on the need to improve workers' living conditions on construction sites and in new towns. There are, however, many interesting projects in "cold storage" for execution at a more appropriate time—schemes for timber and mining development in the BAM zone, for instance. Then, in the years ahead, the Siberian economy should expand in various directions as unexploited reserves (confirmed by geologists) are gradually developed and more manufacturing and light industries are established to cut down the present imports of clothing and other domestic necessities. These developments, however desirable and even necessary, will largely depend on the extent to which the present serious labor shortages can be curbed, perhaps by advanced technology and robots—an open question at the moment.

SIBERIAN AGRICULTURE

From the first years of the Russian conquest of Siberia in the mid-seventeenth century, providing food for the Cossacks, administration officials, and settlers was a main preoccupation of the tsarist government. From the later years of the nineteenth century and the first decade of the twentieth, government-subsidized migration policies promoted a big inflow of peasant settlers to Siberia, to clear the forests and plant crops for food. At the same time, large numbers of other peasants moved there on their own, to establish farms far from the oppression of landlords (who did not exist in Siberia).

Many of these peasants were settled in West Siberia, which contains the most fertile lands in the eastern regions. For years before the revolution, an industrious, thriving Russian peasantry produced a surplus of food. Grain, dairy, and other agricultural products were exported to European Russia and farther west. With the 1917 Revolution, these exports ceased. The once-prosperous Siberian farmers, now labeled kulaks, were removed from their farms by the Soviet collectivization policies of the 1930s. In the struggle against collectivization, many were killed.[22] Planned directives and production targets, largely framed on ideological lines by urban bureaucrats with little or no first-hand knowledge of cultivation methods, ignored the individual farmer's personal knowledge of the region. The results of this politically inspired agrarian policy were long disastrous for Siberian agriculture.

After years of neglect under Stalin (a time when the weight of Soviet interest in Siberia was on industrialization and the new Kuzbas metallurgical base), the first indication of concern about the Siberian agricultural situation came with Khrushchev's 1954 "Virgin Lands" project, which extended widely into southeast areas of West Siberia and the Altai. Large expanses of fallow lands were sown to grain, and at first some excellent crops were produced. Then serious erosion, low yields, and soil infertility began to take their toll. These problems were later attributed to inappropriate methods of cultivation imposed by local bureaucrats. With the rejection of these errors and the removal of compulsory quotas, Siberian grain yields gradually improved (according to official Soviet statistics of 1960–1969), although not to the levels anticipated by Khrushchev and the five-year plans.

Cattle production in West and East Siberia had also suffered great losses as a result of Stalinist policies. The combined effect of low prices officially imposed, severe limits and excessive taxation on private cattle holdings, and the high costs of production had decimated the industry, and the surviving livestock was in a pitiful condition. Khrushchev's efforts to increase Soviet production of meat, butter, and milk (with vigorous claims to surpass American output of these items in 1957) led to some temporary improvements in the Siberian dairy industry. However, attempts to deal with the long-neglected housing problem, to reduce the exodus from rural areas, met with little success. In fact, from 1960 to 1970 the rural population of Siberia declined by 30 percent, 17 percent in West Siberia alone (in line with all-union trends).

Khrushchev's initiatives to raise Soviet agriculture from stagnation failed to reach production targets. They were followed in 1965 by the more realistic Brezhnev reforms—also aimed at higher agricultural productivity but with more practical targets than those set by Khrushchev. Overall investment in agriculture was considerably increased, but it was still not sufficient to put Siberian agriculture on its feet or to redress the long years of meager investment in the industry. Procurement and wage rates were raised for Siberian farmers working in the harsh environments of the north, and steps were taken to improve rural housing and social-cultural facilities: schools, nurseries, medical services, and so on. However, these measures were still inadequate to solve these problems throughout the huge areas of Siberia and the Far East.

A series of poor harvests in the 1970s and the widespread scarcity of food in the Soviet Union seem to have convinced the leadership of the gravity of the problem and the need for thoroughly revising Soviet policies for dealing with it. Thus in May 1982 official policies on agriculture and food were promulgated by the USSR Food Program (1982–1990), which remains the mainspring of current Soviet activities in this field.[23]

The chief provisions of this comprehensive document to a large extent echoed and strengthened the Brezhnev reforms. The need for greatly increasing

TABLE 1.3
Average Annual Production of Basic Soviet Agricultural Products (in millions of tons)

	1961–1965	1976–1980
Grain	130.3	205.0
Sugar beets	59.2	88.7
Vegetables	16.9	26.3
Fruit and grapes	6.5	15.2
Meat (weight for slaughter)	9.3	14.8
Milk	64.7	92.7
Eggs (in billions)	28.7	63.1

SOURCE: *Pravda,* May 25, 1982.

food production was stressed. The failure to satisfy the country's demands for meat and milk products and the inadequate supplies of fruit and vegetables were admitted. Statistics produced in the years 1961–1965, published in the program (see Table 1.3), purported to show that the annual growth in basic foods per capita exceeded the increase in population since 1965 (35 million). Production was allegedly hampered in many collective and state farms by the inadequate levels of complex mechanization, poor use and low quality of agricultural technology, and inadequate supplies of fertilizer. These were some of the "big, complicated, and responsible tasks" calling for solutions by the program.

Massive increases in agricultural investments were therefore allotted, including more funds for rural housing and domestic facilities. Pay for collective and state farm workers was to be raised. "It is important," declared the program, "that every worker sees the precise connection between what he does and what he earns." Payment for workers in agriculture (as in industry) was to reflect the natural climatic conditions of the area, and regional coefficients were to be introduced in areas of Siberia and the Far East. Further financial inducements were offered to specialists prepared to work in unremunerative and loss-taking firms.

The program recognized the considerable contribution of private-plot holders and garden-orchard cooperatives to the production of meat, milk, and fowl, and even more of potatoes, vegetables, and fruit (estimated at about 25 percent of total Soviet production). The program decreed they were to be given much greater help by the government, local soviets, and collective and state farms: "and this help must be shown without fail and systematically." Following years of oppression, this recognition of the private-plot holders' work should encourage them to further efforts. (Their position had already been somewhat improved by the removal of important restrictions on these plots in the decrees of 1977 and 1981.) Procurement prices for cattle, grain, and other agricultural products "do not correspond to necessary production costs," according to the program, and would be raised beginning January 1983. Payments in kind, including grain, should be made to cultivation workers.

The program thus offered many financial inducements to agricultural workers to increase labor productivity and production while shortcomings in the agricultural industry were severely criticized. It was stressed, for example, that all waste must be eliminated, especially the "excessive waste" of food in certain institutions. The "cadres" were allowed too frequent changes in managers in collective and state farms, and "control over democratic principles of production management [should be] strengthened."

This Food Program reflects the determination of the Soviet leaders to raise Soviet agricultural production and improve rural conditions. It offers higher pay to all categories of farm workers, prospects of better housing, help to private-plot holders, and, above all, massively increased investment funds for agricultural development. Two years after the launching of the program, the question of its success inevitably arises.

It is a complex question indeed, one on which volumes might be written. The situation was, however, succinctly reviewed in a major speech by the present party leader, M. S. Gorbachev (then a member of the Politburo and secretary of the Central Committee), in March 1984 at the all-union economic conference on problems of the agroindustrial complex, in Moscow. Briefly, his conclusions were not encouraging. "Production is increasing slowly in many krais and oblasts in the RSFSR. For example, the kolkhozy and sovkhozy in the Altai krai reduced the production and procurement of grain and other types of production in this plan period, in spite of increasing resources," he declared. Notwithstanding large investments allotted for the development of agricultural machine construction, he criticized the relevant ministries for not producing modern types of tractors and other new technology. Many other critical points made by Gorbachev suggest that the improvements in working conditions promised by the program have not yet had the expected response from the farmers or industrial workers.

An explanation of this attitude may at least partly lie in the fact that the program is contained within the constricting framework of the Soviet agricultural system, which governs all basic aspects of production. All major decisions, including production targets, belong to the central planning organs in Moscow and the responsible ministries. The farmers on the spot cannot, for example, decide when to sow and reap, even though they are mostly much better informed about the local soils and climate on which production depends than the Moscow bureaucrats.

Another source of irritation to local farmers is the chain of bureaucrats—mostly party members—appointed to supervise farm work in accordance with orders from Moscow. Even orders revealing ignorance of local conditions and requirements must be followed (though they are often surreptitiously ignored), or penalties are enforced. Under these conditions, Siberian farmers have become frustrated and may lose interest in farming. There are some slight indications that the Soviet government realizes that strict enforcement of these doctrinally based policies may hamper rather than increase agricultural production. The slogan "to be master of the land," now frequently addressed to collective farmers in the Soviet press, and the emphasis on "more democratic management" on farms should give farmers hopes of a greater say in farming matters. Official policy is still far from clear but should be clarified at the twenty-ninth party congress in February 1986.

From the standpoint of Siberia and the Soviet Far East, the major interest of the program surely lies in the much larger investments to be made available for such costly matters as rural housing and social amenities, and better roads between remote villages and towns (especially those in the neighborhood of some new northern Siberian towns), to mention only a few outstanding Siberian needs.

Geographical-climatic conditions for agriculture differ greatly among West Siberia, East Siberia, and the Soviet Far East, and their investment and other agricultural problems vary accordingly. The best natural conditions for agriculture are in West Siberia, which in good years can make a sizable contribution to Soviet food supplies, principally cereals.[24] East Siberia and the Soviet Far East have a harsher climate and often require costly imports of foodstuffs either from European Russia, Canada, or the United States to make good local deficiencies.

Statistics of agricultural production in Siberia are no longer published. In the good years in the 1970s, when official statistics were available, Siberia was estimated to produce some 15 percent of Soviet grain, 11 percent of its meat, and more than 20 percent of its timber. In spite of the hazards of an unpredictable climate—hot summers, winter blizzards, and low precipitation—the good black soil of West Siberia should guarantee favorable harvests when the weather is propitious.

Harmful cultivation methods in the 1970s produced serious erosion, which threatened fertile grain-growing areas of West Siberia in the Kalunda steppe. The erosion was eventually halted, but not before many of the mechanized cadres had fled from the scorched fields. Large-scale amelioration schemes restored cultivation in the Kalunda steppe. The Baraba swamps were drained, and good crops were also produced there. The completion of the Kalunda Canal in 1983 made it possible to irrigate 40,000 additional hectares (98,840 acres), and prospects of grain cultivation there are good.

Apart from the weather, other factors beyond the farmers' control can hamper agricultural production in Siberia—many of them arising from ministerial inefficiency or carelessness. Factors mentioned by Soviet sources are lack of timely supplies of seed, inadequate fertilizer stocks, unreliable rural electrification, equipment unsuitable for Siberian conditions, and insufficient modern technology. The unsatisfactory state of seed preparations for the spring sowings was criticized in 1983–1984. Wheat seed was not quite adequate in West Siberia, and the Tomsk oblast had only 80 percent of the seed required, according to one report. Another report criticized farms in West Siberia, East Siberia, and the economic regions of the Urals for inefficiency in replacing low-quality seeds.[25]

The USSR is second among world producers of mineral fertilizer. Nevertheless, there is an acute deficit of phosphate fertilizer for the Siberian and Far Eastern fields. One reason is that the chief bases of Soviet phosphate and potash supplies are very remote from Siberia (phosphate is produced in the Kola Peninsula and Karatay in Kazakhstan and potash in Solikamsk). This fertilizer shortage was regarded as so serious that the Siberian department of the Soviet Academy of Sciences set up an interdepartmental commission in 1961 to investigate possible phosphate and potash sources in Siberia and the Soviet Far East. Some raw phosphate was discovered hundreds of miles east of Norilsk—inaccessible to the West Siberian agricultural lands that need it until a railway is built there.

According to an expert of the Siberian Agricultural Research Academy, during plowing Siberian soils lose three to four tons of phosphate and ten to fifteen tons of nitrogen per hectare. Good agricultural practice calls for them to be systematically replaced with fertilizers. But the replacement quantities used are far from those required to prevent further exhaustion of Siberian soils, not to speak of any increased productivity. The fertilizer problem in Siberia and the Far East is acute for grain crops, though not for sugar beet or sunflower fields. To import it over thousands of kilometers would be economically unprofitable. And thus, in the view of Academician A. L. Ianshin, fertilizer is one of the serious causes of the relatively low harvests in Siberia. "Siberian fields need phosphorus," he states. "But where will it come from? The region's requirements for phosphorus fertilizer will not be satisfied from local sources till at least the year 2000."[26] In spite of the low level of fertilizer supplied, losses of it are reported from Siberian farms owing to poor storage and careless spreading on the part of the farmers themselves.

Another problem basically affecting Siberian agricultural production (and only incidentally mentioned in the Food Program) concerns technology and the agricultural machinery made of non-frost-resistant steel supplied by the manufacturing ministries to Siberian farms. Plowing, harvesting, and other agricultural machines designed for European Russia frequently break down under the pressure of the harsh Siberian climate. They require costly repairs—if indeed they can be repaired at all. The spare parts necessary for repairs are often lacking and local workshops are ill-equipped to deal with these problems. The constant complaints published in *Pravda* alone since the Brezhnev reform (and for years earlier) expose the lack of coordination between the centralized ministries responsible for the manufacture of agricultural machinery and the Siberian farm requirements. Supplies of even non-frost-resistant equipment are inadequate. These deficiencies will be discussed in more detail in the section below on engineering.

Geographically and climatically, East Siberia is less favored for cultivation of grain crops than West Siberia. It is basically an area for large-scale livestock production, with smaller crops of grain and vegetables. The wide-open expanses of flat grassland provide abundant fodder for the important cattle and sheep industry of the Buryat ASSR, the main administrative unit of East Siberia. Between 1975 and 1981, the production of meat in Buryatia fell.

Some of this meat is processed at the Ulan-Ude meat-packing plant. After years of near-starvation under Stalin's rigid collectivization policies, the Buryat farmers are now in a considerably improved position. The excessive rigors of the Stalinist period, which resulted in enormous losses of cattle, were ameliorated by Khrushchev and then abolished by the Brezhnev reform.[27] Today, East Siberia is a leading Soviet cattle producer and meat exporter. There are still large reindeer herds in the northern part of the region. The adjacent huge area of the Soviet Far East contains a relatively small amount of arable land, mostly the good farming lands of the Amur-Zeya basin (the "granary" of the Soviet Far East) and the Primorye. Farther north, large uncultivated and uninhabited areas of Yakutia fringe the agriculturally bleak arctic territory. The planned expansion of grain and livestock in the farmlands of the Amur basin, lying on the Sino-Soviet frontier, is no longer threatened by the former dangerous flooding of the Zeya River, now largely contained by the Zeya HES dam. Official production statistics are not available, but if these plans are proved successful, Amur grain supplies should be appreciably increased as a result.

In the Primorskiy krai to the east, many varieties of crops and vegetation grow well in the fertile Khanka-Ussuri valleys: rice, sugar beets, soybeans, potatoes, and corn, plus a grain crop important locally but not exported. All are subject to the hazards of the seasonal monsoon climate. Stock breeding is successful in the southern Pacific maritime areas. Valuable fur-bearing animals are a great asset to the economy of the Soviet Far East. Farther north in western Yakutia, around Olekminsk where Russian settlers started agricultural production centuries ago, crops of grain, potatoes, and fodder are still successfully produced. There is a small amount of farming, with cattle and horse breeding, near Yakutsk. In the extreme north of the region, soil and climate impose severe limitations on any form of agriculture, though even in the "pole of cold" at Oymyakon there is (or was, in 1973) a state farm with thousands of reindeer, a number of cows, horses, and a fox farm.[28]

Overall agricultural yields are increasing slowly in the Soviet Far East, where agriculture is mostly confined to the good lands in the Amur-Zeya and Primorskiy areas. The mass of uninhabited land, taiga, and arctic tundra in the region set definite limits to agricultural progress.

Forest and Timber

The forest cover of the Soviet Union is the largest in the world, and 75 percent of this great natural resource is found in Siberia and the Soviet Far East. Only some 35 percent of Soviet output of timber, however, originates there, with an annual cut of about 10 percent. There is thus a considerable imbalance between the major consuming and producing sectors of the industry, both of which are in European Russia,[29] and the immeasurably greater reserves but lower production in Siberia. The European Russian timber industry is better organized than the Siberian, but there has been overfelling in these more accessible European sites and in some forests stocks are becoming exhausted. The trend appears to be for Siberia to become the leading Soviet timber producer, perhaps by the end of the century.

Throughout the thickly forested eastern areas, many different types of trees flourish in the taiga: conifers, aspen (used for matchsticks), and the invaluable larch, providing uniquely hard wood for telegraph poles and railway ties and sleepers.

Timber production in East Siberia and in the Soviet Far East has long been hampered by many factors: inefficient management, lack of hard-surfaced roads through the forests to bring in heavy equipment for felling and removing lumber, and poor working conditions in a bitterly harsh climate on many sites, leading to a quick turnover and occasional shortages of labor. For years criticism in Soviet sources about the poor state of this industry has been evident. Most notable was the attack on the "mountains of waste," unsatisfactory use of new equipment, and obstruction by narrow departmental interests at the big Maklakovo-Yenisei woodworking combine, made by then first secretary of the Krasnoyarsk krai obkom, V. I. Dolgikh, in 1971.[30]

Ten years later, Academician Aganbegian visited the Angara-Yenisei timber industry, in the course of a 1981 expedition, and also noted the waste and inefficiency there. "They cut out the timber selectively, leaving approximately 4 percent of the wood on the site. Moreover, they throw away another 10–15 percent of tops and twigs generally. Some 10 percent is lost in felling. About 54 percent of logs are obtained from the timber and the rest at best go into the fire or are thrown away on the waste land." In Aganbegian's opinion, it would be possible to double or triple the economic position of this industry if cellulose, hydrolysis, or other such production were organized. "Conditions are excellent—the enterprises would work on gratuitous raw material. More than one five-year plan will discuss the question. Meanwhile the volume of timber procurements will grow and with them unproductive waste."[31] The academician was obviously frustrated with the lack of encouragement for this project from the central planning authorities.

In West Siberia, the timber industry, though smaller, is better organized than

TABLE 1.4
Production of Sawn Timber (in thousands of cubic meters)

West Siberia	8,293
Altai krai	1,193
Kemerov oblast	1,561
Novosibirsk oblast	702
Omsk oblast	884
Tomsk oblast	1,696
Tyumen oblast	2,257
East Siberia	16,690
Krasnoyarsk krai	6,574
Irkutsk oblast	7,360
Chita oblast	1,192
Buryat ASSR	1,364
Tuva ASSR	200
Soviet Far East	6,502
Primorski krai	1,567
Khabarovsk krai	2,328
Amur oblast	811
Kamchatka oblast	248
Magadan oblast	231
Sakhalin oblast	619
Yakutsk ASSR	698

SOURCE: *Narodnoe khoziaistvo RSFSR v 1979* (Moscow, 1980).

TABLE 1.5
Production of Paper (in thousands of tons)

West Siberia	1.9
Novosibirsk oblast	1.9
East Siberia	132.1
Krasnoyarsk krai	120.0
Irkutsk oblast	12.1
Soviet Far East	248.7
Khabarovsk krai	9.2
Amur oblast	3.7
Sakhalin oblast	235.8

SOURCE: *Narodnoe khoziaistvo RSFSR v 1979* (Moscow, 1980).

in East Siberia. High-quality pine, fir, and larch are being successfully used for industrial purposes and in the block-house construction plants supplying some of the urgent housing requirements of the north Tyumen oil and gas industry.

In the Soviet Far East, though the cut remains relatively small compared to the huge potential (see Table 1.4), there has been a considerable advance in the numbers of woodworking centers active in the Khabarovsk and Primorski krais. Amursk, the satellite town of Komsomolsk, is notable for its wood chemical plant, the only one in the Soviet Far East, and a large concern containing milling and woodworking factories. A big cellulose and cardboard combine started production there in 1967.

Manufacture of paper is a relatively new industry in Siberia and the Soviet Far East. The Far East is the leader in Soviet paper output in the eastern regions, thanks to production from well-equipped mills seized from the Japanese in south Sakhalin after World War II. (See Table 1.5.)

With the arrival of the BAM in Komsomolsk, the many plans drawn up in advance for the development of the timber industry should soon get underway.

Fur Trapping and Farming

The large forested areas of Siberia from the Urals to the Pacific, where agriculture is not possible, are the natural habitat of Russia's most valuable fur-bearing animals: sable, ermine, mink, and squirrel. All the native peoples of Siberia have traditionally been highly skilled in the crafts of trapping and hunting these animals and before the Soviet revolution produced most of their valuable pelts. By the establishment of the first fur farms by the Soviet government in the 1920s, the fur industry was put on a new basis. Most Siberian fur now comes from caged animals bred in these farms.

The area around Lake Baikal is the habitat of the highly prized Barguzin sable, several times threatened with extinction from overhunting and poaching. They were long considered impossible to breed in fur farms, but after successful experiments in the Moscow Zoo, the sables can now be bred in captivity. The large Sable Natural Reserve on the Barguzin Hills, created in 1916 to restore depleted sable stocks, continues to study sable problems. Soviet conservationists and scientists, keenly aware of the threat to the natural habitats of Siberia's fur-bearing animals from deforestation and mining enterprises, endeavor to avert them, though with little success. A data bank established at the Siberian branch of the USSR Academy of Sciences records the distribution of animals in West Siberia so as to enable experts to evaluate changes in animal habitats induced by forest cutting and other harmful economic activity.

MINING, METALLURGY, AND ENGINEERING

Unlike the relatively meager arable land base available for agriculture, the mining-metallurgical industries of Siberia and the Soviet Far East are based on exceptionally rich and varied mineral reserves. The first metals worked by the

Russians in Siberia after the Russian conquest were gold, silver, and iron ore, which remained of primary interest to the tsarist administration up to the time of the Russian revolution. During the nineteenth century, the operations of the Lena gold fields drew international attention to the richness of Siberian gold reserves, but otherwise there was little interest abroad in Siberian minerals. After the Soviet revolution geological exploration was intensively promoted, to find new materials to supply the defense industries and to cut down costly imports of deficit metals like tin.

Since World War II, officially sponsored geological research throughout Siberia has brought to light some previously unknown ferrous and extremely rich nonferrous resources, mostly in East Siberia and the Soviet Far East. West Siberia, uniquely rich in petroliferous reserves, has not so far been found to contain significant metal resources. Soviet cosmonauts have also been engaged in geological research on land and sea, and have provided new information that has enlarged Soviet geological maps.[32]

Ferrous Metallurgy

Stalin's decision in the 1930s to create a second metallurgical base in West Siberia based on the rich Kuzbas coal fields—the Kuzbas-Urals Combine—was the origin of Siberia's modern metallurgical industry. Early dependence on iron ore from the Urals was later considerably reduced by the development of the iron mines at Temirtau and in the Khakass-Minusinsk areas. The creation of this second metallurgical base at Novokuznets (Kuznets Metallurgical Kombine, or KMK) proved a shrewd strategic move when the Germans invaded the Ukraine in 1941. Restored after the devastation of World War II, the older Ukrainian iron and steel industry eventually outpaced the Siberian Kuzbas plants as the leading Soviet producer of these metals, in spite of the considerable advances made by the Kuzbas industries.

The situation of the coal industry is somewhat different; the center of gravity seems to be shifting to the Siberian Kuzbas and the Kansk-Achinsk coal fields. Recent Soviet measures seem to favor the Ukrainian coal industry, according to the Soviet press, to the detriment of the needs and prospects of the Kuzbas industry. The greater part of all Soviet investment in the coal industry allegedly goes to the Donets Basin, even though the largest increase in coal extraction is found in the Kuzbas. This increase in turn requires expansion of the machine-building base of the coal industry; however, of the six new plants planned to be built in this decade, five are again based in the Donbas and only one in Siberia. Yet the Kuzbas mines supply European Russia with many millions of tons of high-quality coal, and production is increasing, while even with the maximum expenditure the Donbas can only maintain the present declining level of coal output before showing an inevitable fall in production, according to *Pravda*.[33]

Khrushchev's far-ranging plan for a third metallurgical base in Siberia (decided at the twentieth party congress in 1956) did not advance beyond the establishment of the Zapsib (West Siberian metallurgical plant) at Antonovskiy near Novokuznetsk, to which the Czechs contributed valuable modern equipment. Zapsib was the first Siberian plant to produce oxygen-converter steel, and it has a full cycle of production. It also has the most powerful blast furnace in the Soviet Union. According to present Soviet plans, Zapsib should produce 10.6 million tons of pig iron and 12 million tons of rolled metal by 1985. It therefore seems that the poor work discipline, bad management, and costly deficiencies on the Zapsib site noted in the alarming early reports may have been eliminated. Since the 1960s, another source of iron supplies for these Kuzbas plants was provided by the relatively remote Korshunovo "iron mountain" in the Irkutsk oblast and reported to be the largest mine yet developed in Siberia. Though the Kuzbas now has two integrated steel works, the main Soviet ferrous industries are still in European Russia and the Ukraine.

Farther east, the most important iron reserves in production are in the Aldan district in southern Yakutia and the Amur oblast. Smaller mines are scattered throughout East Siberia and the Soviet Far East. Iron ore is among the many minerals reported to exist along the new BAM track, and other important reserves, as yet unexploited, are believed to exist in East Siberia. At present however, Siberian and Far Eastern production of iron ore is only a small percentage (about 6 percent) of the total Soviet production. Though lacking iron ore mines, as far as is known at present the extreme northeastern area of Chukotka is very rich in tungsten. It is actively produced at the Iultin tungsten combine containing modern machinery and an enrichment plant. As there are no industrial centers in the proximity of remote Iultin to use this tungsten, the raw material has to be shipped out through Egvekinot port for industrial use elsewhere in the Soviet Union.

Industrialization has progressed steadily in the southern areas of the Soviet Far East, so much so that there is now an increasing deficit of iron and steel, which has to be imported from the western areas of the country, at high transport costs amounting to 20 million rubles annually.[34]

The Far Eastern steel plant at Amurstal (Komsomolsk-na-Amure) produces only a fraction of the rolled metal the region needs. More steel and rolled metal should become available when the conversion metallurgical works, now under construction at Komsomolsk, is completed. Some Soviet economists have long maintained that the Far East should have its own heavy metallurgical base, since the necessary raw materials (iron, coal, etc.) are locally available. The recent development of the largest known coking coal mines in the region, at Neryungri, near the iron reserves in western Yakutia boosted this prospect. So far, however, there has been no official confirmation of this project.

The nonferrous industries of Siberia and the Soviet Far East are of greater national significance to the Soviet government than the ferrous reserves. Nonferrous mines are widely scattered throughout the eastern areas of the north from Norilsk to the series of mines in Chukotka in the extreme northeast. The most valuable metals produced there are gold, nickel, copper, platinum, tungsten, and tin. Unique sources of Soviet diamonds are in western Yakutia. Nonferrous metallurgy has therefore been justly termed "the backbone of the Far Eastern economy."

For strategic reasons, statistics of nonferrous production are not published in the Soviet Union. Authoritative reports from the producing areas and other Soviet sources suggest that on the whole, production in this industry is satisfactory, though unsuitable equipment or bad living conditions cause occasional fluctuations. Production of some metals, notably gold and tin, has been boosted by "trails" left by prerevolutionary independent prospectors and later successfully followed by Soviet geologists.

Gold

In spite of official secrecy about the volume of Soviet gold production, some information (at best an informed estimate) may be gleaned from news items about the progress of various Far Eastern gold trusts and from reports of Soviet sales of gold abroad. All Soviet gold originates in eastern sources as far apart as the Yenisei and Lena gold fields in East Siberia and the Aldan, Magadan, and Chukotsk deposits in the Soviet Far East. Workers at the Yenisei mines were decorated for good production results in 1983. The once-famous Lena gold fields are still operating, though long eclipsed by more productive, newer mines.

The main Soviet gold-producing area is now the Kolyma Basin in the remote north of the Magadan oblast, with the administrative center at Susuman. Depressing reports appeared in Soviet sources about the working conditions in this industry. Accordingly, the mechanized equipment and the Bel AZ-548 trucks officially supplied, which are not built of frost-resistant steel, cannot stand up to the harsh Magadan climate. Equipment breakdowns are frequent and costly. Passenger and freight transport serving the gold industry is in a poor state; new buses sometimes lack heating facilities.[35] Here, as so often in Siberia, these difficulties are blamed on inefficiency of the centralized supplying ministries in Moscow, and their indifference to local needs.

Some Soviet geologists hold that the tundra wilderness and Chukotka may yet prove to be the most promising of all gold sources and that gold lode offshore may eventually reinforce the Chukotsk placers. All Soviet gold is refined at the Novosibirsk central gold refinery. A gold extraction plant is more conveniently situated for the Far Eastern industry at Nizhni Kuranakh in southern Yakutia.

Tin

For many years the Soviet Union imported most of its tin from abroad. This position was greatly eased by the discovery of rich tin resources in the Soviet Far

East. The great tin belt of the Soviet Union stretches from the Yana River and the Verkhoyanski area to the East Siberian extremity of Chukotka. Tin from the nearby Ese-Khaya ores is concentrated at Batagay, the capital of the important Verkhoyansk tin industry. The cheapest tin in the country is reported to be produced at Deputatski, another Yakutsk tin center, between the Yana and the Indigirka rivers. Farther east, Chukotsk tin resources have been well developed at Iultin, which has a concentrator.

Some tin is also mined around Omsukchan, in what *Pravda* called the "depths of the Kolyma wilderness" where the Dukatsk mining concentration plant was opened a few years ago. When the Dukatsk plant opened, all other tin mining in the Kolyma area ceased. This Dukatsk plant is situated in an area of extremely rigorous climatic and geographical conditions. Living conditions there were also so bad that it was almost impossible to keep workers at the plant in 1982, according to the director's report.[36] "There is a lack of labor," he wrote. "Those wishing to work here from the central areas, we cannot take, there is nowhere to house them. There are millions of capital investments but not one million is spent on housing. Not yet one residential house put up. Not one kindergarten, so many well-qualified women we need cannot work or leave the children." Unfortunately, the reaction of the responsible centralized ministries to this dismal state of affairs is not known.

Tin is also produced in the more clement southern areas of the Soviet Far East at Solnechny and Gorny (Khabarovsk krai) and Khrustalny in the Sikhote-Alin hills (Primorski krai). All Soviet Far Eastern tin is sent for smelting to the smelter at Novosibirsk. According to some foreign estimates, the Soviet production of tin in 1970 and 1980 was 30,000 tons, but official statistics are not available, so these estimates cannot be checked.

Nickel, Aluminum, and Other Resources

The vast Norilsk nickel combine in the arctic zone of East Siberia, with its large smelter, is the chief source of Soviet nickel. As a result of Norilsk production, the Soviet Union has become the second largest world producer of nickel, after Canada. Norilsk also produces platinum, copper, and cobalt. New nickel and other mines are often being developed. All Norilsk mining operations are conducted in extremely difficult conditions of permafrost ground and a harsh climate. There is also a cobalt plant at Norilsk, but neither the copper nor cobalt mined there is of national importance. Siberia's generally low place in the all-union production of copper should be improved when the Udokan copper mines, though difficult and expensive to develop, start production; this is now expected to follow the arrival of the BAM in this area. Cobalt production at Khovu-Aksu in the Tuva ASSR is much more important to the Soviet Union than the Norilsk cobalt.

The relatively new Siberian aluminum industry is of the utmost strategic value to the Soviet Union. Its emergence in Siberia was based on the development since 1954–1967 of the great hydroelectric potential of East Siberia. Aluminum is produced at large plants in Bratsk, Krasnoyarsk, and Shelekhov and is scheduled soon to start at Sayanogorsk, which will have the largest hydroelectric station yet built in the Soviet Union. No official statistics of aluminum production are published, but it is competently estimated that these Siberian plants produce about 80 percent of Soviet aluminum. As Soviet geologists have not found adequate bauxite deposits to feed the aluminum industry, the industry has to work on alumina, nephelines, and occasional imports of bauxite from abroad.

Small lead and zinc mines are scattered throughout East Siberia and the Soviet Far East, but production is mainly centered in the Caucasus and Central Asia, making the Soviet Union the second largest world producer of these metals.

The most important nonmetallic minerals found in Siberia are diamonds and salt. The discovery of the famous Yakutsk diamond pipes in the 1950s made the Soviet Union independent of imports. The center of this industry is at Mirny, now a well-established town in formerly uninhabited taiga and containing a diamond-processing plant. Working conditions are reported to be good there, with no "flight of labor." Other diamond sources are farther north in Yakutia at Udachny (with a diamond separation plant) and Aykhal. The main products of these plants are believed to be bort (industrial diamonds), not gemstones. It was therefore of interest to learn that in 1983 a gemstone of "exceptional beauty" and weighing 95 carats had been found in Yakutia. It was named after the eightieth anniversary of the Second Congress of the Russian Social Democratic Workers' Party.

Engineering

The Siberian and Far Eastern engineering industry has progressed actively since World War II, when the basis of the industry was greatly enlarged by the importation of sophisticated engineering plants from the Ukraine. Considerable restructuring and reorganization are necessary still to enable these industries to deal more effectively with domestic demands and the need for advanced technology. The engineering industries have developed along rather different lines in the three Siberian regions.

West Siberia has a well-developed metallurgical-engineering industry of considerable national importance in the Novosibirsk oblast and Kuzbas areas. Farming equipment and various electrical goods are produced at Omsk, Barnaul, and Tomsk, and railway equipment also at Omsk. Novosibirsk oblast alone produced many types of farming machinery and "almost half of the country's electrothermal equipment, a considerable part of the generators for turbines, and almost a tenth of the heavy electrical machinery in 1983."[37]

The Novosibirsk heavy foundry–equipment works (Siblitmash), however, is the only enterprise in the country that manufactures machinery for pressure casing and molding lines, according to Moscow Radio. The same report criticized other Novosibirsk plants for failing during the current five-year period to fulfill plans for rolled metal and steel pipes (amounting to thousands of tons of metal) and a high percentage of the planned metal-cutting lathes. Problems of excessive manual labor and poor labor discipline were cited in many of these plants and also in the various branches of the construction industries. Novokuznetsk is another major engineering center in West Siberia. Its two integrated iron and steel works are now producing some frost-resistant steel, and the heavy engineering plant makes engines, among other products in this field.

The chief engineering industries in East Siberia are highly specialized; they manufacture equipment for the local mining, woodworking, and transport industries. Mining machinery and woodworking industries are well established in Irkutsk and Krasnoyarsk and are expected to develop further. Ulan-Ude, the capital of the Buryat ASSR, has the largest plant east of the Urals for the construction and repair of diesel locomotives. Farther south, the largest wagon works in the country is at Abakan in the Krasnoyarsk krai. The product range and capacity of the Siberian electrical engineering industries should be greatly enlarged when the big Elektrograd plant now under construction at Sayanogorsk, in East Siberia, starts production. Elektrograd contains a complex of electrical engineering enterprises planned to produce huge turbo and hydro generators, electric motors, and much other electrical equipment, some never previously made in Siberia. It should assist Siberia's economic development in many ways and facilitate the constantly expanding East Siberian hydropower industry.

The timber industry of East Siberia based on the region's huge forest cover is largely located in severe climatic conditions. Much more of the equipment for this timber work (and also for the mining industry), now largely imported from European Russia, could be supplied by the East Siberian engineering and woodworking plants, if they were expanded and allocated the necessary funds and machinery. Such a development could also be a boon to other eastern areas, where predominant industries like mining and timber also rely to a large extent on imported equipment. In East Siberia itself Soviet experts are now optimistic about the extent of the still-unexploited oil reserves, and development seems in sight. Is it foolish to anticipate that in time even the special equipment required for this development might be manufactured by modernized, expanded East Siberian engineering works?

In the Far East, the engineering industries have considerably expanded and diversified, compared to their rather primitive prewar position. Except for mechanical repair shops, engineering plants are almost entirely located in the more clement southern areas of Khabarovsk krai. The following deserve mention: Dal'diesel, which has earned a reputation for reliable production of diesel engines; Dal'selkhozmash, manufacturing agricultural machinery and rice-harvesting combines (largely exported) in Birobidzhan; Energomash, an electric power machinery works; and Amurkabel, producing many types of cable for industry and shipbuilding.

Farther north, there are some major engineering enterprises of more than local importance at Komsomolsk-na-Amure. Amurstal is a fully integrated steel works, the only one in the Soviet Far East; it produces steel used by the fishing and ship-repairing industries. Amurlitmash (Amur foundry) complements Amurstal production with its manufacture of casting, mining, and crushing-grinding equipment. Some has been exported to India and other foreign countries, whereas 33 percent of the total Soviet output of casting machinery came from Amurlitmash in the 1970s. The lifting-equipment works at Komsomolsk produces gantry cranes that have earned a good reputation throughout the Soviet Union where they are also exported.

Against this background, the criticisms voiced by a distinguished economic expert in Khabarovsk of the structure of the Far Eastern engineering industries is of considerable interest.[38] Though there are already enterprises of more than ten branches of engineering and metalworking in the region, in the expert's view production little corresponds to local requirements. Some plants produce items not required locally and therefore almost entirely exported; others are not produced at all. At the same time, the region lacks the machines to supply leading branches of the economy: timber, mining, fishing, fuel, and energy. All this equipment is now brought in from afar. One economist recommended reorienting local industry to meet regional requirements and northern conditions, an investment he believed would be recouped in four to five years, thanks to economies on transport alone. In suggesting a proposal of this magnitude, *Pravda*'s economist failed to mention the many difficulties involved in equipping the Far Eastern engineering industries to supply even the large northern mining trusts with frost-resistant machines. They would apparently solve the labor problem, which might then arise with the formula "more technology, less people."

The provision of more suitable machines and equipment for the northern industries is a problem throughout Siberia, not just in the Soviet Far East. The unsatisfactory situation created by equipment unable to withstand the harsh northern climate has been analyzed in depth by two distinguished Siberian academicians, G. I. Marchuk, and A. G. Aganbegian, in much the same terms. In the first place, both agree that radical changes are necessary to cope with these problems. "For the accelerated development of the economy," states Marchuk, "Siberia needs a regional scientific policy and in the first place the supply of technology adapted to the mining-geological and natural-climatic conditions and not simply a copy of decisions suitable for other areas. Siberia is awaiting a series of machines and equipment designed for deep working of natural resources." It would therefore be advisable, in his view, to create engineering enterprises of purely Siberian specialization. "Meanwhile," he concludes, "the problem of technology for northern use remains acute."[39] Aganbegian agrees with Marchuk that Siberia requires specially adjusted technology. He mentions the heavy excavator factory for the Kansk-Achinsk mines at Krasnoyarsk and the expanded output of drilling equipment at Uralmash as steps in that direction, adding, however, that the greater part of technology in Siberia is little suited to local conditions. He describes many revealing instances of the defects of this technology and the costs to the economy. "Automobiles, bulldozers, cranes break down five to six times more often in northern conditions, their repair is three to four times more costly," he writes. "The annual costs of repairing Chelyabinsk bulldozers coming to the North is twice as high as the cost of making a new one. According to Iakut Filial of the Academy of Sciences, USSR losses from technology unadapted to freezing weather annually amount at present to more than a milliard rubles."[40]

As far as we know, the case so effectively made by Marchuk and Aganbegian in 1981 for a special technological policy for Siberia has not yet been implemented in corresponding government measures, though steps to improve the situation have been initiated by Gorbachev.

CONCLUSION

Since World War II, a number of projects essential for the further economic development of Siberia and the Far East have been successfully initiated, in spite of formidable climatic obstacles and other problems arising from human rather than natural causes.

According to Academician Aganbegian, Siberia and the Far East are developing more rapidly than other regions.[41] A framework has been established for Siberia's industrial expansion in new and old areas of activity. In the first place, the regional energy base has been exceptionally enlarged: witness the development of the north Tyumen oil and gas wells, an increasing number of large hydropower stations in East Siberia, the forward thrust of the Kuzbas coal industry, which now tends to surpass the older Ukrainian coal fields, and the promise farther east of the huge Kansk-Achinsk lignite mines. At the same time the more recently developed Neryungri coking coal adds considerably to the relatively limited known coal reserves in the Soviet Far East.

Backed by Siberia's rich and varied mineral reserves, the mining and engineering industries have considerably expanded in recent years. Presently, however, they are far from able to supply the machines (including frost-resistant equipment) required by the regional oil and gas and mining industries. Such equipment is now mostly imported from European Russia and partly from abroad. For years there have been complaints about the unsuitability of much of this imported equipment to withstand the harsh Siberian climatic conditions. As far back as 1966, for example, Academician Lavrent'ev deplored its defects in much the same terms as Academicians Aganbegian and Marchuk in 1981. So far, such comments have had little effect. Siberian scientists are now calling for the establishment of a "regional scientific-technical policy and not simply a copy of decisions suitable for other regions."

It may be that the failure to solve this long-standing problem is yet another reflection of the tussle of interest between the Siberians and the strongly entrenched European Russian industrial groups, who seem to sense a threat to their dominant position in Siberia's developing economic power. Thus, in one way or another they may endeavor to retard Siberian progress, sometimes even assisted by the centralized industrialized ministries, prone to favor European Russia over Siberian claims. The Siberians are, however, invariably supported by the important Siberian branch of the All-Union Academy of Scientists in Novosibirsk.

In the field of communications, the completion of the difficult 3,115-kilometer Baikal-Amur railway is a major achievement, much needed in the first place to reduce the present excessive load on the old Trans-Siberian railway. Though aviation now links most inhabited places in Siberia, ground transport in this huge area still needs to be greatly improved and extended. The widespread roadlessness between many Siberian villages has now become an acute problem in the Urengoi-Nadym and other difficult boggy sites of the north Tyumen oil and gas industry. No north-south railway yet links the Siberian arctic zone with the southern areas, and the main means of communication continues to be the great Siberian rivers, all of which flow north to the Arctic Ocean but are frozen hard in winter.

Unlike industry, Siberian agriculture presents more problems today than successes. This situation largely arises from decades of official mismanagement and neglect, including lack of investment. Much larger investment funds are now available for Siberian agriculture under the Food Program; agriculture is being assisted technologically and efforts are also in order to improve rural living conditions. Agricultural prospects differ greatly throughout the Siberian regions. West Siberia, with the largest share of the arable land, is the leading producer of grain, dairy products, and cattle. With the unpredictable seasonal weather, grain production can fluctuate from year to year. Arable land is scarce throughout the huge expanses of the eastern regions of Siberia and the Soviet Far East, mostly confined to the fertile Amur-Bureya basin and the Primorye. Siberian scientists have made great efforts to develop types of grain capable of defeating the weather in Siberia. No separate grain production statistics have been published, as formerly, in Soviet official statistical handbooks. According to the report on the fulfillment of the 1983 plan for agriculture, plans for the sales of grain to the government were fulfilled by the majority of union republics, ASSRs, krais, and oblasts, but a later report stated that the wheat sales plan is regularly not fulfilled in the Altai and the Novosibirsk oblasts.

Many Siberian villages are in a state of flux; farmers are leaving the collectives for the more prosperous towns in the vicinity, thus draining the farms of labor, and the official policy of resettling small remote farms into larger, more viable units is proving difficult to implement. The government has awakened to the need for improving the standard of living in Siberian villages by creating better housing and cultural-domestic services including nurseries, kindergartens, and medical facilities and providing a wider range of shops and goods, especially in isolated villages. Clearly such domestic improvements should benefit the agriculture industry, but there is only scrappy information about the progress of this policy in Siberia.

No account of development of Siberian resources would be complete without mention of the harassing problems of labor and management, which still await solution. Shortages of labor have haunted Siberian construction sites for years. Notwithstanding a succession of top-level party and government resolutions aimed at improving the situation, the responsible centralized construction ministries in Moscow and their subdepartments on the spot constantly display indifference to workers' housing, instead giving priority to the more profitable industrial construction. The result is a "flight of labor" when conditions are found intolerable, with most harmful results for construction targets and planned production.

"Youth is not eternally young," *Pravda* pertinently remarked in connection with the flight of workers from the huge Shimanovski works supplying the BAM.[42] "After three or four years the picture sharply changes: the Komsomols have grown up, married, and will not tolerate the bad living conditions normally accepted by enthusiastic 'kids.'" So, regardless of the high pay they receive, many simply walk away from their jobs. "A service of labor," empowered to ensure that government resolutions on living conditions are implemented, as suggested in 1966 by Aganbegian, is still badly needed.

The need to improve management of enterprises at various levels is now widely recognized and discussed in the Soviet Union. Doctrinal delicacy forbids mention of the paralyzing influence of the present rigid Soviet managerial system administered from Moscow by the centralized Gosplan (state planning commission), Gosstroy (state commission for construction), and the all-union responsible ministries. Individual managers' rights of decision on matters directly affecting their own enterprises are still limited by the overriding powers of these superbodies.

The economic experiment introduced by the 1984 plan included measures "to improve planning practice and economic management." It now remains to be seen how far it will actually "extend the rights of productive enterprises in planning and economic activity," as stated by N. K. Baibakov, chairman of Gos-plan.[43] It is at least a high-level Soviet admission that the present state system needs some rectification.

Basic criticism of the harm done to the Soviet economy and the workers by this state managerial system are to be found in an "inside" report by Tatiana Zaslavskaia, a senior member of the Siberian branch of the All-Union Academy of Sciences (leaked to the West in 1983).[44] Among many other points, she argues that the structure of the national economy has now become so complex that it is impossible to regulate it effectively from one center. She attributes the deteriora-tion of economic indices in the majority of sectors and regions to the outmoded system of state management established 50 years ago, no longer appropriate to the changed production relations in the Soviet Union. It also, she believes, has damaging effects on the initiative and the social morale of the workers. Logically, she thinks the group that would be most interested in a transition to economic management methods would be the more qualified and energetic members of the managerial staff of enterprises, whose rights it is proposed to enlarge, and the ordinary workers who could thus work more effectively and receive higher salaries.

Though under the former elderly Soviet leadership abolition of the rigid cen-tralized state management system would scarcely have been a starter, the recent official references, however vague, to more "democratic management," and the economic experiment tentatively introduced in the 1984 plan, suggest that some relaxation of state controls over enterprise management is to be introduced.

Siberia can undoubtedly take credit for an exceptional record of economic achievements in recent decades, but that should not disguise the fact that some major economic problems still await solution. Nevertheless, Siberia has a unique advantage over the older, more developed areas of European Russia in the opti-mism that radiates from this economically youthful and rich country. The farther one goes from Moscow, the greater are the sentiments of a new Siberian patrio-tism and pride in the country's great natural wealth and future promise. Soviet geologists maintain that Siberia has many other valuable, still undeveloped natu-ral resources that in time could be expected to enhance even further the position of the Soviet Union among world leaders of mineral production. Siberia has thus good reason to claim to be the land of the future, nationally and internationally.

NOTES

1. James S. Gregory, *Russian Land and Soviet People* (London: George G. Harrap & Co., 1968).

2. See Philip R. Pryde, "Conservation in the Soviet Union" (Cambridge, England: Cambridge University Press, 1972).

3. Boris Shishlo, "Iukagiry," *Sibirica* (University of Lancaster: British Universities Siberian Studies Seminar, 1983), pp. 8–25.

4. B. P. Orlov, *Izvestiia Ot. A.N.* no. 1, 1973.

5. *Pravda*, February 26, 1983.

6. Academician Abel Aganbegian, "Effektivnost' Sibiri," in *Zadachi stavit Sibir'* (Moscow: Sovetskaia Rossiia, 1982), pp. 59–60.

7. *Pravda*, June 11, 1982.

8. *Pravda*, March 3, 1984.

9. *Pravda*, February 29, 1984.

10. *Pravda*, October 25, 1983.

11. *Pravda*, March 13, 1984.

12. *Pravda*, December 8, 1983.

13. Aganbegian, "Effektivnost' Sibiri," pp. 42–43.

14. *Pravda*, April 3, 1984.

15. *Pravda*, June 2, 1982.

16. Tass in Russian for abroad, April 7, 1983.

17. *Pravda*, June 6, 1982.

18. Aganbegian, "Effektivnost' Sibiri," p. 62.

19. *Pravda*, January 19, 1984.

20. *Pravda*, January 21, 1984.

21. *Pravda*, January 9, 1984.

22. Nikolaus Poppe, "The Economic and Cultural Development of Siberia," in *Russia Enters the Twentieth Century* (London: Temple Smith, 1971), p. 138; H. P. Smolka, *Forty Thousand Against the Arctic* (London: Hutchinson, 1937), p. 27.

23. *Pravda*, May 25, 1982.

24. Aganbegian, "Effektivnost' Sibiri," p. 42; R. K. Saliaev, "Kak Upravliat' Urozhaem," *Zadachi stavit Sibir'*, pp. 222–24.

25. *Izvestiia*, November 26, 1983; and Moscow Radio, January 23, 1984, report on the meeting of the USSR Council of Ministers, Presidium on the Agro-Industrial Complex.

26. A. L. Ianshin, in *Zadachi stavit Sibir'*, pp. 214–20.

27. Caroline Humphrey, *Karl Marx Collective: Economy, Society and Religion on a Siberian Collective Farm* (Cambridge, England: Cambridge University Press, 1983), pp. 144–95.

28. I learned of this farm from Dr. Terence Armstrong, who visited Yakutia in 1973.

29. J. C. Dewdney, *USSR in Maps* (London: Holder and Stoughton, 1982), p. 72.

30. *Pravda*, March 26, 1971.

31. Aganbegian, "Effektivnost' Sibiri," p. 49.

32. *Pravda*, June 8, 1982.

33. *Pravda*, October 6, 1983.

34. *Pravda*, November 26, 1983.
35. Soviet television interview, July 28, 1983.
36. *Pravda*, December 13, 1982.
37. *Pravda*, December 22, 1983.
38. *Pravda*, November 26, 1983.
39. Aganbegian, "Effektivnost' Sibiri," p. 6.
40. Ibid., pp. 50–54.
41. Ibid., p. 42.
42. *Pravda*, October 25, 1983.
43. *Pravda*, December 29, 1983.
44. T. Zaslavskaia, English translation of Novosibirsk Report, with comment by Philip Hanson, *Soviet Studies* (Spring 1984), p. 88.

VICTOR L. MOTE   **2**

The Communications Infrastructure

As impressive as the plans for Siberian regional development are, equally impressive are the physical and economic constraints to those plans.[1] Not the least of those constraints involves a fundamental fact of geography: 80 percent of the demand for the bountiful Siberian resources lies in the European USSR, literally thousands of miles away. In fact, much of East Siberia and the Soviet Far East is closer to Anchorage, Alaska, and Seattle, Washington, than it is to Moscow. The hugeness of the Siberian landscape—57 percent of the total Soviet land area, a region that is over a third larger than the entire United States—embodies the epitome of what some geographers call an anti-resource—a resource that must be overcome before development can take place.

In order to conquer areas of such enormous dimensions, planners must first demand transportation systems of extraordinary lengths and, accordingly, costs. It is absolutely incredible to imagine that until the construction of the Baikal-Amur Mainline (BAM) Railroad during the past decade, an 80-year-old railway, the peerless Trans-Siberian, was the only means of intercity travel for hundreds of thousands of residents of East Siberia and the Soviet Far East. Given the fact that resource development projects have been shifted inexorably farther eastward during this century, the Trans-Siberian, which extends for some 6,600 kilometers (4,150 miles) between Sverdlovsk and Vladivostok, and its associated freight traffic are the principal reasons why the average length of railroad haul in the Soviet Union has increased from 528 kilometers in 1928 to over 900 kilometers in 1983.[2] In fact, when these averages are broken down by economic region, the Siberian lengths of rail hauls are easily twice those for the whole country (ten to eleven times the national average for all types of transportation).[3]

As resources are depleted in the European USSR and new raw materials are developed in Asia, the lengths of haul both for Siberia and the entire country will further expand, and so will the material costs of progress. For nested covertly among the expenditures on individual enterprises are the concomitant costs of infrastructure, not the least of which in Siberia and the Soviet Far East are the requirements for transportation and communications. Indeed, these costs are 40 to 50 percent higher than the country average in more hospitable southern Siberia and several hundred percent higher in the more remote northern portions of the subregion.[4]

RAILWAY TRANSPORT

Far and away the most important transportation option in the Soviet Union is the railroad network. It is also the most heavily used system in the world. For instance, Soviet railways carry three times as much freight per ton-kilometer of railroad track as do their counterparts in the United States. In parts of Siberia the railway is the only form of transport, and literally everywhere in that massive subregion it is the most reliable alternative.

The World Apart from BAM

Like the Great Northern, the Orient Express, the Blue Train, and other great railroads of the world, Siberian lines also have well-known names: Trans-Siberian, South Siberian, Central Siberian, Turksib, BAM, and Little BAM, among others. Of these the Trans-Siberian (Figure 2.1) is the most famous. It is the only railroad, and the only transportation artery except for aviation routes, that connects the east and west coasts of the USSR. Built in fits and starts between 1891 and 1916, it has been the major impetus to Siberian economic development ever since.[5]

Although it officially begins in Moscow, the Trans-Siberian Railroad traces its real geographic origin to the old mining regions of Sverdlovsk and Chelyabinsk oblasts in the eastern Urals. From the mountains it descends onto the world's flattest plain, the West Siberian lowland, laden with grain fields, pastures, cattle, and remnant lakes and swamps. The river junctions of Kurgan (on the Tobol), Petropavlovsk (on the Ishim in northern Kazakhstan), Omsk (on the Irtysh), Novosibirsk (on the Ob), and Krasnoyarsk (on the Yenisei), in their capacities as principal handling centers, where cargoes were shifted from rail to river and vice versa, were and are among Siberia's leading metropolitan centers. At the extreme western end, the gateway cities of Sverdlovsk and Chelyabinsk, on the Iset and Miass rivers respectively, are the two greatest manufacturing and transportation hubs of the central and southern Urals.

For hundreds of miles across the rustic West Siberian lowland, the gradients vary only in inches or fractions of inches. Perhaps for this reason, this branch of the Trans-Siberian is the busiest railroad segment in the entire country, and maybe in the world, carrying almost twice as much freight per unit of track as the Soviet average. The major cargoes on this segment include high-quality coal

FIGURE 2.1

Siblería and the Trans-Siberian Railroad

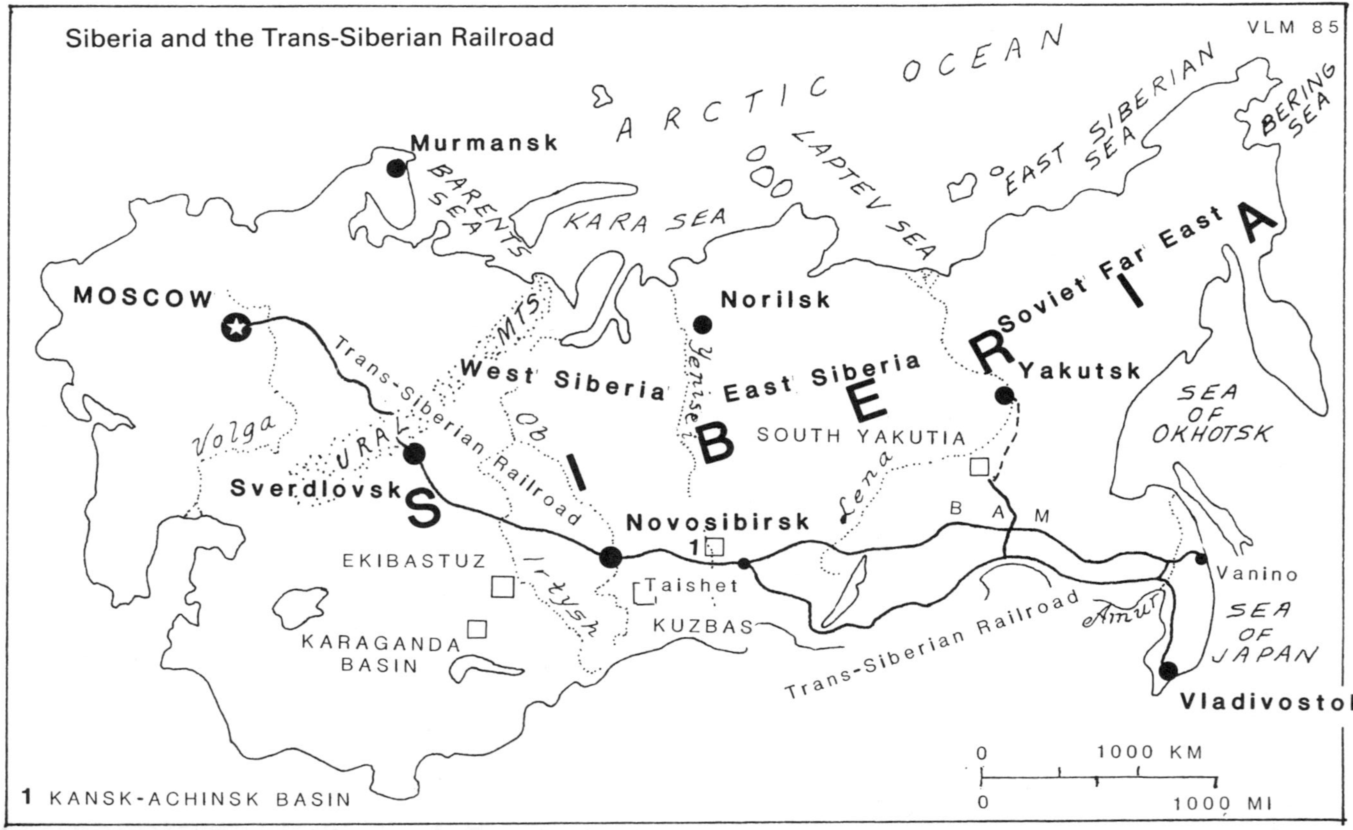

(going west from the Kuznetsk Basin, or Kuzbas), timber from the Lake Baikal region, and grain, for which Novosibirsk serves as the east-west dispatching point. Timber and grain shipments generally increase in tonnage in a westward direction, as the Trans-Siberian is fed by north-south trending lines and rivers at the major railheads. Other important cargoes are oil products going both east and west from refineries at Ufa and Omsk, potash and phosphate fertilizers going east from the central and northern Urals, and building materials from Sverdlovsk and Chelyabinsk. A rapidly growing recent addition to the cargo manifests has been oil- and gas-field supplies and equipment, destined for the Middle Ob oil fields and Lower Ob gas fields from Baku in Azerbaijan and the Volga-Urals ("Second Baku") manufacturing and processing centers.

The monotony of the western plains slowly changes eastward beyond Novosibirsk, as the Trans-Siberian skirts north of the Soviet Union's second greatest coal-mining region, the Kuzbas. Here, the iron horse gently begins to ascend the low ridge, valley, and range provinces of the east. The rise in elevation is barely perceptible, distinguished mainly by a greater frequency of coniferous forests and occasional copses of birches and aspens. Logging camps and lumber towns become apparent, and traffic over the Trans-Siberian thins down, particularly beyond Krasnoyarsk. The commodity mix also changes. In East Siberia timber and oil products are the principal cargoes, with coal a distant third. Both timber and coal are hauled west, while the oil-tanker cars roll east, as do grain and building materials.

Since 1970, there has been a much greater frequency of international container traffic between the Far East and Europe, especially in a westward direction over the so-called Trans-Siberian Landbridge (TSLB). Iron ore is shipped from the Lake Baikal area to the Kuzbas. The Soviet Far East is the recipient of oil and oil products (the largest single category of import into the region), coal from East Siberia and the Kuzbas, and grain from West Siberia. It also represents an *entrepôt*, whose ports at Nakhodka, Vladivostok, Vostochny, Sovetskaya Gavan, and Vanino serve as transit points for outgoing timber, coal, and ore and incoming shipments of fish, finished products, equipment, and containers.

The Trans-Siberian has been improved through the years. During the 1930s it obtained a second track. Its subgrade and rails have been upgraded several times since the 1940s. At the same time, it acquired its first segments of automatic block signaling. Today it is continuously electrified from Moscow to just east of Lake Baikal. Soviet officials hope to electrify the last link of track between Chita and Vladivostok between now and 1990.[6]

A second major east-west link with East Siberia is the South Siberian Railroad (Figure 2.2). At one time ending at the world's largest geographically concentrated iron and steel mill in Magnitogorsk, the South Siberian now extends to the Bashkirian petrochemical capital at Ufa. From there it swings southeastward into the Virgin (or New) Lands, through the Kazakh hillocky country and the

FIGURE 2.2

Railroads of West Siberia

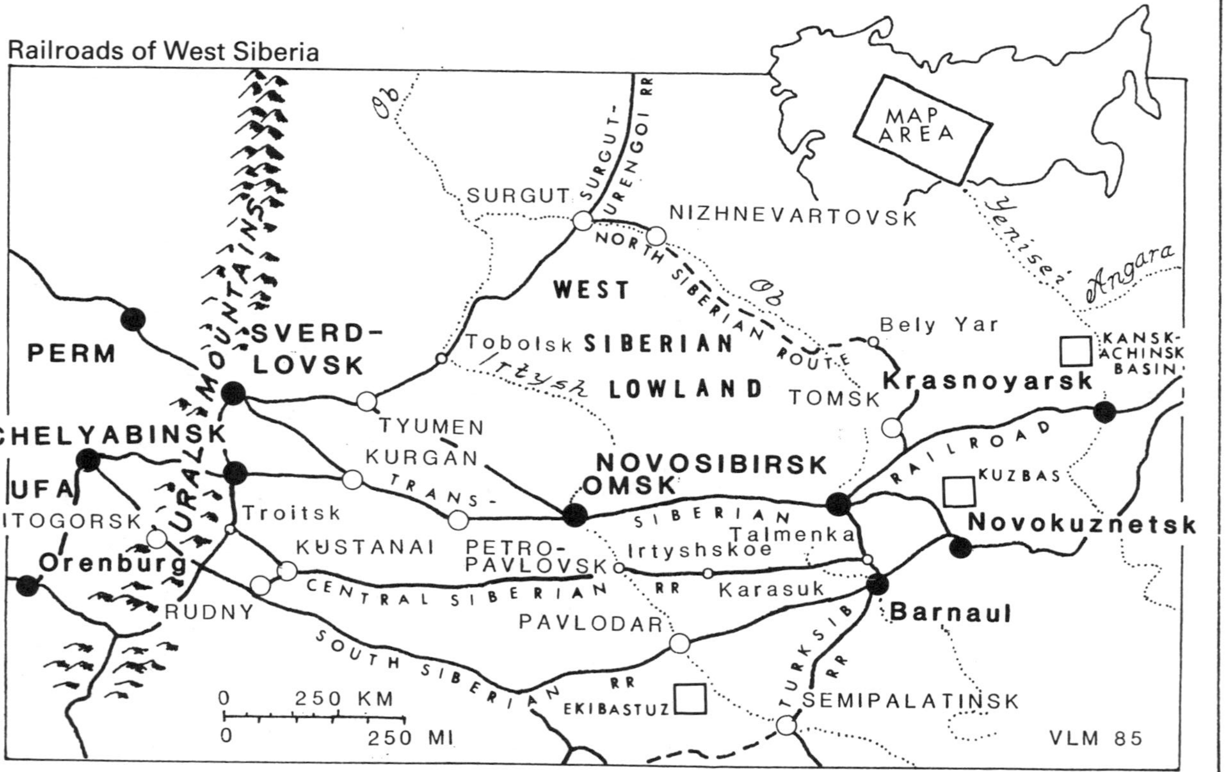

VLM 85

burgeoning Ekibastuz coal basin, to the river junctions of Pavlodar (on the Irtysh) and Barnaul (on the Ob), across the Salair Ridge to Siberia's major center of iron and steel metallurgy at Novokuznetsk in the Kuzbas, through the rugged Kuznetsk Ala Tau and the new energy-development centers of the picturesque Minusinsk Basin, and finally ends at Taishet on the Trans-Siberian. Except for a 500-kilometer stretch between Ekibastuz and Barnaul, the South Siberian is electrified throughout. On its most intensely used sections—the coal-train routes between Magnitogorsk and Tselinograd and between Novokuznetsk and Barnaul—the South Siberian is double-tracked.

Coal and grain are obviously the major commodities on the line, with west-flowing Kuzbas coal substantially augmented by coal moving in the same direction from Ekibastuz and Karaganda. One in four tons of Kuzbas metallurgical coal is mixed with the Karaganda variety to produce the pig iron and steel in the furnaces of Magnitogorsk. The Ekibastuz steam coal ends up as boiler fuel in huge new thermal-power plants in the Urals. The majority of the grain produced in the New Lands moves west, but on the eastern flank of the region, the Altai piedmont, for instance, grain shipments (and livestock products) flow east on the railroad to East Siberian consumers.

Iron ore is an important commodity on the eastern and western extremities of the South Siberian. The ore arrives in Novokuznetsk from iron ore pits east of Taishet and in Magnitogorsk from basins some 200 kilometers south and east of the city at Rudny and from the Kursk magnetic anomaly west of the Urals in the central black earth belt. Iron and steel from Magnitogorsk are used in either Urals or western manufacturing centers. The ferrous metallurgical products from the Novokuznetsk area are dispatched predominantly eastward over the South Siberian and Trans-Siberian to East Siberia and the Soviet Far East and, to a lesser degree, to customers in Central Asia by way of the South Siberian and Turksib railways.

Fertilizers for both the New Lands and the Central Asian cotton fields move east out of the Urals along both the South Siberian and Trans-Siberian to the Turksib and its branch lines. On the South Siberian's eastern extremity, timber shipments are fairly heavy to Barnaul and, to a lesser degree, Tselinograd. From Barnaul the commodity is shipped to Central Asia along the Turksib. Lastly, alumina-bearing materials flow east along the South Siberian to alumina and aluminum refineries in Pavlodar, Novokuznetsk, and points beyond.

The Central Siberian Railroad was built between 1954 and 1980 to serve as a backbone for the transport and distribution of New Lands' grain and supplies. It spans some 1,500–2,000 kilometers of flat to rolling countryside between the Turksib settlement of Talmenka and the Trans-Siberian city of Chelyabinsk. During the harvest season especially, the most important commodity moved is grain, going principally to the west. Throughout the year, however, supplies of agricultural machinery and equipment from such centers of machine construction as

Chelyabinsk, Novosibirsk, Barnaul, and others are readily witnessed on Central Siberian rolling stock.

The route also serves as an alternate east-to-west route for Kuzbas coal, which ofttimes cannot be accommodated by the Trans-Siberian or South Siberian. Iron ore from Rudny is an important west-flowing commodity on the western flank of the Central Siberian. Urals fertilizers are a major eastward cargo for much of the year. The eastern half of the Central Siberian (to Karasuk) is slated to be completely electrified and double-tracked by 1990. In the west double-tracking currently exists only on the segment of the Central Siberian that links the Trans-Siberian with the South Siberian.

These principal east-west mainlines are starting points for major north-south rail routes as well. The north-south spurs traditionally have served as feeders for resource and energy development. The most notable of the meridional lines is the Turksib Railroad, which, as the name obviously implies, connects Siberia with Kazakhstan and Central Asia, where the majority of the Soviet Turkic-speaking peoples reside. One of the major construction projects of the First Five-Year Plan (1928–1932), the Turksib was completed in 1931. Its mission was, and still is, to funnel Siberian grain, timber, and coal over the rail line's 2,500 kilometers to Central Asia in exchange for raw cotton and subtropical foods. Double-tracked from its starting point at Novosibirsk to Semipalatinsk, the Turksib links the Trans-Siberian with the Central Siberian (at Talmenka) and South Siberian (at Barnaul).

Two other north-south routes in West Siberia are the Kuzbas Railway and the Tyumen-Surgut-Urengoi Railway. The Kuzbas Railway is a completely double-tracked, electrified line that runs through one of the world's richest bituminous and anthracite coal basins from Yurga on the Trans-Siberian to Tashtogol in the Gornaya Shoriya iron ore district. It represents one of the most intensely used railways in the world. The region is deficient in iron and other ores, which are imported from eastern areas to bolster Kuzbas metallurgical centers. The coal is clearly in surplus and is the principal export. The byproducts of metallurgy and, more recently, imported West Siberian natural gas now serve as raw materials for the manufacture of nitrogen fertilizers, synthetic rubber, and chemical fibers that are shipped out of the Kuzbas and dependent neighboring regions (Barnaul, for example) to Siberian and other consumers. Alumina is imported from Pavlodar to Novokuznetsk, where it is manufactured into aluminum metal and exported north for distribution to the east and west on the Trans-Siberian.

The Tyumen-Surgut-Urengoi Railroad was begun during the 1960s to supply the Middle Ob oil fields with machinery and equipment for the exploration and development of what has only recently become the Soviet Union's most important producer of petroleum. Completed first as a 660-kilometer, single-track, diesel traction railroad between Tyumen and Surgut, the line has been extended now to the massive Lower Ob natural gas reservoir at Urengoi, 600 kilometers to the north. As such, the railway claims partial responsibility for making the West Siberian Ob region the country's largest producer of natural gas as well as oil. Since most of the fluid outflow goes through oil and gas pipeline, the principal cargoes on the railway are in-shipments of drilling equipment, pipe, pipeline equipment (compressors, gas preparation units, and the like), construction equipment and materials, and food. The single-track line is much overworked, and capacities doubled by 1985. Currently being extended to the Yamburg gas fields, the Tyumen-Surgut-Urengoi Railway eventually may be built as far north as Norilsk.[7]

In 1975 the Tyumen-Surgut segment of the last-mentioned rail route was supplemented by a 268-kilometer single-track, diesel traction spur to the principal oil fields around Nizhnevartovsk. We might not even speak of the line except that it represents the start of the long-awaited North Siberian Railroad, which eventually may link up with the meridional spur between Taiga and Bely Yar and run east to the Yenisei-Angara junction, and thence to the Baikal-Amur Mainline (BAM).[8] Presently the Nizhnevartovsk spur road supplies the Middle Ob oil fields with much of the same equipment inventoried earlier. Some oil no doubt moves by tanker car back to Surgut, Tobolsk, and Tyumen, although most goes out of the region by pipeline. Should the North Siberian ever be completed, it will serve as a major roundwood and lumber export line, as its projected route passes through country that is richly endowed with timber.

The World with BAM

With the exception of a few, relatively minor north-south spur roads, the picture of the Siberian railway system remained pretty much unchanged until the 1970s. Looking at a map of those railroads at that time, a keen observer would have noticed the existence of two key east-west spurs in East Siberia and the Soviet Far East: one, completed in the 1950s, running eastward from the South Siberian terminus of Taishet to the Lena River City of Ust-Kut, and another of World War II vintage running westward from the ports of Sovetskaya Gavan and Vanino to Pivan, just across the Amur River from Komsomolsk.[9] In between the two spurs lay 3,115 kilometers of swamp, permafrost, and northern coniferous forest (taiga)—a wild frontier, dependent almost totally on the Trans-Siberian, sometimes hundreds of kilometers to the south.

Little did our observer realize that Soviet planners and designers had mapped out a route for a new railroad across the seemingly empty expanse as early as the 1930s. Thus, the Baikal-Amur Mainline (BAM) Railroad (Figure 2.3) is an old idea whose time has come. First envisioned in various designs in the last century, the practical realization of building a major trunkline railway in permafrost regions north of Lake Baikal could not be achieved until modern technology was up to the challenge.[10]

FIGURE 2.3

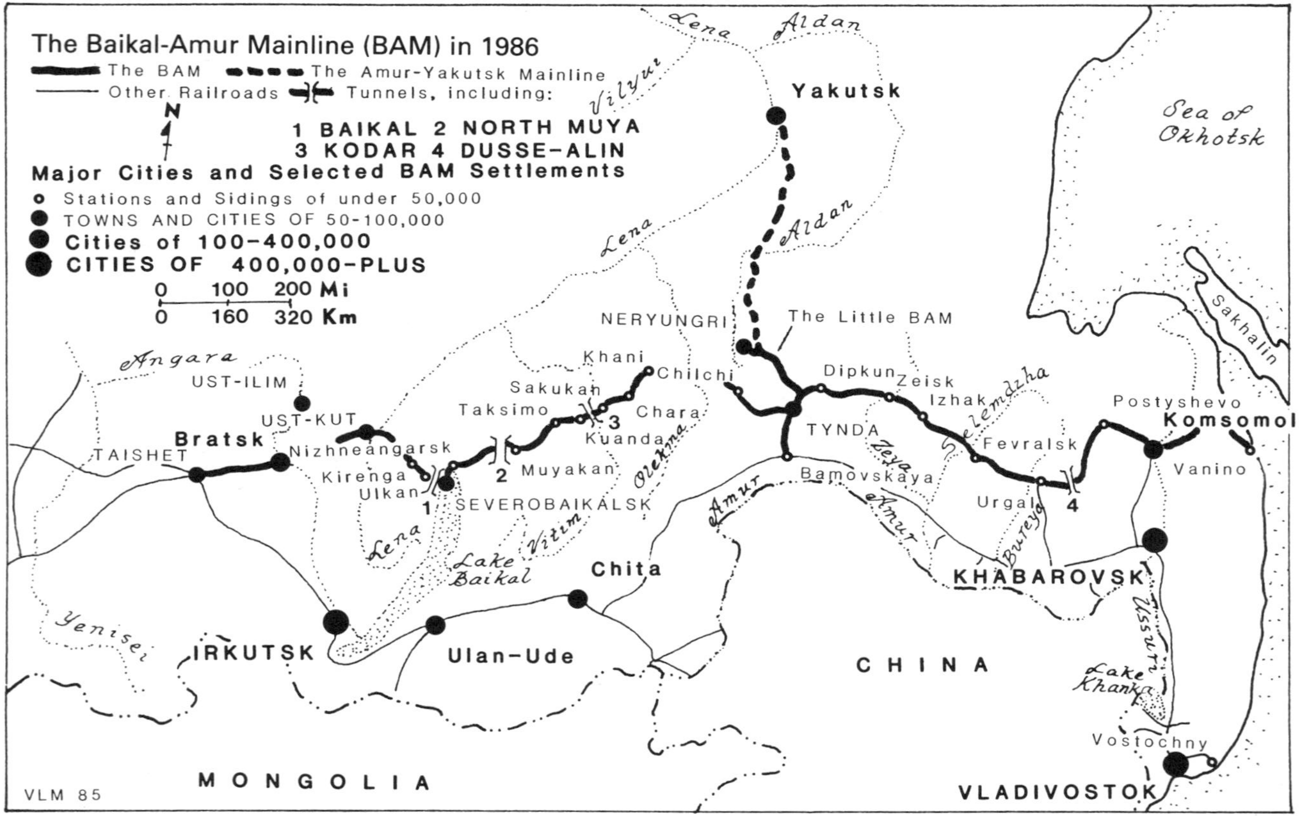
The Baikal-Amur Mainline (BAM) in 1986
The BAM
The Amur-Yakutsk Mainline
Other Railroads
Tunnels, including:
N
1 BAIKAL 2 NORTH MUYA
3 KODAR 4 DUSSE-ALIN
Major Cities and Selected BAM Settlements
Stations and Sidings of under 50,000
TOWNS AND CITIES OF 50-100,000
Cities of 100-400,000
CITIES OF 400,000-PLUS
0 100 200 Mi
0 160 320 Km
Lena
Aldan
Vilyui
Yakutsk
Sea of Okhotsk
Aldan
Lena
Sakhalin
NERYUNGRI
The Little BAM
Angara
UST-ILIM
Khani
Chilchi
Dipkun
Zeisk
Selemdzha
Sakukan
Izhak
Postyshevo
Komsomolsk
UST-KUT
Taksimo
Chara
TYNDA
Bratsk
Kuanda
Fevralsk
TAISHET
Nizhneangarsk
Muyakan
Olekma
Zeya
Vanino
Kirenga
Bamovskaya
Ulkan
SEVEROBAIKALSK
Amur
Amur
Urgal
Lena
Vitim
Bureya
Lake Baikal
Chita
KHABAROVSK
Yenisei
IRKUTSK
Ulan-Ude
CHINA
Ussuri
Lake Khanka
Vostochny
MONGOLIA
VLADIVOSTOK
VLM 85

A harbinger that the BAM would be built sometime in the 1970s and 1980s came with the announcement that a new version of the Little BAM meridional spur was under construction between Bam Station (Bamovskaya) and Tyndinski (Tynda) in 1971.[11] This railroad had been built in the 1930s, but in 1942, during the battle of Stalingrad, the rails were pulled up and hauled to the Volga River, where they were relaid to supply the besieged city from Saratov. Even antitank weapons were forged from Little BAM rails.[12] Today the Little BAM extends to Ugolnaya in the Neryungri-Chulman coal fields of south Yakutia, where it arrived in 1979. The 1930s' plans for the Little BAM included its extension to Yakutsk, where it would serve as a springboard for rail routes east and west to Magadan and Mirny, respectively. Recently, this plan was revived. Track-laying on the 830-kilometer (515-mile) railroad between Ugolnaya and Yakutsk began anew in the spring of 1985 and may be completed as early as 1995.[13]

The official announcement of the BAM construction project finally came on March 16, 1974. The original plan called for completion in 1982 and full operations in 1983. Track-laying was completed instead on September 29, 1984, and full operations may be introduced sometime before 1990.

The BAM in 1985   The Eleventh Five-Year Plan revealed that 1985 would be the revised deadline for the BAM railway. Responding to their new challenge, crew chiefs on the western BAM announced that they would beat the revised target in time for the Komsomol Birthday on October 29, 1984. In the same spirit, eastern BAM railroad army officers vowed to finish their labors in time for Victory Day on May 9, 1984. Crews on each wing of the railroad effected a storming posture (*shturmovshchina*) and easily met or transcended their avowed targets.[14]

Toward the end of 1983 the east-west trunkline of the BAM between Ust-Kut and Komsomolsk-na-Amure was a little over 87 percent complete, with around 400 kilometers of roadbed preparation, bridging, and track-laying remaining out of the 3,115-kilometer distance. Only 120 difficult but manageable kilometers separated the two teams of Soviet army railroad troops on the eastern wing of the BAM, and 280 even more difficult kilometers confronted the Komsomol crews in the west. By mid-December the western BAM units were a total of 38 kilometers short of their 1983 goals of Taksimo, coming from the west (20 kilometers), and Sakukan, coming from the east (18 kilometers). Even at previous record paces it did not appear that the crews would be able to reach these targets. On the other hand, work in November had proceeded at a fever pitch, with one of the teams reaching a track-laying rate of more than a kilometer per day for four days straight. After that, however, the crew was stymied for over a month by a lack of materials, particularly cross-ties. Defying all odds, beginning in mid-December 1983, the two teams, together with a masterful coordination between cross-tie suppliers at Taishet and Ushumun, almost miraculously reached both Taksimo and Sakukan before New Year's Day, 1984.[15]

As of October 1983, about 800 kilometers of main BAM track were fully operational, in terms of both the range and weight of cargoes and train velocities. This represented about 25 percent of the mainline. Another 1,650 kilometers were designated as temporary or workers' service track.[16] This meant that a little more than three-fourths of the BAM could be used for any purpose. On both wings of the BAM, flooding and icing tended to be the most frequent hazards, with stabilization of foundations and subgrades accounting for the delays of full operations. In the past, it has taken from three to four years to convert from temporary to full-service status. Based on this experience, parts of the BAM may not be fully operational until after 1987.

Between 1979 and 1984, attempts were made to estimate when the BAM tracks would be fully laid by projecting the annual track-laying rates.[17] The crude estimates ranged from an obviously wrong May 1990, arrived at when rates were very slow in the late 1970s and early 1980s, to March 1986 and, finally, February 1985, as the pace quickened. In the end, representatives of the party, government, and the entire citizenry rallied to cheer on the BAM track-layers as they completed their work well ahead of their own stated goals.

The storming method has been common in Soviet history. The following summary is provided to illustrate its effectiveness on the BAM railway. Given a remaining distance of 120 kilometers on the eastern BAM and a goal of May 9, 1984, Soviet army troops had to cover their ground at a rate of 790 meters per day or 288 kilometers per year. The best that they had mustered through 1982 had been 214 kilometers per year. Without any insight into the morale of the workers, an analyst would have had to conclude that finishing that segment by May 9, 1984, was not very realistic. Then again, the most important matter was to finish the entire BAM by October 29. The pressure was on the teams working in the west and not on those in the east. Just the same, the army came through when it said it would: in May 1984.

The work on the western wing was crucial. Some 280 kilometers and 320 days remained in December 1983. In order for them to achieve their goals, the Komsomol work crews had to lay track at an overall average of 880 meters per day or 321 kilometers per year. The fact was that both crews had their best years in 1983, with combined rates reaching 280 kilometers per year: 136 on the west-central BAM and 144 on the extreme western BAM.[18] In fact, until December 1983 western BAM crews worked at an average of only about 100 kilometers per year, whereas the west-central crews worked at a higher, but erratic, pace. It was the latter team that laid over a kilometer of track per day at times. Thus, record daily rates were required if the targets were to be met on time. And everything hinged on the efficiency of the supply system. For instance, for want of cross-ties in 1981 and 1982, roughly 130 kilometers of BAM had not been laid (65 kilometers per year), and the situation reportedly had changed little in 1983.[19] By 1984, however, the foremen of both western BAM track-laying crews had made

TABLE 2.1
Annual Accomplishments in the Construction of the BAM 1975–1984

End of Year	West BAM	Central BAM West	East	East BAM	Totals (kilometers)	Estimated Costs (millions of rubles)[a]
1975	64	—	—	80	144	160
1976	71	—	15	75	161	180
1977	73	40	75	75	263	290
1978	83	90	75	70	318	350
1979	50	50	30	168	298	330
Subtotal:						
First five years	341	180	195	468	1,184	1,310
Remaining track	—	—	—	—	1,732	—
1980	80	90	55[b]	40	265[b]	290
1981	116	101[b]	59[b]	44	320[b]	352
1982	113	120	27[b]	114	374[b]	411
1983	136	144	84[b]	100[b]	464[b]	846
1984	130	120	11	48	309	575
Subtotal:						
Second five years	575	575	236	346	1,732	2,294
Total:						
1974–84	916	755	431	814	2,916	3,604

SOURCES: *Gudok,* April 26, 1979, p. 2; September 17, 1980, p. 1; December 26, 1980, p. 1; September 25, 1981, p. 1; December 25, 1981, p. 2; April 2, 1982, p. 2; December 26, 1982, p. 2; February 24, 1983, p. 1; January 8, 1984, p. 2; February 9, 1984, p. 1.

[a] Calculated at a rate of 1.1 million rubles per kilometer except for Chita oblast, where a cost factor of 2.3 was used, based on Iu. A. Sobolev, *Zona BMAa: Puti ekonomicheskogo razvitiia* [The BAM zone: Methods of economic development] (Moscow: Mysl', 1979), p. 128.

[b] Estimates based on reliable primary sources.

personal appeals to their respective cross-tie factories at Taishet and Ushumun. It was this coordination between the suppliers and the railroad men that finally spelled the difference between success and failure.

Analysis of BAM in Time Series   Table 2.1 is a summary of the annual progress made by BAM work crews between 1975 and 1984. The table also limns the estimated annual expenditures in rubles on track-laying alone. Note that through the 1970s progress was relatively slow. Using the BAM crossroads and self-proclaimed headquarters of Tynda as the division point, the combination of west-central and western BAM teams laid track at an average of only 115 kilometers per year between 1974 and 1980. At the same time east-central and eastern BAM teams combined for a slightly higher mean of 126 kilometers. It was apparent that at such construction rates, the BAM could not be finished until the late 1980s. During the next three years, however, with greater investment and bureaucratic pressure, construction proceeded at much higher tempos. The combined average on the western BAM spiraled to 240 kilometers per annum; eastern BAM efforts yielded a mean of 139 kilometers yearly.[20]

Greater work loads manifestly required higher investments. With the exception of those allocations intended for the BAM segment in the difficult environments of Chita oblast, expenditures on track-laying alone ran about 1.1 million rubles per kilometer ($2.3 million per mile).[21] In Chita oblast, with severe permafrost, seismic, and mass-wasting constraints, these costs are estimated to average about 2.3 times higher than elsewhere, or 2.5 million rubles per kilometer ($5.3 million/mile). Calculated investments thus rose from under 200 million rubles per year in the early years to over 400 million rubles per year in the last few. These higher investments, stimuli raised by the Eleventh Five-Year Plan (1981–1985), more efficient organization, and "storming" by BAM workers themselves facilitated the successes of the 1980s.

How Does BAM Spell "Relief"?   Since 1945 freight flows on the Trans-Siberian Railroad have grown 700 to 1,000 percent.[22] To see the gravity of the problem, we need to compare the length of Soviet railroads (which is still under half the amount present in the United States) with the growth of freight traffic since the war years. When we do this, we find that flows have outstripped track by a factor of 24! In other words, rail traffic has not been matched by equivalent units of track. Nowhere is this problem more extreme than in the case of the Trans-Siberian, which on the section between Omsk and Novosibirsk is at 95 percent of capacity. According to the British railway historian J. N. Westwood, "A railway operating at 95 percent of its theoretical capacity is in practical terms, perilously overloaded."[23] Moreover, overloading is not unique to West Siberia. Since 1965, traffic between Irkutsk and Vladivostok has expanded by over 211 percent. Ostensibly, overloading was the reason why the Trans-Siberian could supply only four-fifths of the estimated annual logistical demand of Soviet armed forces in the Far East in 1975.[24]

Among its several goals, the BAM has been built to relieve some of this congestion. According to Soviet geographer F. V. D'iakonov, some 20 million tons or 10 to 20 percent of the freight that is now shipped over the Trans-Siberian Railroad between Taishet and Vladivostok can be skimmed off by the BAM.[25] One distinguished authority, however, believes that such diversions will not occur until "the end of the century."[26]

What will the BAM carry? Approximately how much? In 1981, freight flows over the BAM and Little BAM amounted to 9 million tons, 3 million of which was coal from south Yakutia.[27] The balance of the cargo was composed mainly of timber, wood chips, and other wood products. By the end of 1985, coal output was projected to reach 11.9 million tons.[28] Logging camps and lumber mills reportedly were behind targeted schedules.[29] As of 1983, total traffic on the

BAM and Little BAM probably reached about 15 million tons. Since 300,000 passengers were transported by BAM trains in 1981, at least that many must have been moved in 1983.

Original 1975 freight-flow analyses of the BAM forecasted a possible total of 35 million tons of shipments in 1985. These were to include 25 million tons of West Siberian petroleum, 3 to 6 million tons of East Siberian and Soviet Far Eastern roundwood, some 5 million tons of south Yakutian coking coal, 2 to 4 million tons of wood chips and pulp, and lesser volumes of "minor trade items." In contrast, the Eleventh Five-Year Plan for the BAM in 1985 called for a freight turnover of 25 million tons and for a passenger total of 450,000 persons.[30] Very little, if any, of the cargoes contained West Siberian oil. Until recently, the coal that was circulated by the BAM was predominantly steam coal destined for local power plants; most of the coking coal was still too deep below the ground. When south Yakutian coking coal finally became available in sufficient quantities in 1985, it displaced Kuzbas coal as one of the major Siberian exports to Japan. Total shipments for 1985 amounted to more than 20 million tons, including mainly coal and roundwood. This was close to plan. The five-year plan's targets for passengers were also reached.

RIVER TRANSPORT

For most of the Soviet Union, inland waterways are no longer a significant factor in the overall transportation balance (Table 2.2). The many hazards and disadvantages that are associated with the navigation of Soviet rivers have redounded to the favor of other means of transportation, except in Siberia where, in the absence of other alternatives, the role of river transport has grown in importance. In the West Siberian oil and gas fields, the BAM service area, and Yakutia, rivers are used for navigation in the brief summers and as iced-over "winter roads." Indeed, the share of Siberian river traffic (summer navigation only) compared with the contribution by all Soviet rivers expanded from about 21 percent in 1970 to about 27 percent in 1980. Considering Siberia's meager population, the region's rivers carry two and one half times the per capita freight averaged by the rest of the country (Table 2.3).

As an alternative to the railroad, inland waterways have the advantages of cheapness of use and low initial capital investment. The cost of shipping materials by river in Siberia and the Far East is seven to ten times lower than truck transport and fifteen to seventeen times cheaper than air freight. Initial capital investment is low, for obvious reasons. As long as they are free of ice, silt, and other obstacles, rivers are appealing means of transporting heavy bulk and non-perishable items. According to one source, "the river fleet is the only means of

TABLE 2.2
The Soviet Transportation Balance Percentages of Freight (F) and Passengers (P)

MODE	1913 F	1913 P	1940 F	1940 Pa	1960 F	1960 P	1981b F	1981b P	1990c F Only
Rail	61	93	85	90	80	68	55	37	47
Sea	16	3	5	1	7	0.5	13	0.3	NA
River	23	4	7	3	5	2	4	0.7	NA
Motor vehicle	0.1	—	2	5	5	24	7	43	NA
Pipeline	0.3	NA	0.8	NA	3	NA	20	NA	27
Air	0.0	—	—	1	—	5	—	19	NA

SOURCE: Paul E. Lydolph, Geography of the USSR: Topical Analysis (Elkhart Lake, Wis.: Misty Valley Publishing Company, 1979), pp. 420, 452.

NOTE: Percentages are rounded to the nearest whole number except when they are below 1.0; because of this, some totals will exceed 100 percent. A dash (—) symbolizes trace amounts, if any. NA means data were not available.

a For passenger column only, data are from 1950.

b Narodnoe khoziaistvo SSSR. 1922–1982 (Moscow: Financy i Statistika, 1982), p. 325.

c Projected by Izvestiia, December 19, 1978, p. 2.

TABLE 2.3
Siberian River Freight Turnover (in millions of tons)

RIVER BASIN	TURNOVERa 1970	TURNOVERa 1978	PERCENTAGE 1970	PERCENTAGE 1978
Ob-Irtysh	74	50	100	43
Lena		10		9
Other Siberian and Far Eastern rivers		56		48
Totals	74	116	100	100

SOURCES: For 1970 data: Victor L. Mote, "The Baikal-Amur Mainline and Its Implications for the Pacific Basin," in R. G. Jensen et al., eds., Soviet Natural Resources in the World Economy (Chicago: University of Chicago Press, 1983), p. 139; and Transport i sviaz (Moscow: Statistika, 1972), p. 169. For 1978 data: Gudok, August 29, 1978, p. 2.

NOTE: The 1970 "all-Siberian" figure represented 20.7 percent of the Soviet total. The 1978 figure was closer to 26 percent; by 1980 it was about 27 percent. The population of Siberia remains about 10 percent of the country's total.

a "Turnover" implies the total movement of a good or goods into and out of a region; thus, for example, "freight turnover" in tons, as here, or "passenger turnover" in numbers of people.

mass hauling of cargoes in the northlands of Siberia," especially in the removal of timber from those regions.

On the other hand, river transport is usually slow, circuitous, and, where Siberia is concerned, ice-blocked for five months or more, two to three months longer than in the European USSR.[31] Moreover, most of the Siberian rivers flow from south to north, while the main trade axes tend to align from west to east; in the upper (southern) parts, where economic activity is most intense, the rivers are shallowest, with depths reaching only 2 or 3 meters (6 to 9 feet). They also tend to have highly irregular rates of seasonal flow. The latter pattern is especially true of the monsoonal Soviet Far East, including the Lena and its tributaries. In wet years (years of high snowfall), the meltwater may raise water levels 8 to 13 meters (25 to 40 feet) above normal, with increased velocities of up to 4 meters per second (8 miles per hour). Similar changes may be brought on by a wet Pacific monsoon. For instance, floods have been a long-standing problem along the Amur, Bureya, and Zeya rivers. Finally, most Siberian rivers, and their tributaries especially, require constant dredging because their shallow beds are filled with silt during low-water periods.

These problems are especially hard on small Siberian rivers and tributaries. A case in point is the Nadym River, a stream that flows into the Gulf of Ob through the Lower Ob gas fields and therefore becomes important as a real and potential way to move gas-field equipment. In the warmer months of the year, it is navigable to 117 kilometers from its mouth. The main factor contributing to its volume is the regime of precipitation, which, like most Siberian regions, peaks sometime between May and August. However, the depth of the stream, even during summer, is quixotic. Half the annual flow of the Nadym is funneled through the region from May to early July, when summer rains are bolstered by snow and ice melt; low water comes in July and August, when the river is full of sand bars and shoals. The river can be and is dredged at this time, but after a while the returns on dredging are uneconomical. The river is iced over from October to May.[32]

Despite these constraints the Siberian proportion of Soviet river traffic continues to grow (to almost 30 percent by 1985).[33] In Tomsk oblast rivers carry three-quarters of the industrial transport burden. Since 1960, because of dredging on smaller tributaries and rivers, the length of navigable waterways in the Ob-Irtysh basin, serving the oil and gas regions, has increased by almost a third. Here and in the Soviet Far East, river-borne cargoes on small rivers exceed 25 percent of the total transportation balance.

Waterway development has been spurred considerably by the development of Siberia north of the Trans-Siberian Railroad, especially by oil and gas exploration and extraction, the expansion of the Norilsk nickel and platinum metals complex, the exploitation of the Lena River basin, and the construction needs of the BAM.[34] Let's look at each region separately.

The Ob-Irtysh River Basin

The rivers of this region typically haul primary raw materials to the east-west railways, and then bring finished products back.[35] The raw materials consist of timber from the northern forest zones and grain from the Altai and New Lands. The finished products are equipment and supplies designated largely for the Middle Ob and, with the completion of the Surgut-Urengoi branch line, the Lower Ob. Rivers also provide intraregional transportation, including the transfer of roundwood from the northern coniferous forests to the timber-deficit grasslands of the Kazakh republic. Fulfilling the same purpose, construction materials are funneled from south to north. Thus, timber accounts for half and mineral construction materials (sand and gravel) for one-quarter of all the water-borne cargoes of the Ob-Irtysh basin. In the early 1970s the total north-moving supplies averaged 8 million tons per year, three-quarters of which were shipments on the Irtysh, originating mainly at Tobolsk and Omsk. These included 1.3 million tons generally destined for the far north, of which 920,000 tons went to gas fields in the vicinity of Nadym. When the Tyumen-Tobolsk-Surgut rail spur was completed in 1975, oil-field components of the water-borne cargoes declined somewhat, superseded by gas-field components. By 1980, northbound loadings on the Irtysh River topped 6 million tons, half of which moved to sites in the far north. Most of the traffic consisted of steel pipe for mainline gas pipelines.

The basin is administered by two steamship authorities: the Irtysh Steamship Administration within the appropriate provinces of Kazakhstan and Omsk and Tyumen oblasts, and the Ob Steamship Administration within the rest of West Siberia. The Irtysh firm controls 22,000 kilometers (13,750 miles) of navigable waterway, close to 4,000 kilometers of which were added after 1966 in the "roadless" stretches of the oil and gas regions. In order to increase the carrying capacity of the line in recent years, upward of 120 new river vessels have been added annually to the fleet. The bulk of the new ships are 2,000-horsepower diesel varieties capable of plying through ice of up to a foot thick; accordingly, they can extend the navigation season by a week and a half.

Typically, the ships of the Ob Steamship Administration, some of which reach 3,000-ton capacity, travel in convoy from upstream ports like Tomsk, Kolpashevo, Nizhnevartovsk, and Surgut to Salekhard near the Gulf of Ob. Here they are reloaded onto seagoing vessels for navigation to smaller rivers like the Nadym, Pur, and Taz, where the cargoes are shifted once again to small-capacity river-going craft. The navigation season for such arduous journeys is limited to 125–172 days at Salekhard and 105–152 days on the smaller rivers; the Gulf of Ob is ice-free for only three months. Before the coming of the railroad from Surgut, supplies arrived by ship in Urengoi only once each year.

The most important ports in the southern part of the basin exist at the junctions of river and rail. Omsk is situated on the Irtysh and serves as a major rail junction of the Trans-Siberian and Tyumen roads. Pavlodar is also located on the Irtysh, where it is crossed by the South Siberian. Novosibirsk is on the Ob where the river meets the Trans-Siberian. Barnaul is farther upriver at the South Siberian crossing. Tyumen is on the Tura where the Tyumen branch of the Trans-Siberian trends northwest to Sverdlovsk.

In recent years, these ports and others have been the recipients of new and expanded mechanized moorages. Recent five-year plans have called for even further expansion, with moorages of a combined length of 2 kilometers and capacities of 3.6 million tons per year.

The Yenisei River and the Northern Sea Route

One of the more conspicuous developments in Soviet transportation during the last few years has been the renewed interest in the use of the northern sea route between Murmansk (on the Kola Peninsula) and the mouths of the great Siberian rivers, particularly the Yenisei. A northern passage to the Far East has been the dream of Russian and European mariners since the seventeenth century. Both the Yenisei and Ob rivers empty into the Kara Sea, which on average is totally ice-free only from August 10 to September 25.[36] By late June, however, the ice is thin enough for modern seagoing craft, so that today the navigation season in the Kara Sea persists between the end of June and late October. Conventional icebreakers and reinforced freighters can sometimes keep the waters open into December.

The northern sea route is 2,800 kilometers (1,750 miles) long, fringing the Soviet arctic coast from Novaya Zemlya to the Bering Strait, with connections to Murmansk and to Pacific ports. Several hundred ships negotiate parts of the route during the normal navigation season, but only a few are hardy enough to make the complete transit. Of about 4 million tons of cargo moved yearly through the two dozen or so northern sea route ports, more than half is timber and ore from the Igarka and Norilsk areas (on the Yenisei). Navigation is aided by fifteen icebreakers, supplemented by at least twelve freighters that have been strengthened for limited icebreaking.[37]

Most of the icebreakers are diesel-powered and of the Finnish-built *Yermak* class (36,000 horsepower), but since 1959 three atomic icebreakers have been added to the fleet: the *Lenin* (1959) has a capacity of 44,000 horsepower; the *Arktika,* now *Leonid Brezhnev,* (1975) and *Sibir* (1978) are 75,000 horsepower each. The *Rossiya* (under construction) is also of the *Arktika* class. The freighter fleet also is being upgraded in strength and capacity. With the use of these specialized, nuclear-powered craft, Soviet seamen hope to further extend the utility of the northern sea route to year-round navigation. This they nearly accomplished on the Murmansk-Dudinka section between 1978 and 1980.

Freight transportation is limited to two ports on the Yenisei River, which for some 600 kilometers upstream from its mouth is navigable to ocean ships. This contrasts with the rivers that empty into the Gulf of Ob, where there are no deepwater embayments for moorage. Dudinka, the port of Norilsk, works shipments of nickel, copper, and platinum from the Norilsk polymetallic smelters and refineries. Farther upstream, timber is processed through the port of Igarka, which accounts for 14 percent of the country's export of sawn timber. Northbound movements, destined mainly for Norilsk, also have increased on the Yenisei. These cargoes originate at Krasnoyarsk and Lesosibirsk, whose ports and moorages have been dramatically upgraded in the past decade. As a result, northbound shipments have roughly doubled, from 2.7 million tons in 1976 to over 5 million tons in the early 1980s. The cargoes included supplies for the Norilsk area, timber, and sand and gravel for the expansion of the port of Dudinka. The northbound supplies, however, have not been balanced by equal return shipments. Half the barges and containers return empty, increasing the costs of the exchange.[38]

The Lena River and BAM Waterways

The Lena River is completely navigable to its mouth and main port of Tiksi for at least 60 to 65 days every year. Some of its tributaries, like the Aldan, for example, may be navigable for only 10 to 12 days out of the year because of excessive shoaling. Nevertheless, between 1975 and 1980, transshipments at the port of Osetrovo, the so-called lifeline of Yakutia, increased from 2.8 million to 3.6 million tons, about 40 percent of which went to northeast Siberia. Another million or so tons represented supplies for the BAM construction project, river accesses to which were the Kirenga River (settlement of Kirenga) and the Vitim River port of Bodaibo.

Already experiencing a shortage of longshoremen and handling equipment, the port of Osetrovo consistently unloads fewer freight cars than it must each year. By the end of the brief navigation season on the Lena River, usually close to 2,000 cars remain to be unloaded. Even with improved performance in 1983, more than 1,000 loaded cars stood in the port's marshaling yards. Since the cargoes ordinarily cannot be sent to Yakutia by any means other than river barge, they must remain in Osetrovo's freight yards until the beginning of the next navigation season, seven to eight months later! During that time, they become literal "wheeled warehouses." Sixty percent of the port's freight accumulates in the winter. Siberia's largest and, curiously, most mechanized river port (72 percent mechanized), Osetrovo often is jammed up and overstocked. It possesses neither enough warehouses nor enough freight yards.[39] Completion of the BAM, ironically, will only serve to exacerbate the traffic jams. Probably through 1990, the BAM east of Osetrovo will remain single-tracked, while west of the port it will be double-tracked. The new line is bound to stimulate far greater traffic than exists currently, and Osetrovo, having troubles now, could become a freight-handler's nightmare! For this reason, the Little BAM is being extended to Yakutsk.

In the absence of passable motor roads, summer cargoes must be carried to the north shore of Lake Baikal by lighters (freight capacities of 1,000 tons). Since 1974, when construction of the BAM began, cargoes hauled by the lake fleet have climbed seventeen times (over 150,000 tons), easily nine-tenths of which are destined for the construction sites. A small percentage of the freight goes to the local indigenous population. Wharves and moorages at Severobaikalsk have been improved to handle the traffic.[40]

Throughout its period of construction, the BAM and its service area have been supplied by primitive east–west frontage and meridional "winter roads" and by the many north–south-trending rivers. Although they are much less important today than they were in the 1970s, all the navigable waterways in the zone proved extremely important to the supply of the railroad in the early years.

The Lena and two of its right-bank tributaries (the Kirenga and Vitim) served the western BAM region, although they suffered from erratic flow and low water in August. In addition, the Chara and Olekma rivers have been examined as potential suppliers of the west-central BAM regions. These tributaries of the Lena currently are navigable only along their lower courses. The east-central BAM is crossed by the reservoir created by the Zeya River dam. The reservoir is navigable over its entire extent. The Zeya's major right-bank tributary, the Selemdzha, is being improved for use to its junction with the BAM. Until the mid-1970s, it was navigable to a point 129 kilometers south of the railroad. From there on, navigation conditions were hampered by meanders, vagaries of the current, and submerged obstacles. In the eastern BAM regions, the Bureya and Amgun rivers are also navigable to some extent, but require improvement in order to reach the service area. Two dams are being built on the Bureya, and the resultant reservoirs should be navigable well into the area fed by the railroad.[41]

The Amur Basin

The fourth largest river in Siberia and the Soviet Far East (and simultaneously the USSR) is the Amur River, which forms much of the far eastern border between the Soviet Union and the People's Republic of China. Including its headwater tributaries, the Shilka and Argun, the Amur is navigable all the way to Chita (on the Shilka) and Nerchinski Zavod (on the Argun) or over 4,000 kilometers (2,500 miles). The 1,500-kilometer segment between Blagoveshchensk and Nikolayevsk-na-Amure accounts for the bulk of the shipping. The Amur's major right-bank tributary, the Ussuri, is navigable almost to Lake Khanka. The freight carried—easily on a par with the Lena River's turnover of almost 4 million tons—includes roundwood, ore, and some agricultural produce.

Because of the Far East's monsoonal climate, the rivers of the Amur Basin suffer from irregular flow. The Amur itself rises from a depth of 6 meters to 15 meters between the dry and wet monsoon. In the past this has resulted in four to six flash floods a year. The river is frozen from November to May. Thereafter, the navigation season is hampered by "the march of ice," causing 10-meter floodwaters to inundate floodplains in the middle and lower courses of the river over an area 10–25 kilometers wide for a period of up to 70 days. The worst of the floods have occurred at approximately 30-year intervals in 1897, 1928, 1956, and 1981.[42] Even the largest cities on the Amur (Blagoveshchensk, Khabarovsk, and Komsomolsk) do not escape the ravages of the floodwaters at these times. When not plagued by flood, the Amur at low water is a mass of bars and shoals. Much of the year its waters run rusty with sediment; even the drinking water in places like Khabarovsk is tinged with the color, indicating the presence of superfine clays. In the dry monsoon, the sediment builds into navigational obstacles over much of the lower course of the river.

River Transportation in the Northeast

Rivers, both when they are fluid and when they are solid, are the absolute lifelines for the northeastern regions of Siberia. Here the Yana, Indigirka, and Kolyma serve some of the Soviet Union's most important nonferrous and precious-metal sites, principally gold, tin, and tungsten. In winter these rivers become frozen and provide smooth thoroughfares for truck traffic.

MOTOR TRANSPORT

Because of the harsh environment—becoming increasingly so the farther north and east one travels—and the obvious preference for railroad construction, there are few motor roads in Siberia and the far north. To this day, there is no complete interregional highway across the whole of the USSR. Those who want to cross the USSR on land must do so on the Trans-Siberian Railroad.

When citizens of free-enterprise societies think of the automobile, more often than not they think of their own private car. In the USSR, however, citizens traditionally have associated the idea with trucks, taxis, or public buses. According to the estimates of Holland Hunter, in 1980 there were 25 passenger cars per 1,000 persons in the Soviet Union.[43] Since then, the number may have increased to about 31 per 1,000 (*The Economist* says 36 per 1,000).[44] And although this statistic represents better than a fourfold increase over the ratio for 1970, when there were 7 cars per 1,000 persons in the Soviet Union, it still equals but a sixth of Spain's stock, under a third of Saudi Arabia's, and just over a third of Hungary's. Even when truck stocks are considered, the figure rises to only 52 motor vehicles per 1,000 people, still just over half the *passenger car* stock of Hungary. Clearly, until recently the overwhelming majority of vehicles on Soviet streets and highways were trucks and buses. What is more, perhaps three out of ten of the passenger cars, and most assuredly the luxury models, belonged to the motor pools of the government and party.

The neglect of the automobile as a mode of transportation has been characterized as "the greatest weakness" in the Soviet transport system. The reasons for this neglect are both ideological and economic. First, under a system that dogmatically prefers public over private property, officials do not enthusiastically welcome widespread private-car ownership. Advancing the freedom of the individual or his family, cars do not mesh well with Marxist-Leninist collectivist philosophy. Second, because of scarce monetary capital, the high costs of automobile and highway construction, highway maintenance, and automotive infrastructure surely discourage investments in the sector. Ironically, between 1965 and 1978 investments in the automotive industry led all other categories of Soviet civil machine construction (at 11 percent per year) except for automation equipment and instruments. However, investments in highway construction and maintenance and automotive infrastructure (gas stations, repair garages, and the like) were still inadequate.

Soviet highways always have been few in number and easily rank among the worst in the world. (Most farm-to-market roads in the West are superior to the best Soviet highways.) Although almost three times the size of the United States, the USSR has a road network that is under a third as long, only about half of which is "hard-surfaced," a category including gravel-surfaced, asphalt, and concrete. Gravel roads still compose a large percentage of the hard-surfaced routes.

The inadequacies are nowhere more apparent than in Siberia and the Far East, which have fewer roads per square kilometer than any other region of the country (Table 2.4). Hard-surfaced highways are eight times less prevalent in Siberia than they are in Soviet Europe and two and two-thirds less prevalent than they are in Kazakhstan![45] All of Siberia and the Soviet Far East may have only 25,000 kilometers of hard-surfaced roads—3 percent of the country's total. In many cases provincial capitals are not even linked by highway.

Thus, when compared to the USSR as a whole, Siberia lags behind in the use of automobile transport. For example, whereas automobile transport accounts for 6 percent of all Soviet freight turnover, it is credited with only 4 percent of Siberian freight turnover.[46] Although their capacities have been increasing since the construction of the Kama truck plant at Brezhnev (formerly Naberezhnye Chelny), Soviet (and Siberian) trucks tend to be small five-ton military-type vehicles, not the huge "eighteen-wheelers" so obvious on the highways of the

TABLE 2.4
Ratio of Automobiles to Roadways (1977)

Republic	Roads[a] (km in 1000s)	Roads[b] per km^2	Private Cars[c] (1000s)	Cars per km	Car Loadings per km (Above (+) or below (−) average of 4.1)
USSR	1424	.06	5874	4.1	Avg.
RSFSR	843	.05	3141	3.7	−0.4
Siberia and Soviet Far East	48[d]	.015[e]	—	—	—
Ukraine	164	.27	989	6.0	+1.9
Belorussia	72	.35	189	2.6	−1.5
Uzbek	52	.12	267	5.1	+1.0
Kazakh	97	.04	293	3.0	−1.1
Georgia	22	.31	176	8.0	+3.9
Azerbaijan	24	.28	135	5.6	+1.5
Lithuania	32	.49	168	5.3	+1.2
Moldavia	11	.33	70	6.4	+2.3
Latvia	24	.38	114	4.8	+0.7
Kirgiz	22	.11	53	2.4	−1.7
Tadzhik	13	.09	55	4.2	+0.1
Armenia	9	.30	94	10.4	+6.3
Turkmen	10	.02	41	4.1	Avg.
Estonia	30	.66	89	3.0	−1.1

[a] *Narodnoe khoziaistvo SSSR. 1978* (Moscow: Statistika, 1979), p. 313.
[b] Roads divided by area of the region or republic.
[c] A. Arrak, "The Utilization of the Private Automobile," *Problems of Economics,* vol. 21, no. 6 (October 1978): 30–36.
[d] Estimate.
[e] L. I. Kolesov, *Mezhotraslevye problemy razvitiia transportnoi sistemy Sibiri i Dal'nego Vostoka* (Novosibirsk: Nauka, 1982), p. 175. Kolesov uses the Engel coefficient, which divides the length of roadways in kilometers by the square root of the product of the area of the region in hundreds of kilometers squared and the population of the region in tens of thousands. The result for Siberia and the Far East averages out to 3.73; for Kazakhstan, 9.62; therefore, Siberia has a roadway network that is 2.57 times less adequate than that for Kazakhstan or, in the above example, .015 km of road per km^2.

West. They do not lend themselves to long-distance shipping. On average, a third of the trucks await repairs or spare parts, a situation made worse by the critical lack of repair garages in Siberia. The asphalt and gravel roads are so poor that not only do the trucks suffer a high frequency of breakdowns, they also consume 15 percent more fuel on them than on concrete surfaces. To further emphasize the dilemma, most Siberian paved roads cannot accommodate trucks carrying over four tons of freight.[47]

As it does throughout the Soviet Union, truck transport serves local transportation needs by carrying freight over short distances. The average truck haul in the USSR is about 20 kilometers.[48] Siberian averages are about the same, with a mean daily operating distance of 166 kilometers versus an RSFSR average of 167 kilometers. Trucks carry the specific needs of consumers in and among industrial centers (especially in the Kuzbas), provide supplies to rural areas (the New Lands, Minusinsk basin, Amur oblast, Bureya Plains, and Ussuri basin), supply areas with no other means of transportation (portions of Altai krai and Transbaikalia), aid the oil and gas regions of West Siberia, and haul timber to river and rail terminals. Deadheading by truck is even worse than it is by rail: some 45 percent of the vehicles travel empty.

In the swamp-infested regions of the Middle and Lower Ob and portions of East Siberia and the Soviet Far East, most of the truck transport takes place between November and May. Supply convoys wend their way either over frozen rivers or over makeshift roads that are passable only in winter ("winter roads"). What formal roads exist are at a premium. After eight years of gas production, "only 45 kilometers out of a projected 110 kilometers of road had been built at the Medvezhe field, and only 10 kilometers had been built at Urengoi."[49] Projected roads elsewhere in the gas fields have simply failed to materialize. Similarly,

TABLE 2.5
Service Stations and Repair Garages in Siberia and the Soviet Far East (1982)

PROVINCE	1976		1982	
	Stations	Garages	Stations	Garages
Kurgan oblast	30	2	30	4
Altai krai	73	5	78	12
Kemerovo oblast	27	7	30	12
Novosibirsk oblast	42	3	46	12
Omsk oblast	38	1	41	2
Tomsk oblast	14	1	15	3
Tyumen oblast	26	3	27	3
Krasnoyarsk krai	67	7	70	14
Irkutsk oblast	40	4	40	10
Chita oblast	35	2	40	5
Buryat ASSR	29	3	29	4
Tuva ASSR	13	1	13	2
Maritime krai	28	5	32	9
Khabarovsk krai	14	2	16	7
Amur oblast	24	1	26	2
Kamchatka oblast	4	1	4	2
Magadan oblast	19	2	19	2
Sakhalin oblast	5	1	6	2
Yakutsk ASSR	38	1	38	3
Total	566	52	600	109

SOURCE: GUGKpSMSSSR, 1976 and 1982 *Atlas avtomobil'nykh dorog SSSR* [The highway atlas of the USSR] (Moscow: GUGK).

most of the roads in the BAM construction zone are unimproved and classified as "temporary." Travel on them may be characterized as joint-wrenching, bone-shattering, and slow, averaging under 30 kilometers per hour. As of 1983, there were no gas stations over the entire length of the temporary road network within the BAM service area.

In fact, automobile support facilities are notoriously lacking throughout Siberia and the Soviet Far East. In 1982 there were 600 gas stations and 109 repair garages. Amur and Omsk oblasts had 2 repair garages each.[50] Worse yet, despite the increases in the overall automobile stock—doubling per capita since 1970—automobile support units had increased only slightly since 1976 (Table 2.5). One of the better motor roads in East Siberia, the Never-Yakutsk Highway, which runs 1,177 kilometers from the Trans-Siberian Railroad to the Yakutian capital, has had only ten service stations and one repair garage (in Yakutsk) over its entire length for the last ten years. Obviously, the automobile transport sector in Siberia requires a major overhaul.

AIR TRANSPORT

Despite the high costs, air transportation is used to a much higher degree in Siberia than it is elsewhere in the country, largely because of permafrost and other natural constraints to road travel. In addition, shift work (bringing in short-term workcrews) and, in many instances, the sheer need for delivery speed encourage the employment of aircraft. In fact, more than 70 percent of all passenger traffic in East Siberia and the Soviet Far East is by air. With or without reliable roads, most small Siberian communities have air strips for regular passenger and mail service. All raion centers are connected by regional air service, and villages and towns are linked by mail planes and helicopters. In permafrost-plagued zones of the far north, geologists, fishermen, and hunters are supplied by ski planes during winter and by seaplanes that land on lakes and rivers in summer.

Although they carry only a small percentage of the gross output of Siberian transportation—according to Kolesov, 5 to 7 percent in the 1960s and early 1970s—Soviet heavy cargo aircraft of the Antonov class (An-12, AN-28, AN-72) fly up to 700 kilometers per hour and carry up to 45 tons of freight. Where terrain is too rough or too boggy (Yakutia and northeast Siberia, West Siberian swamps, and parts of the BAM service area), heavy-duty cargo and passenger helicopters of the Mil series (MI-4, MI-6, MI-8) are used. Smaller helicopters are used for range management on certain reindeer collectives. The obvious advantage of air transport over other conveyances in Siberia is that, weather permitting, it can be used virtually all year. The equally obvious disadvantage is that it costs two to sixteen times as much.

As it is with all forms of transportation except the waterways, air transport is most heavily used over an east-west axis. The main airports are at Sverdlovsk, Chelyabinsk, Omsk, Novosibirsk, Irkutsk, Khabarovsk, Vladivostok, and Petropavlovsk-Kamchatski. Important secondary landing sites are at Tyumen, Krasnoyarsk, Yakutsk, Magadan, Norilsk, Anadyr, and Yuzhno-Sakhalinsk. Since the 1970s augmentation of the West Siberian oil and gas fields, landing strips have been added at Nizhnevartovsk, Khanty-Mansisk, Nadym, and Urengoi. Similar landing strips have been added to or are planned for the BAM service area.

PIPELINE TRANSPORT

The most rapidly growing sector of the transport economy is and will continue to be pipelines. Since 1970 the quantities of oil flowing through Soviet pipelines have more than quadrupled. Gas deliveries by pipeline have expanded sevenfold.[51] The combined length of pipelines today exceeds 160,000 kilometers (versus 16,000 in 1955) and increases at a rate of 10,000 kilometers per year. Much of the new increment is attributable to West Siberia. Thus, pipelines now account for the distribution of virtually all the natural gas, 90 percent of the crude oil, and more than 10 percent of the oil products.

Since 1965, the expansion of oil exploration and development in the Middle Ob area of West Siberia has resulted in a half dozen or more large-diameter oil pipelines being built between the oil fields and the east-west trunklines, which proceed all the way to Irkutsk. The Siberian network radiates in three directions southward from the supergiant field of Samotlor: (1) to the east-west (Asia-Europe) Friendship Pipeline system to Eastern Europe; (2) to Omsk and from there to points east and west and now south to Central Asia; and (3) through two conduits to the Kuzbas. Other West Siberian pipelines extend to Novorossisk on the Black Sea and to Ventspils on the Baltic.[52]

Transport by gas pipeline is of even more recent vintage than transport by oil pipeline. Within the last decade, several major wide-diameter (1,220 and 1,420 millimeter natural gas pipelines have been highlighted in the international press. The Northern Lights Pipeline has carried gas from Medvezhe across the northern Urals to Moscow and beyond since the mid-1970s. The Urengoi-Center Pipeline proceeds from the world's largest natural gas reservoir through Perm to Moscow. The Urengoi-Chelyabinsk Pipeline, built in the late 1970s, is designed to feed the southern (Ukrainian and Central Black Earth) main transmission lines. Probably the most famous of all, owing to the controversy surrounding its destinations in Western Europe, is a new bundle of pipelines—there ultimately will be six lying in tandem across the Urals—known as the Urengoi-Uzhgorod Pipeline System. Another set of six is projected to parallel the Urengoi-Uzhgorod network from the Yamburg fields on the Gulf of Ob. These pipelines will figure prominently in supplying Soviet domestic as well as East and West European consumers with Urengoi and Yamburg gas. Finally, an oil field–gas pipeline extends from Samotlor to the Kuzbas, and Yakutsk is supplied with gas from the Middle Vilyui basin gas fields.

OTHER TRANSPORT
AND COMMUNICATIONS

Although the Soviet press occasionally enthusiastically reports the existence of futuristic forms of transportation in the country, existing transport modes should continue to prevail in Siberia and the Soviet Far East well into the next century. Hovercraft, amphibious aerosleighs, and heavy-cargo dirigibles all make news, but they probably won't make a dent in the Siberian transport balance for many years to come (Table 2.6).

Two other forms of advanced communications technology seem to have arrived for good: high-voltage AC and DC power transmission lines, and slurry pipelines. Long-distance (over 1,000 kilometers) high-voltage lines of 1,150 kilovolts (AC) and 1,500 kilovolts (DC) have been under construction between eastern Kazakhstan and the Urals for at least five years. Electric power will be supplied to them by minehead coal-burning power plants with capacities of 4,000 megawatts. It is estimated that 13 percent of the power will be lost en route. Construction of at least two more lines of this type is projected for the end of the decade: one from the Berezovka State Regional Power Plant in the Kansk-Achinsk lignite coal basin to other Siberian consumers, and another from Surgut in the Middle Ob oil fields to customers in the Urals.[53]

An experimental coal-slurry pipeline between Belovo in the Kuzbas and the Novosibirsk Thermal Power Station No. 5 is also under construction. The pipeline is designed to propel 4.3 million tons of coal a year over a distance of 250 kilometers. It will contain a 45:55 coal-to-water mix. If successful, the pipeline will serve as a prototype for longer pipelines, especially those running from the Kansk-Achinsk region to other parts of Siberia and the Soviet Far East.

Lastly, any communications infrastructure includes telephones and radio telecommunications. Information on the former is difficult to find in Soviet literature, probably because the countrywide system is so inadequate. According to *The Economist*, the USSR reflected a ratio of 89 telephones per 1,000 persons in 1981. Only Brazil and Mexico among the major nations of the world reported lower ratios. All the countries of Western Europe recorded more than 300 phones per 1,000 people.[54] It can be expected, therefore, that Siberian citizens had less access to telephones than did their countrymen in the European USSR.

Radio and television communications, on the other hand, are much better

TABLE 2.6
A Comparison of Siberian and USSR Freight Balances, 1960–1980

Years	SIBERIA						USSR					
	% RR	% River	% Sea	% Pipe	% Auto		% RR	% River	% Sea	% Pipe	% Auto
1960	89.7	4.0	0.1	2.3	3.9		79.3	5.3	6.9	3.5	5.2
1965	84.1	4.9	0.1	6.9	4.0		69.0	4.7	13.8	7.4	5.1
1970	76.4	4.9	0.1	14.2	3.8		63.1	4.4	16.8	10.3	5.8
1975	64.9	4.4	0.2	26.7	3.8		59.0	4.0	13.0	17.0	6.0
1980	60.0	4.0	0.3	31.1	3.8		55.6	3.9	13.7	19.7	7.0

SOURCE: For 1980: *Narodnoe khoziaistvo SSSR. 1922–1982* (Moscow: Statistika, 1982), p. 325. (Data for Siberia are estimated.) For all other years: L. I. Kolesov, *Mezhotraslevye problemy razvitiia transportnoi sistemy Sibiri i Dal'nego Vostoka* (Novosibirsk: Nauka, 1982), p. 130.

distributed in the country. The Soviet Union has its own telecommunications satellites. Usually within two years after the establishment of an urban settlement in Siberia (for instance, the BAM service area), television transmitters beam video to residents of the town. Almost all Siberian settlements have access to two or more channels. Currently, the Soviet Union can boast that its televisions-per-capita ratio of over 300 units per 1,000 persons is on par with those of all other advanced industrial countries except the United States, Japan, Canada, and Great Britain.[55]

SUMMARY AND CONCLUSIONS

Clearly, the iron horse is still king in Siberia and the Soviet Far East. This is true despite the steady proportional decline of the railroad in the regional freight balance—some 30 percent since 1960 (Table 2.6). This compares to a drop of only 14 percent during the same years for the Soviet Union as a whole. Note, however, that the big gainer of the time was oil and gas pipeline, conduits that carry only two types of freight. All the other forms of transportation—river, sea, and truck—that theoretically might be competitive with rail have maintained roughly the same shares that they had in 1960.

With the addition of a fully operational BAM sometime before 1990, railroads should reflect even better performance relative to all other means of transportation (except pipelines, which obviously will continue to increase at the expense of the other forms, including rail). The chief beneficiary of BAM's operations will be the 80-year-old Trans-Siberian Railroad. The BAM is expected to siphon off 10 to 20 percent of the heaviest traffic, including timber, coal, and ore, in East Siberia and the Soviet Far East. North-south railroads are also expected to be built beyond their existing terminals: the Tyumen-Surgut-Urengoi perhaps to Norilsk by the year 2000 and the Little BAM to Yakutsk in the 1990s. This will further enhance the railroad's reputation as the most versatile of transport alternatives in the country's eastern regions.

Siberian and Far Eastern rivers continue to be vital to their territories, being far more heavily used on a per capita basis than their counterparts in Soviet Europe. They are especially important in remote backwaters far from the railroads, where they are used both as water and ice roads. This is true in the Ob oil and gas regions and in northeast Siberia, where river transport is supplemented also by the use of the northern sea route.

Motor vehicular transport in Siberia and the Soviet Far East is hampered by a critical shortage of hard-surfaced highways and automotive infrastructure. No other region in the Soviet Union is so poorly endowed with the needs of an efficient automobile transport sector. For instance, not only are decent highways at a premium but also there are far fewer gas and repair stations per kilometer of those highways than anywhere else in the USSR.

Although it carries much more of the burden of transport in Siberia than it does in the European regions, the airplane is still a relatively small overall contributor to the transportation balance of the region. So, although 70 percent of the passenger traffic is accounted for by aviation, only a trace of the much more significant freight traffic is carried by air.

Little is known about the communications infrastructure in Siberia and the Soviet Far East apart from the major means of transportation. For at least twenty years there has been a largely successful attempt to extend high-voltage lines from Siberia's powerful hydroelectric facilities and minehead power plants to cities and towns within the territory. Now transmission lines of much greater capacities are expected to be raised from much bigger power plants based on the cheapest of coal (for example, Kansk-Achinsk lignite). The ultimate goal of these efforts is a unified power grid for the eastern half of the country similar to the one that now exists in the western half. In the next decade coal slurry pipelines may become a reality in parts of East and West Siberia. Curiously, although television ownership is probably as prevalent in Siberia and the Soviet Far East as it is in many of the major countries of Western Europe, the personal telephone continues to be far less uniformly available.

NOTES

1. See any of the works of V. V. Kriuchkov, for example, *Sever: Priroda i chelovek* [The North: Nature and man] (Moscow: Nauka, 1979), pp. 31–76; *Chutkaia subarktika* [The sensitive subarctic] (Moscow: Nauka, 1976), pp. 3–26, 70–134; and *Krainii sever: Problemy ratsional'nogo ispol'zovaniia prirodnykh resursov* [The Far North: Problems of rational utilization of natural resources] (Moscow: Mysl', 1973), pp. 66–152. For a somewhat more dated analysis, see Iu. M. Dogaev, *Ekonomicheskaia effektivnost' novoi tekhniki na Severe* [The economic effectiveness of new technology in the North] (Moscow: Nauka, 1969), especially pp. 33–69. A summary and an analysis of all sources that deal with constraining factors in Siberia are found in Victor L. Mote, "Environmental Constraints to the Economic Development of Siberia," in R. G. Jensen et al., eds., *Soviet Natural Resources in the World Economy* (Chicago: University of Chicago Press, 1983), pp. 15–72.

2. Paul E. Lydolph, *Geography of the USSR: Topical Analysis* (Elkhart Lake, Wis.: Misty Valley Press, 1979), p. 423.

3. P. Bunich, "BAM i razvitie ekonomiki Dal'nego Vostoka" [The BAM and the development of the economy of the Soviet Far East], *Planovoe khoziaistvo* 5 (1975): 29. Bunich claimed that the hauls for all forms of transport for Siberia were ten to eleven times longer than the country average, which in 1973 was 180 kilometers, making them

1,800 to 2,000 kilometers in the Soviet Far East. Data for 1975 indicate an average rail haul of 874 kilometers. "News Notes," *Soviet Geography: Review and Translation* 18, no. 9 (November 1977): 701. By 1979, an average rail haul reached 908 kilometers. L. I. Kolesov, *Mezhotraslevye problemy razvitiia transportnoi sistemy Sibiri i Dal'nego Vostoka* [Inter-branch problems in the development of the transportation system of Siberia and the Soviet Far East] (Novosibirsk: Nauka, 1982), pp. 62 and 92. Thus, Far Eastern hauls over railroads are easily twice the length for the country as a whole.

4. Iu. A. Sobolev, *Zona BAMa. Puti ekonomicheskogo razvitiia* [The BAM zone: Methods of economic development] (Moscow: Mysl', 1979), p. 208.

5. Much of the following description of the major railroads and their principal cargoes is derived from materials and sources in Vladimir Kontorovich, *Case Study of Transport in the Urals–West Siberia–North Kazakhstan Region*, Task B of Holland Hunter, ed., *Soviet Transportation Project* (Washington, D.C.: Wharton Econometric Forecasting Associates, December 1982); and Victor L. Mote, *Case Study of the BAM and East Siberian Transport Capacity Problems*, Task C of Holland Hunter, ed., *Soviet Transportation Project* (Washington, D.C.: Wharton Econometric Forecasting Associates, December 1982).

6. *Gudok,* August 9, 1983, p. 1.

7. V. Ia. Vasilenko, "Programmno-tselevoi podkhod k osvoeniiu zony BAMa" [Program and purpose planning in the development of the BAM zone], in *Baikalo-Amurskaia Magistral'* [The Baikal-Amur Mainline] (Moscow: Mysl', 1977), pp. 46–48.

8. Central Intelligence Agency, *USSR: Coal Industry Problems and Prospects* (Washington, D.C.: National Foreign Assessment Center, 1980), p. 13. Figures 2.1 and 2.2 are adaptations from the two maps in this document.

9. A. I. Alekseev, "Po marshrutam Baikalo-Amurskoi magistrali" [Along the route of the Baikal-Amur Mainline], *Voprosy istorii* 9 (1976): 120, and *Khozhdenie ot Baikala do Amura* [Striding from Baikal to the Amur] (Moscow: Molodaia gvardiia, 1976), p. 176. Both these sources provide deep histories into the precedents and planning for the modern BAM project.

10. Akademiia Nauk SSSR, Komissiia po problemam Severa, *Letopis' Severa* [Chronicle of the North], vol. 2 (Moscow: Geografgiz, 1957), pp. 200–205.

11. Theodore Shabad, "News Notes," *Soviet Geography: Review and Translation* 13, no. 4 (April 1972): 260–62.

12. M. E. Adzhiev, "Ekonomiko-geograficheskie problemy BAMa" [Economic-geographic problems of the BAM], *Priroda* 8 (1975): 5; and Alekseev, *Khozhdenie ot Baikala*, pp. 165–69.

13. *Izvestiia,* March 5, 1981, p. 5.

14. *Gudok,* September 30, 1983, p. 2; and *General Council of British Shipping,* communications of December 1, 1983, reference 43/29A, p. 2.

15. *Gudok,* December 13, 1983, p. 1, November 7, 1983, p. 2, December 28, 1983, p. 2, and December 31, 1983, p. 1.

16. *Gudok,* September 30, 1983, p. 2. There was contradiction between the data provided in this article and the previously cited December 13 article (note 15). According

to this article, 2,850 kilometers of track, including the fully operational 402-kilometer Little BAM, had been laid as of October 1. Subtracting the Little BAM, that would have left 697 kilometers of unfinished road on the BAM. Something was obviously wrong with the data, if the December 13 article was correct: 400 kilometers of unfinished track. That is, 300 kilometers of mainline could not have been laid in two and one-half months.

17. Victor L. Mote, "The Baikal-Amur Mainline and Its Implications for the Pacific Basin," in R. G. Jensen et al., eds., *Soviet Natural Resources in the World Economy* (Chicago: University of Chicago Press, 1983), p. 142. The combined annual rates of the western BAM crews were only 97 kilometers at the time; for the eastern BAM crews they were only slightly higher, at 104 kilometers. Victor L. Mote, "Current and Prospective Status of BAM," in *Wharton Econometric Forecasting Associates CPE Current Analysis*, August 24, 1982, p. 2. The combined rates reached 187 kilometers per year on the western BAM and 123 kilometers per year on the eastern BAM. Victor L. Mote, "Reflections on the BAM: Nine Years and Still Counting," *Soviet Geography: Review and Translation* 24, no. 4 (April 1983): 280–88. The rates used were estimated to be 250 kilometers per year on the western BAM, 17 kilometers too high, but still a record for the time, and 214 kilometers per year on the eastern BAM, which may also have been high.

18. *Gudok*, February 24, 1983, p. 1, December 28, 1983, p. 2, December 31, 1983, p. 1.

19. Mote, *Case Study of BAM*, p. 8; and *Gudok*, September 30, 1983, p. 2.

20. *Gudok*, April 26, 1979, p. 2; includes a summary of construction highlights on the BAM since 1974 through January 1979. See also *Gudok*, September 25, 1981, p. 1, December 25, 1981, p. 2, and December 26, 1982, p. 2.

21. For information on the cost of the BAM and its infrastructure, see F. D'iakonov, "Dal'nii Vostok: Problemy i perspektivy" [The Soviet Far East: Problems and perspectives], *Ekonomicheskaia gazeta* 5 (1975): 13; *Saturday Evening Post*, November 1975, p. 66; Seth Mydans in an Associated Press news release for March 1, 1978; and Charles Bremmer, Reuters News Flash No. 22 JC6343/4, RNR 623, "Rails 4 Alonka," March 1978. The latter news releases were obtained from the *New York Times* foreign desk.

22. Adzhiev, "Ekonomiko-geograficheskie problemy BAMa," p. 4.

23. J. N. Westwood, "Variations in the Transport System at the Regional Level: The Role of the BAM (1)," in *Regional Development in the USSR. Trends and Prospects* (Newtonville, Mass.: Oriental Research Associates, 1979), p. 191.

24. Mote, *Case Study of BAM*, pp. 42–47; and *Congressional Record*, June 15, 1977, pp. E3781–82.

25. F. V. D'iakonov, "BAM—Kompleks krupnykh narodnokhoziaistvennykh problem dolgosrochnoi perspektivy" [The BAM—A complex of major economic problems for the long-range future], in *Baikalo-Amurskaia magistral'* [Baikal-Amur Mainline] (Moscow: Mysl', 1977), p. 23.

26. Quoting Abel Aganbegian, *Gudok*, April 22, 1983, p. 2.

27. *Gudok*, November 10, 1981, p. 1, and December 25, 1981, pp. 1–2.

28. *Gudok*, June 21, 1983, p. 4.

29. *Gudok*, October 29, 1983, p. 1.

30. For information on the early forecasts, see N. P. Belen'kii and V. S. Maslen-nikov, "BAM: Raion tiagoteniia i gruzovye perevozki" [The BAM: The tributary and freight shipments], *Zheleznodorozhnyi transport* 10 (1974): 46; and D'iakonov, "Dal'nii Vostok: Problemy i perspektivy," p. 13. For Eleventh Five-Year Plan goals, see *Gudok,* December 25, 1981, p. 2.

31. Paul E. Lydolph, *Climates of the Soviet Union* (New York: Elsevier, 1977), p. 267; for the previous quote, see V. Degtiarev, V. Zin, and N. Permichev, "Rechnoi transport Sibiri i Dal'nego Vostoka" [River transport in Siberia and the Soviet Far East], *Rechnoi transport* 3 (1978): 21–22.

32. I. Kovrigin, "Reka Nadym: Ee osvoenie dlia sudokhodstva" [The River Nadym: Its navigational development], *Rechnoi transport* 1 (1978): 42–43.

33. V. Postnikov, "Novyi etap tekhnicheskogo progressa" [A new stage of techni-cal progress], *Rechnoi transport* 11 (1978): 32; P. Trifonov, "Na malykh rekakh Tom-skoi Oblasti" [On the small rivers of Tomsk oblast], *Rechnoi transport* 9 (1978): 21; O. Strel'cheniia, "Sozdaem glubokovodnyi put' na Severe" [We're creating a deepwater route in the North], *Rechnoi transport* 6 (1978): 40; A. Puzenko and E. Zin', "Problemy osvoeniia malykh rek Dal'nego Vostoka" [Problems of developing the small rivers of the Soviet Far East], *Rechnoi transport* 10 (1978): 29.

34. Theodore Shabad, "News Notes," *Soviet Geography: Review and Translation* 18, no. 6 (June 1977): 420–28.

35. Most of the following information is derived from Kontorovich, *Case Study of Transport,* pp. 39–43.

36. E. L. Zubashev, "Turkestan-Sibirskaia magistral' i drugie proektiiuremye puti v Zapadnoi Sibiri" [The Turkestan-Siberian Mainline and other projected routes in Western Siberia], *Vol'naia Sibir'* 2 (1927): 159. Novgorodians had investigated the coasts as far east as the Gulf of Ob as early as the 1400s.

37. Central Intelligence Agency, *Polar Regions Atlas* (Washington, D.C.: National Foreign Assessment Center, 1978), pp. 26–27.

38. *Gudok,* May 22, 1978, p. 2; and Shabad, "News Notes" (June 1977), p. 423.

39. *Gudok,* November 21, 1979, p. 2, and November 30, 1983, p. 2. During the summer season, fully "a third" of all the rolling stock in East Siberia "belongs to the port of Osetrovo." About 60 percent of all traffic goes to Yakutia over the Lena River and its tributaries, 18 percent goes by Little BAM, 13 percent by truck, 8 percent by sea, and 1 percent by air. After the completion of the railroad to Yakutsk in 1995, the Lena's share will fall to 15 percent, roughly equaling that carried by marine transport. Railroads will carry 65 percent of all traffic. Shabad, "News Notes" (May 1985): 412–13.

40. M. L. Alekseev et al., *Problemy osvoeniia severa Buriatskoi ASSR* [Problems in the development of the Buryat ASSR] (Novosibirsk: Nauka, 1978), p. 82.

41. Shabad, "News Notes" (June 1977), pp. 425–28.

42. *Bol'shaia Sovetskaia entsiklopediia* [The great Soviet encyclopedia], 3d ed., vol. 1 (Moscow: Sovietskaia entsiklopediia, 1970), p. 544.

43. Holland Hunter and Deborah Kaple, *Current Analysis of Soviet Railroad Prob-*

lems, Task D of Holland Hunter, ed., *Soviet Transportation Project* (Washington, D.C.: Wharton Econometric Forecasting Associates, December 1982), pp. 43, 48.

44. "Nirvana by Numbers," *The Economist,* December 24, 1983, p. 53.

45. Kolesov, *Mezhotraslevye problemy,* p. 175.

46. Ibid., p. 130.

47. Westwood, "Variations in the Transport System," pp. 204–6.

48. Kolesov, *Mezhotraslevye problemy,* pp. 62, 67.

49. Kontorovich, *Case Study of Transport,* pp. 46–50.

50. GUGKpSMSSSR, *Atlas avtomobil'nykh dorog SSSR* [The highway atlas of the USSR] (Moscow: GUGK, 1982), pp. 78–98.

51. Hunter, *Current Analysis,* p. 36.

52. For an excellent exposition of Soviet oil and gas, see Leslie Dienes and Theodore Shabad, *The Soviet Energy System* (Washington, D.C.: Victor Winston and Sons, 1979), p. 72.

53. *Izvestiia,* September 7, 1977, p. 1, August 5, 1975, p. 1, April 24, 1976, p. 1, and March 5, 1981, p. 5.

54. "Nirvana by Numbers," *The Economist,* p. 53.

55. Ibid., p. 55.

The Energy Scene

Since the end of 1977 Soviet leaders have seen themselves in danger of an acute energy crisis and a related squeeze on their hard-currency earnings. They have responded over the last eight years with an emergency program that makes energy the country's top industrial priority. The swing of scarce resources to that sector has been so dramatic that it cramps the development of the rest of Soviet industry (particularly in European Russia) at a time when investment resources have been extremely tight.

Much of the energy program is aimed at accelerating the development of West Siberian oil and gas and, though to a lesser extent, Siberian coal. This raises many policy issues that have deeply concerned Siberian authorities and scientists. First, the energy program has not added to Siberia's total share of investment resources so much as it has redistributed them. The only real beneficiaries have been the oil and gas industries in Tyumen province. Second, despite much talk about moving energy-intensive industries to West Siberia, there has been little action, and in practice planners continue to locate new plants in the European part of the USSR. Third, the oil and gas campaigns have brought a flood of new manpower and activity to West Siberia, but housing and infrastructure for them have been grossly neglected. In short, the accelerated energy program is aggravating the problem of unbalanced development in West Siberia.

The focus of this chapter is on the political challenges that such a large and sudden change in course necessarily raises. We were accustomed to thinking of the late Brezhnev leadership as a stodgy and tired *fin de règne,* a regime of postponed decisions, and in many respects it was exactly that. But, faced with what it evidently regarded as a grave threat, the Kremlin under Brezhnev showed it could respond vigorously, just as it did in defense and agriculture in the 1960s and 1970s. Since Brezhnev's death in late 1982, despite three successions in three years, the leaders' commitment to the energy sector has not wavered.

What exactly is the nature of the threat that Soviet leaders believe they face?

Were they slow in perceiving it and in designing a coherent response? How well thought out is their present program, and how likely to endure and succeed? What do its main features, and the way they are being carried out, reveal about the intentions of the leaders and the choices they have made? How might the program go wrong, and in that case how might it be altered or curtailed? What are its consequences for Siberian development? This chapter will address those questions first by outlining the main features of the present policy, then by recounting briefly the background of the last ten years and discussing the principal decision-making challenges of the current policy.

Some important issues will not be addressed in this chapter, since the emphasis of this volume is on Siberia. First, because a steadily growing share of Soviet energy is exported (about 16 percent at present) and energy exports provide nearly 60 percent of Soviet hard-currency income, it is clear that Soviet policy is influenced by more than domestic considerations alone, although these are stressed in this chapter. Second, the rapid increase in energy investment of the last few years puts heavy pressure on all the industries that supply the energy sector with machinery and materials, so that the energy sector competes with other high-priority programs, including defense. Both these subjects (dealt with elsewhere by this author) will be discussed only passingly here.[1]

DIMENSIONS OF THE CURRENT ENERGY POLICY

Just how seriously the Soviet leaders viewed their energy problems in 1981, when the Eleventh Five-Year Plan began, can be judged by the resources they chose to put into energy development. At a time of unprecedented stringency, in which the five-year growth target of investment was to be held to a record low of 10.4 percent, the Soviet leaders allocated about 67 percent of the total increment to the energy sector. (If one measures the energy increment as a percentage of the industrial increment alone, then energy's intended share came out to a whopping 85.6 percent.) The totals announced by Gosplan Chairman Baibakov in November 1981 called for a 50 percent increase in energy investment, or 132 billion rubles, over five years.[2]

In fact, even before Brezhnev's death the Soviet leaders dropped their low-investment diet. Instead of 10.4 percent, the five-year growth rate of investment now looks to be more like 15 or 16 percent. One plausible explanation is that the initial plan would have virtually frozen the investment budgets of every sector of Soviet industry not related to energy (including some of direct interest to the military). In view of urgent Soviet needs in other industrial branches such as transportation and machine-building, such stringency was clearly unacceptable.

TABLE 3.1
Physical Output Targets for the Eleventh Five-Year Plan

	1980	Draft Plan	Final Plan
Oil[a]	603	620–640	630
Coal[a]	716	770–800	775
Gas[b]	435	600–640	630
Electricity[c]	1295	1550–1600	1555
Hydropower	184	230–235	230
Nuclear	73	220–225	220

SOURCE: 1980 data are from *Narodnoe khoziaistvo SSSR v 1980 g.* Eleventh Plan data are from *Izvestiia,* November 18, 1981.

[a] In millions of tons natural.
[b] In billions of cubic meters.
[c] In billions of kilowatt hours.

At any rate, the higher investment rate reduced correspondingly the burden of the energy program, whose growth thus absorbed only about 38 percent of the total increase, instead of 67 percent as initially planned.

The physical energy output targets, however, have not changed; they are shown in Table 3.1. Note that the 1985 targets for coal and oil are relatively modest: the oil target is essentially the same as the one that the Soviets, back in 1976, had hoped to reach by 1980; the one for coal is even lower.[3] This reflects, first of all, the disappointing performance of those two sectors in the previous five-year plan. But the deeper message conveyed by the low 1985 targets, when set alongside the investment figures, is that the Soviets are having to invest ever-larger amounts of capital for smaller marginal returns. "In recent years," says a high Gosplan official, "capital investment in exploration, extraction, and transportation of energy has grown 50 percent faster than energy output itself, and in the oil and gas industries 60 to 100 percent faster."[4] The planned distribution of investment in the Eleventh Plan reflects this rapid increase in unit costs (see Table 3.2).

To appreciate what the rising investment needs of the energy sector imply for the economy as a whole, one must also take into account the capital and manpower requirements of supporting industries and the expenditures associated with consuming energy as well as supplying it. In 1980, these added another 50–60 percent to basic fuel investment, distributed as shown in Table 3.3. Thus energy, which in the narrow sense now takes up about 40 percent of Soviet industrial investment and 5.5–6 percent of the work force, by the broader definition claims as much as 60 percent of industrial investment and 11–13 percent of total employment. The strain placed on the economy by an abrupt acceleration of

TABLE 3.2
Energy Investment (1976–1985) (in billions of rubles)

	1976–1980 (actual)	1981–1985 (plan)
Fuel and power complex	88	132
investment other than pipelines	66	100
oil	26	43
coal	10	12
gas	10	22
electricity	19	23
pipeline investment	22	32
gas		27
oil		5.3

SOURCE: Robert Leggett, "Soviet Investment Policy in the 11th Five-Year Plan," in U.S. Congress, Joint Economic Committee, *Soviet Economy in the 1980s: Problems and Prospects,* vol. 1 (December 1982): 137.

TABLE 3.3
Distribution of Basic Fuel Investment

	Capital Investment, 1980 (109 rubles)	Manpower (106 workers)
Production, transformation, and distribution of energy resources	22.5–23	6–6.4
Fuel supply[a]	16	2.9
Centralized heat and electricity supply (Minenergo)	4	NA
Power plants and boilers belonging to individual agencies (other than Minenergo)	2.5–3	3.1–3.5
Ancillary branches, supporting operation and growth of fuel and power complex	4–5	5.5–6.5
Investment required for energy consumption	7–9	3.5–4.1
Totals	33.5–37	15–17

SOURCE: Iu. D. Kononov, "Toplivno-energeticheskii kompleks v sisteme narodnokhoziaistvennykh sviazei," *EKO,* no. 4 (1983): 20. Kononov's analysis is given in fuller form in his chapter in L. A. Melent'ev and A. A. Makarov, *Energeticheskii kompleks SSSR* (Moscow: "Ekonomika," 1983), pp. 197–227.

[a] Includes exploration, extraction, processing, and transmission.

energy investment, amounting to a 50 percent increase over five years, can be imagined.

The impact on Siberia is especially great. By 1985 Siberia will supply well over half of total Soviet energy output; it is the only significant source of growth in Soviet fuel supply. More than half the increment in Soviet energy investment during the current plan is slated for West Siberia, even though much of that consists of equipment produced west of the Urals. Yet at the same time Soviet economists observe that Siberia's overall share of investment has grown very slowly, which means that the crash development of Tyumen oil and gas is taking place at the expense of other Siberian industries.[5] Indeed, in the Eleventh Five-Year Plan nearly all the increase in investment for West Siberia as a whole is being allocated to the oil and gas industries in Tyumen province.[6]

The core component of the Soviet energy program is investment in oil, which is planned to rise by 63 percent to nearly 43 billion rubles between 1981 and 1985. The Soviet oil industry managed to keep output increasing slowly in the early 1980s by sharply increasing all inputs (especially drilling) and by transferring its resources to West Siberia, where the greater ease of drilling and the higher flow rate of each new well provided a crucial one-time boost (these effects, however, are now rapidly fading). The oil industry is increasingly squeezed between declining yields and rapidly growing costs, as Figure 3.1 shows vividly. If the Soviet leaders remain determined to keep oil output at its present level, they may have to double oil investment every five years to do so.

Fortunately for them, alternatives are on the way. The largest and fastest-growing component of the energy program is natural gas. Gas was the star performer of the Tenth Five-Year Plan, the only energy source that actually achieved the five-year targets set in 1976. In the Eleventh Five-Year Plan, natural gas is supposed to provide 75 percent of the net addition to the fuel balance,[7] and if current trends hold it may end up supplying much more than that. Natural gas output will easily exceed 630 billion cubic meters per year by the end of 1985, which will put the Soviet Union in first place worldwide. Siberia alone is expected to produce 356 billion cubic meters, 60 percent of the total Soviet output.[8]

To achieve this goal, the Soviet gas industry and the pipeline construction agencies could well spend between them from 35 to 40 billion rubles, more than half of the increment allocated to the energy sector. That is not the Soviets' own figure, because they have not published one, but one can arrive at a rough estimate from the bits and pieces available.

We look first at the record of the last three five-year plans. From 1965 to 1980 the investment budget of the gas industry grew very rapidly, from 4.05 billion rubles in the Eighth Five-Year Plan (1966–1970) to around 21 billion in the Tenth.[9] For the Eleventh, there have been two indirect statements by top officials. At the twenty-sixth party congress, the late minister of gas, S. A. Orudzhev,

FIGURE 3.1
Soviet Oil Investment Compared to Output, 1976–1985

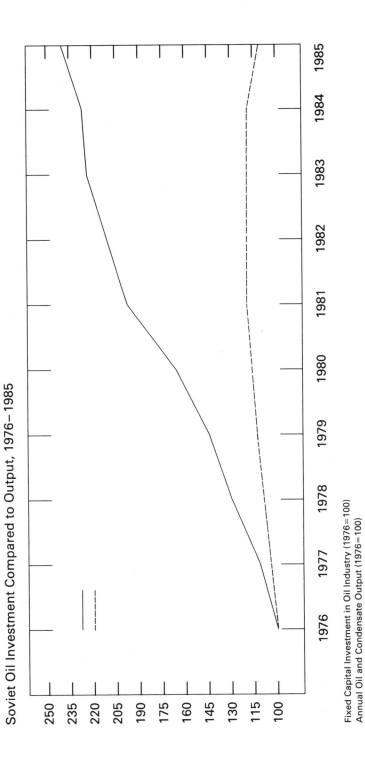

Fixed Capital Investment in Oil Industry (1976=100)
Annual Oil and Condensate Output (1976=100)

SOURCE: *Narodnoe khoziaistvo SSSR.*

TABLE 3.4
Total Investment in the Soviet Gas Industry (1966-1985)

	Billions of Current Rubles
Eighth Five-Year Plan (1966-1970)	4.05
Ninth Five-Year Plan (1971-1975)	10.90
Tenth Five-Year Plan (1976-1980)	20.7-21.5
Eleventh Five-Year Plan (1981-1985)	
Orudzhev's formula	35.7-36.5
Dinkov's formula	41.4-43.0

SOURCE: Thane Gustafson, *The Soviet Gas Campaign: Politics and Policy in Soviet Decision-making* (Santa Monica, Calif.: Rand Corporation R-3036-AF, 1983).

stated that the gas industry would spend as much in the coming five-year plan as in the last three combined, which adds up to around 36 billion rubles.[10] Six months later, after Orudzhev's death, his successor, V. Dinkov (now oil minister), used the formula that gas investment in the Eleventh Five-Year Plan would be double that of the Tenth, around 42 billion rubles.[11] Thus, for the twenty-year period from 1966 to 1985 we have the trend shown in Table 3.4.

About 70 percent of the total is to be devoted to pipelines,[12] much of it to build 20,000 kilometers of 56-inch pipelines from Urengoi. A Soviet rule of thumb is that the six 56-inch pipelines from Urengoi to the West cost roughly one billion rubles per 1,000 kilometers.[13] However, authoritative sources also mention higher figures, particularly for pipeline investment, and this suggests that cost estimates for the gas campaign have been unsettled. M. S. Zotov, chairman of the USSR Bank for Construction, states that for the six main lines from Urengoi, the planners have allocated a total of 31 billion rubles,[14] or 1.5 billion rubles per 1,000 kilometers, 50 percent more than the estimates cited earlier. Similarly, *Pravda* gives the cost of the export line as 7.6 billion rubles, which is closer to 1.7 billion rubles per 1,000 kilometers,[15] although the export line, because it uses imported compressors, is presumably somewhat more expensive than the others. The implication of both figures is that the gas campaign could require some 10 billion rubles more than the range implied by Dinkov, for a total somewhere above 50 billion rubles. In sum, it is a reasonable guess that meeting the projected gas targets will require between 45 billion and 55 billion rubles.[16]

When the five-year targets for the gas industry were first published in 1981, Western observers were skeptical. Could the Soviet gas and pipeline-construction industries successfully handle such a phenomenal inflow of resources in so short a time? The demands placed on them were extraordinary: 40,000 kilometers of major new pipeline, of which 20,000 were to be laid in six

56-inch pipes from Urengoi to European Russia. Nearly the entire increase in Soviet gas production must come from one field alone, Urengoi, whose output was scheduled to increase from 50 billion cubic meters in 1980 to between 250 and 270 by 1985.[17]

The requirement for basic materials such as pipe was equally daunting: a Soviet rule of thumb is that every 1,000 kilometers of 56-inch pipeline require 600 tons of pipe; in other words, the Soviets needed 12 million tons of 56-inch pipe during the Eleventh Five-Year Plan alone.[18] If one adds to that roughly another 8 million tons of pipe for the remaining 20,000 kilometers of smaller-diameter pipeline, the total requirement is about 20 million tons. Most of the larger pipe, and much of the major equipment as well, would obviously have to be imported.

The main battleground was to be in West Siberia, and here the increases in targets were particularly dramatic: the head of Tyumentransgaz, the main pipeline operator in West Siberia, reported that while his organization oversaw the construction of 1,500 kilometers of trunkline in the Tenth Five-Year Plan, it was assigned a target in the Eleventh Plan of 7,500 kilometers, all at 56 inches and 75 atmospheres.[19] The same executive reported that while his organization absorbed 1.1 billion rubles in capital investment during the Tenth Five-Year Plan, he was allocated 7.5 times as much (8.25 billion) for the Eleventh.[20] However, Soviet data suggest that unit costs per kilometer of finished pipeline may be as much as twice as high in the Eleventh Plan as the Tenth,[21] which suggests that the gas industry may be spending even more in West Siberia than the plan called for.

Given these challenges, how have the oil and gas campaigns fared? The gas campaign has been a brilliant success, at least when judged from the overall performance indicators. Pipeline construction stayed right on schedule, thanks in part to the American compressor embargo, which caused the Soviets to accelerate their domestic compressor program. All six of the major 56-inch pipelines scheduled for construction in 1981–1985 are already operating and a seventh is under construction. In sum, what seemed in 1981 like extravagant puffery is turning into an impressive reality.[22]

Oil has been doing less well. Production rose slightly in 1983 to 616 million tons, but actually declined in the last three months of the year, and the decline continued through the end of 1985. What is especially worrisome to the industry is that the recent faltering comes not from the older oil regions, which are actually losing ground less rapidly than planned, but from Tyumen province, which hitherto could always be counted on for above-plan increases. The major bottleneck is not drilling but the long neglect of ancillary tasks, such as well completion, mechanization, maintenance, and repair, as well as road-building and power supply in the oil fields.[23]

The Soviets' achievements in gas and oil since 1978 can be summed up this way: On the positive side, they staved off a peak in oil output for seven valuable years, thus gaining time to prepare alternatives. Simultaneously they have developed the natural gas sector as an all-important bridge to carry the Soviet economy from the age of oil to that of coal and nuclear power. We must give due credit to the Soviet managers' resolve and forcefulness in pursuing these two policies; the results they have achieved have been most impressive.

What is less clear at this point are the hidden costs and constraints whose consequences will only be felt later. The first of these is the long-term impact of the campaign atmosphere in which the oil and gas industries have had to work for the past decade. The second is the strain of so rapid a change in the total energy mix, as the share of natural gas increases from 26 percent in 1980 to 32 percent in 1985. The third is the imbalance caused by a policy that still emphasizes energy supply over conservation.

We shall return to these issues in the final section of this chapter. But first, what made the emergency energy program necessary in the first place? The next section reconstructs the main events that led to the current policy.

EVOLUTION OF SOVIET POLICY
1970–1985

Soviet energy policy over the last fifteen years has been highly changeable. One can count two major shifts in course and a number of minor ones, accompanied throughout by vigorous public debate. Energy policy gives us an exceptionally interesting case study of high-level decision-making at the end of the Brezhnev period, a counterpart in some respects to the agricultural politics that were so prominent at the period's beginning. That earlier issue had been spiced by the rivalry between Kosygin and Brezhnev. When the energy problem arose a decade later, Brezhnev and Kosygin again found themselves on opposite sides, but this time the context was entirely different. Brezhnev's primacy was undisputed and, in any case, both were old and sick. The main reason for the many debates appears substantive and not political. Edward Hewett, in a nice phrase, has called the shifting pattern of decision-making in energy policy not central planning but "central probing," that is, a process of trial and error as experts, planners, and leaders adapt (with varying degrees of enthusiasm and alertness) to the rapidly changing situation in the field.

At the beginning of the 1970s the energy situation as viewed from the Kremlin must have appeared cloud-free. With the development of the major oil and gas fields of the Volga basin and the Ukraine in the 1950s and the even larger fields of West Siberia in the 1960s, the Soviet Union was enjoying the benefits of the era of cheap hydrocarbons, if somewhat later than the West. If one looks back a decade to Soviet publications of 1972 and 1973, it is hard to find any public sign of high-level concern over future energy prospects. In the public summaries of his reports to the December plenary sessions of the CPSU in 1972 and 1973, Brezhnev gave hardly more than a passing reference to the subject. Kosygin, in two of his few published speeches on domestic policy during this period, had equally little to say about energy production or conservation.[24] In September 1972 the deputy prime minister for science and technology, V. A. Kirillin, gave an entire speech to the USSR Supreme Soviet entitled "Rational Utilization of Natural Resources" without more than a passing mention of energy waste, except as a source of pollution.[25] The oil industry, as portrayed in the press at that time, was not without its problems, but they were mainly problems of rapid growth. At the September 1972 session of the USSR Supreme Soviet, for example, speakers criticized slow construction, particularly of oil and gas pipelines and of compressor stations.[26] One of the earliest items to appear in the Soviet press as a portent of things to come was a complaint from the chief of the Tyumen oil industry that funding for oil exploration in West Siberia had been frozen at a constant level for several years.[27]

However, in 1973 concern about inadequate oil exploration in Tyumen province and anxiety about the lack of hard new data on reserves became more prominent. The Middle Ob fields, one technical specialist asserted, could not provide an adequate base for further expansion of Soviet oil output after 1980.[28] Official attention began to shift north and east of Tyumen.[29] The tone was not yet one of panic, but in hindsight 1973 has proved to be a significant year: not one giant oil field has been discovered in West Siberia since.

By 1974 one can find evidence of greater attention to energy policy, at least among technical experts. In that year USSR Gosplan established an Institute of Complex Fuel and Power Problems. In November 1974 energy was the major topic on the agenda of the USSR Academy of Sciences' annual meeting.[30] The energy crisis that had struck the West the year before was clearly on the speakers' minds. Still, in these writings there was no perceptible sense of a crisis, as in the West, but rather an air of unhurried positioning for the future.[31]

If technical experts did not yet perceive a crisis, even less did political leaders. The most eloquent evidence is that the share of the energy sector in industrial investment fell steadily throughout the early 1970s, from 29.4 percent in 1971 to just over 28 percent in 1975. The rumblings coming more strongly from oilmen and geologists in Tyumen province evidently took some time to penetrate the consciousness of the leaders, although one should note that energy's investment share stopped falling after 1975.[32]

By the beginning of the Tenth Five-Year Plan (1976–1980), some of the experts' growing concern began to reach the leaders, but like them, the leaders showed no particular sense of urgency. At the twenty-fifth party congress in February 1976 Brezhnev gave little more time to energy than he had in earlier speeches, such as his report at year-end Central Committee plenums over the previous five years. Kosygin, for his part, stressed the potential role of coal, thus echoing the position taken by the research and development establishment in the previous year or two. Oil and gas, Kosygin declared to the congress delegates, should be saved as much as possible for nonfuel uses. In his conception, large coal-fired power plants would supply the Volga and Ural regions, and the vast reserves of brown coal in Kazakhstan and Siberia would be converted to electricity by mine-mouth plants located nearby, the power flowing to points of demand in European Russia over the world's longest high-voltage transmission lines. To begin this long-term shift toward coal, the guidelines for the Tenth Five-Year Plan called for an increase in coal output of 14–16 percent by 1980.

To understand how the Soviet leaders reacted less than two years later, one should note that what Kosygin was describing to the twenty-fifth congress in 1976 was less an immediate plan of action than a long-term program. For all their public stress on coal, the leaders failed to back their words with an expanded flow of money. The Tenth Plan guidelines projected a continued decline in coal's share of the total energy balance, from 30 percent in 1975 to 26 percent in 1980;[33] coal's investment share was scheduled to decline also. In contrast, the investment share of oil and gas (as defined in the principal Soviet statistical handbook) increased from 51 to 54.6 percent in the first two years of the Tenth Five-Year Plan. If we can assume that the flow of money accurately measures the leaders' perceptions and priorities, it appears they were becoming aware of the rise in energy costs but continued to see oil and gas as the realistic solution, not coal.[34]

The leaders were quite unprepared for the abrupt crisis that broke in the West Siberian oil fields in 1976 and 1977. For the first time, the geologists failed to meet their assigned targets for additions to proved and probable reserves. Other alarm signals went off too: the number of new fields identified, flow rates of new wells, and, most important, the overall growth rate of Siberian oil output—all began dropping. Faced with the possibility that oil output might peak by the end of the decade, Soviet leaders at the end of 1977 realized they had to act.

In late 1977 Brezhnev launched a crash program to speed up West Siberian oil output. In his speech to the December 1977 plenum of the Central Committee, Brezhnev stressed the decisive importance of Tyumen.[35] In the months following, there was a good deal of discussion about the course to take, during which officials with links to Tyumen lobbied vigorously for Siberian oil.[36] It is interesting to note that most major officials in Moscow, including Baibakov and Kosygin, did not immediately follow Brezhnev's line, and during the winter and spring of 1978 Brezhnev did some campaigning, reminiscent of his efforts to launch his agricultural policy in the late 1960s. The new line was apparently consolidated following a Brezhnev trip to Siberia in the spring of 1978,[37] and by a strongly worded speech to the thirteenth Komsomol congress in April 1978. In December an "enlarged session" of USSR Gosplan officials was convened to review the practical issues of speeding up energy development in Siberia.[38]

Over the next four years Brezhnev's role in energy policy grew even more visible, although the initial stress on oil gave way in 1979 to a policy officially described as "balanced," which then led in 1980 to a rapidly growing priority for gas. During the same period, the apparent role of the Central Committee staff grew also. Prior to 1977 it had been the staff of the Council of Ministers and of Gosplan that seemed to be more prominent in energy policy, but from 1978 on, V. I. Dolgikh, the Central Committee secretary in charge of heavy industry, played a steadily larger role in energy matters, and appears today (as we shall see below) to be the leading policy-maker still.[39]

The official investment statistics dovetail neatly with the change in tone of official speeches after 1977. The share of investment in energy development, measured as a percentage of total industrial investment, took a sudden jump after 1977 and has continued climbing rapidly ever since. (See Figure 3.2.) The statistical handbooks also confirm that beginning in 1978 oil investment likewise took a sharp upward turn, increasing its share of industrial investment dramatically, from an average of 9.3 percent in the first half of the 1970s to 17.0 percent in 1982, and more than doubling in the absolute annual amounts invested.

The second turn in Soviet energy policy came in 1980–1981, with the sharp increase in the priority of gas that has already been described. The way had been prepared by several years of modeling and analysis inside Gosplan and specialized research institutes, which showed that shipping gas by pipeline from north Tyumen would be markedly more cost-effective than various schemes for shipping the energy from Siberian coal. At the same time, the results of the previous three years' campaign in the oil fields had not reassured the leaders about prospects in that department. To maintain the share of oil at 44 percent of total energy output, energy experts calculated, would require multiplying oil investment in the Eleventh Five-Year Plan (1981–1985) by a factor of 3.7–3.8.[40] In short, there was no alternative to gas. In February 1981 Brezhnev announced to the twenty-sixth party congress:

> I consider it necessary to single out the rapid development of Siberian gas output as a task of first-rank economic and political importance. The deposits of the West Siberian region are unique. The largest of them—Urengoi—has such gigantic reserves that it can meet for many years both the internal needs of the country and its export needs, including exports to the capitalist countries.

Over the following months, despite evidence (which we have noted) that the gas program's ambitious goals outstripped the modest infrastructure available for achieving them, the leaders' commitment to gas only grew stronger. When the final version of the Tenth Five-Year Plan was published in the fall of 1981, all the other energy targets for 1985 had been cut to the low end of the spreads announced in the draft version unveiled the previous February, but gas was set close to the high end. In November 1981, at the plenary meeting of the party Central

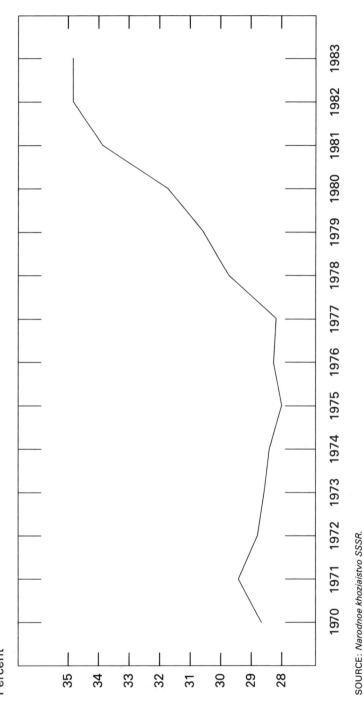

FIGURE 3.2
Investment in the Fuel and Power Sector as a Share of Total Industrial Investment, 1970–1983 (current prices)
Percent

SOURCE: *Narodnoe khoziaistvo SSSR.*

NOTE: Prices exclude most energy transportation and some exploration.

Committee at which the final targets were announced, Brezhnev described the six major Siberian pipelines as "without a doubt the central construction projects of the five-year plan," and he added, "they must be finished on time without fail."[41]

Curiously, earlier in the 1970s the leaders had already twice examined and twice rejected a "big gas" program before accepting it in 1980 as the centerpiece of their policy. Had they missed an important opportunity five or ten years before by not committing themselves to gas earlier? If they had shown more imagination and foresight then, would they have avoided the stress and extra expense of the current campaign?

Probably not. Without giving the Soviet leaders more credit for foresight than they necessarily deserve (we have, after all, many indications of their failure to respond quickly to the gathering evidence of trouble in oil and coal), in the case of gas they probably made the right decision. Consider, after all, the state of knowledge and skills in that industry ten years ago. The technology required to ship gas at 75 atmospheres or higher (without which the proposition is inefficient) was not available in the Soviet Union, so the gas option would have meant even greater dependence on foreign technology than now. The infrastructural base in north Tyumen, skimpy as it is even today, was nonexistent then. Reserves in north Tyumen were not nearly so well known, and the gas industry had little experience in working in such rugged conditions. Thus the costs of a large-scale gas program would have been high and oil, which is cheaper to ship and easier to export, undoubtedly looked much more cost-effective.

ISSUES AND CHALLENGES IN THE PRESENT ENERGY POLICY

With Brezhnev's death in the fall of 1982, Soviet energy policy entered a third phase. Official interest in the demand side of energy policy had been growing for the previous several years,[42] but Andropov's first appearance as general secretary, at the November 1982 plenary meeting of the party Central Committee, marked the first time that the top leadership appeared inclined to put conservation and fuel-switching ahead of energy supply. This impression was strengthened by official statements throughout the following year. In April 1983, the Politburo examined a draft of a long-term energy program that Brezhnev had commissioned in 1979. It gave top priority to restructuring the economy to lessen its energy-intensity.[43]

This stress on demand apparently matched Andropov's own view. In June 1983, when he unveiled the energy program before the plenum of the party Central Committee, he described it as an epoch-making event.[44] Though the evidence is sketchy, through the months of Andropov's failing health the official accent remained on conservation. The November 1983 plenum of the Central Committee and a Politburo meeting that preceded it adopted measures to conserve oil products and commented on the rapidly rising cost of oil production.[45]

Curiously, though the energy program had been official since the previous year, it was not publicly unveiled until a month after Andropov's death,[46] and it looked different from what the previous year's hints might have led one to expect. If one compares it to the recommendations of the energy experts upon whose work the energy program was based,[47] one can see that the program is much more heavily oriented toward energy supply than the experts' recommendations, which had dwelt on demand. It divides the period to the year 2000 into two phases. The first, from the present to 1990, gives top priority to maintaining the growth of oil and gas output and developing nuclear power. The period of the 1990s is to be a decade of coal and conservation, but for the time being the program calls only for "creating the preconditions" (*sozdat' predposylki*) for them. The experts, in contrast, had been quite specific about the urgency of improving measurement, oversight, accountability, incentives, retirement of inefficient equipment, use of waste heat, and improvement of fuel quality (especially coal).[48] On the supply side, the experts had stressed oil's high cost and uncertainty (although without actually going so far as to suggest that oil output should be allowed to peak).[49] Little of that appeared in the program; instead, it committed the leaders to maintaining a steady increase in oil output to the year 2000.

In short, the program showed several signs of retreat toward a more cautious, if expensive, energy policy still heavily based on oil. There are several likely reasons. During 1982 and 1983 the Soviet nuclear program, which is supposed to cover all future growth in electrical capacity west of the Urals, went into a stall.[50] The leaders reacted by sharply increasing investment, but the nuclear sector's troubles must have shown them how vulnerable their diversification strategy was. Then, in the fall of 1983, the Siberian oil industry began reporting the problems we have already described. These two trouble spots together may have convinced the leaders that they dared not run the risk of energy-supply bottlenecks that might strangle economic growth. For those who enjoy Kremlinology, one might add that Chernenko's accession as general secretary raised the stock of Party Secretary V. I. Dolgikh, whose name had been associated with the supply-oriented Brezhnev-era energy program from the beginning.

There is a broader reason, however, why the leaders hesitate to take the plunge into a demand-oriented energy strategy, even though they probably wish very strongly to do so. Conservation and fuel-switching require taking political priority and resources away from the supply side and transferring them to the demand side. That process will take time, and during that time oil output may fall while energy demand remains high. Unless alternatives are ready to fill the gap, the result will be a painful squeeze, with reduced exports abroad and ration-

TABLE 3.5
Share of Energy Investment in Total Soviet Investment

Years	Percentage
1960–1980	13–14
1981–1985	18–19
1985–2000	20–22

SOURCES: 1960–1985: Melent'ev and Makarov, *Energeticheskii kompleks SSSR*, p. 158; "1985–2000: Energy Program," *EG*, no. 12 (1984).
NOTE: Ancillary investment, especially on consumption side, is not included.

ing at home. Hence the leaders' hesitation. Yet the longer they delay the fateful moment, the more resources the oil industry will eat up.

One way to resolve the dilemma is simply to spend more money. The new energy program anticipates that the energy sector (broadly defined to include both the supply and demand sides) will claim a much larger share of total investment in the remainder of the century than ever before (see Table 3.5). In the upcoming Twelfth Five-Year Plan it could run as high as 190 billion rubles, up from 132 billion in the current plan.[51]

But just spending more money will not be enough. The success of the energy program depends on how skillfully the planners manage to deal with three main problems. First, they must provide adequately for near-term policies without crowding out necessary preparation for the longer term. Second, they must limit the strains and waste that necessarily attend a crash reallocation of resources, and prevent them from dissipating their efforts or from driving costs through the roof. Third, they must overcome barriers to substitution among energy sources.

Since 1981 the balance between near and long term has been somewhat sounder. The gas "bridge," as we have seen, is being energetically and successfully developed. Nuclear power is being accelerated. Conservation is being actively studied. But oil policy is still unbalanced in favor of short-term tasks: development displaces exploration, while drilling overshadows all other operations. They resulting imbalance is causing renewed problems in the oil industry and in another few years may do the same in gas.

However, the prime illustration of the difficulty of allocating priority between near and long term is Siberian coal. As with oil and gas, the Soviets have been obliged to seek new sources east of the Urals. Their plans for the year 2000 rely heavily on the enormous Kansk-Achinsk basin in Krasnoyarsk province, which is expected to yield 170–200 million tons a year by the end of the century.[52] Developing the basin's energy and bringing it to consumers, however, will require a large and sustained investment of capital, research talent, and administrative determination. Kansk-Achinsk coal is brown lignite with a high content of water and ash. When burned, it fouls boilers; when shipped, it catches fire spontaneously. Soviet planners have mounted programs to develop special boilers for mine-mouth power plants, high-voltage transmission lines, coal liquefaction and gasification plants, and coal-slurry pipelines.[53] But progress is slow and uncertain. Only a sharp increase in the level and priority of effort will ensure that the coal industry will be ready to shoulder the burden by the year 2000. Yet that would require taking resources away from the all-important oil and gas "bridges," or else stepping up energy investment still further.

Finding a Sound Balance Between
Near and Long Term

Reallocating resources for a crash energy program means not only transferring them across regions and institutions, but also finding the right balance between near-term and long-term programs.

Different people, however, have different ideas about where the optimum lies, and this was one of the causes of the crisis of 1977. The energy experts in Moscow, in advocating a leisurely replacement of hydrocarbons with coal and nuclear, were looking too far into the future and neglecting urgent near-term problems. The planners, obsessed with driving oil output upward year after year while neglecting exploration and alternative sources of energy, were guilty of excess in the opposite direction. It is a difficult problem of dosage, a problem, of course, that confronts energy planners all over the world.

Maintaining Coherence and
Limiting Subversion

In overseeing such a massive shift of resources as the present energy policy calls for, it is no small feat to prevent them from being dissipated. The first enemy is incoherence; the second is bureaucratic inertia, even covert subversion. What steps have Soviet leaders taken to keep their energy program on course, and how successful have they been?

The most crucial front is obviously the gas industry and the pipeline program. Deploying manpower and equipment in north Tyumen resembles nothing so much as landing an invasion force on a foreign shore. Millions of tons of equipment and tens of thousands of workers must be processed through a series of narrow time slots and transshipment nodes imposed by distance and weather. Much of the coverage of the Soviet press is devoted to this logistical aspect of the gas campaign; critical bottlenecks include shortages of electricity to compressor stations and drilling teams, lack of roads and railroads, pileups of equipment and stocks at river ports and landing strips, primitive living conditions, and fragile worker morale with resulting high turnover. Dozens of ministries are involved as suppliers and subcontractors, and the management challenge of forging them into a smooth team is awesome.

To deal with this task Soviet managers made a number of interesting decisions. First, five of the six major pipelines built during the Eleventh Five-Year Plan between Urengoi and European Russia, including the export pipeline to Western Europe, were run along a single corridor (at least in their Siberian portion). This saved valuable infrastructural investment, scarce manpower, and maintenance costs, and more than offset the extra line distances required. This, along with a decision to slow down the development of Yamburg and to concentrate on Urengoi, were two of the most important moves in the gas campaign in the first half of the 1980s.

Next, to oversee the gas campaign, two new administrative entities were created. In Moscow, an energy council for Siberia was attached to the staff of the USSR Council of Ministers; and in Tyumen, an "interagency commission" for the West Siberian energy complex was established, with the status of a Gosplan department.

In addition, the Tyumen party apparatus has been prominently active in the party's familiar roles of overseer, coordinator, and crisis manager. It is possible that the party apparatus has seen the new bodies as rivals. Officials of the Tyumen obkom claim responsibility for several of the major policy decisions we have already mentioned, such as the postponement of Yamburg and the single pipeline corridor, and recently the Gosplan commission has been little heard from.[54]

Career-switching between the state apparatus and the party has been carried as far in Tyumen province as one can find anywhere; this is a familiar technique for putting technical experts in a position of power. The former minister of oil and gas construction (now deputy chairman of the Council of Ministers), Boris Shcherbina, is the former first secretary of Tyumen province, while his successor in that position, G. P. Bogomiakov, was previously director of a research institute in the oil ministry. The staff of the Tyumen obkom party apparatus contains several former officials of the gas and oil industries, as do the party committees of the major gas cities. These officials form an experienced corps of technical experts who have been switched from post to post as the front line moves forward.

One of the problems the overseers of the West Siberian energy programs must deal with is a certain rivalry between the oil and gas industries in Tyumen province itself, which is perhaps due less to intentional subversion than to the fact that normal human and bureaucratic inertia causes people to gravitate (if left to their own devices) toward the relatively more hospitable south of the province, where the oil is, instead of the gas-rich but otherwise uninviting north. Until recently the oil industry was the main business of Tyumen province, while gas ran a poor second. Accounts in the Soviet press suggest that the oil industry still tends to get preference there. For example, *Pravda*'s economic correspondent for West Siberian oil and gas reported that the entire 1981 increment in the work plans of the oil and gas construction organizations was going to the oil industry. He wrote:

> It is necessary, of course, to develop the base for oil extraction; there can be no two opinions about that. But who will fulfill the development program for the gas industry? . . . [Builders are reluctant to go to the far north, where the gas has been discovered. Moreover, there are already well-established relations with the oil industry, and the transportation network in the Middle Ob area (i.e., the oil region of Tyumen province) is a lot easier than in the north of the province. But in the interests of the cause it is essential to shift the construction workers to the new tasks.[55]

Gas officials (and even local party apparatus workers) complain that oil regions in Tyumen province have been systematically favored in road construction, housing, and project infrastructure. Clearly, the prospects of the gas industry in the 1980s will depend not only on its de facto priority in the allocation of resources in Moscow, but also on the extent to which that priority is enforced at the local level as well.

Putting the Siberian energy complex under unified control is a halfway measure that stops short of creating an overall agency for the energy sector as a whole, a step that has had a number of public advocates over the last few years but for which the leaders have evidently not seen a convincing need. There is no overall "energy tsar" on Soviet organization charts in Moscow, but the energy sector's current status as the regime's top domestic priority undoubtedly means that it is receiving concentrated and sustained attention from the party Central Committee, and this fact may obviate the need for a formal energy body. Until 1981 two party secretaries, Kirilenko and Dolgikh, divided up the job of overseeing the energy sector (Kirilenko focusing on power and Dolgikh on oil and gas), but Kirilenko's retirement and Dolgikh's continued presence appear to have unified responsibility for energy in the latter's hands.

On balance, the administrative devices used by the Soviet leaders to implement their energy policy are not substantially different from ones they have used on major campaigns in the past. Their strength is that they guarantee concentration of effort, attention, and resources on the top-priority tasks. Whether the same devices will continue to work in the future depends on two questions: Can they be adapted to the expanded program? Can the concentration of effort on oil and gas development be prevented from disrupting the rest of the energy program, particularly on the consumption side? That is the subject of the next section.

Substitution Among Energy Sources

Perhaps the most important key to success in Soviet energy policy is smooth switching among energy sources.[56] The planners must substitute abundant energy sources for scarce ones, near ones for far ones, high-quality and high-value for low. Above all, fuel-switching means displacing oil, which frees crude oil not only for export but also for conversion to badly needed lighter fractions. In the long run, the energy sector can be compared to a set of communicating vessels: sooner or later, a surplus of one energy source compensates for a shortage of another. But such substitution is neither spontaneous nor rapid, at any rate in the Soviet command economy, where price incentives do not move managers in the same ways as in the West.

For the longer run, as we have seen, the planners' strategy rests on coal and nuclear power. Coal options east of the Urals we have already discussed briefly. West of the Urals Soviet planners are counting on nuclear power, which is supposed to provide the entire increment to electrical generating capacity in European Russia during the Eleventh Five-Year Plan. That would have required bringing about 4.3 gigawatts of new capacity on line each year. But the nuclear industry has fallen far short of that. As a result, Soviet planners have had to resign themselves to a substantial shortfall in nuclear power—about 70 billion kilowatt hours less in 1985 than the 220 billion called for in the Eleventh Plan. However, beginning in 1983 the Soviet leaders began pouring additional resources into nuclear power. It is by no means clear, though, that the nuclear power sector will be able to overcome the problems that have plagued it.

In the short run (that is, for the balance of the 1980s), the fastest and easiest way to displace oil is to substitute natural gas. To judge by overall changes in the fuel balance, such displacement is already moving ahead on a massive scale. The share of gas in the Soviet fuel balance is already nearly 32 percent (up from 26 percent in 1980). So far the Soviet economy has been able to absorb the prodigious increments of natural gas coming from West Siberia. The question is, can it continue to do so throughout the 1980s?

One test is whether oil is being displaced in power plants. In the second half of the 1970s the planners tried and failed. They had intended to displace fuel oil with coal, but bottlenecks in both the coal industry and the railroads prevented the planned expansion of coal deliveries from taking place, and consequently Soviet power plants ended up burning more fuel oil than ever, while the share of coal actually dropped. In 1980 125 million tons of fuel oil went to power stations, representing more than one third of all the fuel value used to generate electricity.[57]

The new energy program aimed to cut the share of fuel oil in power-plant consumption to half the 1980 level, which would be around 17 percent. The proposed substitute is no longer coal but gas. This requires construction of distri-bution pipelines and gas-storage facilities. At this writing there is evidence of considerable activity on the former but much less on the latter, even though stor-age is probably the more important prerequisite for major progress. Yet the gas ministry's targets for gas-storage expansion are modest, and there has been no sign of acceleration. It appears that little net displacement of oil took place in the first half of the 1980s, since at the same time declining coal quality has made it necessary to use more fuel oil as a "spiking" fuel.

A third obstacle to substitution on the supply side is slow progress in devel-oping capacity for catalytic cracking of oil. Hitherto the Soviets have used much of their oil (currently about half) in the form of mazut (heavy fuel oil) under boilers, and have not needed much advanced refining capacity. Current plans, however, call for an increase in what the Soviets call deep refining, so as to end up with a refinery mix with less fuel oil and more light fractions, what the oil industry calls a whiter barrel. The program includes modernization of some existing refineries and construction of several new ones,[58] but its aims are mod-est. Moreover, Soviet planners apparently need all the mazut they can get, which caused the minister of the refining industry, in a recent article, to wonder how much raw material his ministry will be able to get for the catalytic crackers once they have built them.[59]

CONCLUSION

In conclusion, in the three urgent tasks that Soviet energy policy must sat-isfy—maintaining a balance between near and long term, maintaining coher-ence, and substituting among energy sources to alter the structure of demand—the record so far is mixed. The gas campaign is on target so far, nuclear power capacity is growing at about half the planned rate, the oil and coal sectors are barely holding their own, but the task of adjusting among energy sources in the overall consumption mix is lagging. When viewed in perspective, Soviet energy policy as we have described it is evolving much as one would expect a classic Soviet campaign to do: abundant resources are being focused on the tasks that the system performs best and that promise the safest and fastest results (for example, development of new gas output). The more difficult tasks—which require altering microbehavior (as in conservation programs), achieving elaborate horizontal co-ordination (as in substitution programs), or producing major technological inno-vations quickly (as in the development of long-term alternatives)—are all being squeezed by the urgent near-term supply programs.

What are the costs of such a policy? To that question we cannot yet give an answer. The first crucial unknown here is the performance of the economy as a whole. If, for reasons essentially independent of energy availability, the Soviet economy grows less fast than the planners had anticipated, then the policy the Soviets are currently pursuing will easily meet internal and export needs without imbalances. Indeed, if the gas program is fully successful Soviet leaders may even find themselves with an excess of gas, caused by the domestic system's slowness in displacing oil and by a decline in demand for gas in Western Europe. The second crucial unknown is the performance of the Soviet oil industry in the next few years. If oil production can be held to a slow decline through the end of the decade, then the Soviet leaders will have a breathing space in which to implement a systematic program of substitution and conservation, and they will have a comfortable exportable surplus to provide hard currency. It is already clear, however, that the only way all these goals can be met is through continued top-priority investment in the energy sector. This is bound to make choices more difficult in the rest of the economy.

NOTES

1. This chapter is an updated and expanded version of my contribution to the collection published by the Joint Economic Committee of the Congress, *Soviet Economy in the 1980s* (December 1982). Both internal and external issues in Soviet energy policy are analyzed in my forthcoming book, *The Perpetual Campaign: The Politics of Soviet Energy, 1970–1985* (in preparation).

2. Baibakov speech, *Izvestiia,* November 18, 1981.

3. Initial targets for the Tenth Five-Year Plan are taken from the text of the main guidelines, as reprinted in *XXVyi s"ezd Kommunisticheskoi partii Sovetskogo Soiuza* (stenograficheskii otchet) [The Twenty-fifth Congress of the CPSU: Stenographic report], vol. 2 (Moscow: Izdatel'stvo politicheskoi literatury, 1976), pp. 226ff.

4. A. A. Troitskii, "Osnovnye napravleniia razvitiia toplivnoenergeticheskogo balansa elektroenergetiki strany" [Principal directions of development of the fuel-energy balance of electric power engineering], *Teploenergetika,* no. 5 (1981): 2–4. This information cannot readily be checked against the statistics available in *Narodnoe khoziaistvo,* because the investment statistics listed there for the energy sector do not include exploration and transportation.

5. See S. D. Ageeva and B. P. Orlov, "Nekotorye cherty investitsionnogo protsessa v zapadno-sibirskom neftegazovom komplekse" [Some features of the investment process in the West Siberian oil-gas complex], and B. P. Orlov, "Razvitie ekonomiki Sibiri na otdel'nykh etapakh sotsialisticheskogo stroitel'stva" [Development of the Siberian economy at different stages of socialist construction], both in *Izvestiia sibirskogo otdeleniia AN SSSR* (seriia obshchestvennykh nauk), no. 11 (1982): 85–89 and 61–70 respectively.

6. Orlov, "Razvitie ekonomiki," p. 65.

7. A. A. Troitskii, "Osnovnye napravleniia." How Troitskii arrives at this figure is a little puzzling. Edward Hewett, by converting all the Soviet energy targets to millions of

barrels per day of oil equivalent (mbdoe), puts the share of natural gas at 64 percent, or 3.20 mbdoe out of 4.98.

8. Iu. V. Zaitsev (then first deputy minister of the gas industry), "S"ezd profsoiuza rabochikh neftianoi i gazovoi promyshlennosti" [The Trade Union Congress of workers in the gas industry], *Stroitel'stvo truboprovodov*, no. 3 (1982): 5.

9. The figures for the Eighth and Ninth Plans come from R. D. Margulov (currently first deputy minister of the gas industry), *Razvitie gazovoi promyshlennosti i analiz tekhniko-ekonomicheskikh pokazatelei* [Development of the gas industry and analysis of technical-economic indexes] (Moscow: VNIIZ Gazprom, 1976), p. 17. For the Tenth Plan, the late minister of the gas industry, S. A. Orudzhev, gave the figure 21.5 billion ("Zadachi rabotnikov gazovoi promyshlennosti na 1980 god" [Tasks of gas industry workers for 1980], *Gazovaia promyshlennost'*, no. 2 (1980): 5–6). In both cases, incidentally, the figures include pipeline investment and lump together the categories of "productive" and "nonproductive" investment.

10. Orudzhev's speech at the twenty-sixth party congress, reported in *Pravda*, March 2, 1981.

11. V. Dinkov, "Zveno energeticheskoi programmy" [A link of the energy resources program], *Sovetskaia Rossiia*, August 1, 1981.

12. Statements by the gas minister, V. Dinkov, "Gazovaia promyshlennost' na marshe piatiletki" [Gas industry in the realization of the Five-Year Plan], *Ekonomicheskaia gazeta*, no. 2 (1982): 2, and "West Siberia's Gas," *Novoe vremia*, no. 19 (1982): 19.

13. See, for example, Boris Shcherbina, minister of oil and gas construction, in *Stroitel'stvo truboprovodov* 12 (1982): 6.

14. "Vazhnye zadachi finansirovaniia i kreditovaniia kapital'nogo stoitel'stva" [Some important tasks in financing and extending credit in the infrastructure], *Finansy SSSR*, no. 4 (1982): 4.

15. "Urengoi-Uzhgorod: Pervaia tysiacha kilometrov" [Urengoi-Uzhgorod: The first thousand kilometers], *Pravda*, October 4, 1982.

16. One arrives at similar figures if one starts from the gas minister's statements that pipeline construction in Siberia will absorb 70 percent of the investment in the gas sector in the Eleventh Five-Year Plan. Dinkov, "Gazovaia promyshlennost' na marshe piatiletki," p. 2, and "West Siberia's Gas." A statement by Tass uses the figure 67 percent instead of 70 percent (*FBIS*, January 13, 1982).

17. These figures were presented by the newly promoted first deputy minister of the gas industry, R. D. Margulov, at a meeting of the leaders of the labor unions of the oil and gas industries, February 4, 1982, as reported in "Na glavnom napravlenii" [On the principal course], *Gazovaia promyshlennost'*, no. 4 (1982): 5.

18. V. Lisin and V. Parfenov, "Energiia tiumenskogo severa" [Energy resources of the Tyumen north region], *Pravda*, May 7, 1982.

19. E. N. Iakovlev, "Vazhnye usloviia osvoeniia regiona" [Some important conditions of industrialization of the region], *Gazovaia promyshlennost'*, no. 4 (1981): 10–11.

20. Ibid.

21. "Ratsional'noe ispol'zovanie," p. 52. The figure given there is for an unnamed stretch of approximately 1,000 kilometers in West Siberia, quoted from a preliminary planning document submitted to Glavsibtruboprovodstroi (the Pipeline Central Construction Trust of Siberia). Whether it is representative of cost trends for all pipeline construction in West Siberia (let alone elsewhere in the country) is another matter.

22. For a more detailed discussion of Soviet policies on gas and oil, see two monographs by Thane Gustafson: *The Soviet Gas Campaign: Politics and Policy in Soviet Decision-Making* (Santa Monica, Calif.: Rand Corporation, June 1983), and *Soviet Oil Policy, 1970–1985* (Report to the National Council on Soviet and East European Research, Washington, D.C., June 1984).

23. Ibid.

24. On September 30, 1972, Kosygin spoke to an audience of officials of the State Planning Committee and on October 6 to the State Committee for Supply. Unfortunately, only excerpts of these speeches are available. See A. N. Kosygin, *K velikoi tseli* [On the way to the great goal], vol. 2 (Moscow: Izdatel'stvo politcheskoi literatury, 1979), pp. 149–60.

25. V. A. Kirillin, *Pravda,* September 16, 1972. There is equally little mention of the subject in the discussion that follows.

26. Speeches by Deputy P. A. Rozenko (*Izvestiia,* December 20, 1972) and Gosplan Chairman N. Baibakov (*Izvestiia,* December 19, 1972).

27. *Izvestiia,* July 18, 1972, translated in *Current Digest of the Soviet Press* 24, no. 29 (1972): 20. Muravlenko was soon to become known as one of the most pessimistic critics of the oil outlook for Tyumen until his death in 1977. In an article in 1976 he dwelt at length on the daunting infrastructural requirements for meeting the official output targets of the Tenth Five-Year Plan (*Sotsialisticheskaia industriia,* January 1, 1976).

28. *Ekonomika neftianoi promyshlennosti,* no. 6 (1973): 8.

29. The fact that there was communication between technical specialists and at least some leaders over this problem can be seen from the fact that a major meeting on oil exploration, held in Tyumen in late November 1973, was attended by Party Secretary Dolgikh, Gosplan Deputy Chairman Lalaiants, and Minister of Oil Shashin. The Tyumen obkom first secretary, then Boris Shcherbina (he was promoted one month later to the post of minister of oil and gas construction), criticized the geologists for their failure to move north (*Pravda,* November 23, 1973). Oil Minister Shashin voiced the same concern in an article signed at about the same time (*Neftianoe khoziaistvo,* no. 3 [1974]: 4).

30. *Vestnik Akademii Nauk SSSR,* no. 2 (1975): 3–31. This issue carried the speeches of M. V. Keldysh, A. P. Aleksandrov, V. A. Kirillin, and M. A. Styrkovich. Already in Keldysh's introductory address and in Kirillin's article one can find the stress on coal that became the centerpiece of official energy policy at the twenty-fifth party congress in February 1976.

31. Neither was the stress on coal entirely new, as one can see from an article by the economist Tigran Khachaturov, "Natural Resources and the Planning of the National Economy," in *Current Digest of the Soviet Press,* 25, no. 49 (1973): p. 6. Khachaturov observed, "Since petroleum reserves are not as great as coal reserves, their use as fuel

must be limited; petroleum should be used increasingly as a raw material for obtaining products of organic synthesis . . . It will be better to use gas not as a fuel but as a chemical raw material." But it is clear from the context that Khachaturov was writing about what he considered to be a fairly remote future.

32. *Narodnoe khoziaistvo SSSR*, relevant years.

33. See A. M. Nekrasov and M. G. Pervukhin, eds., *Energetika SSSR v 1976–1980 godakh* (Moscow: "Energiia," 1977), p. 149.

34. For background on Soviet coal and on technological innovation in that industry, see the chapter by William Kelly in U.S. Congress, Office of Technology Assessment, *Western Technology and Soviet Energy Availability* (Washington, D.C.: GPO, October 1981); Central Intelligence Agency, *Coal Industry Problems and Prospects*, ER 80-10154 (Washington, D.C.: National Foreign Assessment Center, USSR, March 1980), and *Central Siberian Brown Coal as a Potential Source of Power for European Russia*, SW 80-10006 (Washington, D.C.: National Foreign Assessment Center, USSR, April 1980); and Robert W. Campbell, *Soviet Energy Technologies* (Bloomington: Indiana University Press, 1980), chap. 4.

35. Brezhnev's speech has not yet been reprinted in its entirety. A paraphrase appeared in an editorial in *Pravda*, December 18, 1977.

36. See in particular an article by Tyumen obkom First Secretary G. P. Bogomiakov in *Literaturnaia gazeta*, January 18, 1978, in which he states that the December 1977 plenum had determined precisely Tyumen's place in satisfying the needs of the country for oil and gas, thus settling what Bogomiakov described as "not just a few contradictory judgments in views on the future."

37. Brezhnev's 1978 trip to Siberia was treated by Tyumen "patriots" as a highly symbolic event, as one may see from the words of G. P. Bogomiakov at the sixteenth party congress: "Of fundamental importance have been the instructions of L. I. Brezhnev on the future development of the fuel and power sector, the advice and comments made by him in the course of his trip to the regions of Siberia and the Far East" (*Pravda*, February 27, 1981). At the time the "fundamental importance" was far from plain, since Brezhnev's trip occurred right on the heels of a similar trip by Kosygin, and the energy aspects of both trips received only modest treatment in the press.

38. The Gosplan meeting was followed in June by a big conference at Academic City in Siberia on the same subject, which produced detailed recommendations.

39. In January 1980, for the first time, an article on energy policy appeared under Dolgikh's byline in *Partiinaia zhizn'*. Dolgikh's name has appeared regularly in Soviet accounts of major official meetings on energy, but to my knowledge there have been no further byline articles by Dolgikh since.

40. L. A. Melent'ev and A. A. Makarov, eds., *Energeticheskii kompleks SSSR* [Energy complex of the USSR] (Moscow: "Ekonomika," 1983), p. 165.

41. *Pravda*, November 18, 1981.

42. From 1979 on Brezhnev himself put steadily more stress on restructuring energy demand. His speeches to the November 1979 and October 1980 plenums of the party Central Committee contained strong words in favor of energy conservation (L. I. Brezhnev,

Leninskim kursom [Following Lenin's course], vol. 8, pp. 200, 473), and over the same period two major decrees appeared on recovering waste heat and on saving raw materials and energy.

43. "V Politbiuro TsK KPSS" [In the Politburo of the Central Committee], *Pravda*, April 9, 1983.

44. Andropov called it a "GOELRO for today's conditions," a reference to one of the earliest experiments in countrywide planning in the 1920s: a state program for the electrification of Russia. This reference was intended not only to invoke hallowed precedents but also to suggest how fundamental a restructuring the leadership had in mind.

45. "V Politbiuro TsK KPSS," *Pravda*, October 29, 1983.

46. *Ekonomicheskaia gazeta*, no. 12 (March 1984): centerfold.

47. Melent'ev and Makarov, *Energeticheskii kompleks SSSR*.

48. Ibid., pp. 99–100.

49. Ibid., pp. 160, 165, 176–77.

50. For an overview, see Theodore Shabad, "Nuclear Power Developments," in *Soviet Geography*, vol. 25 (January 1984): 63–64.

51. This rough calculation is based on the assumption that gross investment grows from roughly 750 billion rubles in 1981–1985 to 860 billion in 1986–1990, of which 22 percent (as per the energy program) is earmarked for energy.

52. For a report on the Kansk-Achinsk field, see Theodore Shabad, "Progress Report on Kansk-Achinsk Development," *Soviet Geography*, vol. 24 (1983): 249–56.

53. For a sampling of current Soviet reporting on coal, see M. Styrikovich and V. Popov, "'Ugol': Perspektivy otrasli" [Coal: Some industry perspectives], *Pravda*, October 6, 1983; B. Pustovalov, "Ugol' po trubam" [Coal: Through the pipeline], *Ekonomicheskaia gazeta*, no. 19 (May 1984); V. Sevast'ianov, "Problemy koordinatsii" [Problems of coordination] *Ekonomicheskaia gazeta*, no. 42 (October 1983): 15; and B. Pichugin, "Otstupiv ot zamysla" [Giving up on the original project], *Sotsialisticheskaia industriia*, May 12, 1984.

54. B. Trofimov, "Formirovanie tiumenskogo neftegazovogo kompleksa" [Formation of the gas-oil complex in the city of Tyumen], *Planove khoziaistvo* 9 (1981): 84–88. On the role of party officials in campaigning against development of the more northerly fields, see E. G. Altunin, "Strategiiu vybrat' segodnia" [Strategy to be chosen today], *Ekonomika i organizatsiia promyshlennogo proizvodstva*, no. 2 (1979): 12–22.

55. V. Lisin, "Gaz Sibiri" [Siberian Gas], *Pravda*, June 15, 1981.

56. In this discussion I am somewhat arbitrarily distinguishing between substitution and conservation, although in practice the two overlap closely.

57. Melent'ev and Makarov, *Energeticheskii kompleks SSSR*, p. 167.

58. "Neftepererabatyvaiushchaia promyshlennost'" [Oil-refining industry], *Ekonomicheskaia gazeta*, no. 46 (1981): 2.

59. "Pererabatyvat', a ne szhigat'" [To recycle, not to burn], *Sotsialisticheskaia industriia*, May 20, 1982.

MICHAEL J. BRADSHAW   4

Trade and High Technology

In recent years transfer of technology to the Soviet Union has become a source of disagreement within the Western alliance. This chapter examines the nature of commercial and high-technology trade relations and their impact on the regional development of Siberia and the Soviet Far East. Most studies of East-West technology transfer focus on the impact of Western technology on specific Soviet industrial sectors. The approach adopted here is somewhat different; it concentrates on the composite *regional* impact of Soviet foreign economic relations.

Although the theme of this volume is Siberia, as always it is necessary to examine the development of the region within a national context. Siberian development, in the last two decades, has been dedicated to producing raw materials for domestic and East European markets. Increased foreign trade, in particular with the West, has raised demands for Siberian raw materials. However, at the same time as the resource frontier is being pushed northward and eastward, industrial inertia serves to retain the bulk of manufacturing activity in the European regions of the USSR. Accordingly, the impact of foreign trade on industrial location in the Soviet Union needs to be investigated against the backdrop of domestic locational constraints.

The pattern of economic development in Siberia is conditioned primarily by domestic locational parameters; increased foreign trade serves to amplify many of the locational advantages and disadvantages present in Siberia and the Far East.

SOVIET FOREIGN TRADE AND REGIONAL DEVELOPMENT

Traditional Soviet economic policy stresses the importance of economic self-sufficiency. The strategic necessity of being able to provide all one's domestic needs in time of war, combined with Stalin's policy of "socialism in one coun-

TABLE 4.1
Soviet Foreign Trade by Groups of Countries, 1965–1983 (percentage of total trade)

	Total Trade (millions of rubles)	Communist Countries	CMEA Countries	Developed Capitalist Countries	Developing Countries
1965	14.6	68.8	58.0	19.3	11.9
1970	22.1	65.2	55.6	21.3	13.5
1975	50.7	56.3	51.8	31.3	12.4
1978	63.3	59.8	55.7	28.0	12.2
1979	80.3	56.1	51.9	32.1	11.8
1980	94.1	53.7	48.9	33.6	12.7
1981	109.7	52.8	47.6	32.2	15.0
1982	119.6	54.0	49.1	31.5	14.1
1983	112.5	56.0	51.2	30.1	13.9

SOURCE: *Vneshniaia torgovlia,* various years.

try," fostered an autarchic economic strategy that has only recently been eroded. In the immediate postwar years the majority of Soviet trade activity was among countries of the Eastern bloc. The advent of the Brezhnev-Kosygin era brought a minor revolution in Soviet foreign economic relations. The 1970s witnessed an expansion of trade with noncommunist countries, in particular the developed capitalist countries (see Table 4.1). This increased participation in foreign trade has served as a means of modernizing the domestic economy, consolidating the socialist bloc, and improving East-West relations.

CMEA and Soviet Regional Development

The Council for Mutual Economic Assistance (CMEA), created in 1949, is the official vehicle for increasing economic integration within the socialist bloc.[1] Although the CMEA developed to counter the European community, the dominant position of the Soviet Union has restricted the level of economic integration. Fearing loss of national control, the countries of Eastern Europe have limited the mobility of the factors of production. As a result economic relations are conducted more on the basis of bilateral agreements than through bloc-wide multilateral agreements. But, as Alampiev has noted, economic development is only one of the functions of CMEA integration:

> Socialist economic integration is designed not only to yield definite economic advantages for the countries involved or to enhance the efficiency of the economy and accelerate economic growth, but also to bring about a general consolidation of socialist relations within the community of socialist countries.[2]

The concept of international economic integration, termed in Soviet writings the "international socialist division of labor," was formally adopted by the members of CMEA at their twenty-fifth session of council in July 1971.[3] The comprehensive program, developed to promote increased economic integration, employed four major mechanisms: joint investment projects, specialization and cooperation, interstate economic organizations, and international economic associations.[4] For the purposes of this chapter the first two mechanisms are more significant; the other two are concerned with management coordination and with research and development.

Joint investment projects aim to involve the countries of Eastern Europe in the development of Soviet natural resources. Eastern Europe has become highly dependent on the Soviet Union for energy and raw materials. For example, the Soviet share of total East European oil supply (excluding Romania) was 88 percent in 1978.[5] Even Romania, with its own supplies and a determination to remain independent, has started to import Soviet oil. The burden of this demand and the eastward shift of petroleum production have made it increasingly expensive for the Soviet Union to meet the needs of Eastern Europe. As a result, a number of energy-related joint projects have been carried out. The earliest example was the Friendship Pipeline, built during the 1960s, which delivered oil from the Volga-Urals field to Eastern Europe. Since 1970 West Siberian oil has been fed into the system.[6] Natural gas development initially concentrated on the more accessible western gas fields, with the construction of the Brotherhood Pipeline in 1967 and more recently the Orenburg Pipeline.

The exact nature of the impact of CMEA joint energy projects on Siberian development is difficult to distinguish, but increased output from Siberian oil and gas fields has been necessary to sustain exports to Eastern Europe. Thus, East European energy demands serve to aggravate further the dichotomy between resource-demanding and resource-producing areas. With the exception of the Ust-Ilimsk pulp and paper complex in East Siberia, the majority of joint investment projects have been located in the European USSR, for one primary reason: the desire to minimize transportation costs. In some cases a lower-quality resource has been developed simply because of its proximity to Eastern Europe, for example the development of the potash deposit at Soligorsk in Belorussia to meet Polish needs.[7] In the case of the Iasny asbestos deposit in Orenburg oblast, CMEA joint-project status has rejuvenated a project that was receiving low domestic priority.[8]

In the CMEA joint investment project at Ust-Ilimsk, abundant resources and scale economies have, in theory at least, overcome relatively high transportation costs.[9] The project involves all the East European members of CMEA except Czechoslovakia. Like most other CMEA projects, here the acquisition of foreign technology has been important. At Ust-Ilimsk the East European participants have met some of the foreign currency costs, and one western company has provided plant on a compensation basis.[10] This project alone represented one-tenth of total Soviet investment in the pulp and paper industry during the Tenth Five-Year Plan (1976–1980). The plant, completed in 1980, has a capacity of 500,000 tons of pulp a year. For the first twelve years of operation 205,000 tons per year will be exported to Eastern Europe as compensation payments.[11]

Specialization among the member countries of the CMEA has also favored the European regions of the USSR rather than Siberia. This form of integration involves the manufacture of a product by using facilities in one or more countries cooperatively to supply the entire CMEA market. Examples from the automobile and chemical industries will illustrate these developments.

The modernization of the Soviet automobile industry has led to increasing internationalization. Components and products from the Fiat-built Tolyatti plant have been traded with Eastern Europe. Components for the Zhiguli/Lada car built at Tolyatti and the Volga built at Gorki are supplied from Eastern Europe.[12] Obviously this type of cooperation favors locations in the western regions.

In the case of the chemical industry, given the abundance of hydrocarbons, cheap energy, and water in Siberia, one might reasonably expect a larger degree of Siberian participation. But the existence of pipeline systems moving crude oil and natural gas (rather than refined products) has favored the location of refineries and chemical plants in the European regions rather than Siberia and the Far East. Proximity to domestic and East European markets, the existing infrastructure, and the relative ease of expanding it outweigh the advantages of cheap power and water offered by the eastern regions. As a result, a series of petrochemical works has been constructed in the western border regions, for example at Novopolotsk and Mozyr in Belorussia and Mazeikai in Lithuania.[13] In the case of the so-called ethylene ring, Soviet oil was supplied to a Hungarian refinery on the border at Leninvarosz. Ethylene from the plant was then transported by rail to a polyvinyl chloride plant at Kalush in the Ukraine. A quarter of the output of the Kalush plant was then exported, mainly to Hungary.[14] Even in the case of resource-based industries, CMEA trade has tended to favor the western regions.[15]

In summary, CMEA trade and integration have served to promote Siberian development only in the sense that they have increased demand for Siberian resources. The majority of CMEA-related development has located in what Zaitsev has called the "contact zone" in the western regions of the USSR.[16] However, many of the plants in this contact zone are using Siberian resources, so the indirect contribution of Siberia to CMEA trade and integration is highly significant.

East-West Trade and Regional Development

Soviet desire to obtain foreign currency from exports and to purchase Western plant and equipment has had a substantial impact on the structure of East-West trade (see Table 4.2).

TABLE 4.2
USSR Foreign Currency Trade by Commodity (percentage of total trade)[a]

Exports	1970	1975	1980	1981
Petroleum and products	17.7	40.9	52.1	51.4
Natural gas	0.6	2.7	11.5	16.7
Coal and Coke	4.4	4.9	1.5	0.8
Machinery and equipment	7.9	7.8	6.2	6.5
Ferrous metals	5.7	2.0	1.0	0.7
Wood and wood products	16.0	8.9	6.4	4.3
Chemicals	2.6	2.9	3.2	3.2
Agricultural products	7.9	6.6	2.1	2.3
Diamonds	7.2	5.8	5.5	NA
Other[b]	30.0	17.5	10.5	14.1

Imports				
Grain	3.4	15.9	17.5	23.0
Other agricultural products	22.0	12.1	18.1	19.2
Machinery and equipment	32.4	31.5	23.2	16.3
Rolled ferrous metals	10.2	18.0	13.8	12.9
Chemicals	7.2	5.0	6.3	5.7
Consumer goods	13.1	4.3	4.3	3.8
Other	11.7	13.2	16.8	19.1

SOURCE: Calculated from Directorate of Intelligence, *Handbook of Economic Statistics, 1983* (Washington, D.C.: U.S. Central Intelligence Agency, 1983), p. 68.

[a] May include a limited amount of CMEA trade.

[b] Includes gold.

A recent analysis of Soviet foreign trade identified four major sources of foreign currency: raw-material exports, gold exports, arms sales, and the sale of services.[17] Soviet imports, on the other hand, have been dominated by machinery and grain purchases. What impact has East-West trade had upon Soviet regional development, and what is the role of Siberia and the Soviet Far East in such trade?

Petroleum exports have become by far the most important source of foreign currency. Two trends are apparent. First, because of the recent energy crisis in the West, the export of crude oil has become the most important source of foreign revenue—over 60 percent of foreign revenue, about $16 billion in 1982.[18] Second, more recently natural gas exports have been growing in importance as Soviet oil production has faltered. This trend is likely to continue as more gas pipelines come on stream.

As hydrocarbon exports to the West have increased, so has Siberia's role in their production. At the beginning of the 1970s West Siberia accounted for 9.8 percent of Soviet crude oil production; by 1980 its share of production had increased to 52 percent.[19] The 1985 target was for 68.3 percent of domestic oil production to come from fields in Siberia.[20] Siberia's share of natural gas production is equally impressive; it has been estimated that by the year 2000 the Asiatic USSR (east of the Urals) could account for 54.7 percent of the country's oil production and 88.3 percent of natural gas production.[21] There is little doubt that energy exports from Siberia play a crucial role in Soviet foreign currency earnings. In the future it is likely that oil and gas production in the Soviet Far East will also contribute to energy trade.

Exports of diamonds, timber, and forest products from Siberia and the Far East are also important. Diamonds are the third largest earner of foreign exchange, after petroleum and gold.[22] Since the discovery of diamond-bearing Kimberlite pipes in western Yakutia in 1954–1955, diamond production has been concentrated on three pipes at Mirny.[23] The majority of roundwood exports from the region goes to Japan, but forest products are also exported to markets in Europe. Up to now, poor accessibility has limited the range of eastern resources that have been developed for export. However, Soviet planners envisage that the Baikal-Amur Mainline (BAM) will facilitate expansion of the region's export base.[24] South Yakutian coal is already being exported to Japan, and the copper deposits at Udokan are also slated for export.

During the last decade gold exports have been used to sustain foreign currency reserves. A recent Western analysis calculated that between 1966 and 1979 gold sales accounted on average for 14 percent of the total value of foreign currency exports.[25] Statistics on gold production, like oil production, are now a state secret. Kaser's analysis of Soviet and Western sources suggests that there have been considerable fluctuations in the level of gold exports.[26] This supports the notion that gold sales are used to bolster foreign currency reserves. Gold production from traditional fields in northern Yakutia, Transbaikalia and West Siberia is now supplemented by production from Central Asia. According to Kaser's figures the gold mines in Siberia and the Far East accounted for approximately 60 percent of Soviet production in 1980.[27]

Details on exports of military equipment are also difficult to obtain, but it is likely that such trade is an important component of Soviet economic relations with the developing countries. CIA estimates suggest that foreign currency earnings from military sales were about $1.5 billion per year between 1976 and 1978, or about 11 percent of the total.[28] It is impossible to know what role the eastern regions play in arms production, but one can speculate that much of the high-technology development in Novosibirsk oblast in West Siberia is defense-related. No doubt the vast expanses of Siberia and the Far East are used for weapons testing, as are similar remote regions in North America, such as Alaska and Alberta.

The expansion of Soviet foreign trade has been paralleled by a rapid development of the Soviet merchant fleet. Between 1961 and 1981 the fleet expanded

345 percent, and by 1977 it accounted for 7 percent of total foreign currency earnings.[29] The Soviet Far East is playing an important part in developing the export potential of freight service operations. The trans-Siberian land bridge provides an alternative route for shipping containers from the Far East to Europe, cutting the seaborne journey to northwest Europe by seven to ten days and reducing costs by up to 25 percent. The traffic on the route has increased from approximately 2,000 units in 1971 to 153,000 units in 1981.[30] Japanese involvement in the scheme has been an important factor in its success. Completion of the BAM will likely improve the land bridge service.

Examining the impact of imports is somewhat more difficult because information on final destinations is rarely provided. Nevertheless, it is possible to identify general port and infrastructural developments. The most important component of Soviet imports—machinery and equipment—is the subject of later sections. Here we consider the impact of grain, chemical, and raw material imports. It is likely that most grain imports from the United States, Argentina, and the European community arrive via European ports. But a substantial amount of Canadian grain—2,528,889 metric tons in 1982—is shipped via the port of Vancouver to ports in the Soviet Far East.[31] A small amount of grain from Vancouver is now shipped via the northern sea route to European Russia. Ice-strengthened Norilsk (SA-15 class) freighters built in Finland are used for this traffic.

Raw materials, so abundant domestically, are not substantially imported. One notable exception is in the aluminum industry, where dependence on imported bauxite has risen from 12 percent in 1965 to 50 percent in 1980.[32] The majority comes from Guinea; other suppliers include Greece, Yugoslavia, and Jamaica. A bulk carrier terminal has been built on the Black Sea next to the Nikolayev alumina plant. Alumina produced there will eventually be shipped to a new aluminum smelter at Saian in East Siberia. The plant, originally scheduled for completion in 1984, will probably go into production in early 1986.[33]

Much of the Soviet chemical trade is related to compensation deals and counter-trade agreements. The best-known is the ammonia counter-trade agreement with Occidental Petroleum of the United States, under which ammonia produced at Tolyatti in the Volga region, using Tyumen natural gas, is transported via pipeline to a newly constructed chemical export facility at Yuzhny near Odessa. The ammonia plant was not built in Siberia because the Soviet Union had little experience in building ammonia pipelines and wished to minimize the length of the pipeline. In addition, two new ammonia plants went on stream at Yuzhny in 1979. The same agreement has also stimulated development, based on tanker car deliveries, at the Baltic port of Ventspils. The overall capacity installed in the Soviet Union under the Occidental agreement is 4.5 million tons of ammonia and 1.8 million tons of urea.[34] The agreement is still in force, despite U.S. domestic lobbies and embargoes. Chemical compensation deals have also had enormous impact: between 1975 and 1979 Soviet chemical exports under such agreements expanded roughly 17.8 times, from 6.3 million rubles to 112.3 million rubles.[35] Siberian petrochemical complexes at Tomsk, Tobolsk, and Zima play an important part in such trade.

In reviewing the composite impact of foreign trade, we will use a schema of direct and indirect impacts devised by Robert North, based on empirical evidence and Soviet writings relating to foreign trade and regional development.[36]

Direct impacts are those that result from investment in mines, factories, and transport facilities intended specifically to facilitate exports. They also include the impact of imported plant and equipment. Most direct impacts are felt by the European regions of the USSR, which benefit from a developed infrastructure, a skilled and relatively static labor force, more reliable construction organizations, and the geographical advantage of proximity to European markets. The Ust-Ilimsk complex represents a direct impact on the regional economy of East Siberia. Investment in Siberian and Far Eastern resources above and beyond that needed for domestic demands can be considered a direct impact, in that it is required to facilitate exports. The same is true of pipelines that supply both domestic and export markets.

Indirect impacts are more complex and harder to identify. When export-related infrastructure enhances the attractiveness of certain regions for domestic industries, that is an indirect impact. The location of chemical plants along export pipelines in the European USSR is an example of such impacts. The effect is that it may act as a damper on the expansion of the Siberian chemical industry. A second type of indirect impact may occur when the combination of export and domestic demands makes feasible a change to new technology. Increased demand may also lead to a shift in patterns of supply. Subsequent increased demand may provide economies of scale that enable the development of remote resources. It is likely that the shift to Siberian resources was accelerated by the need to export. Finally, foreign trade may affect different regions in different ways. Thus, the European USSR has mostly benefited from trade-related manufacturing activity, while Siberia and the Far East have received mainly resource-oriented investment. The net effect is to amplify the existing distribution of economic activities. Foreign trade serves to maintain the dominance of the European manufacturing core and boosts the resource economies of the eastern regions. Only in specific instances of border trade or port developments can one really identify changes in the economic geography that are brought about solely by foreign trade.

THE IMPACT OF WESTERN TECHNOLOGY
ON THE SOVIET ECONOMY

A central component of Soviet foreign economic policy has been the desire to purchase Western technology. The Brezhnev-Kosygin era heralded a new phase in Soviet policy of technology procurement. The traditional Stalinist approach, by contrast, minimized foreign contacts and was usually conducted on the basis of individual purchases—periods of trade were often followed by slack periods during which imported technology was assimilated into the domestic economy.[37] Assimilation usually involved reverse engineering and scaling up, the end result being a Soviet-built machine embodying Western technology.

The new approach, called by some the modified systems approach, is in part a response to the increased sophistication of industrial technology, but also represents a new role for Western technology in Soviet economic strategy. According to Hardt and Holliday, the modified systems approach has four characteristics:

1. Long-term or continuous connections.
2. Complex or project-oriented industrial cooperation.
3. Systems-related construction, production management, and distribution.
4. Western involvement in training and in the decision-making process both in the Soviet Union and abroad.[38]

This characterization is based primarily on Holliday's study of the Soviet automobile industry.[39] The long-term nature of the contemporary transfer process is also supported by studies of other industries, such as the chemical industry.[40] Analyses conducted during the 1970s suggest that in certain sectors the importation of Western technology has been crucial to the realization of plan targets and the development of export potential.[41] Soviet writers tend to stress the existence of complementarity between the resource-poor developed capitalist nations and the resource-rich Soviet Union.[42] Increased technology trade is seen as a rational response to the international scientific-technical revolution.[43]

One can identify two distinct features in the structure of Soviet technology trade. The first is a preference for turnkey and coproduction and specialization agreements (see Table 4.3), often financed with compensation payments. In compensation agreements goods and equipment are paid for on a credit basis, with that credit to be paid off by deliveries of the goods or product produced. The most common example is pipe for gas, where large-diameter pipe is purchased and paid for by deliveries of gas. The second feature is the concentration of technology imports within certain sectors (see Tables 4.4 and 4.5). A U.S. study conducted during the mid-1970s reported that compensation agreements were con-

TABLE 4.3
Soviet Industrial Cooperation Agreements Comparison with CMEA, 1975

	PERCENTAGE OF TOTAL AGREEMENTS	
TYPE OF AGREEMENT	USSR	CMEA
Licensing with payment in product	—	26.1
Turnkey	56.6	21.7
Coproduction and specialization	34.8	33.3
Subcontracting	4.3	6.8
Joint venture	—	2.9
Joint tendering	4.3	9.2
INDUSTRY		
Chemicals	31.8	13.5
Transport equipment	13.6	15.0
Machine tools	9.1	5.7
Mechanical engineering	4.6	30.0
Electrical engineering and electronics	18.2	11.6
Other	22.7	22.4

SOURCE: M. Smith, "Industrial Cooperation Agreements: Soviet Experience and Practice," in Joint Economic Committee, Congress of the United States, *Soviet Economy in a New Perspective* (Washington, D.C.: U.S. Government Printing Office, 1977), pp. 772, 775.

TABLE 4.4
Soviet Imports from NATO Countries and Japan

Major Machinery Import Categories	1976–1980 (annual average)	1981
Chemicals	32.1[a]%	15.7%
Metalworking	9.7	12.1
Heavy vehicles	3.7	11.5
Oil drilling and exploration	3.5	3.9
Other machinery[b]	51.0	56.8
Total	100%	100%

SOURCE: U.S. Department of Defense, *Soviet Military Power* (Washington, D.C.: U.S. Government Printing Office, 1983), p. 76.

[a] These imports of Western chemical equipment represented 67 percent of the total Soviet investment in chemical equipment over the five-year period.

[b] Includes over 20 sub-branches of machinery production, ranging from power machinery and precision instrumentation to machinery for the light and food industries.

centrated in the following areas: steel pipe and drilling equipment (repayment with crude oil and natural gas); mining equipment (repayment with coal); chemicals and petrochemicals and an ammonia pipeline (repayment with chemical products); aluminum refineries (repayment with aluminum); and forestry equipment and a cellulose plant (repayment with timber and cellulose).[44] An obvious advantage of compensation agreements is that they provide technology without the expenditure of foreign currency. Often the Western partner is responsible for marketing the product in the West, and therefore has a vested interest in the satisfactory performance of the Soviet plant. Initially, the major advantage from the Western viewpoint was the availability of plentiful, relatively cheap raw materials. However, given the stagnant economic environment in the West, this is no longer such an advantage.

Many technology purchases are made on a turnkey basis: the Western company provides the Soviet Union with an entire factory or production line. The Tolyatti motor works, supplied by Fiat, is an example. In other cases various pieces of plant and equipment are purchased from different suppliers to create an entire complex. The Kama truck complex was created in this way, as were many of the chemical complexes. The major advantage with turnkey projects is that they provide rapid improvements in the technical level of a given industry and, depending on the degree of Western involvement, they *may* circumvent many of the problems associated with domestic construction projects.

On average, imported technology rarely represents more than 3 or 4 percent of total industrial investment in the Soviet Union in any one year.[45] However, the fact that those imports have tended to be concentrated in a few sectors means that they may have a substantial impact on productivity in those industries. For example, the CIA has estimated that in 1975 plants supplied by the West accounted for 40 percent of Soviet output of complex fertilizers, 60 percent of polyethylene production, and 75–85 percent of polyester fiber output.[46] The completion of the Tolyatti motor works just about doubled domestic passenger car production and facilitated exports. Western plant and equipment have also played an important part in the expansion of pipeline systems and the modernization of the aluminum and forestry industries. Thus, within certain sectors importation of Western technology has served to ease bottlenecks caused by neglect or by problems inherent in the domestic economy. The net impact of Western technology goes beyond the immediate benefits of improved techniques, and may have a substantial effect on other industries and regions within the domestic economy.

Within an individual sector it is possible to identify both direct and indirect impacts of imported technology.[47] The direct impact of technology embodied within an imported machine may be seen as "the present value of the flow of output from that machine, over and above what the same resources would have produced using technologies previously available to the USSR."[48] The increased productivity of imported plant is a major reason for its use in Soviet economic plans. Indirect impacts include productivity increases attributable to materials, components, and machinery produced with imported equipment.[49] An example is improved agricultural productivity as a result of using Western fertilizer processes and technology.[50] Using Western plants in a particular industry can produce ripple effects, with technical improvements by material and component suppliers. This may result in higher-quality products or the development of efficient, specialized construction brigades—a factor that may explain the popularity of Tolyatti as a location for Western plants.

The impact of imported technology on the Soviet economy can, however, be reduced, both by a variety of systemic problems and by the nature of the centrally planned transfer process. The centralization of foreign trade may ensure strict control, but it may also hinder the flow of information and requests.[51] Technology procurement is a lengthy process, and decisions made at the center may not be sympathetic to the needs of the individual plant. Despite the high priority assigned to Western plants, one often reads of imported equipment left out in the open because buildings have yet to be completed or because they were built to the wrong specifications. The Tomsk petrochemical complex in West Siberia was delayed a year because of poor site selection.[52] Once installed, the imported equipment may not operate at peak efficiency because of poor management or inadequate training of the labor force. For example, Soviet crews operating sophisticated drill ships, supplied by Rauma Rapola of Finland, have had difficulties mastering the complex equipment on board.[53] Despite these problems it is likely that, once in operation, imported equipment is more productive than domestic alternatives. In addition, imported technology may provide capabilities not available with domestic alternatives.

On a national scale one can identify both resource-releasing and resource-demanding functions relating to technology transfer.[54] The aggregate increased productivity that results from using Western technology may release labor and resources for other projects. For example, Soviet officials have reported that imported chemical plants have cut production costs, increased labor productivity, and reduced labor and raw material demands.[55] The U.S. Department of Defense maintains that the resource-releasing function of imported technology enables the Soviet Union to overcome domestic economic problems without having to reduce military spending.[56] Thus, all forms of technology transfer are seen to have strategic implications.

On the negative side, plants using Western technology may make additional demands on the Soviet economy. This resource-demanding function may include inputs required to operate the plant and equipment, or investments required to use the products produced with imported technology. In the case of Siberian development it could be argued that the efficient use of foreign goods and equipment requires additional investment in the region's economic infrastructure.[57] To quantify such costs for Siberia would be very difficult. However, the lack of sufficient infrastructure is a persistent problem hindering the development of Siberia and the Far East. The initial foreign currency cost of the Kama truck complex at Naberezhnye Chelny (now called Brezhnev) was around $1 billion, and additional domestic expenditure amounted to $2–3 billion.[58]

A final consideration when weighing the advantages and disadvantages of technology transfer is time—to what extent has increased importation of Western technology represented a "quick fix"? In some cases Western technology has been used to improve the performance of a given sector rapidly. This has certainly been the case with the automobile and chemical industries. However, one should not overstate the importance of Western technology in Soviet economic plans. Domestic constraints such as concern for overdependence on the West, foreign currency reserves, and the poor performance of agriculture have limited the level of technology transfer, and will continue to do so. In addition Western political responses to Soviet foreign policy have often interrupted the transfer process. Even if more technology were available, it is likely that a point of diminishing returns would soon be reached because of the resource demands associated with imported plant. Therefore, technology transfer acts as a bandaid to certain industries, rather than a panacea to the entire economy.

REGIONAL DEVELOPMENT AND
TECHNOLOGY TRANSFER

While sectoral case studies have examined the impact of Western technology on certain industries, the spatial implications of technology transfer have been relatively neglected. Here, as a preliminary to detailed examination of Siberia and the Far East, it is suggested that technology transfer may play an important role in the regional development of the Soviet Union.

Soviet postwar regional development has been conducted within the framework of an East Russia–West Russia debate, meaning Siberian and Far Eastern development versus European development.[59] Pro-Siberians have argued that only the comprehensive development of the Siberian economy can ensure the efficient development of resources for the national economy.[60] Pro-Europeans, on the other hand, argue that the comprehensive development of Siberia is too costly, and that the potential of European Russia has yet to be fully exploited.

While this debate was in process, the Soviet leadership announced a change in Soviet economic strategy from the traditional extensive mode to a modern intensive mode of development. This new strategy was to be implemented by the "scientific-technical revolution" (STR), which emphasized quality and efficiency rather than volume of output.[61] In investment terms, the STR has favored renovating existing manufacturing plants rather than new construction. Funds for renovation and expansion of older enterprises rose from 58 percent of industrial investment in 1970 to 80 percent in 1980.[62] Although detailed evidence is hard to come by, there is little doubt that increased technology transfer during the 1970s played an important part in the modernization of Soviet industry, and was an integral part of the STR. Plant modernization and renovation favor European Russia simply because the bulk of manufacturing activity is located there.[63]

The STR can be seen as an attempt to bring about economic change without deep-seated reform. According to Boris Rumer, the program of reconstruction has not been a success. "Not one of the goals of the renovation policy of the 1970s was met. Output failed to increase as planned and there was little saving of resources. The investment process did not become more healthy."[64] Whether a success or not, the combination of the STR and socialist economic integration resolved the East-West debate in favor of European Russia. Siberian investment has been restricted to resource extraction and to a limited amount of primary processing and energy-intensive heavy industries.[65]

Faced with the huge cost of developing the resources of the eastern regions, planners at Novosibirsk have devised an intensive program of investment based on the creation of territorial production complexes (TPCs).[66] The director of the Novosibirsk research team, Abel Aganbegian, has estimated that developing industries, resources, and infrastructure using a TPC-based program could result in savings of 15–20 percent of total capital investment, compared with the cost of a more dispersed location policy.[67] In addition to their cost-saving advantages, TPCs may act as a vehicle for integrating plans. However, lack of political power has often meant that TPCs have suffered from problems of departmentalism and neglect of social infrastructure. In response to these problems, the management of the West Siberian oil and gas complex has been taken over by two new administrative bodies. The commission on development of the West Siberian oil and gas complex is responsible to the presidium of the Council of Ministers in Moscow; the interdepartmental territorial commission on development of the West Siberian oil and gas complex, concerned with regional planning and plan coordination, is responsible to the state planning agency, Gosplan USSR.[68]

This initiative is an indication of the importance attached to the development of Siberian oil and gas, and the official acceptance of the TPC. Whatever the fate of this particular initiative, the success of the TPC approach will probably depend ultimately on whether the central ministries can be persuaded or forced to accept further devolution of power. The importance of the TPC in the eastern regions is illustrated by the fact that of the ten TPCs identified by the atlas of the Eleventh Five-Year Plan (1981–1985), four are located in Siberia and one in the Soviet Far East: the West Siberian oil and gas complex, the Kansk-Achinsk complex, the Saian complex, the Bratsk–Ust-Ilimisk complex, and the South Yakutian complex (see Figure 4.1).[69] Future plans for the development of the

FIGURE 4.1

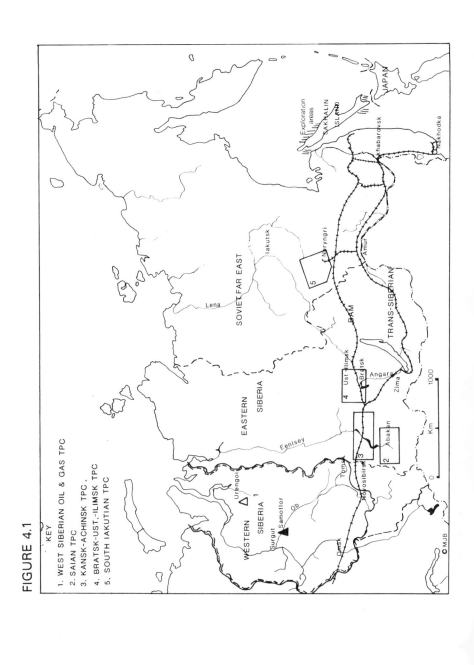

KEY

1. WEST SIBERIAN OIL & GAS TPC
2. SAIAN TPC
3. KANSK-ACHINSK TPC
4. BRATSK-UST.-ILIMSK TPC
5. SOUTH IAKUTIAN TPC

BAM service zone call for the creation of a number of TPCs. As the following section details, acquisition of Western technology has played a key role in the development of resource-based TPCs in Siberia and the Far East.

WESTERN TECHNOLOGY AND EASTERN DEVELOPMENT

West Siberia

Economic geographies of West Siberia describe an economy based on ferrous metallurgy (the Kuzbas), oil and gas (Tyumen oblast), and machine building (see Table 4.5).[70] In recent years development in the region has been dominated by the expansion of the West Siberian oil and gas complex. Table 4.6 illustrates the increasingly important part played by West Siberia in the national energy complex.

Within the West Siberian TPC, oil production is centered on the Nizhnevartovsk-Samotlor area, which accounts for more than 60 percent of total production in Tyumen oblast. Tyumen oblast, in turn, accounts for 90 percent of West Siberian oil production, or about half of national production. Natural gas production is concentrated in fields farther north on the Arctic Circle at Medvezhye and

TABLE 4.5
Structural Change in the Industries of the Eastern Regions of the USSR

	WEST SIBERIA		EAST SIBERIA		FAR EAST	
	1960	1975	1960	1975	1960	1975
Energy complex						
Electric power	3.5%	3.6%	4.9%	7.7%	1.5%	2.8%
Fuel industries	17.6	20.1	10.3	9.2	9.5	5.0
Branches producing and processing natural resources						
Ferrous metals	8.1	5.2	0.9	1.0	0.8	1.0
Nonferrous metals	2.6	1.9	11.4	17.7	7.4	10.4
Chemical industries	4.8	9.4	2.8	4.6	0.7	1.2
Wood products, pulp, and paper	7.2	4.7	20.7	13.8	13.2	11.6
Building materials	3.7	3.5	7.7	5.0	6.4	7.2
Branches producing finished goods						
Machine building	18.3	28.2	10.1	16.2	16.8	21.9
Food industry (including fish)	22.5	14.8	22.2	13.4	38.3	33.7
All Industries	100%	100%	100%	100%	100%	100%

SOURCE: V. I. Mozhin, *Ekonomicheskoe razvitie Sibiri i Dal'nego Vostoka* [Economic development of Siberia and the Far East] (Moscow: Mysl', 1980), p. 208.

TABLE 4.6
Siberia's Share in the Growth of Industrial Output (percentage of national growth)[a]

Branch	1960–1965[b]	1966–1970[b]	1971–1975[c]	1976–1980[c]
All industry	8.2	9.2	9.6	10.4
Electricity	16.1	19.0	18.0	13.9
Fuel oils	23.6	24.1	38.4	59.3
Chemicals and petrochemicals	16.4	6.4	10.0	8.6
Machine building and metalworking	5.6	8.8	6.7	6.6
Forestry	35.5	14.9	17.9	15.3
Construction materials	9.7	9.2	7.5	15.9
Light industry	4.3	6.5	8.6	8.7
Food industry	8.6	6.2	6.0	1.9

[a] Includes East and West Siberia only.

[b] T. B. Baranova, "Osnovye pokazateli razvitiia promyshlennosti sibiri v sed'moi-deviatoi piatilet-kakh" [Main indicators of industrial development in the Seventh–Ninth five-year plans], *Izvestiia Sibirskogo Otdeleniia Akademii Nauk SSSR,* no. 1 (January 1979):32.

[c] T. B. Baranova, "Osnovye pokazateli razvitiia promyshlennosti sibiri v desiatoi piatiletke" [Main indicators of Siberian industrial development during the Tenth Five-Year Plan period], *Izvestiia Sibirskogo Otdeleniia Akademii Nauk SSSR,* no. 11 (November 1982):72–73.

Urengoi. Pipelines from the oil and gas fields move crude oil and natural gas to domestic markets in European Russia, and to Eastern and Western Europe. A series of petrochemical plants was commissioned in West Siberia during the early 1970s at Tobolsk and Tomsk.

Western participation has been important in both the development and transportation of the region's petroleum resources and the development of the petrochemical industry. A recent analysis of technology transfer and Soviet energy availability, conducted by the U.S. Office of Technology Assessment, concluded that "There is no question that Soviet oil production has been assisted by American and other Western technology and equipment, although the impact of the assistance is probably impossible to quantify."[71]

The energy sector is examined in more detail elsewhere in this volume. Here it is sufficient to note that there is considerable disagreement among Western analysts as to the technical level of the Soviet oil and gas industry. A. A. Meyerhoff sees a potential Soviet energy crisis, resulting from the low level of Soviet technology rather than a lack of exploitable reserves. D. Wilson, on the other hand, does not see the level of technology as a limiting factor, and has predicted that the Soviet Union will remain an important supplier of oil to the West well into the next century.[72] Whatever the state of Soviet oil and gas technology, selective importation of Western technology has been important in the rapid expansion of Siberian production. Purchases of energy technology from the West have been in three main areas: large-diameter pipe, compressors, and submersible pumps.[73] Other important items have been drill bits, seismic equipment, exploration equipment, excavators, and pipe layers. In many cases imported equipment has been needed to compensate for the poor performance of domestic equipment in the harsh Siberian environment.[74]

In West Siberia 94 percent of all oil is obtained by waterflooding, and the submersible pumps purchased by the Soviet Union are an essential component of this technique. In the giant Samotlor field, the greatest single contributor to West Siberian output, Soviet pumps proved inadequate and Reda pumps were imported from the United States.[75] Campbell has concluded that the availability of such U.S. pumps was crucial in achieving output goals during the 1970s, though the exact impact of such pumps is impossible to calculate.[76] Western supplies of pipeline equipment were highly publicized during the controversy over the Siberian pipeline to Western Europe.[77] Throughout the 1960s and 1970s the Soviet Union relied on the importation of large-diameter pipe, compressor stations, and pipe-laying equipment to rapidly expand its petroleum pipeline system.

The implications of such trade for Siberian development have been substantial. Without the rapid development of transcontinental pipelines, it would not have been possible to transport vast quantities of oil and gas. Had petroleum transportation been restricted, it is likely that crude oil would have been refined in Siberia and higher value-to-weight petroleum products transported west by rail. The development of such pipelines has also enabled European Russia to maintain its dominance over the eastern regions.

Western contracts for the recently completed West Siberian gas export pipeline from Urengoi to Uzhgorod were spread among the countries of Western Europe: West Germany received contracts worth $1.2 billion, France $664 million, Italy $890 million, the United Kingdom $260 million, and Finland $90 million. The Japanese were not heavily involved in the project, but Komatsu picked up a contract for 500 pipe layers worth $209.8 million when U.S. sanctions prohibited the U.S. Caterpillar Company from providing the equipment.[78] The compressor technology sold to the Soviet Union by West European companies was built using licenses from American General Electric. When the West Europeans refused to stop delivery of pipeline equipment as part of sanctions protesting martial law in Poland, the Reagan administration attempted to bloc the re-export of U.S. technologies. In response to delays and possible embargoes, the Soviet Union pressed ahead with production of its own compressors and built 22, reducing its import order from 33 to 18 stations.[79] U.S. embargoes on the sale of energy technology to the Soviet Union have necessitated a reorientation of Soviet trade, and Japan and Western Europe are now the major suppliers of energy-related equipment.[80] The resultant loss of economic leverage has meant that the United States has had to rely on European acceptance of its views on the strategic implications of energy trade. Obviously West European and U.S. perceptions of the advisability of participation in Soviet energy projects are very different.[81]

Because of the market and infrastructure advantages enjoyed by the European regions of the USSR, the chemical and petrochemical industries of West Siberia have remained relatively undeveloped.[82] The Tomsk petrochemical complex illustrates the nature of Western involvement in this sector. The Tomsk project began in 1974, and the first stage of the complex, a polypropylene plant, went into operation after considerable delay in 1981. The plant, worth $100 million, was supplied by the Italian company Montedison Technimont, which is receiving compensation payments in ammonia.[83] The plant uses natural gas liquids extracted from gas associated with West Siberian oil, and produces approximately 75 percent of total Soviet polypropylene production.[84] The second stage of the complex involves the construction of a giant methanol plant by a British consortium consisting of Davy Powergas, I.C.I., and the West German Klockner company. The methanol plant will have an ultimate capacity of 750,000 tons a year, and will account for 28 percent of total Soviet methanol production. The plant is valued at $275 million, and is financed with compensation deliveries of methanol.[85] The third stage will be a $4 billion petrochemicals complex based on an oil refinery. Negotiations have taken place with German and Japanese companies; however, problems have been encountered over the method of financing, and an agreement has so far not been made public.

Other petrochemical projects in West Siberia using Western equipment include a polystyrene plant and an aromatics complex at Omsk, supplied by the French companies Litwin and Technip. The aromatics complex, which produces benzene, orthoxylene, and paraxylene, is being paid for with compensation deliveries. Developments at Tobolsk are being concentrated on the construction of a synthetic rubber center.[86] Other Siberian plants, such as the tire factory at Omsk, also export to the West.[87]

Siberia's share of East-West chemical trade is relatively small. Nevertheless, Western companies seem to have made a substantial contribution to the development of the chemical and petrochemical industry of West Siberia. Typically the technology transfer process has involved turnkey projects purchased on a compensation basis. But, as Western enthusiasm for compensation deals has waned in the face of recession, it is likely that future development will be restricted by ability to pay.

East Siberia

With the notable exception of the Norilsk metallurgical complex, most development in East Siberia has been in the south. The hydroelectric stations on the Angara-Yenisei river system have served as the basis for a number of industrial complexes. Western participation has been important in the Bratsk–Ust-Ilimsk TPC, the Saian TPC, and at the Zima chemical center.

Construction of a giant forest-products complex at Bratsk began in 1962; by 1975 total capital investment had reached 927 million rubles. A further 420 million rubles were allocated to complete the complex during the Tenth Five-Year Plan (1976–1980).[88] The usual problems associated with large Soviet construction projects were encountered, namely poor coordination and neglect of infrastructure. Purchase of Western equipment via the foreign trade association Prommashimport only complicated the project further, as the forestry ministry has very little say in equipment purchases. The bulk of the Western equipment was supplied by Finnish companies. Despite Finnish offers to store the equipment, Soviet authorities insisted on delivery of equipment well before the sites had been prepared, so the equipment was left out in the open.

Similar problems were encountered in the Kama truck complex, and probably reflect the need for accounting purposes to take delivery of equipment in the same plan-year as it was ordered. At Bratsk such problems only served to aggravate delays and led to criticisms of the scale of the project. The neighboring Ust-Ilimsk complex has been equally problematic. It has not only Western participants, but also CMEA joint-project status. Equipment for Ust-Ilimsk has been supplied by companies in France, Sweden, Finland, and Japan. Finnish companies provided equipment for handling and processing logs; a Japanese company provided a pulp treatment plant. The French participant, a subsidiary of the U.S. multinational Parsons Whittemore, provided a cellulose plant financed with compensation payments of 85,000 tons of cellulose a year.[89]

Western technology has also played a part in the creation of the Saian TPC. Aganbegian maintains that the Saian complex differs from the other Siberian TPCs in that it is a multisectoral complex, combining energy and material-intensive branches of ferrous and nonferrous metallurgy as well as labor-intensive branches of the engineering sector.[90]

Development of nonferrous metallurgy at Saian has centered on the construction of an aluminum smelter by the French company Pechiney-Ugine Kuhlman. The smelter has a capacity of 500,000 tons annually and is being paid for by deliveries of aluminum—100,000 tons a year. Construction delays have led to the stockpiling of alumina at Nikolayev; however, the Saian complex is now expected to start production in early 1986.[91]

Railcar and container manufacturing, related to the trans-Siberian land bridge, now takes place at Abakan, a city within the Saian TPC. Lack of containers and specialized flat cars has contributed to delays on the land bridge.[92] In an effort to solve this problem, a Soviet-built flat car factory, with a capacity of 5,000 cars a year, went into operation at Abakan in 1976. Western companies have cooperated in the construction of two container plants. One at Ilyichensk near Odessa was built by a German company, Industrie Transportsysteme of Lubeck. It was completed in 1978 and is capable of producing 5,000 units a year. The second plant is located at Abakan and was built by a Japanese company, Kawasaki Heavy Industries. It produced 16,000 units in 1978, its first year of operation; ultimately it will be capable of producing 40,000 containers a year.[93]

Western equipment has been important in the construction of a chemical center at Zima in Irkutsk oblast. Ethylene produced by a Soviet-built plant at Angarsk is now transported 230 kilometers (144 miles) via an eight-inch pipeline to Zima. The pipeline was constructed in cooperation with a British company, John Brown Engineering. After considerable delay the plant at Zima went into operation in 1981. At Zima the ethylene is used to produce vinyl chloride, using chlorine obtained by electrolysis from local salt deposits. The vinyl chloride plant was supplied by a West German company, Hoerchst, at a cost of $40 million, and is being paid for with compensation payments of vinyl chloride. The planned capacity of the plant is 270,000 tons a year, but its initial startup date of 1978 was delayed by the late completion of the Angarsk-Zima pipeline. A polyvinyl chloride (PVC) plant, costing $68 million, has been supplied by Klockner. Again the plant is being financed with compensation deliveries of PVC. When fully operational the Zima chemical center will produce 250,000 tons of PVC, raising Soviet PVC production by nearly 60 percent.[94]

As with West Siberia, the transfer of Western technology has facilitated the development of key sectors within the regional economy of East Siberia. A Soviet author has likened the export of Saian aluminum to "exporting the energy of the mighty Siberian rivers in concentrated form."[95] The Soviet penchant for compensation agreements is shown by their dominant role in East Siberian projects. At present, investment in East Siberia is concentrated on the development of the Kansk-Achinsk coal basin. Transportation costs and the nature of the coal deposit have necessitated the construction of mine-mouth power stations and the development of high-voltage transmission lines. The Soviet Union is a world leader in high-voltage transmission technology, and the Kansk-Achinsk complex provides an example of a TPC developing with domestic technologies.[96] A future candidate for Western participation is the copper deposit at Udokan. During the mid-1970s Western companies were asked to submit proposals for development of the copper resource, but nothing came of it. However, during the Eleventh Five-Year Plan detailed feasibility studies are being carried out. It seems likely that the project will come to the fore with the completion of the BAM.

The Soviet Far East

Economic development in the Far East is more dispersed than in Siberia; there is only one official TPC. Since the mid-1960s attention has focused on the export potential of the region's natural resources.[97] Because of the vast distances

TABLE 4.7
Structure of Soviet-Japanese Trade (percentage of total trade)

Imports from Japan	1971	1975	1980
Plant and equipment	35.3	35.2	32.4
Transportation equipment for chemical industry	9.9	2.4	5.0
Rolled steel	7.4	16.7	12.6
Pipe	5.8	16.5	19.2
Chemical products	6.6	4.7	7.9
Silk, including synthetics	6.9	4.3	4.2
Clothing and linen	6.0	1.6	1.6
Other	22.1	18.6	17.1

Exports to Japan			
Plant and equipment	1.3	0.4	0.6
Timber (Roundwood)	35.6	36.7	39.3
Cotton	11.3	14.1	8.0
Scrap iron	3.5	1.2	1.5
Pig iron	1.9	NA	NA
Nonferrous metals	2.2	7.0	NA
Nonmetallic minerals, clay	NA	1.6	0.9
Potassium salts	1.5	2.7	2.1
Oil and oil products	11.3	10.1	11.3
Thermal coal	8.6	16.3	7.3
Other	22.8	9.9	29.0

SOURCE: M. I. Krupianko, *Sovetskogo-iaponskie ekonomicheskie otnosheniia* [Soviet-Japanese economic cooperation] (Moscow: Nauka, 1982), pp. 67, 90.

between the Far East and European markets, the major foreign participant in the Far Eastern economy has been Japan.

The distinct structure of Soviet-Japanese trade illustrates the existing complementarity between the two regions—Japan supplying plant and equipment and the Soviet Union supplying raw materials (see Table 4.7). The specifics of Soviet-Japanese relations are dealt with elsewhere in this volume, and there already exists a large English-language literature on the subject.[98] Therefore, this section briefly reviews the major projects that have come to fruition, concentrating on the trade and technology aspects of such projects.[99] Forestry, petroleum, and coal mining have benefited most from Japanese participation. In addition, port facilities have been expanded to cope with the increased volume of trade between the Soviet Union and Japan.

Forestry Agreements   The mainstay of Soviet-Japanese cooperation in the forestry sector has been a series of agreements on the development of the Far Eastern forest resource. The first was reached in July 1968; subsequent agreements were signed in July 1974 and March 1981. Under these agreements the

Japanese have supplied plant, machinery, equipment, and consumer durables. In return Japan has received timber, mainly in the form of unprocessed roundwood. Thus, these agreements represent compensation deals on a grand scale.

Under the terms of the first agreement, $133 million in construction machinery, vehicles, and vessels for lumbering and transport was provided on the basis of five-year deferred payment.[100] Specific equipment purchases included bulldozers, motor graders, timber carriers, excavators, truck-mounted cranes, and sea dredges.[101] In return Japan received 7,665,000 cubic meters of commercial timber at a constant price between 1969 and 1973 and 320,000 cubic meters of sawnwood between 1971 and 1973. To manage the supply of equipment, fourteen Japanese companies were combined into a consortium called KS Industrial Co. Ltd.[102]

The second agreement, signed in July 1974, was financed by a $550 million loan from the Export-Import Bank of Japan and commercial banks. A similar inventory of equipment was purchased by the Soviet Union, and Japan received 18.4 million cubic meters of roundwood and sawnwood between 1975 and 1979. In contrast to the first agreement, timber prices were set annually.

Negotiations on the third agreement were delayed by Soviet actions in Afghanistan. When finally signed on March 19, 1981, it provided a loan of $910 million to be paid back in deliveries of 12 million cubic meters of roundwood and 1.24 million cubic meters of sawnwood between 1981 and 1986. The lower level of timber deliveries reflects the impact of recession, and also problems related to the technology requirements of the Soviet Union.[103] In addition there has been disagreement over the amount of larch in Soviet deliveries.

The Soviet Union has continually tried to increase the proportion of forest products in trade with Japan. The only notable success has been the wood chips and pulp development project. An agreement signed with Nipon Chip Boeki, in December 1971, provided $45 million in credit for the purchase of equipment for Soviet chip and pulpwood production. Compensation payments involved delivery of 4.7 million cubic meters of pulpwood and 8 million cubic meters of wood chips between 1972 and 1981. Proposals for a second chip and pulp agreement, for modernization of pulp and paper factories on Sakhalin, and for construction of a pulp and paper plant at Khabarovsk have been put forward, but no final agreements have been made public.[104]

Oil and Gas   In the petroleum sector it is fair to say that there has been more talk than action. Of the four projects seriously considered during the last fifteen years (the Yakutian natural gas project, the Sakhalin continental shelf project, the Tyumen oil development project, and the Sakhalin natural gas project), only one—the Sakhalin continental shelf project—has come to fruition. The others have succumbed to political, strategic, and economic problems.[105]

Commercial oil production on Sakhalin began in 1921 and peaked at 2.5 million tons in 1968. By the mid-1970s Sakhalin's output accounted for approximately 20 percent of local demand.[106] Initial discussion on the Sakhalin continental shelf project was conducted between 1972 and 1973. In July 1974 the U.S. company Gulf Petroleum joined the project. On January 28, 1975, a general agreement was signed with the Soviet Union, and the Sakhalin Oil Development Company (SODECO) was created to manage the western component of the project. An initial credit of $100 million was provided to buy and lease the necessary equipment. A further credit of $70 million was awarded in July 1979. The exploration period of the project, scheduled for 1976–1980, was later extended to 1982. The loans were provided at an interest rate of 6 percent, with final payback in deliveries of petroleum. Japan has the rights to 50 percent of the oil and gas discovered by the project, and has agreed to meet half the development costs once production starts.

The harsh natural conditions and Soviet inexperience with offshore exploration have made foreign participation essential to this project. Drill rigs have been leased through Japanese companies, and in July 1980 a Soviet rig, built by Mitsui Ocean Development and Engineering Company of Japan, was put into operation. In the summer of 1982 the Finnish-built drill ship *Mikhail Mirchinsk* was transferred from the Barents Sea to the Far East to explore the region south of Sakhalin Island. Completed exploration off the northern coast has found reserves of 630 million barrels of crude oil, 140.5 billion cubic meters of gas, and 140.5 billion cubic meters of condensate. No startup date has been announced yet, but deliveries of liquified natural gas (LNG) are not expected until the early 1990s. The development phase will involve the construction of a natural gas liquefication plant on the mainland and a pipeline to Japan. Deliveries of LNG are expected to average 3 million tons a year over a twenty-year period.[107]

Because much of the equipment used in the Sakhalin project has been U.S.-built, the project has been susceptible to political embargoes. The Carter administration's response to the Soviet occupation of Afghanistan specifically prohibited the sale of U.S. energy technology to the USSR. As a result U.S. companies lost contracts to supply equipment to the Sakhalin project, and by 1980 Gulf Oil was no longer listed as a member of SODECO. In April 1980, after Japanese pressure, the project was exempted from post-Afghanistan embargoes.[108] When martial law was declared in Poland the Reagan administration countered with economic sanctions; again the Sakhalin project was affected. Part of the 1982 drilling season was lost because one of the rigs the Japanese wished to use, the Hakuryu II, was U.S.-designed.[109] Despite Japanese pressure, it was not until January 1983 that U.S. sanctions on the Sakhalin project were lifted. The subsequent shooting down of the Korean Air Lines jet brought additional exposure to the region, and further aggravated already fragile Soviet-Japanese relations.

However, the commitment already made to the Sakhalin project will ensure continued Japanese participation.

Coal Mining   Japanese involvement in the south Yakutian coal complex can be seen as the first BAM-related project.[110] A June 1974 agreement provided $450 million for the development of the Neryungri coal field in south Yakutia and the modernization of the Kuznetsk basin. The funds have been used to purchase transport equipment, loading and earth-moving machines, and other equipment for the coal field and for construction of the Little BAM, completed in 1978. A further $60 million in credit went to consumer goods and other costs; in addition the rising cost of equipment has necessitated a further loan of $9 million. In payment Japanese companies will receive 84.4 million tons of coking coal from the south Yakutian field and 20 million from the Kuznetsk basin.[111] Due to production problems, delivery of south Yakutian coal was delayed until 1984. In the meantime the Kuznetsk basin is taking up the slack. When at full capacity, the south Yakutian complex will deliver 5.5 million tons per year to Japan, scheduled for a twenty-year period.

Port Developments   Increased trade resulting from Soviet-Japanese cooperation has placed stress on Far Eastern port facilities. Development has concentrated on construction of a new port (sometimes called Vostochny) on Wrangel Bay, east of Nakhodka. Under an agreement signed in December 1970, Japan supplied a credit of $80 million for the construction of a coal pier and comprehensive freight-loading facilities. The new port will ultimately be capable of handling 10 million tons of coal, 500,000 cubic meters of wood chips, and 120,000–140,000 containers annually.[112] Mitsui has supplied the port with two giant gantry cranes and a computer system.[113] The rapid development of the port at Wrangel and the expansion of container facilities at Nakhodka have been essential components of Soviet-Japanese trade relations.

Other Trade   In addition to the major resource projects discussed above, Japanese equipment, such as heavy excavators, has been used in the construction of the BAM. A small amount of coastal trade has also developed between the Soviet Far East and surrounding countries. This local trade is managed through the regional trade association, Dal'intorg, at Nakhodka. Surplus production from Soviet enterprises in the region is traded for equipment and goods. Exports include wood products, fish products, construction materials, and minerals; imports are dominated by equipment and consumer goods such as radios and cameras.[114] The scale of coastal trade is restricted by a lack of Soviet goods for barter and the limited size of the Far Eastern market. Despite the fact that such trade represents only 2 or 3 percent of Soviet trade with Japan, it is important for enterprises in the Far East because it enables them to circumvent central control and obtain equipment on their own initiative.[115]

At first sight the scale of Japanese involvement in Siberian and Far Eastern development may seem impressive. However, Japan has consistently pursued a policy of diversifying suppliers of raw materials, thereby improving its bargaining position and avoiding overdependence. Soviet timber and forest products accounted for 16.1 percent of total Japanese imports in 1979.[116] Other suppliers of forest products included Canada, the United States, Malaysia, Indonesia, and New Zealand. A similar pattern is found with Japanese coal imports. Not only are the Japanese involved in the south Yakutian coal complex, but they are also investing in a similar project at Tumbler Ridge in northern British Columbia, Canada. Likewise, an LNG project similar to the one at Sakhalin is presently being negotiated with Mobil Oil and Petro Canada, again in British Columbia. Therefore, it is likely that intervening opportunities will limit the scale of Japanese investment in the Soviet Union.

From the Soviet viewpoint, Japanese cooperation is an important factor in the development of the resource base of Siberia and the Far East. Through such agreements the Soviet Union receives the technology and equipment needed to ensure the rapid development of the region's natural resources. However, a combination of political and economic factors has served to limit the scale of cooperation well below the level desired by the Soviet Union. In 1983 trade with Japan represented only 7.8 percent of total trade with the developed capitalist nations.[117]

CONCLUSIONS

As we enter the second half of the 1980s East-West trade is at a crossroads. Many of the projects initiated during the 1970s will soon reach a conclusion. The succession of a new Soviet leadership and the beginning of the Twelfth Five-Year Plan (1986–1990) may mark a new direction in Soviet economic policy. At the same time the transfer of technology to the Soviet Union has become a thorny issue among the members of the Western alliance. Thus, it is an opportune moment to examine the impact of commercial and high-technology trade on the Soviet Union.

The evidence presented in this chapter suggests that foreign economic relations have served to perpetuate the core-periphery structure of Soviet regional development. The European core region has benefited from increased integration within the socialist bloc, and has been the major beneficiary of East-West technology transfer. The depletion of the resource base of European Russia and the added burden of export demands have placed further stress on the resource economies of the eastern regions. Not only has the rapid development of Siberia's resources become essential to the domestic economy, but the export of raw materials from Siberia and the Soviet Far East is now a vital part of Soviet foreign economic policy. In some senses Siberian resources have been mortgaged to pay for Western technology used to modernize the manufacturing base of the European regions. Thus, exports from Siberia and the Far East are an integral part of any program that utilizes Western technology to overcome bottlenecks in the domestic economy. The majority of Western technology employed in the eastern regions is dedicated to the exploitation of natural resources and the expansion of the export base.

To substantiate the exact contribution of trade and technology would require a detailed analysis of the entire regional economy of Siberia and the Far East.[118] Nevertheless, there does appear to be a distinct correlation between the location of Western turnkey plants and the establishment of territorial production complexes. Concentrating plants that use Western technology within such complexes may minimize the resource-demanding aspects of technology transfer, while maximizing the resource-releasing benefits. Additional infrastructure demands may be more easily met if plants are concentrated within industrial complexes. The happy coincidence of TPCs and turnkey plants is no surprise given the fact that TPCs are now the official vehicle of economic development in the eastern regions. In all the cases discussed above, the acquisition of Western plants has played a major part in the creation of production complexes. In most instances the sector designated as the specialization for that particular complex has received Western plants and equipment.

The pattern of development and the role of foreign trade is rather different in the Soviet Far East. Remoteness from the industrial core regions of the USSR has restricted the level of development. Traditional exports have been high value-to-weight products, such as furs, gold, and diamonds. However, with the recent emergence of the Pacific rim as an international market, every effort is being made to expand the export base of the Far East. Compensation deals, predominantly with Japan, have served to provide the necessary plant and equipment needed to develop the region's export potential.

The pattern of economic development in Siberia and the Soviet Far East, perhaps more than any other region in the Soviet Union, is affected by external factors as much as by domestic decisions. Western policy toward technology transfer to the Soviet Union has been, to put it mildly, confused. U.S. policymakers have taken to using economic sanctions as a political weapon against the Soviet Union. Time after time those sanctions have backfired, and the Western alliance has suffered as much as the Soviet Union and its allies, if not more. From a policy standpoint, one of the more important findings of this study is the fact that U.S. involvement is no longer a factor in the development of Siberia and the Far East. The major partners in their trade and high-technology arena are now the countries of Western Europe and Japan.

As the Siberian pipeline controversy illustrated, the governments of Western

Europe have a very different perception of the costs and benefits of East-West trade than the policy-makers in Washington. If a coherent and consistent Western policy toward technology transfer to the Eastern bloc is to be achieved, the United States will have to resist the desire to use trade as a political weapon, and the nations of Western Europe and Japan will have to accept the notion that trade with the Soviet Union is a political issue. Trade for trade's sake can no longer be allowed if such trade affects Western security. However, those who would wish to limit trade must be advised of the possible consequences of such a policy. If East-West trade were to be curtailed, not only would the export-oriented industries of the Western nations suffer, but it is also likely that the allies of the Soviet Union would bear the brunt of any economic hardships. If the Soviet Union were unable to produce sufficient resources to satisfy its own needs and those of its socialist partners, it is likely that deliveries of Soviet resources to Eastern Europe would be reduced. (In some areas, this is already the case.) This may force the countries of Eastern Europe to borrow hard currency to import energy resources. Such actions would likely lead to greater economic hardship and possibly political instability within Eastern Europe. Thus, in the interest of continued relative stability, it may be beneficial to the West to continue to trade with the Soviet Union.

Regardless of Western policy toward trade and technology transfer with the Eastern bloc, the Soviet Union will continue to develop the resources of Siberia and the Soviet Far East. The level of Western participation in such development should be determined by both economic reasoning and political policy. If the governments of the Western alliance are able to consolidate their position on technology transfer, then participation in Siberian resource development may provide the West with both economic and political benefits. However, should the present disorganized position prevail, it is likely that the Soviet Union will reap the economic benefits of Western technology while the Western alliance pays the political costs. A total ban on technology transfer would likely slow the rate of assimilation of Siberian resources, but it would not decisively affect the productive capabilities of the Soviet military-industrial complex. Rather, the Soviet populace and the countries of Eastern Europe would suffer any economic hardships resulting from a resource squeeze.

The second half of the 1980s will likely mark a new era in Soviet domestic and foreign economic policy, and Siberia and the Soviet Far East will undoubtedly play a major role. Therefore the question of Western participation in Siberian resource development will continue to remain center stage in East-West trade and technology relations.

NOTES

1. For an examination of the evolution of CMEA, see J. M. Van Brabant, *Socialist Economic Integration: Aspects of Contemporary Problems in Eastern Europe* (Cambridge, England: Cambridge University Press, 1980).

2. P. Alampiev et al., *A New Approach to Economic Integration* (Moscow: Progress Publishers, 1974), p. 38.

3. J. Hannigan and C. McMillan, "Joint Investment in Resource Development: Sectoral Approaches to Socialist Integration," in Congress of the United States, Joint Economic Committee, *East European Economic Assessment: Part 2, Regional Assessment* (Washington, D.C.: U.S. Government Printing Office, 1982), p. 262.

4. For an explanation of these various types of agreement see I. J. Sylvain, "Integration in the Socialist Bloc: CMEA and Cooperative Ventures," in S. McInnes et al., eds., *The Soviet Union and Eastern Europe in the 1980's* (Oakville, Ontario: Mosaic Press, 1978), pp. 277–301.

5. From G. W. Hoffman, "Energy Dependence and Policy Options in Eastern Europe," in R. G. Jensen et al., eds., *Soviet Natural Resources in the World Economy* (Chicago: University Press of Chicago, 1983), p. 660.

6. T. Shabad, "Soviet Regional Policy and CMEA Integration," in P. Marer and J. M. Montias, eds., *East European Integration and East-West Trade* (Bloomington: Indiana University Press, 1980), pp. 228–29.

7. R. N. North, "The Impact of Recent Trends in Soviet Foreign Trade on Regional Economic Development in the USSR," in Jensen et al., *Soviet Natural Resources,* p. 104.

8. Shabad, "CMEA Integration," p. 238.

9. Cost calculations used to justify particular locations are seldom objective and are often manipulated to suit political needs, the classic example being the Urals-Kuznetsk combine.

10. The details of this project are discussed in a later section on technology transfer.

11. Shabad, "CMEA Integration," p. 242.

12. For details of this trade, see G. Chupin, "Integration of COMECON Countries in Auto Production," *Voprosy ekonomiki,* no. 6 (June 1977): 71–78. Translated in *Problems of Economics* 10, no. 7 (October 1977): 81–95.

13. Shabad, "CMEA Integration," p. 227.

14. Ibid., p. 240; and M. I. Gonak, *Sotsialisticheskaia ekonomicheskaia integratsiia i geografiia proizvodstva* [Socialist economic integration and the geography of production] (Lvov: Vishcha Shkola, 1982), pp. 106–7.

15. Obviously the situation is somewhat more complex than this; see R. N. Taafe, "Discussion of T. Shabad, 'CMEA Integration,'" in Marer and Montias, *East European Integration and East-West Trade,* pp. 245–51.

16. I. F. Zaitsev, "Regional'nye problemy razvitiia vneshneekonomicheskikh

sviazey SSSR" [Regional problems in the development of the foreign economic relations of the USSR], in *Metodologicheskie problemy sotsial'no-ekonomicheskogo razvitiia regionov SSSR* [Methodological problems of the socioeconomic development of the regions of the USSR] (Moscow: Nauka, 1979), p. 192.

17. E. A. Hewett, "Foreign Economic Relations," in A. Bergson and H. S. Levine, eds., *The Soviet Union Towards the Year 2000* (London: Allen and Unwin, 1983), pp. 269–310.

18. I. Gorst, "Striving to Maintain Oil Exports," *Petroleum Economist* 51, no. 2 (February 1984): 61.

19. D. Wilson, *Soviet Oil and Gas to 1990* (Cambridge, Mass.: Abt Books, 1982).

20. T. Shabad, "News Notes," *Soviet Geography: Review and Translation* 24, no. 4 (April 1983): 312.

21. R. Campbell, "Energy," in Bergson and Levine, *The Soviet Economy Towards the Year 2000*, p. 208.

22. T. Shabad, "The Soviet Potential in Natural Resources: An Overview," in Jensen et al., *Soviet Natural Resources*, p. 269.

23. Ibid., p. 270.

24. For an assessment of the BAM, see V. L. Mote, "The Baikal-Amur Mainline and Its Implications for the Pacific Basin," in Jensen et al., *Soviet Natural Resources*, pp. 133–87.

25. Hewett, "Foreign Economic Relations," p. 284.

26. M. Kaser, "The Soviet Gold Mining Industry," in Jensen et al., *Soviet Natural Resources*, p. 587.

27. Ibid., p. 559.

28. Quoted in Hewett, "Foreign Economic Relations," p. 287.

29. P. E. Lydolph and H. M. Mayer, "Effect of Soviet Shipping on World Maritime Trade," *Soviet Geography: Review and Translation* 24, no. 2 (February 1983): 100–101.

30. "Trans-Siberian Containers," *International Railway Journal* 23, no. 6 (June 1983): 66.

31. Port of Vancouver, *Commodity Statistics* (1982): 23.

32. T. Shabad, "The Soviet Aluminium Industry: Recent Developments," *Soviet Geography: Review and Translation* 24, no. 2 (February 1983): 89.

33. Ibid., p. 91.

34. T. Shabad, "News Notes," *Soviet Geography: Review and Translation* 22, no. 3 (March 1981): 210–11.

35. T. Shabad, "News Notes," *Soviet Geography: Review and Translation* 21, no. 10 (December 1980): 676–77.

36. North, "The Impact of Recent Trends in Soviet Foreign Trade," p. 99.

37. For detailed analysis of the Stalinist approach, see A. C. Sutton, *Western Technology and Soviet Economic Development*, vol. 3 (Stanford: Hoover Institution Press, 1973); and G. D. Holliday, *Technology Transfer to the USSR, 1928–1937 and 1966–1975* (Boulder, Colo.: Westview Press, 1979).

38. J. P. Hardt and G. D. Holliday, "Technology Transfer and Change in the Soviet Economic System," in F. J. Fleron, ed., *Technology and Communist Culture* (New York: Praeger, 1977), p. 183.

39. Holliday, *Technology Transfer to the USSR.*

40. See V. Sobeslavsky and P. Beazley, *The Transfer of Technology to Socialist Countries: The Case of the Soviet Chemical Industry* (Farnborough, Hampshire: Gower Publishing, 1980).

41. For a review of the literature and findings, see the following works: Congress of the United States, Office of Technology Assessment, *Technology and East-West Trade* (Washington, D.C.: U.S. Government Printing Office, 1979); E. Zaleski and H. Wienert, *Technology Transfer between East and West* (Paris: OECD, 1980); and G. D. Holliday, *Survey of Sectoral Case Studies* (Paris: OECD, 1984).

42. For example, in relation to Soviet-Japanese trade, see: M. I. Krupianko, *Sovetskogo Iaponskie ekonomicheskie otnosheniia* [Soviet-Japanese economic cooperation] (Moscow: Nauka, 1982), p. 120; also, with special reference to Siberia and the Far East, see B. N. Slavinsky, "Siberia and the Soviet Far East Within the Framework of International Trade and Economic Relations," *Asian Survey,* no. 4 (1977): 311–13.

43. For a review of Soviet views, see E. P. Hoffman and R. F. Laird, *"The Scientific-Technical Revolution" and Soviet Foreign Policy* (New York: Pergamon Press, 1982).

44. Council of International Policy, in *East-West Markets* (February 7, 1977), quoted in J. Stankovsky, "Compensation in East-West Trade," from *Creditanstalt-Bankverein Wirtschaftsberichte,* no. 6 (1977): 7–16. Translated in *Soviet and East European Foreign Trade* 13 (1978): 3–25.

45. P. Hanson, *Trade and Technology in Soviet Western Relations* (New York: Columbia University Press, 1981), p. 129.

46. Quoted from Central Intelligence Agency, *Soviet Chemical Equipment Purchases from the West: Impact on Production and Foreign Trade,* in Office of Technology Assessment, *Technology and East-West Trade,* p. 228.

47. This typology is taken from the work of Philip Hanson.

48. P. Hanson, "The Soviet System As a Recipient of Foreign Technology," in R. Armann and J. Cooper, eds., *Industrial Innovation in the Soviet Union* (New Haven, Conn.: Yale University Press, 1982), p. 422.

49. Ibid., p. 423.

50. P. Hanson, "Impact of Western Technology: The Soviet Fertilizer Industry," in Marer and Montias, *East European Integration and East-West Trade,* pp. 252–80.

51. Hanson, "The Soviet System As a Recipient of Foreign Technology," pp. 428–29.

52. T. Shabad, "News Notes," *Soviet Geography: Review and Translation* 22, no. 5 (May 1981): 348.

53. I. Gorst, "Big Boost to Offshore Oil Search," *Petroleum Economist* 51, no. 4 (April 1984): 146.

54. See J. P. Hardt, "The Role of Western Technology in Soviet Economic Plans," NATO Directorate of Economic Affairs, *East-West Technological Cooperation* (Brussels:

NATO, 1976), pp. 315–27; and G. D. Holliday, "The Role of Western Technology in the Soviet Economy," in Congress of the United States, Joint Economic Committee, *Issues in East-West Commercial Relations* (Washington, D.C.: U.S. Government Printing Office, 1979), pp. 57–58.

55. Hanson, "Impact of Western Technology: The Soviet Fertilizer Industry," p. 275.

56. U.S. Department of Defense, *Soviet Military Power* (Washington, D.C.: U.S. Government Printing Office, 1983), p. 75, and *Soviet Acquisition of Militarily Significant Western Technology: An Update* (Washington, D.C.: U.S. Government Printing Office, 1985).

57. Hardt, "The Role of Western Technology," p. 318.

58. Holliday, "The Role of Western Technology," p. 58.

59. For a discussion of this debate, see L. Dienes, "Investment Priorities in Soviet Regions," *Annals of the Association of American Geographers* 62, no. 3 (March 1972): 437–57; and more recently, J. A. Dellenbrant, "The Role of Siberia in Soviet Regional Development Policy," in B. Chichlo, ed., *Siberia I: Siberian Questions; Economy, Ecology, Strategy* (Paris: Institut d'études slaves, 1985), pp. 57–71.

60. For an example of the pro-Siberian position, see A. G. Granberg, "Siberia in the National Economy," *Ekonomika i organizatsiia promyshlennogo proizvoidstva*, no. 4 (1980); 84–106. Translated in *Soviet Review* 22, no. 2 (February 1981): 44–67.

61. There is a vast Russian-language literature on this; for a review of the literature and the implications of the STR, see Hoffman and Laird, *"The Scientific-Technical Revolution" and Soviet Foreign Policy.*

62. Quoted from B. Rumer, "Soviet Investment Policy: Unresolved Problems," *Problems of Communism* 31, no. 5 (1982): 54–55.

63. See N. A. Alisov, "Spatial Aspects of the New Soviet Strategy of Intensification of Industrial Production," *Vestnik moskovskogo universiteta, geografiia*, no. 6 (1978): 23–29. Translated in *Soviet Geography: Review and Translation* 20, no. 1 (January 1979): 1–6.

64. Rumer, "Soviet Investment Policy," p. 59.

65. For a detailed analysis of investment in the eastern regions and an evaluation of Granberg's pro-Siberian position, see L. Dienes, "The Development of Siberian Regions: Economic Profiles, Income Flows and Strategies of Growth," *Soviet Geography: Review and Translation* 23, no. 4 (April 1982): 205–44.

66. See A. G. Aganbegian and M. K. Bandman, "Territorial Production Complexes as Integrated Systems," *Geoforum* 15, no. 15 (1984): 25–32; and M. K. Bandman, *Territorial'no proizvodstvennye kompleksy* [Territorial-production complexes] (Novosibirsk: Nauka, 1980).

67. Quoted in D. S. Kamerling, "The Role of Territorial Production Complexes in Soviet Economic Policy," in Congress of the United States, Joint Economic Committee, *Soviet Economy in the 1980s: Problems and Prospects* (Washington, D.C.: U.S. Government Printing Office, 1982), p. 254.

68. Ibid., p. 255.

69. Glavnoe Upravlenie Geodezii Kartografii pri Sovete Ministrov SSSR, *Atlas SSSR v Odinnadtsatoiy Piatiletke* [Atlas of the Eleventh Five-Year Plan] (Moscow: GUGK, 1982), pp. 8–9.

70. See, for example, B. P. Orlov et al. *Sibir' v edinom narodnokhoziaistvennom komplekse* [Siberia in the national economic complex] (Novosibirsk: Nauka, 1980); V. P. Mozhin, *Ekonomicheskoe razvitie sibiri i dal'nego vostoka* [The economic development of Siberia and the Far East] (Moscow: Mysl', 1980); and A. D. Danilov et al., *Ekonomicheskaia geografiia SSSR* [Economic geography of the USSR] (Moscow: Vyshaia Shkola, 1983).

71. Congress of the United States, Office of Technology Assessment, *Technology and Soviet Energy Availability* (Washington, D.C.: U.S. Government Printing Office, 1982), p. 357.

72. A. A. Meyerhoff, "Soviet Petroleum, History, Technology, Geology, Reserves, Potential and Policy," in Jensen et al., *Soviet Natural Resources*, pp. 306–62; and D. Wilson, *Soviet Oil and Gas to 1990*.

73. R. W. Campbell, *Soviet Energy Technologies Planning, Policy, Research and Development* (Bloomington: Indiana University Press, 1980).

74. Iu. Perikin, "Tyumen Needs Special Oil, Gas Machinery," *Pravda* (November 14, 1979): 2. Translated in *Current Digest of the Soviet Press* 32, no. 46 (1980): 11.

75. Wilson, *Soviet Oil and Gas to 1990*, pp. 93–101.

76. Campbell, *Soviet Energy Technologies*, p. 223.

77. For an excellent analysis of the pipeline issues, see J. P. Stern, "Specters and Pipe Dreams," *Foreign Policy*, no. 48 (Fall 1982): 21–36. See also T. Gustafson, *Soviet Negotiating Strategy: The East-West Gas Pipeline Deal, 1980–1984* (Santa Monica, Calif.: Rand Corporation, 1985).

78. J. B. Hannigan and C. H. McMillan, *The Soviet–West European Energy Relationship: Implications of the Shift from Oil to Gas*, East-West Commercial Relations Series, Report no. 20 (Ottawa: Institute of Soviet and East European Studies, Carleton University, 1983), pp. 76–77; "Komatsu Clinches Big Soviet Deal," *Far Eastern Economic Review* 119, no. 13 (1983): 10.

79. *Ekonomicheskaia gazeta*, no. 40 (1983): 2.

80. J. Bougher, "1979–82: The United States Uses Trade to Penalize Soviet Aggression and Seeks to Reorder Western Policy," in *Soviet Economy in the 1980s: Problems and Prospects*, pp. 419–54.

81. A. Stent, "Economic Strategy," in E. Moreton and G. Segal, eds., *Soviet Strategy Toward Western Europe* (London: George Allen and Unwin, 1984), pp. 204–38; and J. Guillaume, "A European View of East-West Trade in the 1980s," in *Economic Relations with the USSR* (Lexington, Mass.: Lexington Books, 1982), pp. 135–52.

82. B. Rumer and S. Sternheimer, "The Soviet Economy: Going to Siberia?" *Harvard Business Review*, no. 1 (January–February 1982): 30–32.

83. J. Barclay, "U.S.S.R.: The Role of Compensation Agreements in Trade with the West," in Congress of the United States, Joint Economic Committee, *Soviet Economy*

in a Time of Change (Washington, D.C.: U.S. Government Printing Office, 1979), pp. 480–81.

84. T. Shabad, "News Notes," *Soviet Geography: Review and Translation* 2, no. 5 (May 1981): 346–47.

85. Ibid.

86. Sobeslavsky and Beazley, *The Transfer of Technology to Socialist Countries,* p. 138.

87. T. Tishina, "Siberia's Export Base," *Foreign Trade,* no. 2 (February 1977): 38–43.

88. Quoted from Soviet source in K. Braden, "The Role of Imported Technology in the Export Potential of Soviet Forest Products," in Jensen et al., *Soviet Natural Resources,* p. 445.

89. Ibid., p. 463; and V. N. Sushkov, "Trade and Economic Cooperation with Capitalist Countries in the Construction of Large Industrial Projects in the USSR," *Foreign Trade,* no. 2 (February 1977): 2.

90. A. G. Aganbegian, "Towards an Integrated Approach to Research into the Development of Siberia's Productive Forces," in *Regional Studies for Planning and Projecting: The Siberian Experience* (The Hague: Mouton Publishers, 1981), p. 246.

91. From Adeichev, *Geografia proizvoditel'nykh sil SSSR,* p. 170; Barclay, "U.S.S.R.: The Role of Compensation Agreements," pp. 468, 476; and T. Shabad, "News Notes," *Soviet Geography: Review and Translation* 20, no. 2 (February 1979): 124.

92. E. B. Miller, "The Trans-Siberian Landbridge, A New Trade Route Between Japan and Europe: Issues and Prospects," *Soviet Geography: Review and Translation* 19, no. 4 (April 1978): 233.

93. T. Shabad, "News Notes," *Soviet Geography: Review and Translation* 19, no. 2 (January 1978): 67, and 20, no. 2 (February 1979): 124.

94. Details obtained from Sobeslavsky and Beazley, *The Transfer of Technology to Socialist Countries,* p. 140; and T. Shabad, "News Notes," *Soviet Geography: Review and Translation* 24, no. 1 (January 1983): 77.

95. Tishina, "Siberia's Export Base," p. 43.

96. D. Drach, *Tapping the Energy Wealth of Siberia: A Case Study of the Kansk-Achinsk Coal Basin,* Discussion Paper no. 51 (Syracuse, N.Y.: Department of Geography, Syracuse University, 1978).

97. For a discussion of the problems and prospects of Far Eastern Development, see R. N. North, "The Soviet Far East: New Centre of Attention in the U.S.S.R.," *Pacific Affairs* 51, no. 2 (Summer 1978): 195–215.

98. Recent examples include R. L. Edmonds, "Siberian Resource Development and the Japanese Economy: The Japanese Perspective," in Jensen et al., *Soviet Natural Resources,* pp. 214–31; K. Ogawa, "The USSR's External Economic Relations with Japan," from *Sekai Shuho* (February 15 and 22, 1983): 30–39 and 30–40. Translated in *Japanese Economic Studies* 12, no. 1 (1983): 26–53; and N. Nobuhara and N. Akao, "The Politics of Siberian Development," in *Japan's Economic Security, Resources as a Factor in Foreign Policy* (Aldershot, Hampshire: Gower, 1983), pp. 197–215.

99. Apart from the projects outlined here, many other projects, such as pulp and paper plants, steel mills, oil and gas extraction, and transportation projects, were discussed but never came to fruition.

100. Edmonds, "Soviet Resource Development," p. 216.

101. V. Spandarian, "The Development of Soviet-Japanese Economic Relations," *Foreign Trade* no. 4 (1975): 26.

102. S. B. Chung, "Japanese-Soviet Economic Relations," in *Le Courier des pays l'est,* no. 183 (1975). Translated in *Soviet and East European Foreign Trade* 11 (1976): 17.

103. Details from Braden, "The Role of Imported Technology," p. 455; Edmonds, "Siberian Resource Development," p. 217; and Nobuhara and Akao, "The Politics of Siberian Development," p. 199.

104. Nobuhara and Akao, "The Politics of Siberian Development," p. 200.

105. For a detailed analysis of these projects, see P. Egyed, *Western Participation in the Development of Siberian Energy Resources: Case Studies,* East-West Commercial Relations Series, Report no. 22 (Ottawa: Institute of Soviet and East European Studies, Carleton University, 1983).

106. L. Dienes and T. Shabad, *The Soviet Energy System* (Washington, D.C.: V. H. Winston and Sons, 1976), p. 61.

107. Details from Gorst, "Big Boost," p. 146; and Egyed, *Western Participation,* pp. 51–56.

108. Egyed, *Western Participation,* p. 55.

109. *The Economist* (June 12, 1982).

110. For a discussion of this complex, see V. Borovikov and O. Krivoruchko, "Formirovanie territorial'no-proizvodstvennykh kompleksov v zone BAM (na primere Iuzhno-Iakutskogo TPK)" [Formation of the TPCs in the BAM zone, the example of the South Iakutian TPC], *Voprosy ekonomiki,* no. 2 (February 1984): 54–60.

111. Spandarian, "The Development of Soviet-Japanese Economic Relations," p. 27.

112. Slavinsky, "Siberia and the Soviet Far East," pp. 326–27.

113. Miller, "The Trans-Siberian Landbridge," p. 237.

114. Mozhin, *Ekonomicheskoe razvitie,* p. 250; and Slavinsky, "Siberia and the Soviet Far East," p. 328.

115. Edmonds, "Soviet Resource Development," p. 225.

116. Ibid., p. 218.

117. V. Klochek, "Vneshniaia torgovlia SSSR v 1983 gody" [Foreign trade in the USSR in 1983], *Vneshniaia torgovlia,* no. 5 (1984): 12.

118. Such a study is now being conducted by the author.

Linkage with Europe

Controversies about the political and economic usefulness of trade with the East have for many years marred European–U.S. relations. The West European nations, particularly the Federal Republic of Germany, have always adopted a more positive attitude toward East-West trade than the United States. (There is, of course, a solid foundation for this attitude: European nations have traditional links (Mannesmann AG of Germany sold pipes to the Russians even before 1900, when the Caspian Sea oil reserves were developed), proximity to Eastern Europe, and export-oriented foreign trade policies.)

The United States political stance on this trade (represented, for instance, by the new Soviet–West European natural gas project) is, of course, a reflection of U.S.-Soviet relations after World War II. In the United States, trade relations with the Soviet Union (and other CMEA countries) have essentially been regarded as a means to achieve political ends. This view was based on the assumption that the denial of trade could induce the Soviet Union to decide for a policy of good conduct outside and even inside its sphere of influence. Beginning in the 1960s, détente in East-West relations led to the definition by Nixon and Kissinger of a new concept of the linkage between trade and foreign policy. According to the new approach, trade with the East, in particular the USSR, was based on a strategy of incentives for restraint: rewarding the East with a given set of trade arrangements for a given conduct under given circumstances. Designed for more stability in U.S.-Soviet relations, this policy called for an expansion of trade, including energy trade.

During the mid-1970s, political developments such as Soviet activity in Vietnam and Angola prompted U.S. congressional action (the Jackson-Vanick amendment, the Stevenson amendment, and the Church amendment) demanding a more rigid application of the linkage concept by punishing Soviet aggression. In the United States, trade sanctions were considered a tool that could and should be used to influence Soviet conduct.[1]

The West European nations, on the other hand, did not wish to endanger the progress achieved by détente during the 1970s and conceived their trading policies more strongly to suit their own interests, arguing that trade would have a stabilizing effect on overall East-West relations. The trade restrictions imposed by President Carter after the Soviet intervention in Afghanistan in late December 1979 and by President Reagan after the declaration of martial law in Poland were rejected by the countries of Western Europe; they viewed these restrictions as a declaration of economic warfare with an uncertain outcome.

This divergence of opinion on trade with the USSR climaxed between 1980 and 1982, when the Soviet–West European natural gas project was the bone of contention. The economic sanctions against the Soviet Union decided by President Reagan in December 1981 and June 1982 brought the dispute between the West European nations (particularly France and the Federal Republic of Germany) and the United States to a head. The countries of Western Europe took particular exception to what they saw as extraterritorial application of U.S. legislation and refused to accept any encroachment on their sovereignty. They also believed that the U.S. action would threaten industrial and technological cooperation between the United States and Western Europe. In the second half of 1982, the controversy culminated in U.S. trade embargoes, although gas purchase contracts and contracts for the sale of equipment had already been signed.[2]

It would, of course, go beyond the scope of this chapter to review and to analyze the principles underlying the embargo policy, the Coordinating Committee (COCOM) negotiations, the military and strategic implications of technology transfer, and the financial aspects of East-West relations, including the foreign exchange issue and credit arrangements. Here we will address only trade relations between the USSR and Western Europe, particularly from a West German viewpoint, and discuss the role played by West Siberia in East-West cooperation. The huge natural gas reserves in West Siberia will remain a vital element for the expansion of trade between the USSR and Western Europe.

This chapter will also discuss the importance of the new natural gas project for the West European nations. The United States had objected to the deal, maintaining that the project would create an unacceptable dependence by Western Europe on the USSR, increase Soviet foreign exchange income beyond reasonable limits, and give the Soviet Union an opportunity to obtain strategic goods and high-technology equipment, either directly or indirectly through the income earned. In this chapter we will therefore examine these arguments (which were also studied for many years by international organizations, such as the International Energy Agency [IEA] and the European Economic Community [EEC]. Finally, this chapter will set the political and strategic objections against the background of the facts of the project.

THE DEVELOPMENT OF
SOVIET TRADE WITH THE WEST

Soviet foreign trade with the industrialized nations of the West has grown at a rapid pace since the early 1970s. From 1970 to 1983, Soviet exports to the West increased from $2.4 billion to $26.3 billion, and imports rose from $2.8 billion to $25.2 billion. Since trade between the USSR and its other trading partners (CMEA countries, developing countries) has not developed at the same rate, the importance of the West for Soviet foreign trade has risen. Its share in overall Soviet imports rose from 24 percent in 1970 to 35 percent in 1980 and ran at 32 percent in 1983; imports by the West accounted for 19 percent of all Soviet exports in 1970, 29 percent in 1983 (see Table 5.1).

Apart from the political climate, crucial elements of Soviet trade with the West include trading partners and the goods traded. If we are to understand this trade fully, we must also consider how it developed over time.

In the first half of the 1970s the ground was prepared for more trade between the USSR and the West. Soviet exports to the West rose from $2.4 to $8.5 billion, and imports from the West jumped from $2.8 to $13.5 billion. The Soviet balance of trade with the West thus ran up a deficit of $5 billion in 1975. In the latter

TABLE 5.1
Soviet Foreign Trade with the West (in billions of U.S. dollars)

| | | | | PERCENTAGE OF TOTAL FOREIGN TRADE | |
	Export	Import	Balance	Export	Import
1970	2.4	2.8	−0.4	19%	24%
1971	2.8	2.9	−0.1	20	23
1972	3.0	4.2	−1.1	20	26
1973	5.0	6.2	−1.2	24	30
1974	8.3	8.1	+0.2	30	33
1975	8.5	13.5	−5.0	25	36
1976	10.4	14.4	−4.0	28	38
1977	12.0	13.5	−1.5	27	33
1978	12.8	16.1	−3.3	25	32
1979	19.1	20.2	−1.1	29	35
1980	24.3	24.1	+0.2	32	35
1981	23.9	25.1	−1.2	30	34
1982	25.9	26.1	−0.2	30	33
1983	26.3	25.2	+1.1	29	32

SOURCES: Deutsche Bank, "Sowjetunion," Frankfurt, January 1983; Wharton Econometric Forecasting Associates, "UdSSR, Entwicklung des Aussenhandels mit westlichen Industrieländern 1981–1987."

TABLE 5.2
East-West Trade by OECD Countries

	EXPORTS TO EAST AS PERCENT OF GNP	SHARE OF TOTAL OECD EXPORTS TO EAST		SHARE OF EAST IN COUNTRY'S TOTAL EXPORTS	EXPORTS TO EAST AS PERCENT OF IMPORTS FROM EAST		
	1982	1979–80	1982	1982	1970–79	1980–81	1982
Finland	7.83	5.4	10.4	28.8	82	100	100
Austria	2.62	5.0	4.8	11.1	116	80	80
Iceland	2.30	0.2	0.2	8.4	69	67	59
Germany[a]	1.14	23.8	20.9	4.3	145	106	97
Belgium-Luxembourg	1.09	3.0	2.5	1.7	115	78	49
Greece	0.84	1.1	0.9	7.7	77	72	63
Sweden	0.84	3.5	2.3	3.0	87	77	52
Switzerland	0.80	2.9	2.2	3.1	141	70	71
Netherlands	0.72	3.2	2.8	1.5	85	55	30
Italy	0.71	7.6	6.8	3.3	82	52	47
Canada	0.71	2.7	5.7	3.0	315	736	1,156
New Zealand	0.60[b]	NA	NA	2.0[b]	NA	391	NA
Turkey	0.57	0.8	0.8	5.3	57	54	76
Australia	0.53	2.1	2.4	3.8	708	996	892
France	0.52	10.0	7.8	3.0	128	72	65
Denmark	0.45	1.1	0.7	1.6	56	61	34
Japan	0.42	8.7	12.4	3.2	140	173	241
Norway	0.39	0.9	0.6	1.2	77	69	37
Portugal	0.39	0.2	0.2	2.1	50	35	62
Ireland	0.38	0.1	0.2	0.8	30	72	49
United Kingdom	0.31	5.7	4.2	1.6	70	101	76
Spain	0.25	1.1	1.2	2.1	78	83	51
United States	0.12	10.7	10.0	1.7	285	275	337
OECD	0.47	100.0	100.0	3.1	118	99	91

SOURCE: Stephen Marris, "East-West Economic Relations," OECD Observer, May 1984.
[a]Excluding intra-German trade.   [b]1981.

part of the 1970s, this deficit was gradually reduced: imports rose only some 80 percent between 1975 and 1980, and exports almost trebled. In 1980, a small surplus was even recorded.[3]

Although the political climate and overall economic conditions determining East-West trading have since deteriorated, Soviet trade with the West has continued to grow.[4] However, the importance of East-West trade relationships is often overrated because of the political implications and the effect of technology transfer on the Soviet Union.

In terms of overall exports by members of the Organization for Economic Cooperation and Development (OECD)—$110 billion to OPEC countries, $180 billion to developing countries—exports to the East are almost marginal: a mere 0.5 percent of the sum total of the gross national products of all OECD members, but of course this percentage varies considerably from country to country (see Table 5.2). The significance of trade with the East for the economy of the Federal Republic of Germany remains limited. For a number of years, some 5 percent of all West German foreign trade has been with the East.

A number of critics suggest that the importation of high-technology products by the USSR has often been overestimated. Soviet trade with the West has not reached any proportion that would indicate dependence on supplies from the West. In spite of the high growth rates, Soviet exports to the industrialized nations of the West (as well as Soviet imports from the West) still equal only approximately 2 percent of the gross national product of the Soviet Union.

In the early 1970s, trade between the USSR and the West was essentially an exchange of Soviet energy and raw materials for capital goods from the West. However, as a result of growing grain imports, now largely secured by long-term contracts, patterns of trade have changed fundamentally. The Soviet Union now imports $12–$13 billion worth of agricultural products (grain, fodder, meat), half from developing countries. Machinery and similar products are approximately one quarter of total imports; products of the iron and steel industry (mainly steel tubes for pipeline construction) are in third place.

Energy is still the primary export. Crude oil, oil products, and natural gas (exported mainly to Western Europe) were as much as 80 percent of overall 1983 exports—up from 25 percent in the early 1970s. The Soviet Union has not been able to make any major sales of machinery and capital goods to the West; they represent less than 5 percent of all exports. The importance of Soviet energy exports is reflected by the large surpluses earned by the USSR in bilateral trade with the major buyers of Soviet energy.[5]

In 1983, the Federal Republic of Germany was the largest trading partner of the Soviet Union, followed by Finland and Italy. Even so, West German exports to the USSR, totaling $3.86 billion, were only 2.6 percent of the country's total exports, and imports from the Soviet Union ($3.73 billion) were only 3 percent of all West German imports. The exchange of machinery, iron and steel products,

TABLE 5.3
West German–Soviet Trade by Goods

	IMPORTS FROM THE USSR		EXPORTS TO THE USSR	
	1982	1983	1982	1983
Total (million DM)	11,358	11,864	9,395	11,245
Foodstuff	0.7%	0.6%	8.7%	5.1%
Raw materials	19.9	23.0	0.5	0.7
Semifinished products	71.6	69.9	4.0	3.0
Finished products	6.6	5.4	86.6	91.0

SOURCE: West German Ministry of Economics, "Der deutsche Osthandel 1983," May 1984.

and chemical products on the one hand for crude oil, oil products, and natural gas on the other is also typical of bilateral trade between the Federal Republic of Germany and the Soviet Union (see Table 5.3).[6]

ENERGY TRADE BETWEEN THE USSR AND WESTERN EUROPE

Following two major oil crises in the 1970s, energy markets in the OECD countries passed through a period of fundamental change, and today total OECD energy consumption is still only slightly higher than in 1973.

West European primary energy demand is approximately 16 percent of the total world demand. It is covered by oil (47 percent), coal (23 percent), gas (15 percent), nuclear power and other sources of energy (15 percent). Unlike the United States, which imports only 13 percent of its energy, the West European nations, with inadequate domestic reserves, are highly dependent on imported energy. In 1983, imports supplied well over 40 percent of all energy consumed; in 1973 it was more than 60 percent.

In response to the OPEC policy of the 1970s, the West European nations stepped up exploration and production of their domestic energy reserves (oil, natural gas, and coal) and developed a consistent policy of diversifying their energy imports. In 1973, 90 percent of the oil used in Western Europe was still imported from the Middle East, and only 3 percent came from West European fields. Ten years later, in 1983, the share of OPEC oil had dropped to 52 percent, and West European production had risen to some 30 percent (see Table 5.4).

During the same period European Economic Community (EEC) crude imports from the Soviet Union rose from 14 million metric tons to 29 million met-

TABLE 5.4
Sources of West European Primary Energy Supplies

	1983			1973		
	Oil	Coal	Natural gas	Oil	Coal	Natural gas
Indigenous	30%	82%	80%	3%	88%	97%
OPEC	52	—	7	90	—	2
Eastern Europe	9	3	13	3	7	1
OECD	—	10	—	—	4	—
Others	9	5	—	4	1	—

SOURCE: Various statistics, OECD, International Energy Agency.

ric tons, giving the USSR a share of 7 percent in overall EEC oil supplies. In terms of overall EEC primary energy consumption, the share of Soviet oil is around 3 percent. In the Federal Republic of Germany, Soviet oil accounts for 6.7 percent of all crude-oil imports, making it sixth among the 23 nations from which West Germany receives crude.

Soviet natural gas increased its share in West European supplies from 1 percent in 1973 to 12.5 percent in 1983—from approximately 2 billion cubic meters to about 29 billion.

THE ENERGY INDUSTRY OF THE SOVIET UNION

The Soviet energy industry, especially the crucial development of Siberian resources, is discussed elsewhere. This chapter will briefly review Soviet oil and coal production and electricity generation, but will analyze somewhat more comprehensively the Soviet gas industry, including the huge Siberian production potential, and Soviet cooperation with the gas industries in Western Europe.

The energy industry is increasingly becoming a key sector of the Soviet economy, both in domestic production targets and potential exports to the West. The USSR's energy program, with overall objectives for the 1980s and the 1990s, foresees adequate domestic energy supplies through a sustained high level of oil production, the increased use of Siberian gas (implying a considerable expansion of output and transmission facilities), and the construction of new nuclear power stations. The Soviet Union also plans considerable investments in coal mining.

The energy program calls for large investment in the energy industry and in the industries that supply equipment for energy projects, for increasing man-

TABLE 5.5
Soviet Primary Energy Consumption, 1973–1990

	1973	1975	1980	1985[a]	1990[a]
Million Metric Tons of Coal Equivalent					
Oil	465	526	638	675	751
Gas	287	335	452	650	740
Coal	409	432	437	430	450
Nuclear energy	4	8	29	52	115
Other primary electricity	45	46	66	70	90
Other	55	55	42	40	28
Total	1,265	1,402	1,664	1,917	2,174
Million Metric Tons[b]					
Oil	325	368	446	472	525
Gas	241	282	381	547	622
Coal	596	625	634	623	649
Nuclear energy[c]	2	3	12	21	47
Breakdown of Energy Sources by Percent					
Oil	36.8%	37.5%	38.3%	35.2%	34.5%
Gas	22.7	23.9	27.2	33.9	34.7
Coal	32.3	30.8	26.3	22.4	20.7
Nuclear energy	0.3	0.6	1.7	2.7	5.3
Other primary electricity	3.6	3.3	3.9	3.7	4.1
Other	4.3	3.9	2.6	2.1	1.3
Total	100	100	100	100	100

SOURCES: Soviet statistical yearbooks; estimates from German Institute for Economic Research, June 1984.

[a] Estimate, assuming an average annual gross national product growth of 3.5 percent and an energy ratio of 0.8 between 1981 and 1985 and 0.7 between 1986 and 1990.

[b] Gas expressed in billion cubic meters and nuclear energy in 1,000 megawatts.

[c] Annual average generating capacity.

power for energy production and transportation, and for improved management training in the various sectors of the energy industry.[7]

Soviet energy consumption totaled some 1.7 billion tons of coal equivalent in 1983, and is estimated to rise to some 1.92 billion by 1985 (see Table 5.5).[8] In 1983, the primary energy demand was covered by oil (36 percent), gas (31 percent), coal (27 percent), nuclear power (2 percent), and other sources (the remaining 4 percent). Current plans for 1985 give oil a share of 39 percent, gas 32 percent, coal 21 percent, nuclear power 6 percent, and others 2 percent.

Forecasts of future oil development, and hence oil exports to the West, are extremely difficult. Although oil output rose from 491 million metric tons in

1975 to 616 million in 1983, and although the Soviet Union is still the world's largest oil-producing nation, there is information that oil production is no longer growing. Thus it seems doubtful that the Soviet Union will be able to achieve the 1985 production target of 630 million metric tons (nearly two-thirds from West Siberia) stipulated in the current five-year plan (see Table 5.6). The USSR therefore gives priority to gas, coal, and nuclear power over oil on the domestic market. This will allow the country to expand oil exports to the West, and in so doing to compensate for losses in foreign exchange income through declining world oil prices.

Soviet coal production has practically stagnated for ten years. The output of 645 million metric tons in 1983 is far from the 1985 target of 775 million. Power generation and nuclear-generating capacities are also unlikely to reach the levels fixed in the 1981–1985 five-year plan, primarily because of inadequate coal supplies and delays in construction of nuclear power stations.

It is too early to say whether the objectives of the new energy program will be incorporated in the 1986–1990 five-year plan and will thus become recognized targets of the Soviet economy. The progress achieved by the energy indus-

TABLE 5.6
Soviet Energy Consumption and Production

Primary Energy Consumption by Source		
	1983 (actual)	1985 (planned)
Natural gas	31%	32%
Oil	36	39
Coal	27	21
Nuclear energy	2	6
Others	4	2
Energy Production		
	1983 (actual)	1985 (planned)
Natural gas (billion cubic meters)	535	630
West Siberia		357
Oil (million metric tons)	616	630
West Siberia		399
Coal (million metric tons)	645	775
Nuclear energy (billion kilowatt hours)	110	130

SOURCE: Various Soviet statistics.

try in West Siberia is nonetheless remarkable. The region's contribution to overall Soviet oil and gas supplies had grown from less than 10 percent in 1970 to more than 50 percent by 1983. It seems certain Siberian energy production will continue to grow in importance during the years to come.

The Natural Gas Industry of the USSR

The natural gas industry of the USSR has witnessed record growth rates during the last fifteen years. From 1970 to 1983, gas reserves more than trebled, gas production rose from 230 to 635 million tons of coal equivalent (tce), and consumption increased from 226 to 567 million tce. Natural gas exports were stepped up during the same period from 4 to 70 million tce. Some 54 percent of this gas is delivered to CMEA nations, 46 percent to Western Europe (see Table 5.7).

The gas industry of the USSR has thus met the standards set by the current five-year plan. Further increases in gas production are scheduled for 1984 and 1985, raising output to an annual 630 billion cubic meters by the end of 1985. This amazing growth represents an annual increase of as much as 200 billion cubic meters during the 1981–1985 period alone.

The great success of the Soviet gas industry is essentially attributable to a consistent policy of exploration and development. Between 1979 and 1983, the Soviet Union improved its gas resource base by more than 55 percent. Reserves of almost 40,000 billion cubic meters give the country by far the largest gas resources in the world—44 percent of the world's total reserves (Iran has 15 percent, the United States 6 percent, and the Netherlands 2 percent). Additional resources not yet discovered are estimated at 60,000 billion cubic meters. With such a huge potential, it is practically impossible for the nation to deplete its reserves.

Until the early 1970s, Soviet natural gas was almost exclusively produced in the European part of the USSR in the Ukraine, in the northern part of the Caucasus Mountains, and in the Volga region. West Siberia became the country's most important gas-producing area in the late 1970s. Like the nation's oil resources, most of the Soviet natural gas reserves—approximately 80 percent—are located in the West and East Siberia. A further increase in gas production, provided for by the new energy program but not yet quantifiable by outside observers, would necessitate new exploration and development activities in Siberia. It seems likely that future exploration will increasingly integrate medium-sized and small fields in the Siberian gas-supply network.

During the period covered by the next five-year plan (1986–1990), targets will probably include an increase in output from the huge Urengoi field, and also development of the Yamburg field and other reserves in the north Tyumen region.

TABLE 5.7
The Soviet Natural Gas Industry

	1970	1975	1980	1981	1982	1983
Natural gas reserves (billion cubic feet)	12,000	22,650	26,050	32,850	35,110	39,640
Natural gas production (million tce)	230	335	505	540	600	635
Natural gas consumption (million tce)	226	329	450	483	520	567
Natural gas exports (million tce)						
CMEA countries	4	23	64	68	69	70
	3	13	35	35	37	38
Western Europe (including Yugoslavia)	1	10	29	33	32	32

FIGURE 5.1
Natural Gas Transmission Systems in the U.S.S.R.

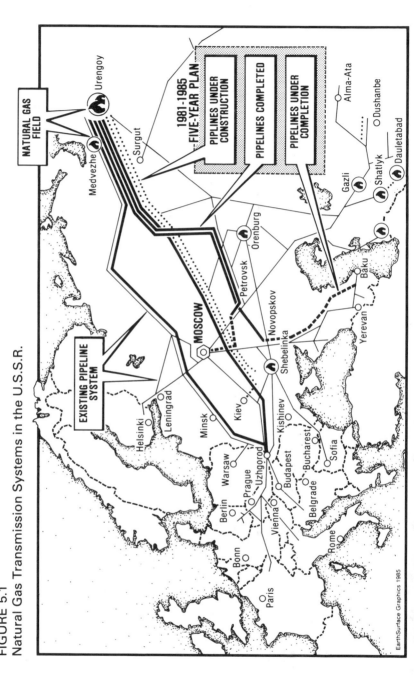

NATURAL GAS
FIELD

EXISTING PIPELINE
SYSTEM

1981-1985
FIVE-YEAR PLAN

PIPLINES UNDER
CONSTRUCTION

PIPELINES COMPLETED

PIPELINES UNDER
COMPLETION

Urengoy
Medvezhe
Surgut
Orenburg
Petrovsk
MOSCOW
Novopskov
Shebelinka
Yerevan
Baku
Gazli
Shatlyk
Dauletabad
Alma-Ata
Dushanbe
Helsinki
Leningrad
Minsk
Kiev
Kishinev
Bucharest
Sofia
Uzhgorod
Budapest
Warsaw
Belgrade
Prague
Berlin
Vienna
Bonn
Rome
Paris

EarthSurface Graphics 1985

The logistical and environmental problems involved in this major Siberian effort will be enormous.

Regarding gas transportation, the current five-year plan calls for the construction of six huge natural gas transmission lines from West Siberia to the west for domestic supplies and for export to Western Europe. According to official Soviet data, four of the six pipelines have already been completed; the Urengoi-Grjasovec line (2,438 kilometers), the Urengoi-Makhachkala line (2,730 kilometers), the Urengoi-Novopskov line (3,345 kilometers), and the Urengoi-Uzhgorod line (4,665 kilometers). The remaining Urengoi–Center 1 and Urengoi–Center 2 lines were commissioned in 1984–1985. *Pravda* reported on July 1, 1984, that the last section of the 3,020-kilometer Urengoi–Center 1 line had been tested and was ready to go into operation, eighteen months ahead of schedule. The Urengoi-Uzhgorod line has been in operation since mid-1983; apart from gas for domestic supplies, this line will carry the gas recently purchased by a number of West European gas utilities.

The total length of the Soviet pipeline system was reported to be 166,000 kilometers at the end of 1984 (see Figure 5.1).[9]

EUROPEAN-SOVIET COOPERATION
IN THE NATURAL GAS SECTOR

The Soviet-European cooperation in the natural gas sector, which has existed for some fifteen years, breaks down into two main phases: (1) deliveries under old contracts between 1968 and 1983; and (2) deliveries (beginning in 1984) called for by the new Soviet–West European natural gas project.

Contracts Between 1968 and 1983

The rapid expansion of natural gas use in Western Europe began in the late 1960s and the early 1970s, when the huge Dutch natural gas reserves were developed. After the first oil crisis in 1973–1974 and the policies calling for the substitution of gas for oil and the diversification of energy imports, natural gas strengthened its position on the West European energy market and increased its market share from 6 percent in 1970 to 15 percent in 1983.

Austria was the first West European country to import gas from the Soviet Union; deliveries to ÖMV AG began in 1968. In West Germany, Ruhrgas AG has been receiving gas from the USSR since October 1973, under two contracts signed in the early 1970s. Soviet exports to Italy (SNAM S.p.A.) and to Finland began in 1974, and Gaz de France has been importing gas from the USSR since early 1976.

As more Soviet gas was imported in the mid-1970s, major West European

TABLE 5.8
Soviet Natural Gas in Western Europe[a]

	1968	1970	1973	1975	1979	1980	1983
Primary energy consumption (million tce)	1,303	1,471	1,683	1,593	1,807	1,746	1,670
Natural gas consumption (million tce)	51	93	176	214	261	258	253
Natural gas share in primary energy consumption	4.0%	6.0%	10.0%	13.0%	14.0%	15.0%	15.0%
Soviet natural gas supplies (million tce)	0.2	1.1	2.3	9.2	25.7	28.4	31.5
Share of Soviet natural gas in total natural gas supplies	0.4%	1.0%	1.0%	4.0%	10.0%	11.0%	12.0%
Share of Soviet natural gas in total primary energy supplies	—	0.1%	0.1%	0.6%	1.4%	1.6%	1.9%

[a] Including Yugoslavia.

fields, especially reserves in the British and Norwegian sectors of the North Sea, were developed. West European gas has largely remained an indigenous source of energy; local fields supply currently some 80 percent of all gas used. The share of Soviet gas in overall West European supplies rose from 1 percent between 1970 and 1973 to some 12 percent in 1983. The remainder comes from Algeria (6.7 percent) and Libya (0.4 percent); see Table 5.8.

The New Project

The first meetings to discuss the new Soviet–West European natural gas project—a new pipeline from West Siberia to Western Europe—were held at a time when relations between the two superpowers were beginning to deteriorate. Before these negotiations began, the Soviets had discussed among themselves at length whether priority should be given to the exploration and development of oil reserves and increased oil exports, or to the development of the huge natural gas reserves of West Siberia. The final decision was for more gas, both for domestic supplies and for export. The 1981–1985 five-year plan, prepared in 1980, targeted an increase in natural gas output of approximately 200 billion cubic meters.

The talks about the Urengoi–Western Europe project were conducted at a time when two other major West European natural gas projects had failed. One project was the Iranian deal struck by Ruhrgas AG, Gaz de France, ÖMV AG, and National Iranian Gas Company (NIGC) in Tehran on November 30, 1975. The arrangements agreed provided for the annual export of 11 billion cubic meters of Iranian gas to Western Europe. Deliveries (by way of transit through the USSR) were scheduled to commence in early 1981 and to continue until the year 2003. The contracts for this project were canceled by the new Iranian regime in 1979. The second project that had failed was the exportation of Algerian natural gas to the Federal Republic of Germany and the Netherlands. The contract signed by Sonatrach and West German and Dutch gas companies in mid-1977 was terminated by the Algerians in 1980. Notwithstanding the agreements concluded, Sonatrach had expressed that they would be unable to raise the funds required for the liquefied natural gas facilities to be built in Algeria and offered the delivery of the gas through a pipeline from Algeria through Tunisia, the Mediterranean and Italy to West Germany and the Netherlands at prices that were unacceptable and hence rejected by the West European utilities concerned.

The original Soviet plans for the annual export of 40 billion cubic meters of West Siberian gas to Western Europe have not materialized. Contracts have been negotiated with West European gas companies for approximately 27 to 28 billion cubic meters—70 percent of the original goal. The following annual deliveries have been agreed: 11.2 billion cubic meters for the Federal Republic of Germany (including West Berlin) reduced to 8.75 billion; 8 billion for France; 6 billion for Italy; 1.5–2.5 billion for Austria; and 0.4 billion for Switzerland.

Deliveries of new gas to France began on January 1, 1984, and the first to Austria on July 1, 1984. Ruhrgas AG received the new Soviet gas destined for the West German market on October 1, 1984 (October 1, 1985 for West Berlin). The new exports to Italy started in October 1984; deliveries to Switzerland will not start until 1988. The agreed points of delivery are the Czechoslovakian borders with West Germany and Austria. The Soviets will thus be fully responsible—both in legal and in commercial terms—for the transportation of the gas through the USSR and Czechoslovakia.

The Soviet gas exports to Western Europe will increase slowly, reaching the plateau level of 57 billion total cubic meters in the late 1980s and the early 1990s.

U.S. CRITICISM OF THE SOVIET–WEST EUROPEAN NATURAL GAS PROJECT

Hardly any commercial project in modern industry has been the subject of such heated political and strategic debates as the Soviet–West European natural gas project during 1981 and 1982. These debates were preceded in the 1970s by the controversy between OPEC and the industrialized nations of the West. The grave consequences of this controversy for economic development and growth in the industrialized world are still felt today. On the world's energy market, the oil crisis initiated structural changes that in Western Europe led to a reorientation of energy policy and a re-evaluation of the role of natural gas.

Space is far from sufficient for presenting, let alone analyzing, the multiplicity of meetings and conferences held in Western Europe or in the United States between 1979 and 1984 to discuss the Soviet–West European natural gas project. The issue was on the agenda of three summits (in Ottawa, Versailles, and Williamsburg) and at the heart of practically all European-American conferences at all levels. The political, commercial, and academic worlds and, above all, the mass media had found a political issue that apparently never lost interest. After the Williamsburg summit in May 1983, U.S. opposition to the gas deal gradually moderated, but the press and the other media occasionally still voice criticism of the project.

U.S. criticism of the natural gas project focused on various issues, primarily energy (dependency, alternative energy supplies, economics), technology transfer, and foreign exchange. We will examine some of the main issues in detail.

Dependence on Energy Imports from the USSR

The new Soviet gas exports will increase the share of Soviet gas in overall West European gas supplies to some 19 percent by 1990, or 3 percent of overall West European energy supplies, up from 2 percent currently. In the Federal Re-

TABLE 5.9
West German Energy Imports from the USSR (in million metric tons coal equivalent)

	1970	1975	1980	1981	1982	1983
Natural gas	—	3.7	11.7	12.8	11.4	11.8
Crude oil	5.0	4.5	4.1	1.4	5.0	6.4
Oil products	3.3	6.1	5.5	5.6	7.0	8.9
Coal	—	0.2	0.2	—	—	0.1
Total	8.3	14.5	21.5	19.8	23.4	27.2
West German primary energy consumption	336.8	347.7	390.2	374.1	361.5	362
Share of Soviet natural gas in primary energy supplies	—	1.1%	3.0%	3.4%	3.2%	3.3%
Share of Soviet energy in primary energy supplies	2.5%	4.2%	5.5%	5.3%	6.5%	7.5%

SOURCE: Ministry of Economics, Bonn, 1984.

public of Germany, gas from the Soviet Union, now about 20 percent of all gas supplies, will increase its share to some 30 percent by 1990. In overall primary energy terms, Soviet gas currently represents 3 percent of all supplies and will contribute 5–6 percent in 1990 (see Table 5.9).

Considering these figures, it is by no means true to say that Soviet gas is vital for West European or West German primary energy supplies. Further, since it is the nature of this and any other natural gas project to forge close technical and economic ties between the seller and the buyer, no unilateral dependency will be created. The gas contracts do not give the Soviet Union a tool for pressuring Western Europe.

The issue of West European dependence on Soviet natural gas and the security of gas supplies were examined in a number of national and international studies. These investigations have shown that even a hypothetical interruption of natural gas deliveries, entailing considerable commercial risks for the Soviet exporter due to the contractual arrangements, would not result in a serious disruption of West European or West German gas supplies. This was, for instance, the conclusion of a study made by the International Energy Agency of Paris for the Williamsburg summit.[10] The Commission of the European Communities also examined West European gas supplies in summer 1982 and investigated several scenarios; for example, interruptions of 10 percent and 25 percent of gas supplies over a six-month winter period. The conclusions, presented in October 1982, included these points:

> Natural gas will continue to play an important role in meeting Community energy needs, in diversifying the Community's energy supplies and in helping to reduce the Community's dependence on oil.
>
> Very considerable efforts are in hand in the gas industry of the member states to assure the security of natural gas supplies. On the basis of information returned by the member states, the measures currently envisaged could deal with a major interruption in supplies (at least 25 percent during a period of six consecutive months) with a minimum of repercussions for the final consumer. The gas deficit would then be partially covered by supplementary supplies of oil. The Commission will continue to follow the evolution of the situation in consultation with member states.[11]

To cope with any such hypothetical interruption of service, the gas industry in Western Europe has several tools available, including:

1. Flexibility under all supply contracts.
2. An integrated and highly efficient natural gas transmission system.
3. Adequate storage facilities, which are being expanded.

4. Flexibility at the sales end of the market, through interruptible contracts with dual-fuel customers.

Potential alternatives to the natural gas project were examined in detail by the West European importers at the time the Soviet contracts were negotiated. They concluded that no available alternative could replace the Soviet project. They felt that natural gas from Algeria, West Africa, and the Arabian Gulf area (OPEC countries) would be no alternative to the Soviet project. Nor would natural gas from Canada be an alternative; the earliest date for initial imports would be the mid- or late 1990s. Furthermore, major quantities of gas from the Norwegian sector of the North Sea (Troll field) will not be offered for delivery to continental Western Europe until the mid-1990s. Gas companies from continental Europe, including Ruhrgas AG, will give priority to negotiations for the purchase of this gas.

Nuclear energy and coal were also considered. The use of nuclear energy will in any case be stepped up as far as economic and political restraints allow. Additional coal imports (for instance from the United States) are also called for in the energy programs of the West European nations, but are hardly likely to have any major impact in view of the restrictions imposed by the market potential and the need to protect domestic coal production.

The only real alternative to the Soviet natural gas project would have been additional oil imports. But that would have conflicted with the planned reduction of oil and the policy of energy diversification that has been pursued by politicians and industry in Western Europe for many years.

Economics

The economic viability of the new Soviet natural gas project has often been disputed by certain U.S. analysts. The West German gas industry has purchased the Soviet natural gas on the condition that it be able to resell the gas to consumers in the highly competitive West German market. This guarantee has been incorporated in the earlier contracts and in the contract for the new gas. The principle that the Soviet gas must be competitive in the marketplace applies whether oil prices rise or fall and irrespective of the actual transportation cost incurred by the Soviets.

Unlike the United States, where natural gas prices are regulated, prices charged to users in the Federal Republic of Germany do not require any government or other approval. The contracts agreed by V/O Sojuzgazexport and Ruhrgas AG are therefore strictly commercial arrangements, and the importer is exposed to the full risk of selling the gas to consumers at a price that is determined by competition on the energy market.

The structure of the West German energy market and the key role played by competition has, on a number of occasions, been presented by senior West German executives to a U.S. audience. Dr. Klaus Liesen, the chairman of the executive board of Ruhrgas AG, has, for example, commented on the issue on a number of occasions.

> The opinion was voiced that the price arrangements made for the Soviet project will result in a loss for the importer as oil prices are falling. Reasons put forward for this view are outlined in the *Wall Street Journal* editorial run on March 15. Fortunately, though, the author's understanding of the price conditions does not at all correspond with the real price conditions—and therefore the conclusions he draws are fortunately as wrong. To stop the spread of misconceptions, I state quite frankly and without reservation that the terms and conditions of the new Soviet natural gas sales contract allow the West German importer to sell the gas to end users economically at a competitive price, even when oil prices decline and irrespective of the cost incurred by the Soviets for producing and transporting the gas to the West German border.[12]

It is important to note in this context that the West German gas industry has not undertaken any financial commitments, such as credits, interest subsidies, or capital contributions, in connection with the importation of the Soviet gas. The credit arrangements made between the Soviets and West German banks were merely to finance the purchase of equipment by the Soviets in the West.

The natural gas contract has no legal or other ties with these credit facilities. On the contrary, the gas contracts are cost insurance freight contracts, and the West German importer will pay only for the gas actually received. Soviet natural gas is in no way subsidized by the West German taxpayer or gas user.

Export credit arrangements in Western Europe differ from country to country. In the Federal Republic of Germany, Hermes-Kreditversicherungs-AG, a private-sector company, has provided insurance coverage for exports since 1949; it was not specifically set up for exports to the USSR or to other countries in Eastern Europe. Insurance coverage of this type is a necessary tool in an export-oriented nation and available for orders received from any country in the world. Hermes insurance premiums remain the same whether the guarantee is for the sale of equipment to the East or to the West and whether interest rates are high or low.

In Italy, in the United Kingdom, and, above all, in France (COFACE, the state-owned insurance organization), subsidized export credit facilities of different types have for many years been a recognized part of foreign trade policy. Efforts have long been made in the OECD and at meetings between the United States and European governments to coordinate export credit guarantee facilities and to classify minimum interest rates.[13]

The Foreign Exchange Issue

The foreign exchange earnings of the Soviet Union from the new Soviet–West European natural gas project have also been a source of criticism. Naturally, the USSR will benefit from the project. If this were not the case, the Soviet Union would certainly not have gone ahead with the scheme. However, some misconceptions seem to exist about the amount of foreign exchange earned by the USSR. An annual foreign currency flow of $10–15 billion was mentioned in the United States. The foreign exchange income of the USSR for annual deliveries of some 28 billion cubic meters of gas—a level that will not be reached until around 1990—will, however, be considerably lower. Since Soviet oil exports will decline, the real-term foreign exchange income earned by the Soviet Union in 1990 from energy projects will therefore be below today's level. The value of the increased natural gas exports will not be as high as the income lost by the USSR as a result of the decrease in oil exports.[14]

The Technology Transfer Issue

No technology with strategic implications was exported to the USSR for the new Soviet–West European natural gas project. Since the mid-1970s, the USSR has already imported more than 280 turbine-driven compressor units, all based on U.S. technology. The equipment exported by countries of the West for the new Soviet–West European project (pipes, plant components, compressor units) is, in actual fact, standard technology that has already been developed in the Soviet Union.

The USSR does not depend on the technology of the West for its gas and oil operations (exploration, development, production, and transmission) in the harsh West Siberian permafrost environment, as current production levels in this region demonstrate. The temporary difficulties with respect to delivery of Western compressors and turbines to the Soviet Union, following the U.S. embargo, have not substantially delayed the construction of transmission pipelines from West Siberia to Western Europe.

The Soviets declared in a very early phase that they would begin gas deliveries as agreed in the contracts and replace Western products by their own equipment, if necessary. The early completion of the Urengoi-Uzhgorod pipeline—to which the Soviets gave, of course, considerable political priority—shows the quick response of the USSR to embargoes or other trade restrictions. Witness the case of the pipe embargo in 1962–63. George W. Ball, quoting Soviet Ambassador Anatoly Dobrynin from a conversation in 1964, concisely expressed the adaptability of the Soviet system under embargo conditions:

> I wish to thank you on behalf of my government. When you got the Germans to renege on their contracts you forced my country to do what we should have

done long before—build a mill to make wide-diameter pipe. Now we are independent of the world. So we are grateful to you.[15]

The Soviets have accelerated the development and production of their own 25-megawatt compressor stations and have already installed these units along their pipelines from Siberia to the west.

SUMMARY

It is, of course, natural that industry accepts the primacy of politics over business. In a speech delivered in Washington, Otto Wolff von Amerongen, chairman of the German East-West Trade Committee, characterized the interaction between politics and business in the pipeline project by saying:

Let me assure you that in the case of the pipeline gas deal, my government, my business colleagues, and I discussed the political and security implications long before the matter became an issue in the United States. The fact that our conclusions were different from those of some members of the present Administration of the United States does not make us less responsive or less responsible. In the case of a conflict between policy guidelines of our respective governments and legal orders, we owe our loyalty to our own government and obedience to our laws. We would not like to be drawn into conflicts between our governments. There can also be no choosing of allegiance according to the economic or political advantage of the day.[16]

The West European business community introduced certain aspects of the Soviet–West European natural gas project into the political and strategic discussions at a very early phase:

1. No dependence on energy imports from the Soviet Union.
2. No increase in the foreign exchange income of the USSR.
3. No transfer of sensitive technology.
4. Equitable contractual arrangements.

Together these are designed to make the energy supply, industrial, commercial, and economic implications of the project uncontroversial. The scope of traditional West European–Soviet cooperation is actually widened by a project that serves the economic best interests of both partners and forms a basis for long-range collaboration.

NOTES

1. Hanns-Dieter Jacobsen, *Die Ostwirtschaftspolitik der USA, Möglichkeiten und Grenzen einer "linkage"-Politik* (Ebenhausen: Stiftung Wissenschaft und Politik, 1980); see any of the works of Heinrich Machowski, for instance, *Soviet–West German Economic Relations, The Soviet Perspective* (Berlin: German Institute for Economic Research, 1984); and Werner Beitel, *Die Aussenwirtschaftsbeziehungen der Sowjet-Union unter dem Gesichtspunkt der Ost-West-Zusammenarbeit* (Ebenhausen: Stiftung Wissenschaft und Politik, 1980).

2. Hanns-Dieter Jacobsen, *Die Ost-West-Wirtschaftsbeziehungen als Deutsch-Amerikanisches Problem* (Ebenhausen: Stiftung Wissenschaft und Politik, 1983).

3. Deutsche Bank, *Sowjetunion* (Frankfurt, 1983).

4. Wharton Econometric Forecasting Associates, *UdSSR, Entwicklung des Aussenhandels mit westlichen Industrieländern 1981–1987.*

5. Deutsche Bank, *Sowjetunion* (Frankfurt, 1983).

6. West German Ministry of Economics, *Der deutsche Osthandel 1983* (Bonn, 1984).

7. *"Energeticheskaia programma v deistvie"* [The long-range energy program], *Ekonomicheskaia gazeta,* vol. B (Moscow, 1984).

8. Wharton Econometric Forecasting Associates, *UdSSR, Entwicklung des Aussenhandels mit westlichen Industrieländern 1981–1987;* Jochen Bethkenhagen, *Soviet Energy Supplies as a Factor in East-West Relations* and other publications (Berlin: German Institute for Economic Research, 1984).

9. Esso AG, "Oeldorado 1983" (Hamburg, February 28, 1984); Vassilij Dinkov, speech reprinted in *Ost-West-Commerz,* June 8, 1984.

10. International Energy Agency, Communiqué of meeting of governing board at the ministerial level (Paris, May 8, 1983).

11. Commission of the European Communities, "Communication from the Commission to the Council on Community Natural Gas Supplies" (Brussels, October 15, 1982).

12. Klaus Liesen, "Natural Gas and International Trade: What Are the Issues?" (Dallas: Center for International Business, April 13, 1983).

13. Jacobsen, *Die Ost-West-Wirtschaftsbeziehungen.*

14. See studies of the OECD, the CIA, and the Congress of the United States in 1981 and 1982.

15. George W. Ball, "On Cutting Pipelines—and Our Own Throat," *Washington Post,* March 11, 1982.

16. Otto Wolff von Amerongen, Speech at Georgetown University, Washington, D.C., April 26, 1984.

Economic Relations with Japan

Political relations between Japan and the Soviet Union have been generally cool and lacking in harmony throughout the 40 years since World War II, more so than can be explained by the fundamentally different political, economic, and social systems. Although diplomatic relations between the two countries were restored in 1956, contacts have never been marked by genuine friendliness.

For the Japanese there are a number of reasons for this political coolness. First, there is a lingering distrust that stems, in part, from the Soviet entry into World War II against Japan during the closing days of the war, in disregard of a mutual nonaggression pact. A second and related reason is the Soviet detention of hundreds of thousands of Japanese soldiers after the war. Then there are Japan's close ties with the United States. In every facet of political and economic relations, Japan has given the highest priority to aligning her foreign policy with that of the United States.

There are other factors as well, among them the issue of the Northern Territories and the closely related fishery problems. Soviet military intervention in Afghanistan in December 1979 and its uncertain future have further antagonized Japanese public opinion toward the Soviet Union. The Japanese government followed the example of the United States and imposed sanctions on the Soviet Union, prohibiting the Japan Export-Import Bank from issuing new credits and banning the sale of high-technology products to the Soviet Union. These actions have clearly had a negative impact on the development of Japanese-Soviet trade in the early 1980s.[1]

The Soviet Union has reacted to what it perceives as Japan's anti-Soviet policy with a hardened attitude. Moreover, Moscow's age-old chauvinistic superpower attitude and heavy-handed diplomatic posture have often rubbed the Japanese public the wrong way, thus aggravating the situation.

Despite these difficult political circumstances, the complementary trade relationship between Japan and the Soviet Union has remained in surprisingly good shape, and both nations see mutual benefits in its further development. Except for a few years, bilateral trade has grown steadily through the 1960s and the 1970s (see Table 6.1). Economic and trade relations are at the base of Japanese-Soviet relations; Japanese-Soviet relations without economic and trade links would be very fragile indeed. It is in this light that Japan and the Soviet Union have recently been urged to pay more attention to this exchange channel and to redouble their efforts to maintain and expand it.[2] The future development of Japanese-Soviet relations depends unquestionably on the favorable growth of economic and trade relations between the United States and the Soviet Union.

The progress of joint economic development projects for Siberia and the Soviet Far East has been the most important factor in expanding Japanese-Soviet economic and trade relations through the 1960s and 1970s. Many large-scale Siberian projects between Japan and the USSR have been initiated, and one can be sure that some of these projects will continue to play an important role in future Japanese-Soviet trade.

Since the early 1980s, when Japan opted for stable economic growth, Japan's interest in Siberia's natural resources has decreased compared with the period of Japanese economic growth. The Soviet Union, for its part, suffered from chronic economic depression and an attendant slump in its development projects, and so greatly limited its investments in East Siberia and the Soviet Far East. The Soviets apparently are now placing a low priority on the development of these areas. The result is that cooperation in Siberian development is not as intense as it was earlier.

This chapter will examine the mutually beneficial nature of Japanese-Soviet economic and trade relations and the basic attitudes on both sides toward their maintenance. Also discussed are the significance and purpose of cooperation in Siberian development, the historical background, the substance and problems of individual cooperation projects, and, finally, future prospects.

JAPANESE-SOVIET
ECONOMIC RELATIONS

Table 6.1, which details the evolution of Japanese-Soviet trade since World War II, demonstrates that bilateral trade grew steadily through the 1960s and the 1970s. Although trade with the Soviet Union accounts for only some 2 percent of Japan's total trade volume, and is therefore rather minuscule, the Soviet Union has always ranked somewhere between the eleventh and the fifteenth place among Japan's foreign trade. From the 1960s to the beginning of the 1970s, Soviet exports to Japan increased more rapidly than Japan's exports to the USSR, resulting in a favorable balance of trade for the Soviets. After 1970, however, Japan's exports took a dramatic upturn and Soviet exports to Japan showed little sign of growth, causing a huge surplus in Japan's favor.

TABLE 6.1
Growth of Trade Between Japan and USSR, 1946– 1985 (in thousands of U.S. dollars)

Period	Year	Japan's Exports	Japan's Imports	Total Volume
General Headquarters–supervised trade	1946	24	0	24
	1947	140	2,004	2,144
	1948	4,385	2,670	7,055
	1949	7,360	1,933	9,293
Private-level nonagreement trade	1950	723	738	1,461
	1951	0	28	28
	1952	150	459	609
	1953	7	2,101	2,108
	1954	39	2,249	2,288
	1955	2,710	3,070	5,780
	1956	760	2,860	3,620
	(October 19, 1956: Restoration of Soviet-Japanese relations)			
	1957	9,294 (100)[a]	12,324 (100)	21,618 (100)
	(December 6, 1957: Treaty of Commerce and Trade Payment Agreement)			
Government-level agreement trade	1958	18,100 (195)	22,150 (180)	40,250 (186)
	1959	23,026 (248)	39,490 (320)	62,516 (289)
	(1960– 1962 Trade Payment Agreement signed)			
	1960	59,976 (645)	87,025 (706)	147,001 (680)
	1961	65,380 (703)	145,409 (1,180)	210,789 (975)
	1962	149,390 (1,607)	147,309 (1,195)	296,699 (1,372)
	(1963– 1965 Trade Payment Agreement signed)			
	1963	158,136 (1,701)	161,940 (1,314)	320,076 (1,481)
	1964	181,810 (1,956)	226,729 (1,840)	408,539 (1,890)
	1965	168,358 (1,811)	240,198 (1,949)	408,556 (1,890)

Year						
(1966–1970 Trade Payment Agreement signed)						
1966	214,022	(2,308)	300,361	(2,437)	514,383	(2,379)
1967	157,688	(1,697)	453,918	(3,683)	611,606	(2,829)
1968	179,018	(1,926)	463,512	(3,761)	642,530	(2,972)
1969	268,247	(2,886)	461,563	(3,745)	729,810	(3,376)
1970	340,932	(3,668)	481,038	(3,903)	821,970	(3,802)
(1971–1975 Trade Payment Agreement signed)						
1971	377,267	(4,059)	495,880	(4,024)	873,147	(4,039)
1972	504,179	(5,425)	593,906	(4,819)	1,098,085	(5,079)
1973	484,210	(5,210)	1,077,701	(8,745)	1,561,911	(7,225)
1974	1,095,642	(11,789)	1,418,143	(11,507)	2,513,785	(11,628)
1975	1,626,200	(17,497)	1,169,618	(9,491)	2,795,818	(12,933)
(1976–1980 Trade Payment Agreement signed)						
1976	2,251,894	(24,230)	1,167,441	(9,473)	3,419,335	(15,817)
1977	1,933,877	(20,808)	1,421,875	(11,537)	3,355,752	(15,523)
1978	2,502,195	(26,923)	1,441,723	(11,698)	3,943,918	(18,244)
1979	2,461,464	(26,484)	1,910,681	(15,504)	4,372,145	(20,225)
1980	2,778,233	(29,893)	1,859,866	(15,091)	4,638,099	(21,455)
(1981–1985 Trade Payment Agreement signed)						
1981	3,259,415	(35,070)	2,020,706	(16,397)	5,280,121	(24,425)
1982	3,898,841	(41,950)	1,682,017	(13,648)	5,580,858	(25,816)
1983	2,821,249	(30,356)	1,456,001	(11,814)	4,277,250	(19,786)
1984	2,518,314	(27,096)	1,393,987	(11,311)	3,912,301	(18,096)
1985	2,750,583	(29,595)	1,429,255	(11,597)	4,179,838	(19,335)
(1986–1990 Trade Payment Agreement signed)						

SOURCE: Soren Too Boeki Kai, "NisSo Boeki Tokei," *Soren Too Boeki Chosa Geppo*, [Japan Association for trade with Soviet Union and Socialist countries of Europe, "Japan-Soviet trade statistics," *Monthly bulletin on trade with USSR and Eastern Europe*] February 1986:27.

[a] Numbers in parentheses are indices of trade change, with 1957 equal to 100.

In the 1960s and the early 1970s, Japan experienced a high annual growth rate and expanded its importation of industrial raw materials, including items from the Soviet Union. The 1973 oil crisis, together with the fundamental changes in the international economic environment suggested above, prompted Japan to turn to a policy of stable economic growth and restricted importation of raw materials across the board.

In the same period, the Soviet economy was expanding, and with it Japan's export to the USSR. The Soviet Union's Siberian energy development was the most important factor responsible for this expansion in Japanese-Soviet trade. During the second half of the 1970s, imports of Japanese machinery and materials, including large-diameter steel pipes for rapid transmission of natural gas, rose substantially. In 1970, Japan was the Soviet Union's largest trade partner, and from 1971 through 1979, the second largest (after West Germany). Clearly, Japan's machinery and steel had come to play a very important role in the Soviet economy.

The general trend in Japanese-Soviet trade during the second half of the 1970s basically remained unchanged into the early 1980s. While Soviet exports to Japan showed a slight decline, Japan's exports to the USSR grew dramatically each year between 1980 and 1982. Yet during this period, reaction to U.S. economic sanctions in response to the Soviet military intervention in Afghanistan dealt a heavy blow to Japan's trade with the Soviet Union. Specifically, Moscow canceled many large-scale plant projects that had been negotiated between the two countries, thereby curtailing the progress of Siberian development cooperation. As a result, Japan's exports to the USSR in 1983 registered the first large decrease, a 27.6 percent decline from the previous year. While attributing all responsibility for the present sluggish Japanese-Soviet trade to the Japanese, the Soviet authorities have taken every opportunity to criticize Japan's economic sanctions against the USSR and to call for their removal.[3]

JAPAN'S POSITION AND INTERESTS

Japan and the Soviet Union are neighbors that face each other across the Sea of Japan. This fact alone is reason for the two countries to deepen their economic relations and develop trade, despite obstacles arising from different social and economic systems. Indeed, notwithstanding many knotty political problems, the Japanese government, bureaucracy, and business circles have made efforts to keep at least proper economic relations with the Soviet Union. Moreover, the critical reason for the expansion of Japanese-Soviet trade since the late 1950s is the fact that Japan exports primarily manufactured goods—machinery, equipment, and steel—and imports industrial raw materials and fuels.

Development of economic relations with the Soviet Union was motivated by

Japan's need to diversify export markets. The Soviet Union was seen as a good candidate for a larger, long-term export market and, at the same time, a significant source of the raw materials essential to Japan's economy. In short, the character of Japan's exports and imports basically matches Soviet trade requirements. This basic pattern of complementary bilateral trade will probably continue through the 1980s.

It was the Soviets who proposed negotiations on large-scale plant and steel imports in conjunction with Siberian development projects. Progress in Soviet Siberian and Far East development and the materialization of Japanese-Soviet cooperative projects led to massive Japanese exports of machinery and materials as well as consumer goods (mainly secondary textile goods) for Siberia's local population. Conversely, Japan began importing raw materials and fuel from the USSR on a large scale.

Let us take a closer look at the commodity structure of Japanese-Soviet trade. Japan mainly exports to the Soviet Union industrial products: steel (primarily large-diameter pipes in recent years), machinery, plants, textiles, and chemical products. Industrial plants and steel are especially important. The Soviet Union is Japan's second largest market for steel, after the United States, and the Soviets are the number one importer of Japanese steel pipes—between 1976 and 1980, approximately four million tons. Also imported from Japan, from the mid-1960s through 1980, were more than 50 plants, mainly petrochemical plants.

The Soviet Union's chief exports to Japan are timber (largely logs), raw cotton, coal, coking coal, nonferrous metals, and gold. If and when the Siberian development projects make headway in the 1980s, then natural gas may rise to the top of the Soviets' most important export items to Japan.

The Soviets have endeavored to sell consumer items to Japan, but they have not been successful. Japanese businesses take little interest in Soviet manufactured products, which lack appeal and are not competitive in the Japanese market. Obviously, the market factor is the key to the expansion of Japanese-Soviet trade and will, no doubt, remain so in the future.

Evidence of Japan's consistent business interest in expanding trade with the Soviet Union was the establishment in 1965 of the Japan-Soviet Economic Committee. The committee has held joint sessions with its Soviet counterpart, the Soviet-Japan Economic Committee, and has initiated a number of cooperative Japanese-Soviet projects for Siberian development. There are also other promising, highly feasible cooperative projects on the agenda for the future.

The Japanese government's policy of expanding trade with the Soviet Union began with the Trade Payment Agreement, first reached in 1957 and renewed every five years since 1966. It has provided a framework for stable growth of trade relations. (The agreement was curtailed after Soviet military intervention in Afghanistan, but these restrictions were recently modified.) The very fact that the Japanese government agreed to a large and long-term credit to the Soviet

Union via the Japan Export-Import Bank—approximately $1,000 billion between 1974 and 1982—suffices to confirm Japan's official policy. Japan's policy toward the Soviet Union, which may look very inflexible at first glance, is in fact quite flexible and practical in the field of trade.

SOVIET ECONOMIC STRATEGY TOWARD JAPAN

Economic and trade relations with Japan are of major significance to the Soviet Union, even though its share of total foreign trade has been small—about 2 or 3 percent. Soviet tactics to expand economic relations with Japan have been consistently very active. The Soviet leadership hopes to use Japan's superior economic capability and industrial technology—through the implementation of economic cooperation and the expansion of trade—to develop the Soviet economy, especially Siberia's, as much as possible. How much economic cooperation can be secured from Japan is the critical question that decides Soviet economic strategy toward Japan.

Leonid I. Brezhnev was reported to have revealed his strong expectation of Japan's active participation in Siberian development at the special economic talks held in Yalta in the summer of 1976, citing various specific projects.[4] The Japanese side in these talks, headed by Toshio Doko, was represented by the Federation of Economic Organization.

V. B. Spandarin, the chief Soviet trade representative to Japan from the beginning of 1975 until the spring of 1986, has long played a key role in Japanese-Soviet trade. In a lengthy article entitled "Trade and Economic Relations between the USSR and Japan," he wrote:

The interdependence of the trade structure, the high economic, scientific and technological levels of the two countries, and the geographical proximity between Japan and the rapidly developing Soviet East—these objective conditions create the necessity for successful development of USSR-Japan economic relations on a long-term basis as well as on a large scale.[5]

He also pointed out:

Trade and economic cooperation between the two countries have continuously expanded, so that the value of Soviet-Japan trade in 1979 surged 100 times as much as that recorded in 1957, the year when the Soviet-Japan Trade Treaty was signed.[6]

A Soviet scholar has tried to provide a theoretical basis for economic cooperation with Japan, and has stated the following:

The regional distribution of natural resources in the USSR is first of all characterized by its unevenness; a major part of the resource reserves are in large-scale mines in Siberia and the Soviet Far East. This high concentration of valuable mineral resources in Siberia and the Soviet Far East enables us to develop natural resources on a large scale and organize their processing not only for satisfying domestic demand, but also for producing ample raw materials for export. This is why economic cooperation with Japan in developing resources in Siberia and the Soviet Far East is useful for the USSR. Such cooperation will help the USSR to facilitate the solution of various important problems concerning the location of production units and the improvement of regional imbalances in national economy. It also will help the USSR to promote the establishment of large-scale regional production complexes in the East, and the expansion of the export infrastructure based on long-term agreements. The creation of the infrastructure, and the additional mobilization of resources for export of this kind make it possible to take advantage of the Japanese market. Thus, the USSR can better meet the demand for producer goods and consumer goods indispensable for the Soviet economy.[7]

The Soviet Union made active and persistent efforts to improve economic relations with Japan between 1980 and 1982. Speeches by Soviet leaders and the tone of the press with regard to Japan remained deliberate and moderate during this period. Considering the fact that the Japanese government had imposed economic sanctions in response to Soviet military intervention in Afghanistan, this mild attitude should be seen as evidence of the great importance Moscow assigns to economic relations with Japan.

TRENDS IN JAPANESE-SOVIET TRADE, 1980–1983

Japanese-Soviet trade in the early 1980s was severely restricted by Japan's support for U.S. economic sanctions against the Soviet Union. Japan's exports to the USSR nevertheless went up, showing a rapid increase of 12.9 percent in 1980, 17.3 percent in 1981, and 19.7 percent in 1982. This resulted mainly from brisk sales of Japanese steel pipes, machinery, and equipment to meet active development demand within the Soviet Union, associated in large part with the Far East forest resources development project. Economic and commercial motives can override political factors.

The 17.5 percent growth in 1981 was especially noteworthy since total Soviet imports from the advanced capitalist industrial countries increased only 8.7 percent that year (based on the Soviet trade statistics). Soviet imports from West Germany, France, Italy, and the United Kingdom all marked negative growth. In fact, Soviet imports from Japan in 1981 were third largest, behind Finland and

West Germany. Japan might have taken the top position, if not for a reported $1 billion loss of export opportunities.[8]

Japanese imports from the Soviet Union, on the other hand, continued to fall through the same three-year period, chiefly because Japan's main import items— raw materials and fuels—were susceptible to Japan's business fluctuations. The slump in the Japanese lumber market, for example, caused a drastic decrease in Japan's imports of Soviet lumber, the leading import item. Though Japan's customs clearance statistics show an 8.7 percent increase in imports from the Soviet Union in 1981, this was due to the inclusion of 37 tons of gold bullion.

Japanese-Soviet trade in 1982 showed nearly the same pattern: substantial growth of 19.7 percent over the previous year, including a remarkable increase in Japanese export of steel, machinery, and plant equipment. Japan's imports from the Soviet Union, on the other hand, declined 17 percent from the previous year.

In spite of this steady growth in exports, the economic sanctions against the USSR cast a dark shadow on Japanese-Soviet trade. As a result, plant export negotiations with the USSR were not particularly productive, nor was there actual progress in Japanese-Soviet negotiations on Siberian development and cooperation projects. This situation, with its negative influence on Japan's exports to the USSR in 1983, raised much concern. The establishment of a higher yen exchange rate in 1978 had already notably weakened the competitive position of Japan's exports on the world market. The deterioration of general export environment, due to the economic sanctions and Japan's related ban on the extension of new credits, brought about total cessation of plant exports to the USSR. In fact, because of a drastic decrease in the export of machinery, equipment, and seamless pipes for oil wells, Japanese exports to the USSR in 1983 registered a large decline (a fall of 27.6 percent from the previous year) for the first time.

Japan's imports from the USSR in 1983 also continued the downward trend, showing a 13.4 percent decline from the previous year. In contrast, Soviet trade with West European countries in 1983 expanded remarkably. Soviet imports from France, West Germany, Italy, and Austria recorded a sharp rise of 15–40 percent over the previous year. This was the result of a Soviet policy to place a higher priority on imports from Western Europe as a tradeoff for the recent surge in the West European purchase of natural gas and oil, and the huge Soviet trade surplus that followed.

The trend in Japanese imports from the Soviet Union will greatly affect the future possibility for expanding Japanese-Soviet trade. It is thus important to expedite two ongoing Siberian development projects: one involving south Yakutian coking coal and the other petroleum and gas off Sakhalin. Obviously, this would also lead to an expansion of exports to the USSR. However, a rapid recovery of Japanese-Soviet trade cannot be expected without an easing of the severe confrontation between the United States and Soviet Union, and an improvement of East-West relations in general.

As has been noted repeatedly, the planning and implementation of Siberian development and cooperation projects have been the mainstay of Japanese-Soviet economic relations since the mid-1960s, and the key to the expansion of Japanese-Soviet trade. The cooperation projects have their origin in the Soviet proposal for joint exploitation of the Garinskoe mine in the Soviet Far East, presented in 1961 by then Deputy Premier A. I. Mikoyan while on a visit to Japan. The next year a large delegation of Japanese businessmen, headed by Yoshinari Kawai, went to Siberia to confirm the feasibility of economic cooperation between the two countries in Siberian development. Following a series of active exchanges of personnel, the Agreement of Japan-Soviet Economic Joint Sessions was signed in July 1965. The first joint session of the Japan-Soviet Economic Committee, for discussing basic issues of cooperation projects for Siberian development, was held in Tokyo in March 1966.

Agreement by Japanese industry to embark on the Siberian development and cooperation projects was signaled with the establishment of the Japan-Soviet Economic Committee on the initiative of Keidanren (the Federation of Economic Organizations). Since then, Keidanren has consistently played a leading role, so much so that the Japan-Soviet Economic Committee, the secretariat of which is located in Keidanren, has become almost synonymous with Keidanren itself.[9]

The Japan-Soviet Economic Committee has so far held eight sessions, the last one in Moscow in September 1979. Key issues on the agenda at each session are cited below.

First Joint Session (Tokyo, March 1966)   The Japanese explained the condition and characteristics of the Japanese economy, and expressed Japan's view on a desirable state of Japan-Soviet trade (including coastal trade) and the exchange of technology. The Soviets similarly outlined the condition and the prospects of their country's economy and stated their views for the development and prospect of Soviet foreign trade, especially with Japan, and on such issues as the promotion of Soviet-Japanese technological exchanges, the improvement of port facilities, and the transportation of oil.

Second Joint Session (Moscow, June 1967)   Concrete measures toward Japanese-Soviet economic cooperation in the following areas were discussed:

1. The development of forestry in the Far East.
2. The exploitation of the Udokan copper mine.
3. The exploitation of Siberian oil and its transportation.
4. The expansion and modernization of Soviet Far Eastern port facilities.

Third Joint Session (Tokyo, December 1968)   Concrete proposals on the following issues were presented:

1. The improvement and modernization of ports in the Far East.
2. The expansion and improvement of the transportation network.
3. The development of broadleaved timber for industrial chips and pulp.
4. The exploitation and supply of natural gas, iron ore, and coal.
5. The exchange of scientific technology.
6. The development of Japanese-Soviet trade.

Fourth Joint Session (Moscow, February 1970)   Each side exchanged views on the following issues:

1. The modernization and expansion of ports in the Far East.
2. The development and supply of natural gas and of broadleaved timber for chips and pulp.
3. The financing of credits.
4. The development and supply of iron ore and coal.
5. The exchanges of scientific technology.

Fifth Joint Session (Tokyo, February 1972)   Each side exchanged views on the progress in implementing recommendations given in the fourth session, and on the following issues:

1. The supply to Japan of Tyumen oil.
2. The construction of pipelines leading to Nakhodka and of a wharf for oil transportation.
3. The development of Yakutian coal.
4. The exploration of oil and gas on the continental shelf off Sakhalin.
5. The exchange of scientific technology.
6. The conclusion of basic contracts for the construction of Wrangel Port (Vostochny).
7. The supply to Japan of industrial wood chips and broadleaved pulp.

Sixth Joint Session (Moscow, October 1974)   The following issues were discussed:

1. The interim report on the implementation of basic contracts for the construction of a port in Wrangel Bay, the supply to Japan of industrial chips and broadleaved timber for pulp, and the development of forest resources in the Far East.
2. The results of negotiations on the two basic contracts for cooperation in the development of south Yakutian coal and the expansion of the development of forest resources in the Far East, along with the supply of

bank loans by the Japan Export-Import Bank to the Soviet Foreign Trade Bank.

3. The progress in preparation of the basic contracts to prospect for oil and gas on the continental shelf area off Sakhalin, and geological exploration of Yakutian natural gas.

4. The preparation of an agreement on the supply of oil by the USSR to Japan.

Seventh Joint Session (Tokyo, September 1977)   Progress in implementating the following issues was discussed:

1. The construction of Vostochny Port in Wrangel Bay.
2. The supply to Japan of industrial chips and broadleaved timber for pulp.
3. The development of south Yakutian coal.
4. The development of forest resources in the Far East.
5. The implementation of geological prospecting for natural gas in Yakutsk.
6. The prospecting for oil and gas on the continental shelf off Sakhalin.
Also discussed were problems of scientific and technological exchange.

Eighth Joint Session (Moscow, September 1979)   Progress in implementating basic contracts on these issues was reviewed:

1. The production of industrial chips and broadleaved timber for pulp.
2. The development of the south Yakutian coal field.
3. The development of forest resources (the second basic contract).
4. The prospecting for Yakutian gas.
5. The prospecting for oil and gas on continental shelf off Sakhalin.

Both sides expressed interest in cooperative improvement of the paper and pulp-manufacturing industry on Sakhalin, as well as the construction of a paper-manufacturing complex at Amur in the Far East. Each side also made a preliminary statement on the prospect for future economic cooperation on a compensatory basis in the following areas: the development of Molodezhnoe asbestos mine, the construction of an iron-manufacturing complex in the Soviet Far East, and the construction of a mining and processing complex based on the Udokan copper mine.

The Ninth and Tenth Joint Sessions held in December 1984 (Tokyo) and April 1986 (Moscow), respectively, pursued somewhat more limited goals of economic cooperation for reasons suggested in the following pages.

PROGRESS OF SIBERIAN
DEVELOPMENT PROJECTS

The first Japanese-Soviet Siberian development cooperation project involved the First Far East Forest Resources Development Project, agreed in 1968. This project, commonly known as the KS Project (for Kawai and Sedov, the chiefs of the original Japanese and Soviet delegations), significantly expanded Japanese-Soviet trade; almost one-fourth of Japanese exports to the USSR between 1969 and 1970 was accounted for by goods related to the KS Project. In 1969, 52 percent of Japanese machinery and metal goods exports to the USSR were related to the project, 63 percent in 1970.[10]

Japanese-Soviet cooperation for Siberian development saw further progress in the early 1970s and took on added significance when the Japanese government decided to supply bank loans to the projects on the occasion of Prime Minister Kakuei Tanaka's visit to Moscow in October 1973.[11] The Japan-China Peace and Friendship Treaty signed in the summer of 1978 created excessive expectations for the growth of trade between the two countries, prompting Japanese businessmen to neglect Soviet trade somewhat. Early in 1979, however, Japanese-Soviet trade received an impetus for a comeback.

The eighth joint session of the Japanese-Soviet Economic Committee was held in Moscow in September 1979. The main topics included a review of four projects already underway, discussion of three projects still pending, and a preliminary survey of three newly proposed projects. The four projects already in progress were:

1. The Second Far East Forest Resource Development Project.
2. The Chip and Pulp Wood Development Project.
3. The South Yakutian Coking Coal Development Projects, and
4. The Sakhalin Continental Shelf Oil and Natural Gas Exploration Project.

The three projects under negotiation since the seventh joint session in September 1977 were:

1. The Third Far East Forest Resource Development Project.
2. The Construction Project of Pulp and Paper Industry in Sakhalin, and
3. The Vostochny Port Expansion Project for Loading Containers and a Coal Berth.

In addition, the Soviets proposed the following three projects as new target items for further cooperation:

1. The Far East Steel Mill Construction Project.
2. The Udokan Copper Project for exploration and construction of a Dressing and Smelting Complex, and
3. The Molodezhnoe Asbestos Mine Development Project.

A final agreement to begin even part of those projects, each requiring a huge amount of work, would pave the way to a new epoch in economic cooperation between Japan and the Soviet Union.[12]

Soviet military intervention in Afghanistan chilled this favorable climate, and Japanese economic sanctions were imposed against the USSR. However, in December 1980 Japan and the Soviet Union reached a broad agreement on the Third Forest Resource Development Project, to be carried out between 1981 and 1986; the agreement was officially signed in March 1981. Because this project included the extension of $1 billion in bank loans from Japan, the prospects for Japanese-Soviet trade became brighter; and a significant growth in Japan's export to the USSR will in fact bring it about in due course.

As for the Sakhalin oil and gas project, the existence of promising continental oil and gas reserves has been confirmed, and full-scale development already has been put on the agenda. Most of the drilling equipment was to be imported from the United States, however, and U.S. economic sanctions against the Soviet Union prevented its timely arrival, resulting in an unexpected delay in 1982. Japan had already invested 60 billion yen, including government funds, and risked failing to accomplish the drilling according to the contract terms by the end of 1983. In the event of failure, Japan would have been charged with noncompliance, threatening Soviet cancellation of the entire enterprise. Fortunately for Japan, however, the softening of the sanctions in November 1982 relieved Japanese fears and rekindled the expectations of successful completion of the contract projects.

The Sakhalin project is still in the exploration stage, but if it goes into full operation, the total cost involved is estimated at $3 billion or even as high as $4 billion. Commercial production of natural gas and oil from this project is scheduled to begin in 1988, and annual shipments of three million tons of Sakhalin liquefied natural gas to Japan are projected for the next twenty years. Sales of Sakhalin oil to Japan, although not yet scheduled, are also a distinct possibility in the near future. The problem is, however, that Japanese business circles are not very attracted to the project while the international oil market is glutted and oil prices are low. Electric utility companies, big customers for natural gas, were never enthusiastic about this project; there are as yet no buyers for the natural gas. The Japanese direct contractor, SODECO, a quasi-governmental agency, is nevertheless devoting all its efforts to realization of the project.

Promotion of the south Yakutian coking coal development project has begun. However, because of the many difficulties encountered by the Soviets in the development process, commercial production is likely to run substantially behind schedule. As a result, shipment of a total of 100 million tons of high-quality coal to Japan, originally scheduled to start in 1983, was set back to 1985.

The three cooperation projects relating to the iron and steel complex in the Far East, the Udokan copper mine, and the Molodezhnoe asbestos mine are among others that are expected for a startup during the Twelfth Five-Year Plan (1986–1990). A good deal of patient negotiation between Japan and the Soviet Union will be necessary before cooperation on these future projects is agreed upon. Moreover, Japanese industrial circles still appear to be cool to the projects.

Japan's Interest in Siberian Development

It is clear that Japanese-Soviet economic cooperation is mainly aimed at Siberia and the Soviet Far East regions, hence the name Siberian–Far East Development Cooperation, or Siberian Development Cooperation for short. Japanese interests and motivations are varied. First, the Soviet plan for large-scale development of Siberia and the Soviet Far East will conceivably create a massive demand for Japanese equipment, machinery, material, and consumer goods, thereby raising the expectation in Japan that Siberia and the Far East will become a large export market. At the same time, Japan's earlier expectation of continued high economic growth prompted the perceived need for increasing access to raw materials. Consequently, the Japanese considered acquisition of resources the most urgent economic problem, and adopted a policy aimed at diversifying the country's source of supplies. To implement this policy, Japan came up with the idea of developing the abundant natural resources in Siberia and the Soviet Far East. This was the basis for Japanese business consensus on Siberian development, and was the cornerstone for Japanese-Soviet trade throughout the 1960s and the mid-1970s. Among Japanese business circles, that enthusiasm has cooled now that demand for raw material has decreased to an extremely low level as the result of Japan's option for stable economic growth.

At any rate, it was this idea of cooperation for Siberian development that led to joint Japanese-Soviet economic consultations, and that gave impetus to project-based trade, based on the "product sharing" or, more commonly, especially in the USSR, "compensation trade" formula. The latter entitles Japan to receive a share of the developed resource over a long period in exchange for supplying necessary equipment, machinery, material, and supplies for the project, or to purchase the resource at a low interest rate and with deferred payments. Such project-based trade can effectively expand Japan's exports to the Soviet Union. In 1974 the Japan Export-Import Bank extended bank loans worth $1.5 billion, which the Soviet Union used to purchase machinery and materials from Japan for Siberian development. This, in turn, produced an expansion of Japan's exports to the Soviet Union in the latter half of the 1970s.

The point here is that prices in ordinary trade transactions are determined by the terms of payment deferral and rate of interest. For Japan the question is to decide what amount of the capital investment funds originally committed to Southeast Asia and other areas should be reallocated to the Siberian and Far East projects. This decision hinges on such questions as to what degree Japan could cooperate in Siberian development and whether such cooperation benefits Japan from the view of political economy. This is a commercial choice, but it is a choice that affects the allocation of capital funds, as the benefits of Japanese-Soviet trade are weighed against these derived from other foreign economic activities. It may also be considered a highly political choice, since it determines the degree of Japan's participation in economic cooperation with the Soviet Union. The larger the scale of Siberian and the Far East development and individual project-based trade becomes, the greater significance this choice assumes.

Prospects for Siberian Development into the 1990s

The benefit that the Soviets derive from the Siberian development and co-operation projects is the availability from Japan of a significant portion of the necessary funds and materials. Siberian resources have taken on a more dominant role in the Soviet economy, and the export of those resources to Japan is the essential condition for expansion of Soviet trade with Japan, thus multiplying the benefits from the projects.

The next critical question for the Soviets concerns the prospects for the growth of Siberian development through the 1990s. This matter is also of major significance to Japan. (Soviet journals have published a number of good articles on the role of Siberian development in the Soviet economy.)[13]

Siberia's present-day role in the Soviet economy is a relatively small one. As Table 6.2 shows, the region's contribution to total industrial output is only a bit more than 9 percent. What is more, the annual growth of this share did not increase at all through the latter half of the 1970s; the position of Siberia in the processing industry (such as food and metalworking) has even shown a downward trend. Siberia's harsh natural environment, its remote location that makes transportation extremely difficult, and the necessity of additional payments for local labor, force a higher capital investment per given unit of net products. Therefore, it is extremely important for Siberia to specialize in products that are either highly competitive or indispensable to the Soviet national economy. This means that it is impossible to invest in several sectors at the same time.

Does this imply that the importance of Siberian development for the Soviet economy has diminished? On the contrary, it has been rapidly increasing, and its growing importance in the future is a certainty.

Siberian development today is synonymous with energy development—oil,

TABLE 6.2
Contribution of Siberian Industrial Production to the Soviet Total (1960–1980)

	1960	1965	1970	1975	1980
Industry total	8.1%	8.2%	8.5%	9.0%	9.2%
Electric power industry	11.3	13.6	15.5	15.3	15.0
Fuel industry	12.8	14.6	17.0	21.2	26.7
Chemical and petrochemical industry	6.2	12.0	9.5	9.4	9.2
Machine and metalworking industry	9.7	7.5	8.1	7.7	7.4
Wood processing industry	12.6	14.9	14.9	16.0	16.0
Building materials industry	8.7	9.0	9.1	9.0	9.5
Light industry	4.2	4.2	5.0	5.4	5.9
Food industry	6.4	6.9	6.7	6.3	6.0

SOURCE: Data for 1960–1970 compiled from T. B. Baranova, "Osnovnye razvitiia promyshlennosti Sibiri v Sed'moi-Deviatoi Piatiletkakh," *Izvestiia Sibirskogo Otdeleniia Akademii Nauk SSSR,* no. 1, 1979, p. 30. Data for 1975 and 1980 compiled from T. B. Baranova, "Osnovnye pokazateli razvitiia promyshlennosti Sibiri v Desiatoi Piatiletke," *Izvestii Sibirskogo Otdeleniia Akademii Nauk SSSR,* no. 11, 1982, p. 73.

gas, and coal. Siberia's mining industry, unlike the Soviet Union as a whole, has had a growth rate surpassing the processing industry. The rate of increase in oil and gas production in Siberia, especially West Siberia, has been larger than that for the Soviet Union as a whole. It offsets not only the total increase in demand for energy resources, but also compensates for the fairly rapid decrease in production in other districts of the Soviet Union.

It is therefore expected that Siberian development in the 1980s will focus on energy resources, and that investment will be concentrated on the development of oil and gas in West Siberia. However, because of shortages in capital, labor, and food supplies, not enough energy resources will be available for the development of Siberia's processing industries through the 1980s.[14] This situation might compel the Soviets to call for Japan's economic cooperation more actively than before. In fact, one Soviet author, Iu. I. Maksimov, has argued that by the 1990s or 2000s the regional balance in Siberian economy should be changed, and that a major effort of prospecting and mining in East Siberia will be urgent to meet the total energy demand in the Soviet Union.[15]

JAPANESE-SOVIET TRADE
AT THE CURRENT CROSSROADS

In February 1983, more than 230 Japanese traveled to Moscow to meet with Soviet representatives and discuss bilateral economic and trade relations. The Japanese delegation was headed by Shigeo Nagano, the former president of the

Japan Chamber of Commerce and Industry. The Soviets stressed the importance of cooperation in Siberian development, and requested that Japan take part in large-scale development projects for natural resources, including the Far East Steel Mill Construction Project. The Soviets also proposed four new, relatively small-scale cooperative projects, noting that prospects of implementation would facilitate compensation and financing. The projects included a plant to manufacture aluminum from nepheline, sawmills and mobile equipment to manufacture fuel (briquette) from waste lumber, and facilities for processing secondary materials such as waste cables and used tire cords.

The Soviets listed a broad range of areas for development under the forthcoming Twelfth Five-Year Plan (1986–1990). They announced that they had already begun negotiations with West European and U.S. companies, and expressed their desire for the same kind of negotiations with Japanese businesses.[16] The response from Japanese business circles was not enthusiastic.

Since the signing of an agreement for the Third Far East Forest Resource Project in March 1981, against a backdrop of generally unfavorable East-West relations, not a single Japanese-Soviet Siberian development and cooperation project has been concluded, nor have there been any active moves toward their conclusion. A large-scale Japanese-Soviet conference on economic and trade problems, originally scheduled for April 1984, has been postponed indefinitely by the Japanese, with no date set for the next meeting. In short, cooperation in Siberian development is now sluggish.

There are various reasons for Japan's negative response to the Siberian development. Especially critical, for it touches on the future progress of a wide range of Japanese-Soviet Siberian development and cooperation projects, is the fact that it is impossible for private companies to commit financing as high as $2–$3 billion without the aid of government funds. This leads to the conclusion that the future of the projects depends on Japanese policy toward the Soviet Union, which in turn depends on the trends in U.S.–Soviet relations. The United States has sought to tighten restrictions on export of high-technology products to the Soviet Union and has urged the West Europeans and the Japanese to follow suit. Moreover, the guidelines of the Organization of Economic Cooperation and Development (OECD), which ask that the member nations voluntarily refrain from providing the Soviet Union with competitive low-interest financing, are still in effect.

The list of high-technology products that the United States has demanded be embargoed is quite broad; it includes many machines and equipment that Japan has readily provided to the Soviets in the past. Consequently, a shift to improved U.S.–Soviet relations is very much the key to growth of Japan-USSR trade.

We must remember, too, that the importation of Siberian resources has become less attractive to Japan. The Siberian development and cooperation projects were all planned and blueprinted during the period of Japan's high economic growth; in the 1960s and early 1970s concern over the tight supply of natural resources under the expected continuous high-growth economy prompted recognition of projects for development and import of natural resources as "national" projects. The present situation in the 1980s is dramatically different. A protracted, severe depression characterized by low economic growth has caused Japanese big business to be cautious about participating in large-scale Siberian development projects.

Finally the Japan Association for Trade with the Soviet Union and Socialist Countries of Europe pointed to the qualitative change in cooperation for Siberian development, when it published the results of a study involving companies concerned with Japanese-Soviet trade. The association proposed to broaden the range of cooperation for development by including manufacturing industries (presupposing the import of value-added middle raw materials in return) in parallel with such large-scale projects as the development of coal, oil, natural gas, or timber. The association also proposed a scaling down of projects, and enumerated the following as possible new "mini projects":

1. A project for processing marine products in the Pacific region along the Sea of Japan.
2. Japanese cooperation in improving Siberia's agricultural system in exchange for raw materials.
3. A project for development of port facilities.
4. A project for constructing ironworks, oil refineries, and petrochemical plants.
5. A project for cooperation in coldproof technology.
6. A project for overall utilization of lumber.
7. The collaborative study on an overall project including civil construction.

Some of the mini projects are already under negotiation between Japanese companies and the Soviet organization. In the future, it will be necessary to plan a number of projects that can be carried out by the private sector. This can be done by widening the scope of projects to include processing industries, the service sector, and transportation.

Other mini projects that have been put on the agenda include:

1. The export of fishing equipment and machinery for processing marine products such as crabs, sea urchins, and scallops, and the import of the finished products.
2. The export of bone meal.
3. Construction of a bark-compost plant.
4. A project for increasing the production of soybeans and buckwheat.

5. The export of food-packing machines and the import of the finished products.

6. The development and export of steam coal from Sakhalin.

7. A project for effective utilization of peat.

8. The export of a small-scale wood processing plant and the import of sawn lumber.

9. A project for producing biocube (solid fuel).

10. The export of machines for producing bark dust.

11. A cooperation project for producing plywood.

12. The export of equipment for reclaiming scrapped covered electrical wires.

13. The export of equipment for reclaiming tires.

14. The development and export of structural sand and gravel from Sakhalin.

CONCLUSION

Japanese-Soviet economic relations, complementary and mutually beneficial, are the widest and most solid channel of Japanese-Soviet interaction. Given that both Japan and the Soviet Union should make every effort to secure and develop this channel, it seems clear that Japan is relatively indifferent on this matter, whereas the Soviets are much more active. The Soviet Union wants closer bilateral economic relations with Japan, now even under Mr. Gorbachev's new leadership, something that is surely desirable for Japan as well. Although it is certainly important for Japan to act in concert with the United States, this policy should be tempered if the consequences are a cooling-off of Japanese-Soviet relations and raised tensions between the two countries.

NOTES

1. On the views of specialists and businessmen in both Japan and the Soviet Union on this point, see Soren Too Boeki Kai, *NisSo Keizai Senmonka Kaigi Hokokusho* [Reports on the interchanges of specialists on Japanese-Soviet economic relations] (Tokyo: Soren Too Boeki Kai, 1978–1983).

2. Kazuo Ogawa, "Japan-Soviet Economic Relations: Present Status and Future Prospects," *Journal of Northeast Asian Studies* 2, no. 1 (March 1983).

3. For example, P. D. Dolgorukov, "SoNichi Keizai no Hatten to Shyomondai" [Development and problems of USSR-Japanese economic relations], *Soren Too Boeki Choosa Geppoo* [Monthly bulletin on trade with the USSR and Eastern Europe] 28, no. 6 (June 1983): 27–32. For an excellent analysis of the evolution of Japanese-Soviet trade

after World War II and its motives; a four-type classification of Japanese-Soviet trade (general trade, cooperative trade, coastal trade, and Siberian development project trade [a special form of general trade]); the relationship between Siberian development projects and Japan-Soviet trade; the relationship between Japan's dependence on external raw materials and Siberian development, and its future prospects; and also the relationship between Japanese-Soviet trade and Japanese-Chinese trade, see Richard Louis Edmonds, "Siberian Resource Development and Japanese Economy: The Japanese Perspective," in Robert G. Jensen, Theodore Shabad, and Arthur W. Wright, eds., *Soviet Natural Resources in the World Economy* (Chicago: University of Chicago Press, 1983), pp. 214–31.

4. Ryoo Kiire, *NisSo Boeki no Rekishi* [*The history of Japanese-Soviet trade*] (Tokyo: Ningen Sha, 1983), p. 173.

5. V. B. Spandarian, "Sovetsko-iaponskie torgovo-ekonomicheskikh otnosheniia," *Problemy Dal'nego Vostoka*, no. 3 (1980): 91–97.

6. V. B. Spandarian, "Perspektivy sovetsko-iaponskikh ekonomicheskikh otnoshenii," *Problemy Dal'nego Vostoka*, no. 2 (1972): 28–43.

7. M. I. Krupianko, *Sovetsko-iaponskie ekonomicheskie otnosheniia* (Moscow: Nauka, 1982), pp. 124–26.

8. On my visit to the Asian Affairs Bureau of the USSR Foreign Trade Ministry in Moscow in July 1981, one of the high officials told me that Japan had lost $1 billion worth of export opportunities due to the economic sanctions Japan imposed on the Soviet Union.

9. Kiire, *NisSo Boeki no Rekishi*, p. 88.

10. Tsusho Sangyo Sho, *Tsusho Hakusho: Sooron* [White paper on international trade] (Tokyo: Okura Sho, 1971), p. 276.

11. For details on one of the projects, Tyumen oil exploration, and the process leading to its cancellation, see Kazuo Ogawa, *Siberia Kaihatsu to Nippon* [Siberian development and Japan] (Tokyo: Jiji Tsushin Sha, 1974), pp. 219–22; and Hisaya Shirai, *Gendai Sobieto Koh* [A study of today's Soviet Union] (Tokyo: Asahi Evening News Sha, 1981), pp. 397–400.

12. Kazuo Ogawa, *Siberia Kaihatsu to Nippon*, pp. 167–71.

13. Iu. I. Maksimov, "Toplivno-energeticheskii kompleks Sibiri," *Ekonomika i organizatsiia promyshlennogo proizvodstva* [*EKO*], no. 10 (1982): 97–108; B. P. Orlov, "Razvitie ekonomiki Sibiri na otdel'nykh etapakh sotsialisticheskogo stroitel'stva," *Izvestiia sibirskogo otdeleniia Akademii Nauk SSSR*, no. 11 (1982): 60–70; and A. Gladyshev, V. Loginov, and V. Savel'ev, "Razvitie ekonomiki Sibiri i Dal'nego Vostoka," *Voprosy ekonomiki*, no. 11 (1982): 28–37.

14. Orlov, "Razvitie ekonomiki Sibiri," pp. 67–70.

15. Maksimov, "Toplivno-energeticheskii kompleks Sibiri," pp. 105–7.

16. Soren Too Boeki Kai, *The Japanese Trade and Economic Delegation to the USSR (Records)* (Tokyo: Soren Too Boeki Kai, February 1983), pp. 32–41.

The Siberian Military Buildup
and the Sino-Soviet-U.S. Triangle

The Soviet ruling elite's strategic assumptions about Siberia have inevitably been strongly conditioned by the evolution of the Soviet Union's relationships with its neighbors in the Far East and, above all, with China. Many factors have contributed to the long-term process through which the Soviet military position in Siberia has been and is still being transformed. The most important factor, however, has undoubtedly been the Soviet decision in the mid-1960s that the regime that had emerged on Siberia's southern borders fifteen years earlier was likely to be a major geopolitical rival and opponent of Soviet ambitions in Asia for the foreseeable future. The story of the militarization of Siberia over the last two decades was thus launched by this momentous Soviet discovery in the first place, and has ever since been directly affected by the course of Soviet dealings with the People's Republic of China (PRC).

This chapter seeks to trace the relationship between these two trends—the military buildup in Siberia and the interaction with China—over the last twenty years.[1] It attempts, at the same time, to identify the consequences for the Soviet military posture in Siberia that have been produced since the late 1960s by the interaction of both the Soviet Union and the PRC with a third power—the United States. In conclusion, it will discuss the likely future of the Siberian military buildup against the background of present trends in this strategic triangle.

GENERAL CHARACTERISTICS
OF THE BUILDUP

Three points can be made at the outset about the general characteristics of the Soviet military buildup in Siberia and the Far East.

The first is that this process, in progress since about 1965, has obvious elements of long-term planning and continuity. The allocation of the human resources required has clearly been an important factor in the five-year planning cycles of the Ministry of Defense and of the ministries supervised by the Military-Industrial Commission. The buildup cumulatively absorbed a large portion of the total increase in the Soviet ground forces during the Brezhnev years. The Soviets have surely had to make broad estimates of these requirements, forecast long in advance, to be correlated with manpower induction and retention policies and with an anticipated range of needs for other military manpower and for the economic labor force.

The effects on the matériel side are even more powerful. It is reasonable to suppose, for example, that over the years, targeting of China has consumed an increasing share of the total mix of the evolving Soviet IRBM and ICBM (intermediate-range and intercontinental ballistic missiles) capability and has therefore entered increasingly into the production plans for these missiles. Certainly such items as the concrete required for military airfields or large-scale defense fortifications in the Far East and the planes and weapons that will ultimately be used at such installations must be planned for long in advance. Even the planned capacity of future plants intended to produce a wide variety of such items must be affected to some degree by the projected requirements of the Chinese front. Planning for the Chinese task, like the other major Soviet military missions, must therefore reverberate forward for many years into the future, inevitably affecting a complex network of resource allocation decisions.

Second, the buildup, despite the factors making for long-term continuity, has not been evenly paced or uniform, particularly regarding additions of manpower. It seems fair to say, however, that any overview of the buildup must take into account not only the pace of the increase in troops assigned to the anti-China mission, but also changes in the pace of fortification, construction, and replacement of equipment, and changes in the rate of formation of new skeletal divisions that could be used for rapid mobilization. Use of any one of these three criteria in the absence of the others is likely to produce a misleading view of the Soviet overall effort and intentions. With this caveat in mind, we may conclude that, broadly speaking, the buildup has gone through four phases to date:

1. An initial period of gradual expansion after 1965 from the base of some seventeen to twenty divisions inherited from the Khrushchev era.
2. A period of some acceleration in all three categories—manpower, units, and equipment—for a few years around the turn of the decade.
3. A period of much slower growth—and gradual improvement of the equipment and manpower levels of under-strength units—between the early 1970s and 1977.
4. Some movement off this near-plateau in the period since 1978, characterized by modest increases in total combat manpower in combination with significant reorganization and some forward deployment, increases

in the number of new skeletal divisions deployed, and marked acceleration in the pace of modernization of equipment and stockpiling of materials.[2]

In the process, the number of Soviet divisions of all strength levels appears to have mounted from 20 or less at the outset of the buildup to about 40 early in the 1970s to roughly 52 in 1983.[3] A disproportionate share of the manpower—the bulk of the ground combat troops present today—was apparently in place by the early 1970s.[4]

The third general characteristic is that the mix of factors motivating the Soviets to conduct the buildup has not been static, but has changed considerably over time with changing circumstances. The fundamental conclusions the Soviets drew from their dealings with Mao through 1964 and 1965 were thus supplemented in turn by a series of factors: their experience in the 1969 border crisis; their reaction to Sino-U.S. rapprochement in 1971–72; their evaluation of Chinese behavior during the 1971 India-Pakistan war; their perception of Chinese behavior on the Sino-Soviet border during the 1970s; their discovery late in the decade of a Soviet geopolitical interest in deterring China from action against Vietnam; their decision to take steps to offset the worst-case possibility of eventual Sino-U.S.-Japanese military collusion against them; and finally, their perception of the heightened importance of their strength in the Far East as a result of both changes in SLBM (submarine-launched ballistic missile) technology and the new opportunities for power projection from the Far East that have emerged in Southeast Asia and beyond.

As each of these factors successively began to affect Soviet thinking about the force levels needed in Asia, there was an effect upon Soviet judgments about the level of risk that was acceptable in dealing with the Chinese. The discussion that follows will attempt to track the evolution of Soviet assumptions on both points.

THE BREZHNEV REGIME

The Brezhnev regime appears to have decided, not long after taking power, to begin a military buildup against China. This decision reflected the interaction of three factors.

First, the post-Khrushchev Politburo reached an overall conclusion that Chinese hostility—at least while Mao remained—was likely to be implacable and enduring. This assessment was strongly reinforced by the collapse of the hopes the new regime had harbored that it could reach a modus vivendi with Mao as a result of Khrushchev's removal. The failure of two exploratory talks on the overall relationship (held by Zhou Enlai with the Soviet leaders in Moscow in November 1964 and by Kosygin with the Chinese leaders in Beijing in February 1965) made it clear to the Brezhnev leadership that there was little chance that Mao would abandon his intransigence. This conclusion was reinforced a year later when Mao in early 1966 broke party-to-party relations, and thereafter ceased reference to the Sino-Soviet treaty or the Sino-Soviet alliance.

Second, superimposed on all this was the specific fact that Mao had publicly challenged the legitimacy of the Sino-Soviet frontiers, and just before Khrushchev's ouster had ostentatiously reiterated this challenge in such a fashion as to torpedo the first Sino-Soviet negotiations about the border. Negotiations about the eastern border had begun in early 1964—in the wake of the Chinese public disclosure in 1963 that China had an unsettled account with the Soviet Union over tsarist and Soviet land grabs at Chinese expense. These talks were initially stalemated by Soviet unwillingness to admit—as the Chinese demanded—that the existing border treaties were "unequal." The talks were then terminated by the Soviets after publication of a Mao interview that made a frontal assault on the USSR's right to its holdings in the Far East.[5]

Khrushchev and his successors reacted to these Mao statements with fervent vows that the Soviet Union would take all measures necessary to ensure "the inviolability of its frontiers,"[6] and Khrushchev, a month before his removal, added a threat that the USSR would use "all means at its disposal" to defend its borders, including the "up-to-date weapons of annihilation" it possessed.[7] This was apparently the first Soviet nuclear threat against China. But the Chinese furnished an effective reply to this threat in mid-October 1964, the day after Khrushchev was removed, when they exploded their first nuclear device.

Thus, from the start, Khrushchev's successors had a clear view of the dimensions of the problem they had inherited. They apparently responded with an early decision to begin a long-term strengthening of their military position in the Far East, both to ensure the "inviolability" of the frontiers they claimed and more broadly to create the means to exert pressure on Mao.

Third, Brezhnev, unlike Khrushchev, was predisposed to furnish the new resources deemed necessary to deal with the problem. While it is not impossible that Khrushchev himself, had he remained, would have felt compelled to begin a large-scale buildup against China, he had certainly indicated throughout his tenure in office a very strong reluctance—to put it mildly—to divert to the ground forces the large additional sums that were ultimately required by the anti-China effort.[8] The considerable increase in the size of the ground forces carried out over the ensuing years, in large part consumed by the buildup against China, took place in the context of more general expansion of all categories of Soviet military strength. This "all-azimuth, all-service" approach to military spending, into which the new anti-China program fit so neatly, was of course at first facilitated for Brezhnev by the rapid growth of the Soviet economic pie in the late 1960s and the increasing availability of resources for the military as a whole. These favorable trends were later to prove ephemeral. Brezhnev's initial approach, however, reflected a conviction that expanding all branches of Soviet military power would pay dividends for the enhancement of the Soviet Union's worldwide geopolitical position. One result was the militarization of the Soviet conflict with China.

The Principal Arenas

Mongolia   One of the first steps was to secure a Soviet military position in Mongolia. Brezhnev paid a visit to Ulan Bator in mid-January 1966, and soon thereafter a new mutual assistance treaty was signed. *Pravda* then informed Beijing that the USSR and Mongolia would henceforth "jointly" take all necessary measures, "including military measures," to defend the territory of both states.[9]

This decision served multiple purposes. On the political level, the establishment of a permanent Soviet military presence in Mongolia served to guarantee, once and for all, both the continued loyalty of the existing pro-Soviet Tsedenbal regime and its continued hold on power in the face of any future conceivable Chinese intrigues within the Mongolian party. While the first consideration was not a major concern (Tsedenbal's loyalty was not seriously questioned), the second was of some long-term importance: clashes within the Mongolian leadership some years earlier had produced the purge of some Politburo members considered favorable to Beijing. In short, like the Soviet forces in Eastern Europe, the Soviet forces in Mongolia would not only serve to confront and to intimidate the antagonist across the border, but would also ensure the stability of the local Soviet political base.[10] There would thus be no chance that political circumstances could ever force the Soviets to give up this strategic asset, as they had forced the USSR to abandon its conquests at Port Arthur and Dairen twelve years earlier.

At the same time, the introduction of Soviet forces into Mongolia served immediately to secure the flank of the Transbaikalia Military District (MD). These deployments strengthened the Soviet capability both to defend and eventually to attack at the northern Mongolian trijunction with the USSR and Manchuria, focal point of a historic attack corridor between Russia and China and the scene of well-remembered Soviet battles with both Chinese warlords and the Japanese at different periods before World War II and again with the Japanese in the last month of that war.

Beyond this, Mongolia served not only as a strategic buffer against China, but as a platform from which the Soviets could menace the north China plain and the approaches to Beijing, particularly after Soviet tank forces had been stationed in Mongolia. The potential vulnerability of the Chinese capital to such an armored assault from Mongolia was over the years to become a matter of increasing political importance, and eventually a focus of demonstrative Soviet efforts to intimidate the PRC.[11]

The Far East and Transbaikalia   The buildup in Mongolia proceeded in general synchronization with the strengthening of the Soviet position in the two easternmost military districts of the Soviet Union—the Far East and the Transbaikalia MDs. The preponderant weight of Soviet efforts was thus consistently placed on the eastern portion of the Sino-Soviet frontier, because of the extraordinary concentration there of vulnerable assets on both sides. On the Soviet side, these included the isolated salient of the Soviet Far East (Primorski krai), with its cities, population, and naval facilities; the Trans-Siberian Railway, precariously close to the Amur and Ussuri, the two border rivers; and the many contested islands in the rivers themselves, which because of geography sometimes had strategic importance in Soviet eyes.

Particularly notable was the large island that the Chinese call Heixiazi, at the confluence of the Amur and Ussuri (see Figure 7.1). Although this island lies on the Chinese side of the main channel, it is immediately adjacent to Khabarovsk and the Trans-Siberian Railroad, which passes through the city. Khabarovsk would be highly vulnerable to fire from hostile forces on Heixiazi. The Soviets have therefore been determined to ensure at all costs that the Chinese never occupy this island, whatever the legal equities.[12]

The eastern sector of the Sino-Soviet border has also been very important to the Soviet military planners because directly opposite, on the Chinese side, lies the primary Chinese industrial base of Manchuria. This is also a vulnerable salient, and therefore a prize worth menacing from the Soviet side, but for that very reason defended by large Chinese armies whose presence has served further to justify Soviet deployments opposite them.

The Far East Military District had always been the site of the largest Soviet concentration of force in Asia, even in Khrushchev's time, when its primary mission was to defend Vladivostok and to confront the United States and Japan. With the advent of the anti-China buildup, this district retained its primacy as its strength increased under Brezhnev, but became progressively more dual-purpose and dual-oriented, looking west and south as well as east. The mission of the Transbaikalia Military District, on the other hand, now became unambiguously anti-Chinese. Although remaining second in the local allocation of forces, this district probably gained the most from the buildup in comparison with its strength before the advent of Brezhnev and the anti-China task.

Partly because of the asymmetrical effects of geography upon the military needs of the opposing sides, and partly because of the Chinese perception of their firepower inferiority, the main Soviet forces have been deployed over the years much closer to the eastern river frontiers than have their Chinese opposi-

FIGURE 7.1
Heixiazi and Damansky/Chenbao Islands

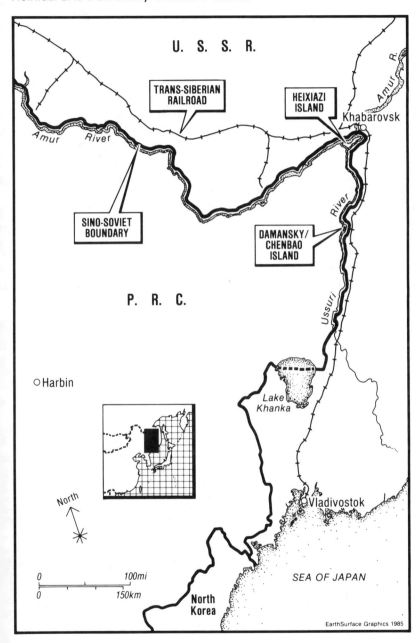

tion on the other side.[13] The disposition of Soviet strength, regardless of Soviet intentions, has therefore always implied a threat to China.

The Xinjiang Sideshow   Farther to the west, the confrontation along the border between Soviet Central Asia and Xinjiang was to remain very much of a sideshow, with somewhat less at stake for both contestants, and therefore smaller forces on both sides. Both sides knew that because of the significant Soviet local firepower advantage and even greater logistical advantage, Xinjiang was highly vulnerable to the Soviet Union in the event of large-scale fighting and might be regarded by China as temporarily expendable in a protracted struggle. Despite its less vital military importance, this sector of the Sino-Soviet border confrontation remained a political tinderbox—because of the history of past Soviet efforts to dominate Urumchi; past (and continuing) Soviet attempts to incite local minorities against Beijing; the existence of several small, actively disputed points along the border; and because of a large Chinese claim to the Soviet-controlled Pamir Mountains adjoining Afghanistan.

The Chinese Response

Against this background, the Soviet buildup in the first few years of the Brezhnev regime encountered what probably seemed to Moscow a paradoxical response from the Chinese side: increased pugnacity combined with reduced capability.

The Chinese Army's Difficulties   In terms of absolute military capabilities, the Chinese threat in the initial years of the buildup did not significantly increase, and in relative terms it may well have declined as Soviet reinforcements arrived in the Far East and new Soviet weapons were deployed, and as much of Chinese military attention was necessarily diverted because of U.S. participation in the war in Vietnam.

Moreover, these were the years of the Cultural Revolution. Although Chinese military spending for research and development apparently was maintained at a high level under the aegis of Defense Minister Lin Biao, any accomplishments are likely to have suffered considerably because of the frenetic atmosphere engendered by the Cultural Revolution even in military research organizations. Procurement of new military equipment decreased at first for the same reason, although it then rose rapidly after 1968.[14]

More important, the combat proficiency of the People's Liberation Army (PLA) as a whole is likely to have suffered considerably. The extreme politicization of the armed forces, the denigration of professionalism, the purges of successive chiefs of staff, the diversion of many military cadres to civilian administrative and political tasks previously performed by the shattered party machinery, and, above all, the pressure on the armed forces to take sides in the factional struggles waged by rival Red Guard organizations throughout the country, all surely had an adverse effect on military morale and capabilities.

The Chinese Posture Toward Moscow   What must have been difficult for Soviet political and military leaders to understand was that it was precisely in this period, when political chaos was attenuating the PLA's capabilities, that Chinese baiting of the Soviet Union multiplied. In early February 1967, the Soviet embassy in Beijing was besieged and isolated for more than a week. *Pravda* accused the Chinese of seeking to force a break in diplomatic relations, and such a break may in fact have been averted only as a result of the intervention of Zhou Enlai, who brought about an end to the siege. On several occasions during the next two years, Soviet and East European diplomats were manhandled in Beijing and Soviet merchant ships detained in Chinese ports. Meanwhile, along the Sino-Soviet border, all this was supplemented by occasional Red Guard demonstrative forays against Soviet border guards.[15]

More important, in 1966 and 1967, amid the chaos of the Cultural Revolution, the Chinese leadership appears to have gradually authorized Lin Biao to make more of an effort, through border guard patroling, to assert an occasional presence on islands in the Amur and Ussuri border rivers that were claimed by China (often with a strong legal case) but that the Soviets had long regarded as their own. While both sides enforced a rule against shooting until March 1969, border guard shouting, shoving, and clubbing confrontations evidently grew gradually more frequent during the long winters of 1966, 1967, and 1968, when the frozen rivers made mutual access to disputed islands easier for both foot patrols and military vehicles.[16] Such confrontations became particularly common at places, such as the island of Damansky/Chenbao in the Ussuri, that were normally uninhabited and were close to the Chinese shore, and where the Chinese therefore felt, with some justification, that they had a particularly strong claim.

The Soviets in those years claimed that the border treaties gave them title to the entire width of the Manchurian border rivers to the Chinese shore, including all the hundreds of islands in the rivers, no matter how close they were to China; and their border patroling sought to enforce this title. Although the Soviets knew that their legal case was weak, and they were willing to give up some of the islands on the Chinese side of the main river channels as part of a negotiated settlement, they were unwilling to give up many others that they considered of economic or strategic importance. Moreover, they were reluctant to give up anything at all without a general settlement and Chinese abandonment of all other claims.

The Effects of the Soviet Invasion of Czechoslovakia   Against the background of the growing Soviet buildup in the Far East, the Soviet use of force against Czechoslovakia in August 1968 had a galvanizing effect on the Chinese. By demonstrating the lengths to which the Soviets were prepared to go, it dramatized the danger to Chinese security and thereby enabled Zhou Enlai to persuade

Mao that a continuation of the Cultural Revolution chaos was a luxury China could no longer afford. At the same time, this event appears to have convinced the Chinese that they had to show the Soviet Union that they were not cowed by what had happened to the Czechs and would not be bullied. In addition to condemning the Soviet invasion and exhorting the PLA to strengthen border defense work, the Chinese now began calling attention to Soviet practices along the border, such as overflight violations, about which they had previously been silent.

On September 16, 1968, Beijing for the first time publicized a note of protest to the Soviet Foreign Ministry about Soviet border overflights, asserting that there had been an extraordinary increase in such violations between August 9 and 28.[17] It is credible that Soviet military reconnaissance may indeed have made frequent shallow violations of Chinese airspace in the past—reflecting a calculated and intimidating contempt for the capabilities of Chinese air defense—and it also is likely that there was a precautionary increase in such reconnaissance against China during the period surrounding the Czech invasion. By publicizing this phenomenon, the Chinese were also making an implicit admission of their weakness—their inability or unwillingness to take risks to put an end to such alleged violations.[18] On September 29, responding to this implication, Zhou Enlai again asserted that overflights were taking place "more frequently," alluded to Soviet "massive troop concentrations" on the Sino-Soviet and Sino-Mongolian borders, and announced that Soviet "military threats and war blackmail" would have "no effect whatever" on China.[19]

It seems likely that the Chinese leaders, determined to show that they were not intimidated, overcompensated with more vigorous attempts to assert through border guard patroling their title to those particular islands in the border rivers where they felt their right to be undeniable. This applied, above all, to Damansky/ Chenbao, where, as earlier noted, the Chinese legal case was especially strong. The Soviets, for their part, confident in their superior strength, were resolved to give not an inch. The result was a gradual escalation in border guard confrontations, from arguing, to shoving, to club-swinging,[20] until the Chinese at last staged a shooting ambush on Chenbao in early March 1969.

THE 1969 BORDER CRISIS

Soviet behavior during the protracted crisis with China over the Sino-Soviet border between March and September 1969 was conditioned by a conflict between two fundamental and opposing Soviet national interests. On the one hand, the Soviet leaders saw an urgent need to find a way to make the Chinese desist from efforts to enforce their claims on Soviet-held or Soviet-claimed territory— without a war, if possible. On the other hand, they wished to minimize the U.S. ability to extract an advantage in Soviet-American dealings from the Soviet dilemma. During the crisis period, the urgent first need took precedence over the second. The discussion to follow will suggest that despite the Soviet anxiety to avoid enhancing U.S. leverage over the Soviet Union, before the crisis was over, the Soviets in fact thought it necessary to try to involve the United States, if only as expert witness to the seriousness of their threats against China.

In the first place, the Soviets were astonished and greatly disturbed at what they regarded as the incomprehensible temerity of the Chinese in accepting— and, in some cases, provoking—armed combat with a greatly superior opponent. This was particularly striking in the way the sequence of clashes began.

As already suggested, the firefights of 1969 appear to have broken out during expanded patroling by both sides at the many disputed points customarily controlled (if not always inhabited) by the Soviets but claimed by the Chinese. More directly, however, the train of firefights was put in motion because the Chinese, in the first key clash on March 2, set a precedent by escalating border guard encounters to the shooting level.

Because the Chinese, having set an ambush, had much the better of this first shooting incident on Damansky/Chenbao Island, the Soviet leadership felt obliged to reply in kind at the next highest level. Thirteen days later, a much larger Soviet ambush at the same spot, undoubtedly approved by the Politburo and coordinated in advance from Moscow, produced the required bloody Chinese defeat. The Soviet attitude, like that of the Chinese toward Vietnam a decade later, was one of "teaching a lesson" to the weaker party.

This event did not, however, put an end to competitive Chinese patroling in the disputed areas. Under the circumstances—that is, given the extent of the blood that had just been spilled, and given Moscow's propensity in these circumstances to "lean forward" to defend all the territory it considered Soviet more vigorously and with more aggressive patroling—further incidents were virtually inevitable. A long series of larger or smaller firefights ensued in March, April, May, June, and August, alternating between the disputed islands in the Amur and Ussuri border rivers to the east and the Xinjiang-Central Asian border to the west. While firing in some of these clashes appears to have been initiated by the Soviets, it is likely that the Chinese began the shooting in other cases.[21]

The net result, for many in Moscow, was to confirm the impression of Chinese irrationality and unpredictability that had been fed by Chinese conduct over the preceding three years. More than anything else the Soviets were disturbed by the implications of the apparent Chinese willingness to act in disregard of the great Soviet advantage in both conventional firepower and nuclear striking force. Themselves inclined to give decisive importance to their ability to calculate forces and risks accurately, the Soviets are likely to have seen in the risky behavior of the Chinese a contention that the Soviets were bluffing. If the Chinese were not irrational, the only credible interpretation of their conduct was that they felt the apparent risks were illusory. The Chinese seemed to be implying that despite

loud talk, the Soviet leaders were not, in fact, willing to accept the possible consequences of a war with China, and that Chinese local actions in defense of what
Beijing saw as Chinese rights therefore need not be constrained by the threat of
escalation.[22] There was enough truth in this to be particularly infuriating to
Moscow; the Soviet leadership was indeed reluctant to become involved in a
large-scale war with China.

Soviet Threats of Escalation

A central aim of Soviet policy from March through September 1969 was
therefore to create credibility for the threat of escalation, through a combination
of means.

Behavior in the Border Encounters   First, the Soviets provided evidence
of credibility through practice, by demonstrating readiness to use somewhat
higher levels of force when reinforcements were deemed necessary in border encounters. The most notable such occasion was the second clash on Damansky/
Chenbao on March 15 when the Soviets apparently employed considerably
greater strength than the Chinese, including heavy use of artillery and rockets.[23]
In most of the subsequent patrol encounters in 1969, the Soviet forces appear to
have been larger than those of the PRC.

Advertisement of Reinforcements   Second, the USSR not only took steps
to reinforce its dispositions facing China but, more to the political point, took
measures to ensure that this reinforcement was discreetly advertised. The border
clashes appear to have caused some acceleration of the pace of the Soviet buildup
and of military resource transfers to Asia, although it is not clear that they materially altered the interim goals for the buildup that were in effect before March
1969. But although the Soviets continued efforts to improve their firepower advantage over the Chinese, their more urgent need was to extract practical political leverage from the sizable advantage they already possessed. To this end, they
allowed foreign visitors and journalists to observe and report on aspects of the
reinforcement process, so as to multiply the political effect.[24] In addition, Soviet
media during the crisis months occasionally alluded to recent Soviet military exercises in Asia; this was also somewhat unusual.[25] Moreover, the Soviets also
appear to have encouraged widespread rumors that circulated after the Soviet
victory in the second battle of Damansky Island on March 15, erroneously con-
tending that the Chinese losses in this battle had been multiplied by Soviet use of
terrible and mysterious new weapons, hitherto unknown.[26] Obviously the Soviets
intended to encourage exaggerated awe and respect for their firepower advantage.

Precedents for Conventional Attack   Third, the Soviets repeatedly reminded the Chinese of three past occasions when the Soviet Union had indeed
escalated to large-scale combat in the Far East.

1. The Soviets several times during the 1969 crisis pointed to the sharp defeat inflicted upon Japanese forces in a short undeclared war fought 30 years earlier at Khalkin-Gol near the Manchurian-Soviet-Mongolian trijunction.[27]
2. The earlier rout of local "Chinese militarists" by a specially formed Soviet army in 1929 was similarly used as an object lesson for Maoist "adventurists," notably by Col. Gen. V. F. Tolubko in a well-known article published not long after his transfer to command of the Far East Military District.[28]
3. The Soviets also brought to Chinese attention a much larger-scale Soviet attack: the Soviet conquest of Manchuria from Japan at the close of World War II. Chief of the General Staff Marshal Zakharov, in an article entitled "An Instructive Lesson," recalled the "two converging strikes" into Manchuria that overwhelmed the Japanese, and said that this "graphically testifies" to what could happen to others.[29]

The Threat of Nuclear Attack   Fourth, in addition to citing precedents for large-scale conventional attack, the Soviets sought to convince the Chinese leaders that there was a real possibility of a Soviet nuclear attack. In general, however, they approached this task in a much more gingerly fashion, conveying the message primarily by innuendo and implication, through occasional statements in nonauthoritative Soviet sources,[30] and, above all, by manipulating a crescendo of Western speculation and assertions on this subject. The Soviets clearly wished to have their cake and eat it too. They desired to avoid or minimize the negative political consequences that they believed they might incur, in world public opinion as a whole and within the Chinese elite,[31] if they were to make brutally unequivocal and authoritative threats of nuclear attack against China. To this end, they went so far as to issue repeated denials that they had any such intention.[32] At the same time, they did their utmost within the constraints described to persuade the Chinese leaders to disbelieve their formal denials. This dual campaign was ultimately successful.

To fully convince the Chinese of the reality of the risk of Soviet nuclear attack, the Soviets found it necessary to invoke the testimony of others on the credibility of their threat. First, during the summer of 1969, they apparently transmitted letters to certain communist parties in the West raising the possibility of a Soviet pre-emptive strike at Chinese nuclear installations.[33]

Second, and probably not without certain misgivings, the Soviet Union sought to involve the United States. On August 18, a Soviet embassy official in Washington asked a State Department official what would be the U.S. reaction to a Soviet assault on Chinese nuclear facilities. In putting this question to the United States, the Soviet leaders were most unlikely to have expected support or approval for such a step; they had good reason to expect U.S. support would not be forthcoming. Rather, the Soviets were probably hoping that the U.S. reaction to the question, even if adverse, would reach the Chinese, and would serve as independent testimony to the gravity of the Soviet menace to China. This hope was borne out when, on August 27, the director of the United States Central Intelligence Agency revealed to diplomatic correspondents that the Soviet Union had been sounding out foreign Communists on the possibility of an attack on China.[34] He indicated genuine concern about the matter.

However, it was not until September 16—a few days after the Beijing airport meeting between premiers Zhou and Kosygin had finally defused the crisis—that the Soviets made their most explicit and elaborate threat in the West to use nuclear weapons against China, using a technique that was intended to be both sufficiently authoritative to be completely frightening, yet disavowable. They published in the *London Evening News*, under the byline of their well-known agent Victor Louis,[35] a story that had probably been carefully vetted for Louis in the international department of the Central Committee, and possibly drafted there. This story cited "well-informed sources in Moscow" as asserting that "Russian nuclear installations stand aimed at the Chinese nuclear facilities," that "the Soviet Union prefers using rockets to manpower" in responding to border clashes, that the USSR "has a variety of rockets to choose from," that the Soviets have a "plan to launch an air attack on Lop Nor," and that "whether or not the Soviet Union will dare to attack Lop Nor, China's nuclear center, is a question of strategy, and so the world would only learn about it afterwards."[36] These statements were apparently timed to provide impetus to Chinese agreement to enter border talks, a matter then under consideration in the wake of the Zhou-Kosygin meeting.

The Resolution and Aftermath of the Crisis

The cumulative result of all the measures adopted in the Soviet credibility campaign was that the Chinese were, in fact, gradually intimidated. The repeated intimations of the nuclear strike threat appear to have impressed the Chinese somewhat more than the more explicit Soviet trumpeting about past large-scale invasions of China. The Chinese have since 1969 more than once expressed the conviction that the Soviets would be most reluctant to risk becoming bogged down in a long-term conventional land war in China, and that China would have the capability to ensure that any large-scale Soviet invasion would become such an open-ended struggle.[37] It is possible, however, that Chinese confidence in the effect of this claim wavered in 1969 in the face of Soviet military conduct and public statements. At the least, doubts on this score are likely to have added weight to the arguments of those (presumably led by Zhou Enlai) who successfully argued at the close of the summer that steps be taken to reduce the existing tension.

In any case, the nuclear strike threat clearly had an important effect on Chinese private calculations. From May 1969 on, Chinese pronouncements made frequent reference to Soviet "nuclear blackmail," Soviet missile deployments against China, and, finally, to the possibility of a Soviet surprise nuclear attack.[38] While to some extent these Chinese public statements were self-serving, intended to further blacken the Soviet image inside and outside China, they nevertheless almost certainly also reflected a genuine and increasing concern of the Chinese leadership. The Soviet steps taken in August to advertise in the West the possibility of such an attack appear to have added some verisimilitude to this possibility in the minds of the Chinese. One effect may therefore have been to encourage doubt about the adequacy and survivability of the Chinese nuclear deterrent, which in 1969, five years after the first Chinese nuclear explosion, did not yet include the 1,500-mile CSS-2 IRBM capable of reaching most major Soviet cities in Siberia, let alone the 3,500-mile CSS-3 limited-range ICBM, which is capable of reaching Moscow.[39]

In the aftermath, the experience of 1969 may therefore have lent urgency to subsequent efforts to achieve Chinese operational status for the CSS-2, accomplished two or three years later, and for the CSS-3 thereafter. The events of 1969 probably also reinforced Chinese determination to develop basing modes for the growing mix of Chinese strategic weapons that would permanently assure sufficient Soviet uncertainty about Chinese strategic survivability to guarantee the Chinese deterrent.[40] The upshot, for the Soviets, was to be the evolution of a strategic environment in which they knew that the kind of nuclear blackmail they successfully practiced against China in 1969 would never again be quite as credible.

Results of the 1969 Crisis

For more than one reason, therefore, from the Soviet perspective the net results of the 1969 crisis were mixed, with significant minuses as well as pluses.

The Cessation of Aggressive Patroling   The minimum Soviet objective was attained. After Mao had consented to allow Zhou to meet with Kosygin in September, the PRC was at last induced to halt the aggressive patroling intended to assert Chinese claim to hundreds of points claimed and held by the Soviet Union. In return, the USSR made a small tacit concession: in the case of a few river islands where the Soviet legal claim was obviously exceptionally weak and the Soviet strategic and economic interest small, the Soviets themselves apparently ceased patroling, in effect ceding control to Beijing. Damansky/Chenbao Island, the scene of the first two firefights, was one such case; it has remained in the hands of the Chinese ever since.[41] The Soviets undoubtedly judged this a small price to pay; they had averted the perceived danger that the border would be kept continuously aflame, and they had managed to do it without giving up control of the vast majority of the disputed points and without going to war with China. They surely judged this a major achievement.

The Resumption of Border Talks   In addition, the Chinese were induced in October to begin a new series of border negotiations with the Soviet Union, in effect resuming the talks that had been broken off in 1964. But although the occurrence of the negotiations was itself useful to the USSR as a symbol of reduced tensions along the border, the Soviets soon became aware that they were unlikely to get a settlement they were willing to accept, a settlement ratifying Soviet title to most of the disputed points. Instead, the Chinese from the outset demanded a Soviet military evacuation of all disputed territory prior to demarcation of an agreed frontier. The PRC in the years since has never relinquished this position. Thus, while the Soviets at the close of the 1969 crisis got the Chinese to halt their military challenge to the Soviet version of the border, they did not get the PRC to abandon its political challenge to the legitimacy of the existing Soviet holdings along the frontier. Instead, the border negotiations were to become a new Chinese vehicle for charges of territorial thievery against the Soviet Union. Soviet leadership statements over the next few years were to suggest that the Soviets found this prolonged impasse discouraging, and a source of ongoing vulnerability for Soviet dealings with the United States.

The ongoing Soviet buildup and the implied threat of nuclear attack on China—the advantages that had produced the Chinese backdown in 1969—now became a target of Chinese demands in the border negotiations. When the Chinese made it clear that no fundamental concessions were to be expected under conditions of nuclear blackmail, the Soviets, who had no intention of abandoning what they saw as necessary military leverage upon China, offered the Chinese instead a series of paper substitutes: proposals for nonaggression and no-use-of-force treaties. The Chinese invariably countered what they naturally regarded as a propaganda ploy by insisting that any such paper pledges be incorporated into a Soviet agreement to make a unilateral preliminary military withdrawal from all the areas China claimed to be in dispute. There the matter rested.

In practice, the Chinese were not asking the Soviets to evacuate the vast areas in the Far East that China claimed Russia had stolen in the past. Nor were the Chinese demanding, as is sometimes supposed, a uniform Soviet pullback of any given distance all along the border. Rather, the Chinese since October 1969 have requested a Soviet withdrawal from those particular places and areas Beijing claims tsarist Russia and the USSR have occupied, above and beyond the territory given Russia by "unequal treaties"—in effect, the hundreds of islands in the eastern border rivers and the large Pamir tract in the west.[42]

Meanwhile, for the Soviet leaders, the growth of U.S. maneuverability relative to the Soviet Union was the major drawback of the way the 1969 crisis was resolved. From the outset, the Soviets were concerned that U.S. leverage might be enhanced, but felt obliged to give priority to efforts to isolate China from the United States. Thereafter, over the next two years, while the Soviet buildup against China continued at a fairly rapid pace, the Soviet leaders explored the implications of the evolving situation in the Sino-Soviet-U.S. triangle. They apparently were suspicious throughout of the possibility of secret Sino-U.S. negotiations, and they sought to head off the chance that their two adversaries would combine against them, by making secret proposals to each.

The Politburo made repeated secret attempts to make personal contact with the Chinese leaders. Perceiving themselves in a race to try to "normalize" relations with the PRC before the United States did, the Soviets made proposal after proposal for a summit meeting with Mao or Zhou.[43] The Chinese, however, went on with the secret negotiations that eventually produced a Sino-U.S. summit,[44] while rejecting Soviet feelers for a Sino-Soviet summit out of hand.[45]

Approaches to the United States   Unsuccessful on one side, the Soviets tried the other. In July 1970, after the SALT I negotiations with the United States had been under way for only nine months, the Soviet SALT delegation surfaced a proposal for Soviet-U.S. "joint retaliatory action" against any third nuclear power that undertook "provocative" action against either country.[46] Against the background of the Sino-Soviet border crisis of the preceding year, this momentous proposal was transparently aimed at China. The Soviets were seeking, in effect, to lock in a Soviet-American combination against Beijing before the PRC could come to an agreement with the United States that would isolate the Soviet Union.

A quick American rejection put an end to these hopes for the time being, but four years later the Soviets were to revive the essence of this notion outside the SALT context and in somewhat different form. Richard Nixon states that at his last summit with Brezhnev in Moscow in July 1974, Brezhnev privately proposed "a U.S.-Soviet treaty which others could join where each country would come to the defense of the other if either country or one of its allies were attacked."[47] It thus appears that at both the opening and the closing stages of the détente relationship, Moscow unsuccessfully floated security proposals to the United States that were aimed at isolating the PRC and either pre-empting or breaking the American connection with China.

THE STRATEGY IN THE
FIRST HALF OF THE 1970s

Over the next few years, Soviet strategy toward China became in essence a holding action. The buildup slowed down markedly. The Soviets were unsuccessful in further attempts to line the United States up with them against China, but on the other hand they were relieved to see that despite the precedent set during the India-Pakistan war, Sino-U.S. rapprochement did not evolve rapidly into anti-Soviet security cooperation. The Soviets now waited for the death of Mao and pinned their hopes on the conjecture that this event, when it finally came, might extricate them from their unfavorable position in the triangle.

The Slowdown in the Buildup

It is difficult to pinpoint the beginning of the slowdown in the buildup, but it appears that at least by 1972, the large-scale reinforcements seen earlier had been reduced to a much smaller flow. Although major military construction continued, the Soviets seemed to concentrate thereafter on gradually filling out and improving the capabilities of units already in place. Equally as important as this deceleration in the flow of military personnel eastward was the slowdown, persisting over the next several years, in the rate of establishment of new division structures in the Far East. This change in the slope of the curve appears to have occurred as Soviet force levels allocated to the anti-China and anti-Japan missions in Asia (in the Central Asian, Siberian, Transbaikalia, and Far East military districts and Mongolia) rose toward 400,000 ground combat personnel, and as the rough total of divisions at all strength levels assigned to these areas approached 40.[48]

Reasons for the Slowdown

Possible Achievement of Interim Force Goals   There may well have been several contributing reasons for the slowdown. It is a reasonable conjecture that one very important consideration was that the first-stage, interim force goals established by the Brezhnev regime in 1965 had been mostly, if not entirely, achieved during the Eighth Five-Year Plan, 1966–1970. It is not impossible that this happened sooner than expected because of an acceleration over planned rates in 1969 and 1970 as a result of the 1969 border crisis. In any case, it is plausible that the military planners for the Ninth Five-Year Plan, which was to be carried out from 1971 through 1976, felt by late 1970 and early 1971 that they would soon have accumulated sufficient margin in Asia to permit them over the coming period to allow the anti-China buildup to continue at a more moderate pace. This would in turn permit them, after 1972, to divert a larger share of the scheduled growth of the ground forces to other purposes, including, among other things, an enlargement of the size of all Soviet divisions.

Meanwhile, it was not long after the Soviets began to slow down the buildup that they also decided to commit the enormous resources required to build a second Siberian railroad—the Baikal-Amur Mainline (BAM) project. This major undertaking, announced by Brezhnev in 1974, was to be begun in the Tenth Five-Year Plan (1976–1980). The decision testified to Soviet determination to expedite the economic development of the east and also, of course, to strengthen support for military forces there. In a sense, it supplemented the buildup and partly compensated for the slower growth of those forces in the mid-1970s.

Perception of Greater Border Stability   It also seems likely that the Soviet leadership felt able to decelerate the buildup because the situation on the Sino-Soviet border appeared, at least temporarily, somewhat more stable. The 1969 sequence of firefights had stopped; Chinese competitive patroling had been curtailed; and border incidents had become much more infrequent. The border negotiations, although going nowhere, were at least a useful token of stability. Moreover, although the new thrust of Chinese foreign policy under Zhou Enlai's aegis remained thoroughly anti-Soviet (and much more effective), the Soviets could console themselves that at least the irrationality and unpredictability they associated with the Cultural Revolution had vanished. Finally, Lin Biao was also gone. Since the Soviets may have associated Lin with pugnacious Chinese behavior on the border in 1969, his death, and the associated disruption in the Chinese high command, may well have been seen as also promising continued Chinese caution.

In this connection, it should be noted that the pace of Soviet military preparations against China was never simply a function of the Soviet view of Chinese military strength, or even of the Sino-Soviet military balance. On the contrary, the Soviets had accelerated those preparations in precisely those years when PLA morale and energies were devastated by the Cultural Revolution, when China did not yet have a deployed missile capable of reaching Soviet cities, and when the diversion of Chinese strength in response to a U.S. buildup in Indochina to the south was increasing. Paradoxically, the USSR began to decelerate the buildup in the years when the U.S. presence and threat on the Chinese southern flank was declining, when the PRC was reinforcing and strengthening its forces facing north, and after the Chinese had for the first time deployed a missile (the CSS-2) that gave them a more than trivial deterrent against Soviet nuclear attack.

Clearly, the Soviet view of what was required by the Chinese military "threat" was never simply a function of the Soviet estimate of the Chinese order of battle. At least equally important was the Soviet subjective appraisal, at the time future deployments were being planned, of what could be expected of Chinese behavior and Moscow's assumptions at each stage about what it wanted to deter the Chinese from doing. By 1972, reviewing the results of the 1969 border crisis and the 1971 India-Pakistan crisis, the Politburo was evidently satisfied with the level of deterrence it had achieved, for the time being. But this satisfaction was only provisional and, as later events proved, temporary.

Hopes for Improvement After Mao   In addition, the Soviet leaders had not quite given up hope of a significant improvement in their relations with the Chinese, once Mao Zedong had also departed the scene. From long experience they had come to look upon Mao as the implacable driving force behind Chinese hostility. They continued to hope that there were elements in the Chinese elite, particularly in the PLA, that desired a reduction of Sino-Soviet tensions, and that these preferences, submerged under Mao, would surface once Mao was dead. They hoped that divisions within the Chinese leadership might then open the possibility of a settlement of Sino-Soviet differences based on significant Chinese concessions to the Soviet Union. With this in mind, through the mid-1970s they continued vehemently to deny that they had made nuclear threats against China in 1969 and to denounce those—like Joseph Alsop—who reminded the world that the USSR had sought out American approval for a possible Soviet nuclear strike at the PRC.[49] At the same time, they showed remarkable patience after a Soviet helicopter crew was captured and detained in China in March 1974 and not released until December 1975.[50]

THE BUILDUP
SINCE THE LATE 1970s

In 1977 and 1978, however, considerations of different kinds began to influence the Soviet leaders to give a heightened priority to their strength in East Asia. Some of these factors concerned China; some the United States and Japan; some, the three together. Gradually and cumulatively, the joint effects of all these inputs to Soviet thinking began to be more and more visible after 1978.

The Scope of Changes

In retrospect, it appears that by early 1978 at the latest, the Soviets had decided that it was necessary to give heightened importance to the size, structure, organization, deployment pattern, and rapid mobilization potential of their forces confronting China.[51] This changing priority was symbolized, and perhaps also given impetus, by the highly unusual public visit Brezhnev and Minister of Defense Ustinov paid to the commands at Khabarovsk and Vladivostok in April 1978.[52] In the years since, the effects of this decision have been reflected in a variety of ways:

First, by the widely reported large-scale renewal of Soviet military hardware in Siberia, Mongolia, and the Far East with next-generation equipment—a process that was particularly notable in the case of aircraft.[53]

Second, by an acceleration of the process of deploying new, low-category, thinly manned divisions facing China.[54] This process had the advantage of significantly augmenting both the rapid mobilization potential of the anti-Chinese forces and the threat perceived by China without a comparable immediate expenditure of increasingly scarce military manpower resources.

Third, by carrying out a major reorganization of the Soviet command structure opposite China. By 1979, a high command was established[55] for the Far East theater of operations, which appears to exercise authority over the Far Eastern, Siberian, and Transbaikalia military districts, including Soviet forces in Mongolia.[56] It is plausible to conjecture that under wartime conditions, if not sooner, the Pacific fleet and the Central Asian Military District might also be subordinated to this command. In view of the dual mission of the Far East Military District—facing both China and Japan—the establishment of the high command imposed a single focus on the tasks of opposing China, Japan, and U.S. forces in the Far East. In addition, it was a long step toward recognizing the inescapable permanence and need for self-sufficiency of the Far Eastern theater, a subject to which we shall return later.

Fourth, by augmenting what the Chinese have regarded as the demonstrative and threatening deployment of forces in Mongolia. The PRC has reacted bitterly and publicly to what it sees as an increased and gratuitous Soviet threat to the north China plain since 1979, as well as to the unprecedentedly large Soviet exercise held in and around Mongolia in the spring of 1979.[57]

And fifth, by making more visible to China the threat of strategic weapons of mass destruction through the deployment of the SS-20 IRBM and the Backfire bomber. Notable in this connection was an unusual facet of the deployment trend of the SS-20 after 1979. This IRBM, which has also been deployed against Europe, appears to devote more nearly equal targeting to China and the Far East than have previous such weapons systems.[58] Parallel with this has been the gradual, piecemeal discovery over the same period—through the revelations of Soviet conduct in Afghanistan and Indochina—that the Soviet Union may have been preparing and testing in action chemical and biological agents to which China is potentially particularly vulnerable.

Meanwhile, there was simultaneously an acceleration of naval and air deployments to the Far East directed against Japan and U.S. forces in the area. The naval buildup was dramatized by the temporary deployment to Vladivostok of the antisubmarine warfare (ASW) carrier *Minsk* and the large troop carrier *Ivan Rogov* in 1979. Probably of more fundamental long-term significance for U.S. naval forces in the Pacific was the fact that the Backfire was deployed with antiship as well as deep-theater bombing missions. The aspect of these changes that had the most immediate political consequences, however, was the Soviet decision to begin fortification and garrisoning in 1978 of the southern Kuril Islands claimed by Japan, despite the adverse political effect this had on Soviet relations with Japan.

The Multiple Causes

Why did the Soviet leaders begin this multifaceted effort in 1978? A combination of four reasons seems likely.

The Heightened Role of the Sea of Okhotsk Bastion   One factor was simply the powerful effects of advancing technology. The advent at about this time of very-long-range, submarine-launched ballistic missiles (such as the SS-N-8 and later the SS-N-18) made it possible for the first time for Soviet ballistic missile submarines to target the United States without leaving "bastion areas"—that is, partially sheltered bodies of water immediately adjoining the Soviet Union, such as the Barents Sea in the northwest and the Sea of Okhotsk in the Far East.[59] This fact gave added strategic importance to nearby land areas— the Kola Peninsula in the northwest and the Soviet Primorski province, Kamchatka, and the Kuril chain in the east. The heightened role of the Sea of Okhotsk made it increasingly important for the Soviet Union to deny U.S. access to this sea in time of war and to guarantee its own egress. This growing sensitivity about the bastion area in turn contributed to the Soviet decision to begin the fortification of the southern Kurils and to accelerate the naval, air, and ground force buildup along the surrounding coasts.

Presumptive Insurance Against Sino-U.S.-Japanese Cooperation   It is also likely that the Soviets by early 1978 had already begun to take out insurance against a worst-case contingency of Sino-U.S.-Japanese security cooperation. Even before the successive alarm bells were rung in Moscow by the visit of U.S. presidential security adviser Brzezinski to China in May 1978, the signing of the Sino-Japanese friendship treaty in August, and the announcement of Sino-U.S. normalization in December, the Soviet leaders seem to have begun to fear that their efforts to retard the drawing together of these three powers would ultimately be unsuccessful. It is thus entirely plausible that resources allocated and military plans made during the 1977 finalization of the Tenth Five-Year Plan (1976–1980) ere in part influenced by the desire to prepare for this contingency. The projected increase in Soviet strength in the Far East, in combination with the new Soviet organizational cohesion, was clearly expected to give the Far Eastern theater an independent viability against the potential combined forces of its adversaries, and a significant advantage if those adversaries did not combine.[60]

Although the Sino-U.S.-Japanese security combination feared by the USSR has not in fact yet materialized, the Soviets probably now view the steps they have taken as serving a prophylactic purpose. The menacing new Soviet deployments in Mongolia and the Kurils have in common, among other things, the goal of intimidating two prospective members of this hypothetical alliance. The potential to intimidate is enhanced by the concrete military advantages these deployments would give the Soviets against their prospective adversaries in wartime—in the Chinese case, quicker access by Soviet armor to the north China plain, and in the Japanese case, greater possibilities to achieve and maintain control of the Soya Strait.

In general, this recent effort to intimidate regional opponents through the Far

East buildup bears a close resemblance to the analogous function already served by the Soviet buildup in Europe.

The Heightened Importance of Indian Ocean Support   The new activism in the Soviet deployments and organizational measures taken in the Far East also reflected the heightened importance of the Far East in supporting Soviet efforts to exploit new opportunities opening up in southern and western Asia. Apparently because of the uncertain reliability of the Suez Canal, Soviet naval operations in the Indian Ocean have had to be largely supported and controlled from distant Vladivostok. In view of the events that unfolded in both Iran and Afghanistan in 1978, and the geopolitical opportunities created for the USSR by the weakening U.S. position in Southwest Asia, the Soviet Far East took on additional significance in the worldwide Soviet contest with the United States as the essential base for future Soviet naval deployments southward and westward.

The Wish to Increase Leverage on China Concerning Vietnam   The Soviets were also influenced to give a higher priority to the Far East buildup by a felt need to increase their leverage on China, in connection with trends in Indochina in the wake of the expulsion of the United States from the peninsula in 1975. The Soviet leaders undoubtedly watched eagerly the approach of geopolitical opportunity through 1977 and 1978 as they observed the rapid decay of Sino-Vietnamese relations and the parallel growth in Soviet-Vietnamese association, which were to culminate in Hanoi's entry into the Council for Mutual Economic Assistance (CMEA) in June 1978 and the signing of the Hanoi-Moscow treaty in November. Since 1975 the Chinese had been warning—correctly, as it turned out—of the Soviet thirst for access to the former U.S. naval facilities at Cam Ranh Bay.[61] Even before the opportunity to cash in on these facilities materialized, the Soviets are likely to have vaguely foreseen that circumstances might well evolve in which they could reap geopolitical profit by underwriting Vietnamese ambitions in Indochina and protecting Vietnam against the PRC. Over and above all other motives, the strengthening of the Soviet ground, air, and naval position in the Far East after 1978 was intended to serve this purpose: increasing Soviet deterrent pressure on China to restrain China's actions to the south.

It was against this background that a test of the Soviet deterrent capability suddenly appeared in Indochina in late 1978.

THE 1979 CRISIS IN INDOCHINA

Factors in Soviet Calculations

It seems likely from the circumstances surrounding the signing of the Soviet-Vietnamese "friendship" treaty on November 3, 1978, that the Soviet leaders were well aware from the outset of the Vietnamese intention to attack and conquer Cambodia. They were aware also that if the PRC responded in kind against Vietnam and in defense of its Cambodian client, Soviet choices would be limited. Even in the unlikely event that it should want to do so, the Soviet Union could not bring significant ground force strength to bear in Vietnam itself for many weeks or even months because of the great logistical difficulties. Consequently, the central issue created by the 1978 treaty was the implicit Soviet threat to take military action of some kind across the Sino-Soviet border, whether by land or air or both, in the event of Chinese action against Vietnam.

From the Soviet perspective, the state of their military matchup with China in 1978 had both favorable and unfavorable implications for the venture they were about to take in Indochina by associating themselves with Hanoi's plans to act. On the one hand, Chinese nuclear capabilities had significantly improved since the border crisis of 1969. In view of the entry into operational status of both the Chinese CSS-2 and CSS-3 surface-to-surface missiles, and their deployment in modes likely to diminish Soviet confidence in the total effectiveness of any disarming strike, the Chinese deterrent against any Soviet attack had been considerably augmented since 1969. Moreover, the Soviets had every reason to suspect that the Chinese also thought so. Consequently the Soviets could not expect indirect nuclear threats of the kind employed against China in the 1969 crisis to have the same degree of credibility again. Meanwhile, despite the continued growth of the Soviet firepower advantage, the Soviets are likely to have retained their reluctance to become involved in a land war with China from which they might not be able to extricate themselves.

On the other hand, despite these Chinese improvements, the Soviets entered the new crisis with a relative firepower advantage over China (both conventional and nuclear) that had in fact grown rather than diminished since the first crisis in 1969, when they already had a great advantage in both respects. In addition, it seems probable that they were encouraged by the memory of their experience with China during the India-Pakistan war of 1971. On that occasion, China did not come to the assistance of Pakistan when it was attacked by India with the support of the Soviet Union. In 1971 as in 1978, the attacking state had signed a treaty of friendship with Moscow shortly before launching its attack. Although the U.S. government, according to Henry Kissinger,[62] was seriously concerned during the India-Pakistan war that China would respond militarily against India, possibly unleashing a subsequent Sino-Soviet conflict that could involve the United States, the PRC did not in fact take such action, and the Soviets are likely to have concluded that this inaction was largely due to the Soviet deterrent. As the Indochina crisis of 1978 unfolded, the Soviets are therefore likely to have assumed that the threat they posed in Siberia, to China's north, would probably again paralyze Chinese reaction to events to the south.

At the same time, the Soviets may have been in some doubt as to what role the United States might play in a new Soviet crisis with China. The experience of the past decade again pulled in two directions, and paradoxically gave the Soviet leaders cause for both confidence and concern. On one side of the ledger was the Soviet perception that the world power position of the Soviet Union, compared with that of the United States, had been significantly improved since 1969. In the decade gone by, trends in both the strategic and conventional military balances had been encouraging to the Soviet leadership. The growth of Soviet power projection capabilities and a simultaneous decay of U.S. and Western influence at a number of points in the Third World previously strongly oriented toward the West had permitted an unprecedented expansion of the Soviet presence around the world. From this perspective, seizure of a new Soviet political opportunity in Indochina is likely to have been seen by the Soviet leadership as an action fitting into a pattern of precedents in which Soviet boldness had been rewarded and the U.S. response increasingly constrained.

On the other side of the ledger, however, Soviet leaders in November 1978 had cause to believe—remembering the shock of the U.S. opening to China in 1971—that the United States was capable of unpleasant surprises. One result of the deterioration of Soviet-U.S. relations since 1975 had been a reversal of the trend of declining U.S. military spending; another had been the beginning of a trend toward somewhat closer Sino-U.S. dealings. During 1978 this trend toward greater Sino-U.S. cooperation had seemed to accelerate, notably with the visit of Brzezinski to Beijing in May 1978, and the U.S. encouragement of Japan to sign the Sino-Japanese friendship treaty, essentially on Chinese terms, in August. The Soviets meanwhile observed the inauguration of gradual unwelcome changes in the U.S. position regarding Western arms sales to the PRC. Although it is likely that the Soviets did not foresee, when the Soviet-Vietnamese treaty was signed in early November, that Sino-U.S. normalization would be completed only a month later, they were surely well aware of unusual stirrings in the relationship.

The net result of the interplay of all these considerations was that initially the Soviet leaders probably somewhat underestimated the risks latent in their actions, and had no "worst-case" plan in mind at the outset. The evidence of their behavior just before and during the crisis, reviewed below, suggests surprise and temporizing. This pattern of hesitancy and caution during the Chinese "counterattack" also suggests that the Soviet leaders had not previously decided on the course of action they would take to save the Hanoi regime if worse came to worst. On the whole, it seems likely that they were somewhat misled by their easy experience with China in 1971, and therefore partially miscalculated the Chinese reaction in 1979 to the more severe provocation created by the overrunning of Cambodia.

The Ambiguity of the Treaty Commitment

Nevertheless, the Soviets took care to ensure sufficient ambiguity in the treaty signed with Vietnam to preserve their options, including the option of in-action. Unlike all other Soviet treaties signed with communist states, the pact with Vietnam was not called a "mutual assistance" treaty and did not pledge Moscow to provide "immediate aid," including "military" aid, in the event of an attack on Vietnam. Instead, as they had done in the case of India, the Soviets promised to "consult" with the Vietnamese and to take "appropriate effective measures." This language, once again, was intended to enable the Soviets to have their cake and eat it: to imply a threat against China without formally committing the Soviet Union to any military response.

But also, as in the case of the 1971 India-Pakistan crisis, the Soviets knew that this legal safeguard would not protect them from the severe dilemma that would arise if Vietnam should ever find itself in desperate need of Soviet action. Moreover, because Vietnam, unlike India, was a communist regime, the political pressure on Moscow to take dangerous military risks in such an extremity would be much higher.

The Treaty and Soviet Military Pressure

However ambiguous their deterrent against China, the Soviet leaders did not intend to sell it to Vietnam cheaply. The atmosphere surrounding the final nego-tiations that produced the treaty in Moscow in early November strongly sug-gested that the talks included hard bargaining.[63] Although the evidence is not conclusive, it is a reasonable speculation that one of the matters under contention involved the guidelines for the special military rights that the Soviet Union sub-sequently obtained in Vietnam for the first time: the right to conduct naval port visits, to use and enlarge naval support facilities in Vietnamese ports, to build and operate electronic facilities at Cam Ranh Bay, and to use Vietnamese air-fields to stage long-range naval reconnaissance flights from the Soviet Far East.[64] All these Soviet privileges emerged in the immediate aftermath of the Sino-Vietnamese fighting. It appears likely that the details of the Soviet activities, which may have been broadly sanctioned on a contingent basis by these under-standings, were spelled out in Soviet-Vietnamese contacts only during and after the fighting. For example, the spacing of Soviet TU-95 reconnaissance flights to Vietnam and the length of the stay of these aircraft in Vietnam may well have become the subject of continuing conversations between Moscow and Hanoi.[65] Nevertheless, agreement in principle on the broad framework of these new Soviet activities, to be phased in if need later arose, is likely to have been part of the Soviet-Vietnamese bargain from the outset, and an essential if unpublicized por-tion of the treaty package finally agreed upon.[66]

In the aftermath, the Soviets have evidently believed that the risks associated with their support of Vietnam have been outweighed by the value their new privileges in Vietnam offer to Soviet power projection capabilities. The facilities eventually obtained in Vietnam offer the Soviets major conveniences for the deployment into the Indian Ocean of naval forces based in and controlled from the Soviet Far East, help the Soviets to support frequent deployments in the South China Sea, and give a significant assist to Soviet submarine and antisubmarine warfare operations within a wide radius of Vietnam.[67] Beyond all this, the Vietnam facilities have a historical significance to the Soviet leaders: they are the first points of support for naval operations that the USSR has been able to obtain in the Pacific outside its home territory since the Soviet Union was forced to surrender Port Arthur and Dairen in the 1950s.

The Evolution of Soviet Behavior in the Crisis

Once the Vietnamese blitzkrieg into Cambodia began in December 1978, the Soviets watched the evolving Chinese reaction with great reserve. Although the Soviets were surely aware of the growth of the Chinese military buildup in areas near Vietnam as it developed in late December and throughout January, they initially said very little about this. They were reticent about the Chinese troop movements partly because they did not want to raise the issue of their own intentions, but also partly because they may at first have continued to hope that the Chinese were bluffing and were merely seeking to intimidate Vietnam, in the same way that they themselves had for a long time sought to intimidate China through their buildup on the Chinese frontier.[68]

By late January 1979, however, the Soviets seemed to attach greater credence to the possibility that China would really attack, and Soviet editorials and broadcasts denouncing the Chinese took on a tone of greater alarm. Nevertheless, no Soviet statement specified what the Soviets might do if the Chinese marched, or referred directly to the possibility of any military Soviet action. The closest approximation to such a threat was far removed indeed—one journal's appeal to "international public opinion" to prevent Beijing "from overstepping the forbidden line."[69]

After the Chinese did attack in early February 1979, the Soviets issued a government statement demanding that the Chinese stop "before it is too late," insisting that the Vietnamese have "reliable friends," and asserting that the Soviet Union would "fulfill the commitments it assumed" under the treaty with Hanoi.[70] Neither the statement nor any other Soviet public comment, however, chose to be more specific about the nature of those commitments, nor to refer, through the period of the fighting, to Article 6 of the treaty, the clause that promised "consultations" with Vietnam if it were attacked and "effective measures" to "eliminate the threat." Although the Soviet minister of defense later termed the government statement a "serious warning" to the Chinese, he too refrained from any hint as to what the Soviets proposed to do if this warning were ignored and the Chinese continued their assault.[71]

The Chinese View of the Risks

The Chinese, however, do not appear to have had great confidence that the Soviets would not act, and they seem to have become more nervous about this as the fighting went on. All in all, although the Chinese leadership appears to have made a considered judgment, before crossing the Vietnamese border, that the Soviet Union would probably not take military risks in response to the kind of limited Sino-Vietnamese engagement Beijing envisioned, the PRC nevertheless appears to have seen at least a marginal chance of a Soviet attack.

Beforehand, the Chinese did what they could to minimize the risk. They reinforced in Xinjiang, evacuated civilians on a large scale from exposed areas near the border, and put forces facing the Soviet Union in a posture of enhanced readiness—all steps that they knew the Soviets would see, and that they hoped would remind Moscow of the risks involved in any precipitate action.[72]

Most important of all, they advertised in advance, as widely as possible, the limited nature of their objectives, both in space and time.[73] As the fighting developed, the delays in the Chinese timetable occasioned by the stubborn Vietnamese resistance therefore apparently evoked not only embarrassment in Beijing but also increased concern about the Soviet reaction, since these delays inevitably tended to make ultimate Chinese objectives seem more ambiguous and the Chinese promise of a short "lesson" and an early pullout somewhat less credible. It was not until March 5, after the fall of Long Son—an event evidently necessary for Chinese pride—that the Chinese announced that they had taught Vietnam its "lesson" and would now retire. The long delay in achieving the fall of Long Son was apparently largely responsible for the delay in the Chinese withdrawal.

The Soviet Military Response

During the Sino-Vietnamese war the Soviets assisted the Vietnamese in Vietnam with air and coastal transport,[74] increased their naval air reconnaissance from the Soviet Far East,[75] maintained the naval intelligence collection vessels already deployed in the vicinity of Vietnam,[76] and moved a naval flotilla down from the Soviet Far East as far as the East China Sea. There, however, the flotilla remained; it did not venture into the South China Sea during the fighting.[77]

There is no evidence, and no reason to believe, that during the hostilities major threatening gestures were made by the Soviet Union along the Chinese border.[78] Not long after the fighting ceased, the USSR during the spring of 1979 staged a large-scale military exercise in the Soviet Far East, Siberia, and Mongolia,[79] and no doubt hoped (with good reason) that aspects of this exercise would be observed by the Chinese and would incidentally help in Moscow's ongoing efforts to intimidate China. But in view of the long lead time probably required to prepare such exercises,[80] it appears most unlikely that this one was organized in response to the events of the previous few months in Indochina, or had intimidation as its primary purpose.

Although the Soviet war effort was thus confined largely to logistics, intelligence, and rhetoric, it can be argued that little more was required by the Vietnamese, given their own impressive resistance and the limited Chinese objectives. Afterward, the Soviets could claim—and no doubt said so privately to Hanoi—that their primary contribution had been to ensure that the Chinese objectives were indeed limited and remained so. Nevertheless, it is difficult to believe that at the outset of the fighting, when some uncertainty necessarily existed about Chinese intentions, the Vietnamese would not have welcomed a more forthright deterrent warning from Moscow to Beijing, including warning gestures on the Sino-Soviet border.

Subsequent Defensive Soviet Rationalizations

Both during and after this 1979 episode, some Soviet statements about what the USSR had and had not done seemed somewhat defensive. In a speech on March 3, Brezhnev protested that "no one should doubt" that the Soviet Union would live up to its treaty commitment, evidently reflecting a belief that some doubts had arisen. Some Soviet editorials later stressed that the Soviet deterrent had worked, and that "the Peking leadership had to reckon with the serious warnings addressed to it by the Soviet Union."[81] Other Soviets, after the fact, passed dark hints implying that forthright and threatening Soviet actions, which they were unable to specify, had indeed been taken during the crisis.[82] Yet others implicitly denied this, claiming that Moscow's "vigorous diplomatic activity" had been all that was needed and that in so doing, "our country, acting in accordance with the Soviet-Vietnamese treaty, gave fighting Vietnam all the help which was necessary in the Vietnamese comrades' opinion."[83] At least one Soviet writer admitted that Soviet behavior had been conditioned by risks implicitly involving the United States.[84]

THE AFTERMATH IN THE TRIANGLE TO DATE

Since the 1979 Sino-Vietnamese fighting, there have been changes in certain aspects of the Sino-Soviet-U.S. triangular relationship that modified the main trends seen in the late 1970s.

The steady decline in Soviet-American relations since the mid-1970s has continued in the 1980s, and for a time even accelerated.[85] Because of the further contraction of U.S. maneuvering room in the triangle, the intrinsic importance to the United States of the role played by the PRC has continued to increase.

Meanwhile, the growth in the Sino-U.S. relationship, in vigorous progress since 1978, was temporarily halted in 1981, largely as a result of new prominence given to the Taiwan issue by both sides. Apparently mainly for this reason, the Chinese in 1981 and 1982 moved increasingly to a public posture of criticism of both the United States and the Soviet Union. The geopolitical realities, however, remained asymmetrical. The PRC continued to maintain economic and other relations with the United States that were qualitatively different from those with the USSR; and Moscow, not Washington, continued to develop a strategic threat to Chinese interests on the northern, southern, and western borders of the PRC. The United States thus continued to be very important to Beijing as the essential offset to Soviet geopolitical pressure against China in East Asia, and as a long-term source of the dual-use advanced technology needed to strengthen China's military industrial capabilities against the Soviet threat. These underlying realities were reflected in a considerable improvement in Sino-U.S. relations in 1983, and in a striking series of high-level visits and contacts, culminating in the visit of President Reagan to Beijing in April 1984.

Although this presidential visit was primarily of symbolic rather than substantive importance, the visit nevertheless represented an important watershed for both sides. On the American side, it symbolized Reagan's coming to terms with China's strategic importance to the United States despite his reluctance to abandon support for Taiwan. On the Chinese side, it demonstrated recognition that despite China's assertion of an independent foreign policy, its rejection of a formal alliance with the United States, and its efforts to reduce tensions with the USSR, a reasonably good relationship with America remained important for Chinese national interests in view of the likelihood of an enduring Soviet strategic threat to those interests.

Moreover, despite the ongoing frictions in Sino-U.S. relations and Chinese explicit disavowal of a U.S. alliance, Chinese dealings with the United States in 1983 and early 1984 continued to pose before the Soviets the prospect of increased Sino-U.S. security cooperation. This message was conveyed by the visit of U.S. Defense Secretary Weinberger to Beijing in September 1983, by the visit of Premier Zhao Ziyang to Washington in January 1984, and, most strikingly, by the long-delayed visit of Chinese Defense Minister Zhang Aiping to the United States in June 1984.[86] From the Soviet perspective, the likelihood that a U.S. transfer of military technology to the PRC would actually materialize was now greater than it had ever been before.

These developments took place against the background of an ongoing stalemate in the broad Chinese strategic confrontation with the Soviet Union in Asia. Chinese forces have continued to confront hostile armies on two sides, to the north and the south. Although Hanoi has been unable to put an end to Khmer Rouge resistance to the Vietnamese occupation of Cambodia, on the whole and for the time being the Vietnamese, with Soviet help, have made good their effort to assert control over the Indochinese peninsula. In this sense, the Chinese effort to "teach the Vietnamese a lesson" has failed. The Soviets have consolidated and expanded the military benefits they acquired on Vietnamese soil at the close of the Sino-Vietnamese fighting, and now maintain a semipermanent naval presence in the South China Sea. The Vietnamese have meanwhile strengthened their military position in their northern border provinces facing China, thus probably making any prospective new Chinese attack much more difficult and costly.

The Sino-Soviet border stalemate also continues, and the Sino-Soviet border talks in progress since 1969 halted after 1978, although they have recently been scheduled to resume in 1987. In the spring of 1979, the Chinese gave notice of abrogation of the long-dormant Sino-Soviet treaty of alliance. Moreover, in December 1979 the Soviet Union, through its invasion of Afghanistan, added yet another item to the list of issues on which Soviet and Chinese policy conflict in Asia.

The Process of Limited Sino-Soviet Improvement

Nevertheless, since 1981, and particularly since the fall of 1982, there has been a perceptible trend of gradual improvement in certain aspects of Sino-Soviet dealings. This trend evidently evolved in part because of the aggravation of Sino-U.S. differences over the Taiwan issue with the new Reagan administration, and the consequent Chinese inclination to create some distance between the PRC and the United States. More fundamentally, however, the Chinese leaders have sought to improve their business dealings with the USSR as a means of easing some of the pressure on China created by the ongoing Soviet buildup and China's two-front confrontation with Vietnam and the USSR. At the same time, Beijing has sought to use the gradual expansion of state-to-state contacts on secondary matters as a means of enticing the USSR into making concessions on the issues China considers of primary importance: the reversal of the Soviet buildup, the abolition of Soviet military pressure against China, and the abandonment of those geopolitical gains the USSR made in Asia in the 1970s that injure Chinese interests.

To this end, since 1982 mutual contacts in sports and cultural affairs have grown; a handful of Chinese students have gone to the USSR to study; Sino-Soviet cross-border trade has resumed; total trade turnover has significantly risen; China has agreed to have the USSR re-equip a few old Chinese plants; and a series of semiannual talks on contentious issues have been instituted at the deputy foreign minister level.

But despite these advances in certain aspects of the Sino-Soviet relationship, until the summer of 1986 China had still made no progress in getting the Soviet leaders to offer even token concessions to any of the three demands Beijing poses as prerequisites for a more fundamental improvement of relations:[87]

> **1.** Removal of all Soviet troops from Mongolia and the reduction of the Soviet force posture east of the Urals down to the level of Khrushchev's day—that is, a complete undoing of the Soviet buildup discussed in this chapter.
>
> **2.** Cessation of Soviet support for Vietnam's effort to consolidate its conquest of Cambodia (and, implicitly, elimination of the Soviet military presence in Vietnam).
>
> **3.** Removal of Soviet forces from Afghanistan.

In practice, the Chinese leaders would no doubt be pleased to obtain something less than these extreme demands. The Chinese have appeared particularly eager to secure the withdrawal of Soviet forces from Mongolia, where they perpetually threaten the invasion route to the north China plain and Beijing. The PRC has also placed particularly heavy stress on the need for the USSR to exert significant pressures on Vietnam to secure a radical change in Hanoi's intransigent posture.

In July 1986, Soviet general secretary Gorbachev at last raised the possibility of token concessions to certain of the Chinese security demands, but none that seemed likely to bring China an early respite for the growth of Soviet geopolitical pressure.[88] He stated that the USSR has been "discussing" with Mongolia the withdrawal of a "considerable" part of the Soviet troops there. He did not say that he would in fact pull back part of these forces, or when, but it seems likely that having raised the matter, he intended to do so in the not distant future given a minimally encouraging Chinese response. Gorbachev also did not say how many troops he would withdraw, or to where they might be moved. The most likely possibility—a pullback of one or two of the five divisions to neighboring Siberia—would not reduce the total of Soviet forces opposite the PRC or materially alter the Soviet force posture confronting China. Thus this Gorbachev gesture, while of some political symbolic importance, appeared to have only minimal military significance.

At the same time, Gorbachev also for the first time proposed to begin negotiations with the PRC about "balanced" reductions in conventional ground forces in the Far East. In contrast to the notion of a partial pullback from Mongolia, however, this proposal was apparently not envisioned as leading to unilateral action. Gorbachev evidently desired to draw Beijing into negotiations analogous to the long-frozen MBFR talks in Europe, and to demand a still unspecified price for even token Soviet reductions. He was surely aware of the problems this would pose for Beijing, particularly in view of the great asymmetries in the nature and disposition of the forces involved. As earlier noted, the much larger Chinese forces facing the Soviet Union rely mainly upon their superior numbers—and China's space—to help offset a great Soviet advantage in conventional and nuclear firepower. Prospects for agreement in any such MBFR-type talks were rendered still more problematical by the fact that the most important aspect of that threatening Soviet firepower—Soview nuclear weaponry in Asia—would apparently be withheld as a subject of such negotiations.

In sum, although it is possible that the Soviet Union may eventually make some token gestures to China in the form of small-scale local pullbacks in Mongolia or elsewhere, it seems unlikely that Moscow will soon begin to halt, much less reverse, the Siberian buildup. Meanwhile, as of the fall of 1986 the Soviet geopolitical attack on Chinese interests around the Chinese periphery showed no sign of slackening. During the 1980s, those Soviet policies to which the PRC objected had in many respects in fact significantly intensified.

In Afghanistan, the Soviet punitive war on China's western frontier continues, with no end in sight. In Indochina, an area much more important to the PRC, despite some ongoing friction between Moscow and Hanoi the Soviet Union appears unwilling to endanger the strategic benefits it has obtained in Indochina by pressuring Vietnam to give up its domination of Cambodia and to accept a Cambodia settlement tolerable to Beijing. The Soviets have evidently been unwilling to jeopardize the bird in the hand—their growing military advantages in Cam Ranh Bay—for the sake of the bird in the bush—the conjectural rewards of Chinese good will. Fresh evidence of this Soviet attitude was furnished in November 1983, when for the first time Soviet-manned TU-16 medium-range Badger bombers were deployed from the Soviet Far East to Cam Ranh Bay.[89] These aircraft offer Vietnam an added measure of Soviet protection against any possible Chinese move against Vietnam in the South China Sea, and they also offer the Soviet Union a new instrument against American naval operations in the area. The PRC, meanwhile, is likely to interpret Vietnamese consent to this important expansion of the Soviet presence at Cam Ranh Bay as a quid pro quo for the Soviet refusal to abandon support of Vietnam at China's behest.

To the north, meanwhile, the Soviet ground force buildup in Siberia and the Far East traced in this chapter has apparently continued in the early 1980s at the measured pace seen since the early 1970s. According to the estimates of the Japanese government, the seventeen to twenty divisions stationed in Asia when Brezhnev came to power had grown by 1983 to fifty-two, and the 180,000 ground force combat troops had risen to nearly 500,000.[90] The process of modernization of the Soviet forces facing China is gradually serving to widen further the gap that already exists in the conventional firepower potential of the two states. Chinese weaponry, still fundamentally composed of 1950s and 1960s technology, now must oppose such recent arrivals in Siberia as the SU-24 fighter-bomber, the MIG-23 and MIG-27 fighters, and the T-72 tank. Thus on the whole, although the Chinese do appear to be making some progress in military modernization, they do not seem to be advancing rapidly enough to remain in the same place relative to the Soviet forces they confront. This increasing Chinese vulnerability on the ground is likely to be further accentuated as the new tactical weapons systems the Soviets have begun to deploy in Europe—the SS-21, -22 and -23 short- and medium-range surface-to-surface missiles—begin to make their appearance in Asia.

Finally, the Chinese are well aware that the Soviet strategic nuclear threat based in Siberia is continuing to grow rapidly. At the same time that Sino-Soviet talks have unfolded in the 1980s and while Sino-Soviet contacts and trade have grown, there has been a significant increase in Soviet-theater nuclear capabilities in Asia, evidently directed partly at Japan and U.S. forces in East Asia, but primarily at China. There are considerable grounds to suggest that the Soviet leaders made use of the resources released by the temporary moratorium on new European SS-20 deployments announced by Brezhnev in 1982 to carry out an acceleration of construction for fresh Asian deployments of this missile. By 1986, some 171 of these three-warhead missiles were reported to be deployed in Siberia.[91] Moreover, Western press reports have alleged that missile facilities placed under construction would eventually further enlarge that figure.[92] This trend has clearly had an alarming effect on Beijing, which since the spring of 1983 had joined Japan in repeatedly protesting Soviet SS-20 deployment policy. The Chinese have also raised the issue in their periodic bilateral talks with the Soviet Union, evidently without result.

In sum, by the fall of 1986, there seemed little fundamental change in the factors that have impelled Soviet strategic policies in Siberia and the Far East and that continued to attack Chinese interests. Although improvements in certain aspects of Sino-Soviet dealings appeared likely to go on, they seemed thus far to have had minimal effect upon the underlying conflict of Soviet and Chinese geopolitical interests in East Asia.

CONCLUSIONS

The panorama we have examined suggests that the mixture of Soviet motives for the buildup has changed over the years, and the relative weight of different Soviet motives has shifted as well.

During the first five or six years of the buildup after 1965, the Soviets were overwhelmingly concerned with creating the military capabilities east of the Urals deemed necessary to inhibit the Chinese from challenging the Soviet version of the Sino-Soviet frontier. These capabilities were intended to ensure that the USSR would overmatch the Chinese at every step up the ladder of escalation, and to ensure Chinese recognition that they would be overmatched. Since October 1969, the threat conveyed by this buildup has succeeded in deterring the Chinese from attempting aggressive border patroling to assert the Chinese version of the frontier.

The original purpose of the buildup—protection of the frontier—has endured, but in recent years has been accompanied, and more and more overshadowed, by new purposes:

1. To ensure, through the threat constantly posed on China's northern borders, that the PRC was inhibited from undertaking effective military action to counter initiatives by Soviet clients on the PRC's southern borders. We have seen that this function of the Soviet buildup first came into effect during the 1971 India-Pakistan war, and has been more fully displayed since the 1978 Vietnamese invasion of Cambodia.

2. To ensure that Soviet military capabilities in the Far East retain an advantage against any combination of Soviet adversaries, particularly in the event of the development of Sino-U.S.-Japanese military collaboration.

3. To ensure that the Soviet Far East can serve as an effective platform to assist in the exploitation of opportunities for Soviet geopolitical advance in South and Southwest Asia.

In sum, the Soviet buildup in the Far East has evolved from relatively simple beginnings to more and more complex purposes. It increasingly defends not only the Soviet version of borders with China and Japan, but also a steadily widening circle of Soviet geopolitical interests elsewhere. The troops and weapons deployed against China have come to embody pressure on the PRC not only to accept the status quo on the Sino-Soviet frontier, but also to accept a new status quo more recently imposed in Indochina that is a fresh challenge to Chinese interests. Similarly, the Soviet planes and ships dispatched to the Far East not only challenge the Japanese and American position in the area, but assist Soviet prospects in Southwest Asia by exerting pressure on American military resource allocation. That is, they confront the United States with the alternatives of either accepting a less and less favorable naval and air balance in the northwest Pacific—with the adverse geopolitical consequences that may follow there—or of restricting carrier transfers from the Pacific to the Indian Ocean intended to partially offset the imposing Soviet ground and air advantage in Southwest Asia.

The Far East Theater Is Here to Stay

The Soviets are thus now driven by so many mutually reinforcing reasons to continue strengthening their position in Siberia and the Far East that it is unlikely they will soon stop. Enormous inducements will be required to halt, much less reverse, this momentum. In any case, it seems clear that a second major military arena—with permanent requirements that are almost, if not quite, comparable to those of the European theater—has become a permanent fixture in Soviet military planning. As we have noted, this geopolitical fact has now been given organizational recognition.

A Wartime Ground Force "Swing Strategy" Is Now Unlikely

As a corollary, the evidence suggests that the Soviets have become pessimistic that in time of war they would be able to use much of their Far Eastern ground forces as a reserve pool for a "swing strategy," as they did in World War II.[93] Far Eastern troops flowed steadily westward throughout the war to help defeat Hitler, until a rapid reverse transfer of troops eastward in the closing months of the war made possible the overwhelming surprise assault on Japanese forces in Manchuria. There is reason to suspect that in the early years of the Brezhnev buildup against China, some Soviet military leaders continued to nourish hopes that the bulk of these forces could be regarded as a potential reserve for a "swing strategy" to be employed in case of need. If so, these hopes have probably now dwindled, and this change is formalized in the inauguration of a permanent Far Eastern theater.[94]

In this regard, the Soviets are probably now governed by three considerations:

1. While surely still far from enthusiastic about the possibility that they might become engaged in a two-front war in Europe and the Far East, the Soviets apparently now consider it essential to prepare for that contingency. They also probably judge it unlikely that the forces so laboriously assembled in peacetime that now cover this contingency could be significantly and safely drawn down in wartime. They seem to believe that they must shape their permanent force posture to allow for the possibility, however unlikely, that they might eventually have to fight the PRC during a war with the United States, wherever such a war began.
2. The Soviets apparently believe that even if this worst case did not materialize, and China remained aloof from such a struggle, large forces would still be required to deter the PRC and ensure its continued neutrality.
3. In addition, Soviet analysts appear to assume that the Soviet Far East

would be far more vulnerable to China than heretofore in the aftermath of a devastating and exhausting Soviet clash with the United States.[95] They must therefore also guard against this final alternative. The establishment of the new Soviet high command in the Far East reflects all these considerations.

U.S. and PRC Security Interests
Have Become Interdependent

The record of Soviet behavior since the Far East buildup began also supports the conclusion that even at the present very limited level of Sino-U.S. security cooperation, the security interests of the PRC and the United States have become, to some extent, mutually dependent.

On the Chinese side, two concrete and ongoing geopolitical benefits from this relationship stand out. There seems little doubt that the growth of Beijing's American connection has over the years increasingly complicated Moscow's risk calculations regarding China. The vivid contrast between the kind of threats used against China during the 1969 border crisis and the extraordinary Soviet reticence during the Sino-Vietnamese crisis ten years later appears to derive at least in part from the growth in Soviet concern about the U.S. reaction, along, of course, with other factors.

Other considerations include the fact that the Soviets are naturally more sensitive to Chinese behavior on their own border than to Chinese actions against Vietnam, the fact that the Chinese nuclear deterrent had significantly improved in the ten years between 1969 and 1979, and the fact that the Chinese had advertised limited intentions in Vietnam. While all these factors contribute to explaining the contrast in Soviet behavior on the two occasions, they are not the whole story. As discussed above, the Soviets were also considerably more wary of what the United States might do in 1979, particularly in the light of Deng's visit to Washington.

In short, however ambiguous U.S. intentions remain in the event of a Sino-Soviet conflict, the issue has become sufficiently important to Moscow to have some constraining effect on Soviet risk-taking. Indeed, it is likely that Brezhnev's efforts at summit meetings in 1972, 1973, and 1974 to head off the development of a U.S. security association with China reflected, at least in part, a long-standing Soviet belief that this process would tend to reduce Soviet ability to bully China.

In addition, the Chinese ability to continue to resist Vietnamese and Soviet consolidation of a fait accompli in Indochina—a cornerstone of present Chinese foreign policy—has become increasingly dependent on American diplomatic support as the stalemate in Cambodia has continued. In view of the restiveness already shown toward this policy by some ASEAN (Association of Southeast

Asian Nations) states that are friendly to the United States but suspicious of China, pressures on the United States to modify the policy are likely to grow in the future. By continuing to resist these pressures, at some political cost, U.S. policy encourages and reinforces the position taken by Thailand, which for geographical reasons is vital to Chinese efforts to resist the assertion of Vietnamese hegemony in Indochina.

On the other side of the ledger, the evolution of events over the last decade has undoubtedly increased the importance of the PRC to U.S. security interests. As already suggested, one side effect of the deterioration of Soviet-U.S. relations in the 1970s was an inevitable reduction of the maneuverability in the strategic triangle that the United States enjoyed in the early 1970s, when it had better relations with both the PRC and the USSR than they had with each other.[96] This narrowing of U.S. alternatives in the triangle as a result of the hardening of the American posture toward the Soviet Union has been useful to Beijing. But, as already suggested, the worsening of Soviet-U.S. relations did not fundamentally result from the process of Sino-U.S. rapprochement, as the Soviets sometimes allege. (On the contrary, the downhill slide of Soviet-U.S. relations commenced during the October 1973 Arab-Israeli war, and began to accelerate sharply in 1975—all long before Sino-U.S. relations had evolved very far from the initial improvement achieved with the Nixon visit in 1972.) Rather, it resulted from the continued outward pressure of Soviet foreign policy to expand Soviet presence and influence everywhere possible, most often at the expense of the interests of the West in general and the United States in particular.

This is the same worldwide process that also presses on Beijing's interests on its periphery, and Beijing's resistance occupies a major segment of Soviet energies. There is little reason to believe that this broad and fundamental impulse underlying Soviet policy will soon disappear. Consequently, the security interest of the United States in the continued viability of Chinese resistance to Soviet military pressure remains an objective fact whose significance is likely to grow over the next decade, along with the Soviet military presence in Asia.

NOTES

1. This chapter is an updated, revised, and expanded version of Harry Gelman, *The Soviet Far East Buildup and Soviet Risk-Taking Against China,* R-2943-AF (Santa Monica, Calif.: Rand Corporation, August 1982).

2. Japan Defense Agency, *Defense of Japan 1980* (Tokyo: Japan Times, 1980), pp. 49–58; *Defense of Japan 1981* (Tokyo: Japan Times, 1981), pp. 76–86. In a notable article in the summer of 1981, Chief of the General Staff Ogarkov placed heavy emphasis on the need for lightly manned peacetime units capable of extremely rapid wartime mobilization. He therefore underlined the need for predisposition of "planned reserves of per-

sonnel and equipment." This discussion was accompanied by stress on the need for new forms of military organization, particularly the new "larger-scale form," the theater of military operations ("Na strazhe mirnogo truda [Guarding peaceful labor], *Kommunist,* no. 10 [July 1981], pp. 80–91).

3. Japan Defense Agency, *Defense of Japan 1983* (Tokyo: Japan Times, 1983), p. 30.

4. More detailed estimates of divisional totals at different periods of the Soviet buildup will not be found in this chapter because they would convey a misleading sense of precision. The best and most commonly used published sources, the estimates supplied annually by the International Institute for Strategic Studies, while useful as to trends, do not appear to be an adequate guide to the pace of small incremental changes.

5. This interview, given to Japanese journalists on July 10, 1964, was published in *Sekai Shuho* (Tokyo) on August 11. Mao said, "About 100 years ago, all areas east of Lake Baikal, including Khabarovsk, Vladivostok, and the Kamchatka Peninsula, were incorporated into Soviet territory. We have not as yet settled these matters with the Soviet Union." In addition, Mao told the Japanese that the southern Kurils held by Moscow "must be returned to Japan," and observed that in general the Soviet Union had occupied "too much territory" all around its periphery—in Europe after World War II as well as in Asia. He cited Poland and Finland, as well as Japan, China, and Mongolia, as Soviet victims.

6. *Pravda,* September 15, 1964, and October 21, 1964.

7. *Pravda,* September 15, 1964.

8. This is not intended to imply any generalizations about Khrushchev's attitudes on military spending as a whole—a more complex subject—but merely to note that he demonstrated, through both his successful and his unsuccessful efforts to cut the ground forces, a consistent inclination to give them a lower priority in resource allocation than did his successors.

9. *Pravda,* January 19, 1966.

10. On this ground alone—and apart from all purely military considerations—the Soviets are extremely unlikely ever to satisfy the Chinese demand that they remove all their forces from Mongolia.

11. Liu Keming, director of the Chinese Institute of Soviet Studies, wrote in 1979: "The Soviet Union has dispatched large numbers of troops to station in Mongolia, and most of them are stationed in areas bordering China. The Soviet Union has built military bases including missile bases in Mongolia and has staged frequent joint Soviet-Mongolian military maneuvers there with China as the imaginary target of attack. Many of the Soviet Union's leading military personnel often go to Mongolia to carry out military activities against China. The stationing of Soviet troops in Mongolia constitutes an important component part of the Soviet Union's entire anti-China military strategic deployment" ("Soviet Foreign Policy: On Sino-Soviet Relations," a paper prepared for the Sino-American Conference on International Relations and the Soviet Union, Washington, D.C., November 8–11, 1979). This rhetoric conveys a strong sense of a feeling of special vulnerability to the Mongolia deployments.

12. See Harry Gelman, "Outlook for Sino-Soviet Relations," *Problems of Communism,* 28, no. 5–6 (September–December 1979): 50–66.

13. *New York Times,* July 25, 1972; Harry Harding, "The Evolution of Chinese Military Policy," in Frank B. Horton, Anthony C. Rogerson, and Edward L. Warner, eds., *Comparative Defense Policy* (Baltimore, Md.: Johns Hopkins University Press, 1974), pp. 228–29; Japanese Defense Agency, *Defense of Japan 1981,* p. 96. In addition, in contrast to the eastern sector, some parts of the western Sino-Soviet border are so mountainous that neither side can maintain a sizable military presence close to the border.

14. *Chinese Defense Spending, 1965–79,* SR 80-10091 (Washington, D.C.: National Foreign Assessment Center, July 1980).

15. The first detailed account of such Red Guard actions on the frozen Ussuri was provided in *Pravda,* July 19, 1967.

16. *Pravda,* March 12, 1969; *People's Daily,* March 15, 1969.

17. New China News Agency (NCNA), September 16, 1968.

18. There is no evidence in the public record that Chinese interceptors have ever attempted to down a Soviet reconnaissance plane. The Chinese are well aware of their qualitative inferiority in the air, and they may have believed that such an incident would be particularly likely to escalate. (Partly for somewhat analogous reasons, they did not employ air power during the 1979 Sino-Vietnamese war.) Chinese and Soviet statements both suggest that the military helicopter seized by the Chinese in 1974 was captured only after it had spontaneously become disabled and was obliged to land in Chinese territory.

19. TANYUG (Belgrade), September 29, 1968.

20. *Pravda,* March 12, 1969.

21. Henry Kissinger disagrees; he argues (*White House Years* [Boston: Little, Brown & Co., 1979], p. 177), apparently solely on the basis of the Soviet logistical advantage along the Central Asian–Xinjiang border, that the Soviets were initiating all the shooting. This appears to me to oversimplify the picture. In a situation in which aggressive border patroling was being conducted by both sides, against a background of repeated recent firefights, the initiation of new firing is likely to have varied from incident to incident with changing tactical circumstances.

22. As already suggested, from Mao's perspective it was especially important, precisely because of the genuine Chinese alarm over the implications of the Soviet invasion of Czechoslovakia the year before, to demonstrate that China was not cowed by the Czechoslovak precedent and could not be bullied.

23. The Soviets boasted of the "mighty rain of artillery" employed against the PRC units (*Pravda,* March 17, 1969), and the Chinese complained of the Soviet use of artillery fire (Chinese Foreign Ministry Note of March 5, 1969, NCNA, March 15, 1969).

24. A correspondent for the Japanese *Asahi Shimbun,* for example, was allowed to visit Khabarovsk in July, and duly reported that "military buildup was seen everywhere," and that "some 30 military trucks and field guns were seen on freight trains at Khabarovsk railway station, and MIG fighters were flying overhead." He added his impression that there had been some "mobilization" of reserve tanks and troops (quoted in *Washington Post,* July 16, 1969). In view of the well-known Soviet attitude regarding military secrets,

it is not credible that they would have permitted the visits had they not wished to encourage such reporting.

25. See, for example, *Krasnaia zvezda,* March 8, 1969.

26. Soviet agent Victor Louis later wrote: "The Soviet Union prefers using rockets to manpower. She has a variety of rockets to choose from, depending upon the terrain and other circumstances. For instance, in the case of a Chinese attempt to occupy an island, the whole surface of the island was burned together with any Chinese troops and equipment already ensconced there" (*London Evening News,* September 16, 1969).

27. This precedent was cited in a series of *Pravda* articles in early May that used history as testimony for the credibility of escalation and that drew the lesson that Chinese provocation would invite immediate retaliation (Konstantin Simonov, "Thinking Out Loud," *Pravda,* May 3 and 4, 1969). *Pravda,* on August 18, celebrating the anniversary of this 1939 victory, termed the rout of the Japanese at the Khalkin-Gol River "a warning to the Chinese adventurists."

28. *Krasnaia zvezda,* August 6, 1969. Tolubko took the occasion to emphasize that Soviet troops remained in Manchuria "for some time." This episode was recalled again in *Sovetskaia Rossiia,* September 19, 1969.

29. *Izvestiia,* September 2, 1969.

30. The most nearly explicit such threat in the Soviet press appeared at the very outset, soon after the first Damansky/Chenbao battle. An emotional rehash of the battle in *Krasnaia zvezda* on March 8 included a statement that "the rocket troops showed at the important exercises just completed that the formidable weapons entrusted to them by the motherland for defense of the Far Eastern frontiers are in strong, reliable hands. Let any provocateurs always remember this." A week later, a broadcast in Mandarin by Moscow's Radio Peace and Progress—which purports to be unofficial—declared that "the whole world knows that the main striking force of the Soviet Armed Forces is its rocket units," and went on to emphasize that in any contest between Soviet and Chinese nuclear-missile forces, "Mao Tse-tung and his group . . . would certainly end up in utter defeat." The Soviets then apparently decided that this language was unwise, and for several months thereafter, both official and nominally unofficial Soviet media were more circumspect in allusions to the possible use of nuclear weapons. In midsummer, the Soviet revelation that the deputy chief of the Strategic Rocket Forces had been transferred to command the Far Eastern Military District was itself a broad hint of a connection between the two; but Tolubko's August 6 article admonishing the Chinese did not allude to rocket-nuclear forces. On August 28, however, a *Pravda* editorial declared that if a war with China did break out, it would involve "lethal armaments and modern means of delivery" that "would not spare a single continent," strongly implying the inevitability of the use of nuclear missiles against China in any such war.

31. The Soviet leadership had by no means given up vague hopes of someday finding Chinese leaders with whom it could improve relations. The Soviets therefore had the difficult and delicate job of intimidating the current leadership without permanently destroying all such hopes.

32. For example, a week after Radio Peace and Progress called attention in its Mandarin broadcasts to the Soviet nuclear arsenal in the context of the border clashes, a March

21 Radio Moscow broadcast in English derided "the provocatory false rumor" of threatened Soviet nuclear action against China as an invention of British propaganda. On August 13, *Literaturnaia gazeta* denounced Western "lies" about Soviet readiness to use nuclear weapons against China.

33. *Washington Star,* August 28 and 29, 1969; Kissinger, *White House Years,* p. 184.

34. Kissinger, *White House Years,* p. 184.

35. The Soviet attitude regarding the Western treatment of Victor Louis is two-sided. On the one hand, Moscow wishes Louis's nominal status as a simple Soviet "free-lance journalist" to be sufficiently respected to make his statements nonbinding, and also to assure him continued access to Western institutions, like the *London Evening News,* that might feel obliged to deny him employment if he had an official Soviet title. On the other hand, Moscow also wishes Louis's actual status as an agent and spokesman for the Soviet regime to be sufficiently well recognized to lend attention and weight to his published statements.

36. Lop Nor is well known to be a nuclear weapons test site. Louis presumably singled it out as a symbolic example familiar to the public.

37. An unusually pithy statement of this oft-repeated Chinese view was furnished in 1977 by Vice-Premier Li Xiannian, who told the editor of a British newspaper: "Russia will get into trouble if it starts a war with China, as our territory is so vast. They know the way we would fight. We would mobilize the masses of the civilian people and get them bogged down in China . . . Even if Russia occupied half of China, we would go on fighting. Should the Russians put one foot on Chinese territory, they would find themselves in a swamp" (*The Sunday Times,* London, March 27, 1977).

38. For example, PRC government statement, May 24, 1969 (NCNA, May 24, 1969); NCNA, June 2, 1969; NCNA, July 6, 1969; NCNA, August 1, 1969; NCNA, August 14, 1969. A Chinese slogan issued for PRC National Day on September 16 for the first time in the use of such slogans called attention to the possibility of Soviet attack on China in which nuclear weapons would be used; and a joint *People's Daily–Liberation Army Daily–Red Flag* anniversary editorial on September 30, 1969, defiantly insisted that China would not be intimidated by "nuclear blackmail." After the Victor Louis threat discussed above, the October 7, 1969, Chinese government statement that formally accepted negotiations warned that "if a handful of warmongers dare to raid China's strategic sites, that would be war . . . and the Chinese people will rise up in resistance." This was probably meant to imply that any "surgical strike" would inevitably become a long-term land war. Eight years later, a *People's Daily* article on May 13, 1977, recalled in bitter detail the Soviet "nuclear blackmail" used against China in 1969.

39. Defense Intelligence Agency, *Handbook on the Chinese Armed Forces,* DDI-2680-32-76, July 1976, pp. 8-1, 2; A-50. In 1969, Chinese nuclear delivery systems were limited to the 600-mile CSS-1 MRBM and a fleet of aging bombers using technology obtained from the Soviet Union in the 1950s (Ibid., A-41).

40. In October 1981, a CIA analyst testified to Congress that the PRC "strategic missile force's deterrent value has been increased by concealment and dispersal in remote areas" (Senate Foreign Relations Committee, *The Implications of U.S.-China Military Cooperation* [Washington, D.C.: U.S. Government Printing Office, 1981], p. 23).

41. As early as the late spring of 1969, PRC official documents implied that the Chinese were back on the island and claimed that the Soviets were threatening to fire at them (Chinese government statement, May 24, 1969 [NCNA, May 24, 1969]; Chinese Foreign Ministry note, June 6, 1969 [NCNA, June 6, 1969]). In the years since the 1969 crisis, Chinese propaganda has frequently made it clear that the PRC retains physical possession of Chenbao.

42. Chinese Foreign Ministry statement, Xinhua, October 9, 1969. For more details, see H. Gelman, "Outlook for Sino-Soviet Relations," *Problems of Communism.*

43. O. Borisov, "Who Is Preventing Normalization?" *Izvestiia,* May 16, 1974.

44. Kissinger, *White House Years,* pp. 187–91, 684–732.

45. *Izvestiia,* May 16, 1974.

46. John Newhouse, *Cold Dawn: The Story of SALT* (New York: Holt, Rinehart & Winston, 1973), p. 189; Henry Kissinger, *White House Years,* pp. 547–48.

47. Richard M. Nixon, *RN: The Memoirs of Richard Nixon* (New York: Grosset and Dunlap, 1978), p. 1030. Kissinger reports that Nixon instructed him, in the presence of the Soviets, to consider the idea of such a treaty for subsequent exploration with the Soviets; but Kissinger was adamantly opposed and Nixon, soon to be overwhelmed by the Watergate crisis, never referred to the matter again. It is extremely unlikely that this notion would have been long considered by either man under any circumstances since, as Kissinger points out, such a treaty would have had the "clear implication that the United States was giving the Soviet Union a free hand to attack China" (Kissinger, *Years of Upheaval* [Boston: Little, Brown & Co., 1982], pp. 1173–74).

48. See *The Military Balance* (International Institute for Strategic Studies), issues for 1970 through 1977. In the spring of 1977, a Chinese Foreign Ministry official discussed the Soviet buildup in an interview in Beijing. He repeated the somewhat exaggerated Chinese standard rhetorical claim that Soviet armed forces "in the east as a whole" reached 1 million men (even counting all the other Soviet services besides the ground forces east of the Urals, this is inflated). But he also asserted that there had been "no" increase in the manpower deployed since 1972, although, he added, Soviet military equipment had improved (*New York Times,* March 25, 1977).

49. For example, *Pravda* on February 6, 1972, September 23, 1972, and February 8, 1973, carried vituperative articles denouncing Alsop for recalling this Soviet behavior.

50. As noted earlier, it is probable that the helicopter was, in effect, thrust into Chinese hands by becoming disabled and making a forced landing on Chinese territory. As the Soviets probably suspected, it is likely that the disposition of this machine and its crew subsequently became a political issue within the Chinese leadership.

51. It should be emphasized, however, that these changes in the Far East went forward as part of a broader, nationwide program to modernize the Soviet armed forces and to improve their structure.

52. See *New York Times,* April 10, 1978. The lengthy, well-reported Brezhnev-Ustinov rail tour of economic and military facilities in Siberia and the Far East was apparently intended to serve notice, both to the Chinese and to local Soviet officials, of the heightened strategic importance the Soviets assigned to the development and defense of

the eastern portion of the USSR. In Vladivostok, Brezhnev and the defense minister visited the fleet; at Chita, they had "discussions" with the commanders of the Transbaikalia
Military District; and at Khabarovsk, on the Chinese border, the local Soviet commanders
staged what was termed a "combined-arms tactical exercise" for the two leaders (*Pravda,*
April 4, 6, 8, 1978). The Chinese minister of defense reacted to this visit by writing that
Brezhnev had "personally sneaked into Siberia and the Far East to encourage the Soviet
troops and issue war cries" (Xu Xiangqian, "Heighten Vigilance, Be Ready to Fight,"
Red Flag, no. 8, 1978, as reported by NCNA, July 30, 1978).

   53. Japan Defense Agency, *Defense of Japan 1980,* pp. 51–53; *Defense of Japan
1981,* pp. 78–79.

   54. Ibid.

   55. Initially, this command was under General Petrov, the prestigious commander of
the successful Soviet-Cuban operations in Ethiopia in 1977–1978, subsequently chief of
Soviet ground forces, and then deputy minister of defense (*Boston Globe,* March 28,
1979).

   56. Japan Defense Agency, *Defense of Japan 1980,* pp. 51–53. This authoritative
Japanese publication asserted that "a new combined command was established to control
the Far Eastern, Transbaikalia and Siberian military districts as well as the troops stationed in Mongolia." It added that "in establishing the combined command . . . the Soviet
Union has apparently taken into consideration the need to cope with any contingency not
only on the Chinese front but also in the Pacific theater."
   The Chinese have also taken public note of this change. On October 9, 1981, NCNA
stated that as a "first step" in "building up an independent command structure for war in
the Far East . . . the Soviet Union set up in 1978 the Far Eastern Theater Command near
Lake Baikal to assume unified command of troops in the Far East, Transbaikalia and Siberian military districts and in Mongolia as well as the naval and air forces in the region"
(FBIS, *Daily Report—China,* October 14, 1981, D-1).

   57. This exercise was first described in *New York Times,* March 17, 1979. It was
further reported by the Japanese *Yomiuri Shimbun* on March 27, citing a Japanese Foreign
Ministry and Defense Agency statement, by the *Boston Globe* on March 28, and finally
by NCNA on March 29.

   58. See John M. Collins, *U.S.-Soviet Military Balance* (New York: McGraw-Hill,
1980), map 4, p. 134. In addition, there has been an increasing Soviet tendency in recent
years to modernize weapons systems in Asia at roughly the same pace as in Europe. In the
east, as in the west, the arrival of the Backfire bomber has complemented the strategic
threat presented by the SS-20 deployments.

   59. "While YANKEE-class SSBNs must operate in the eastern Pacific to strike the
United States, DELTA-class SSBNs in the home waters can hit almost any target in the
United States with their SS-N-18 SLBMs" (Maj. Gen. James C. Pfautz, "The Soviet Military Presence in Asia," paper presented at the Security Conference on Asia and the Pacific, Palm Springs, Calif., January 8–10, 1982).

   60. In his earlier-noted 1981 article, Ogarkov made unusually explicit references to
the new status of the "theater of military operations," emphasizing that it had now replaced the "front" as the new Soviet "basic form of military operations." He also asserted

that what he claimed was "the expansion of the military-political ties between the United States and China and Japan" was creating "a long-term military threat to our Eastern borders" (*Kommunist,* no. 10 [1981]: 80–81).

61. As early as June 1975—only a few weeks after the American evacuation of Vietnam—Deng Xiaoping publicly warned that "the other superpower insatiably seeks new military bases in Southeast Asia," and told a visiting Thai premier that it was "highly probable that that superpower may request the use of bases in South Vietnam" (NCNA, June 30, 1975; *The Nation,* Bangkok, July 3, 1975). Three years later, not long before the signing of the Soviet-Vietnamese treaty, Deng was continuing to warn of the Soviet desire to make use of the "dozens of naval facilities and airports" in Vietnam "that were built by the United States during the war" (*Asahi Shimbun,* Tokyo, September 7, 1978).

62. Kissinger, *White House Years,* pp. 906–7.

63. Moscow Radio described the atmosphere of the first session of talks as one of cordiality, mutual respect, and "comradely frankness," a phrase that almost invariably indicates disagreement. Contrary to custom, there was no welcoming banquet for the Vietnamese after the first session. Only after the final session, when agreement had been reached, did Moscow Radio announce "full unanimity of views"; only then did the USSR provide the missing banquet.

64. On Soviet use of these facilities, see *Soviet Military Power, 1984* (Washington, D.C.: U.S. Government Printing Office, 1984), p. 66. Beijing has repeatedly and bitterly complained about these Soviet base rights in Vietnam (e.g., *People's Daily,* May 9, 1979; FBIS, *Daily Report,* May 11, 1979; and *People's Daily,* June 3, 1979; FBIS, *Daily Report,* June 8, 1979).

65. These flights evolved out of shorter flights from the Soviet Far East conducted during the Chinese incursion that went only as far as the East China Sea. See Japanese Defense Agency, *Defense of Japan 1979,* pp. 38–40.

66. The Soviets from the outset of 1979 thus walked a fine line between their thirst for military bases and their perception of risk for themselves. They had a vested interest in a heightened Vietnamese fear of China sufficient to bring about a Soviet military presence in Vietnam, yet they had not decided how to respond to the dangers that might be created by the kind of Chinese actions that would heighten Vietnamese fears.

67. Department of Defense, *Soviet Military Power,* 1981, p. 93. *FY 83 Report of the Secretary of Defense to Congress,* p. II-20.

68. A Soviet broadcast on January 3 thus referred in passing to alleged reports "from foreign correspondents in Beijing" about Chinese troop movements to the borders of both Vietnam and the Soviet Union, and characterized this, in generalized fashion, as efforts "to whip up tension on the borders with the country's neighbors." Until the last week of January, the Soviets contented themselves with minimal reportage of the Chinese buildup and with unspecific condemnation of Chinese efforts at "intimidation." As late as January 27, a television broadcast by Leonid Zamiatin, chief of the Central Committee's International Information Department, claimed that the Chinese themselves were spreading reports about the possibility of a Chinese "lightning strike" into Vietnam "in order to exert political and military pressure on Vietnam." Zamiatin seemed still to be adhering to the bluff theory.

69. *New Times* (Moscow), February 8, 1979.

70. Tass, February 18, 1979.

71. Ustinov electoral speech, Tass, February 23, 1979.

72. *Tien Tien Jih Pao,* Hong Kong, February 20, 1979; *Daily Telegraph,* London, April 17, 1979; *New York Times,* September 30, 1979.

73. They implied that they would go only a short distance into Vietnam and stay for only a modest amount of time. This had some credibility because of the precedent of Chinese behavior in their clash with India in 1962, when they had voluntarily withdrawn after routing Indian forces in the Northeast Frontier Agency. In practice, the main test applied now by all concerned was whether the Chinese would seek to descend from the Vietnamese border highlands into the Red River delta to menace Hanoi.

74. *Washington Post,* March 10, 1979; *New York Times,* March 16, 1979.

75. Japan Defense Agency, *Defense of Japan 1979,* pp. 38–40.

76. *New York Times,* February 8, 1979.

77. Japan Defense Agency, *Defense of Japan 1979,* pp. 39–40. See especially the map, p. 39.

78. The Chinese later did tell Western journalists that during the Sino-Vietnamese fighting they had observed Soviet local reinforcements opposite Xinjiang (*New York Times,* September 30, 1979), and opposite Inner Mongolia (*Daily Telegraph,* London, April 17, 1979), but that "the Russian threat came to nothing," and "there were no armed clashes." It seems unlikely that these local troop movements constituted a Soviet attempt to intimidate the PRC.

79. *New York Times,* March 17, 1979; *Yomiuri Shimbun,* Tokyo, March 27, 1979; *Boston Globe,* March 28, 1979.

80. See, on this point, the views of U.S. military experts cited in *Boston Globe,* March 28, 1979.

81. *Far Eastern Affairs,* no. 3 (1979): 10.

82. Recounting an interview with the Soviet Foreign Ministry officials Kapitsa and Sladkovsky, the Polish editor Rakowsky wrote: "The Chinese leaders . . . in their view of Soviet capabilities and its ability to counter military aggression are realists, no doubt. One of my very responsible interlocutors said: 'You can write down that in the days when China committed an aggression against Vietnam we took practical steps in the Far East which were very well understood in Beijing'" (*Politika,* April 14, 1979).

83. A. Bovin, *Izvestiia,* March 21, 1979.

84. In his *Izvestiia* article, Bovin, unlike many other Soviet writers, alluded to dangers that may have indeed preoccupied the Soviet leadership: "Moscow, like Hanoi, understood that the situation which had arisen was fraught with dangers on a global scale. Of course, the concrete choice of means to influence the situation was dictated by concrete circumstances." This was clearly an allusion to the possibility of U.S. involvement.

85. For an extended discussion of the factors that contributed to this result, see Harry Gelman, *The Brezhnev Politburo and the Decline of Detente* (Ithaca, N.Y., and London: Cornell University Press), 1984.

86. *Washington Post,* June 15, 1984; *New York Times,* June 12, 1984.

87. For a more detailed discussion of the issues involved, see Harry Gelman, "Soviet Policy Toward China," *Survey,* vol. 27 (118/119), (Autumn-Winter 1983): 165–74.

88. Tass, July 28, 1986.

89. *Washington Post,* December 21, 1983.

90. Japan Defense Agency, *Defense of Japan 1983* (Tokyo: Japan Times, 1983), p. 30.

91. *Baltimore Sun,* February 25, 1986.

92. *Los Angeles Times,* May 8, 1983.

93. Some Soviets evidently regret the abandonment of the swing strategy. As recently as 1979, one Soviet author reviewed in some detail "the contribution of the troops of the Far East to the overthrow of the German-Fascist invaders" (S. Isaev, *Voenno-istoricheskii zhurnal* [Military historical journal], no. 8, August 1979). Although he did not draw conclusions as to the practicality of making such transfers in the future, he emphasized that in World War II it proved possible to deter a Japanese attack while furnishing large reserves for the struggle in the west.

94. As already noted, Marshal Ogarkov stressed in his July 1981 *Kommunist* article the decisive importance of the "theater of military operations" as the new basic Soviet strategic unit of operations, and implied that the theater must have an independent wartime viability. The voicing of this generalization was clearly given impetus by Ogarkov's assumption that the Far East high command, operational since at least 1979, would continue to face what Ogarkov termed a "long-term" threat from the United States, China, and Japan. The implication was surely that the forces assigned to the theater organization were now considered fairly permanent.

95. This point was raised by Soviet analysts during extensive interviews conducted in Moscow by an American specialist in 1981. See Banning N. Garrett, *Soviet Perceptions of China and Sino-American Military Ties* (Arlington, Va.: Harold Rosenblum Associates, 1981), pp. 48, 60.

96. Kissinger has persuasively argued that in 1971 the United States gained practical fruits from this early advantage, which apparently caused the Soviets to accelerate coming to final agreement in the Berlin talks (Kissinger, *White House Years,* pp. 837–38). It must be remembered, however, that thereafter the United States never again obtained comparable benefits from its position in the triangle. Particularly after 1972, the Soviets proved unwilling to make tactical concessions because of China.

The Soviet Far East, East Asia, and the Pacific—Strategic Dimensions

THE CONTEXT AND
STRATEGIC PARAMETERS

It is conventional to view the dramatic escalation in Soviet strategic attention to Siberia and the Soviet Far East as reactions to the 1969 border clash with China and to the 1972 Sino-U.S. rapprochement. While there can be little question as to the seriousness with which Moscow viewed its mini-war with China, a closer look at the big picture suggests a larger strategic rationale. The stepped-up strategic-military development of Siberia and the Soviet Far East must be read as the logical extension of Soviet communications, ground forces, air, naval, merchant marine and missile capabilities to the East Asian/Pacific region, as part of the Soviet Union's metamorphosis from a European to a global power.

The much overworked term "strategy" may, of course, be defined in a number of ways. In its broadest sense, the term is customarily used to cover all aspects and dimensions of national power (the "strategic" ramifications of technology transfer, for instance). In a narrower sense, the word is applied to war and war-game situations, as in strategy versus tactics. The phrase "strategic dimensions" as used in this chapter centers on the tangible middle ground: those political, economic, and military elements that have direct or indirect bearing on Soviet power, capabilities, policies, and options in the Soviet Far East and the Asian/Pacific arena.

Geography and history provide the strategic keys. Northeast Asia is the only region in the world where the interrelated strategic interests of four of the major powers—the United States, USSR, China, and Japan—interact directly, overlap critically, and often clash head-on. The world's six largest armed forces are either in or adjacent to the region, including four nuclear powers. The presence in the same potentially explosive environment of a hostile, heavily armed North Korea, a Taiwan uncertain as to its future, and, to the south, an aggressive, Soviet client-state, communist Vietnam, adds a clearly disquieting dimension to that historically troubled region.

We hardly need be reminded that, in terms of East-West confrontation, the Far Eastern arena has accounted for an impressive share of the major military conflicts that have continued to punctuate the peace since the end of World War II: the internationally charged communist-nationalist conflict in China (1945–1949), the Korean War (1950–1953), and the war in Vietnam, to cite but three classic examples. In each case, the Soviet Union has played an important role, directly or indirectly, and in each Moscow's "anti-imperialist" goals have been served to a greater or lesser degree.

The transformation of Siberia and the Soviet Far East, largely within the last two decades, into a substantial military-industrial complex with now-formidable communications, military (naval, ground, air, and missile), and commercial capabilities, and the parallel development of the Soviet Pacific fleet and adjunct merchant marine, provide the rationale for characterizing the Soviet Union as both a European and now an Asian-Pacific power.

Historical Perspectives

Soviet strategic concern with postwar Asia began to emerge even as events at home and in Europe necessarily occupied the lion's share of Soviet attention. Though yet another debate on the wisdom or folly of the West at Yalta and Potsdam need not be joined here, one is reminded of the late Philip E. Mosely's wise counsel proffered when President Roosevelt was literally pleading with Stalin to join the war in the Pacific.[1] "The question," Dr. Mosely cautioned at the time, "is not how to get the Soviets into the Pacific War, but how to keep them out."[2] To the victor goes the spoils! Soviet "spoils" as a consequence of the two-week strategically irrelevant military participation against Japan were and are significant: addition to (or reconfirmed as part of) the Soviet sphere of Outer Mongolia, the southern half of Sakhalin, and the Kuril Islands. (Concessions in Manchuria were later returned to China.)

The major strategic issues that concerned the Soviets in East Asia during the last years of the Stalin era (1945–1953) were China, the Korean War, and the Allied (read U.S.) occupation of Japan. If Soviet plans for China were badly conceived and ultimately counterproductive (including the 30-year Treaty of Friendship and Alliance), Soviet policy and practice for Korea and Japan must be judged equal, if not greater, failures—although Moscow may take some justifiable solace in having denied North Korea to the West. Siberia at this time was still (as we shall see) perceived by Moscow as a remote and distant land. The Soviet Pacific fleet was not yet even a future plan. Soviet eastern military forces were minimal.

Two issues dominated Soviet strategic concern with the East Asian scene during the Khrushchev decade (1954–1964): the ongoing China problem, and Japan's reassertion of sovereignty, accompanied as it was by a security treaty with the United States. Soviet plans to bring South Korea under communist military control had been checkmated by U.S., UN, and South Korean military action and determination.

When I was in the Soviet Union for a month during the summer of 1957 visiting centers of Chinese studies, it became increasingly clear to me that Moscow was seriously concerned over its relations with China, although nothing suggesting concern had yet appeared in the press of either country.[3] Even before the end of the Khrushchev era, the 13,000 Soviet economic and military advisers had been withdrawn from China, the joint nuclear research center in Moscow had been closed down, and there were abundant other signs that Sino-Soviet relations, never really good, were by 1958 or 1959 rapidly disintegrating. Indeed, Khrushchev's inability to "manage" the China problem is generally thought to be one of the factors contributing to his political demise.

Moscow's policy and practice toward the new Japan proved an even more conspicuous failure, as Japan moved from occupation to independence with a democratic, multiparty system and a security treaty with the United States. Moreover, political pronouncements and public opinion in Japan, with only a few noisy exceptions, displayed an unmistakably anti-Soviet flavor. Even the Communist Party of Japan—despite a long history of ties with Moscow—proved ineffective, unreliable, and ultimately "independent."[4] A high-ranking Japanese government specialist on the Soviet Union (who shall remain nameless) said to me about this time, "The Soviets seem ideally unsuited for dealing with Japan."

The aftermath of the Korean War (which had seen the introduction of some one million Chinese military "volunteers" into the picture) produced a confused political situation in North Korea. If the issue of Moscow versus Peking orientation was (and remains) cloudy, one thing was clear: the North Koreans were early dedicated to a major military buildup using both Soviet and Chinese economic and military aid.

The Khrushchev era witnessed, as we shall see, some fairly general plans for the economic development of Siberia and the Soviet Far East, but the region east of the Urals had not yet been assigned a top strategic priority. The concept of a Soviet Pacific fleet was just beginning to take shape. The strength of Soviet ground forces in the east remained at about twenty divisions, few of them at a high-readiness state.

It was during the two decades of Brezhnev chairmanship that the region of Siberia and the Soviet Far East came into its strategic own. That period, 1964–1982, witnessed some bold initiatives and dramatic developments with unmistakable strategic implications for the West. Among the more significant of these were:

1. The joint Soviet-Japanese economic development projects (dating from 1966), including Siberian timber, pulpwood and chips, natural gas, coal, iron, oil, and construction of port facilities in the Soviet Far East, in exchange for Japanese industrial knowhow and equipment, high technology, and long-term credits.

2. The Soviet-Chinese mini-war of 1969 and related subsequent Soviet troop buildup from 20 to 52 divisions in Mongolia, Siberia, and Soviet Far East.

3. The construction of a second trans-Siberian railway, the Baikal-Amur Mainline (BAM), begun with a crash program in 1974 and officially completed in 1984 but still not fully operational.

4. An intensified Soviet program for the acquisition of Western military and dual-use technology (from the United States, Western Europe, and Japan), some of it related to the development of the new military-industrial establishment in the east.

5. The substantial upgrading of ground, naval, and air establishments and weapons systems on Sakhalin and the Kuril Islands (dating from as early as 1978).

6. The development of the Soviet Pacific fleet and the expanded Soviet merchant marine.

7. Expansion and upgrading the Soviet Pacific air forces; and deployment of the SS-20s.

8. The substantial Soviet upgrading of Vietnam (Cam Ranh Bay and Danang) as a major Soviet naval and air base.

The brief Androprov (1982–1984) and Chernenko (1984–1985) periods saw essentially a continuation of Brezhnev-era policy. The most dramatic and worrisome innovations have been the deployment in Siberia and the Soviet Far East of some 135 SS-20s (170 by the end of 1986) and construction in Siberia of a huge ABM-mode battle management radar.[5] The substantial upgrading of all weapons systems and the increased appearance of Backfire and other newer types of weapons in the region during the Gorbachev era attests to the seriousness with which the Soviets are pressing their increased strategic interests in the east.

THE STRATEGIC SIGNIFICANCE OF THE EAST

Preoccupation with recovery from World War II, the vast distances and the communications void beyond the Urals, urgent problems with East European satellites, the sheer enormity of the developmental task, and other bureaucratic, systemic, and economic constraints served to relegate East Siberia and the Soviet

Far East to a low strategic priority in Soviet planning until well after the end of the Stalin era.

Beginning with the Khrushchev decade, however, the increasingly enhanced perception of the potential role of Siberia and the Soviet Far East in the economic and strategic scheme of things may be seen in the projections, promises, and practices of successive Soviet regimes.

When Soviet documentation is examined against the record of achievement (or nonachievement), several things become evident. First, there is an obvious gap between promises and practice, between plan and performance (especially in the earlier postwar years), but, at the same time, some of the ambitious plans for the eastern regions that are now economic and strategic accomplishments were conceived as early as the mid-1950s. Second, despite economic setbacks and the celebrated opposition to many of his programs (such as the Virgin Lands scheme), Khrushchev and his regime (1954–1964) projected programs and launched piecemeal projects for "eastern development," especially in industrialization, oil, natural gas, electrification, and forest and mineral resources. These programs, to varying degrees, contributed, if modestly, to the progress of the Soviet economy as a whole. Third, the mini border war with China (1969) marked the watershed in Soviet strategic concern with its eastern flank; it was a major catalyst, but not the sole rationale, for the subsequent strategic buildup in Siberia and the Soviet Far East. Fourth, these same years (1967–1969) marked the initiation of the strategically significant joint economic projects with Japan. Fifth, a second trans-Siberian railway (BAM) with a crash construction program announced in 1974, was perceived by Moscow (quite correctly, I think) as the key to the larger economic and strategic development of the Eastern region. Sixth, Brezhnev's highly publicized and extensive tour of Siberia during the spring of 1978 could leave little doubt that Siberia and the Soviet Far East had come of age strategically, particularly as Brezhnev was accompanied by Minister of Defense Ustinov. Seventh and finally, the parallel expansion and upgrading of Soviet naval, air, and missile installations and forces in Siberia, the Soviet Far East, and the Pacific area marked the Soviet Union unmistakably as both a European and an Asian-Pacific power.

Now to the post-Stalin documentary record, in capsule form. A speech by the chairman of the USSR state planning commission, N. K. Baibakov, in February 1956 reflected the essence of Soviet concern with Siberia and the Soviet Far East during the Khrushchev decade: "In improving the geographical location of production in the Sixth Five-Year Plan," Baibakov said, "the main task, as Comrades N. S. Khrushchev and N. A. Bulganin noted in their reports, is the further powerful advance of productive forces in the eastern areas and enhancement of their roles in the country's economy." Baibakov concluded that during the new five-year plan period "the volume of capital investment will increase more than 2.5 times in Western Siberia and 2.8 times in Eastern Siberia."[6] The importance of these figures is mainly what they tell us about early Soviet perceptions of the future economic and strategic role of the "east."

Some five years later (in November 1961), in his "Report on the Program of the Communist Party of the Soviet Union," Khrushchev, after painting a positive picture of general Soviet economic progress and plans, focused on what he terms the "distribution of productive forces." It was here that the ambitious and optimistic Soviet view of the future role of Central Asia, Siberia, and the Soviet Far East emerged in bold relief. "It is planned," the reports noted:

- "to create mighty fuel and power bases in the area of Siberia . . . where coal can be mined and hydroelectric resources . . . put to use . . .
- to transform Central Asia into a major power-producing region . . .
- to create mighty new metallurgical bases so that by 1980 there will be five all-Union bases: in the Urals, the Ukraine, Siberia and the Soviet Far East, Kazakhstan and the central regions of the European part of the USSR [and]
- to organize large chemical industry complexes [in the same areas] and Siberia and Central Asia.[7]

At this time, it should be noted, Siberia and the Soviet Far East were still seen as part—a newly developing part—of a balanced national program for the exploitation of Soviet economic and strategic resources. They were not yet cast in the extravagant terms with which the region's protagonists somewhat later were to characterize them: "treasure house of resources" and "key to the economic future."

The directives of the twenty-third CPSU congress for the five-year plan approved by that Congress and published in February 1966, with Brezhnev and Kosygin now in command, were more explicit on the importance of Siberia and the Soviet Far East. Moreover, the international dimensions, just then in the planning stage, were underlined by the reference to the seaports. Among the indicators of the enhanced importance with which the region was by this time viewed: a separate section of the document is devoted to "accelerated development of productive forces **in the regions of Siberia and the Soviet Far East** [bold-face type in the original document]. This section outlines development plans for oil and gas, forests, electric power, mineral development, fish, whales and marine animals (35 percent of all-union total), and the seaports of Vladivostok, Nakhodka, and Vanino."[8]

The so-called Draft Plan for the Development of the National Economy 1971–1975 put forward at the twenty-fourth CPSU congress (February 1971) devoted an even more substantial and specific section (some 1,200 words) to plans for Siberia and the Soviet Far East. In summary, the plan proposed to:

- Ensure high growth rates for the metal, chemical fuel, electric power, construction, and other industries.
- Create the country's largest petroleum-industry base in Western Siberia . . . and accelerate the development of the extensive gas deposits of the northern Tyumen province.
- Improve coal extraction and metallurgical plant construction.
- Accelerate petroleum refinery construction (at Achinsk, for example) and expand territorial hydroelectric, steel, aluminum, and railroad-car plants and production.
- Continue work on the accelerated development of productive forces in the *Far East* (underlined in the original). (A long list of particulars followed, ranging from hydroelectric development to seaport construction)
- Create conditions for a further influx of population to the Far East and Eastern Siberia for the permanent settlement of cadres in these areas.[9]

Between the twenty-fourth and twenty-fifth party congresses, an article appeared in the Soviet press (during the summer of 1973) by B. P. Orlov entitled "Objectives of Long-Range Development of Siberia, 1976–1990." At the time, Orlov was affiliated with the Institute of Economics and Organization of Industrial Production of the Siberian Branch of the USSR Academy of Sciences in Novosibirsk. The article is unusual in at least two ways. First, "long-range" is really long range—1976–1990. Second, and more to the point here, the linkage is now explicitly made between the economic and strategic dimension in the role projected for Siberia and the Soviet Far East. Consider the "four general objectives" for the development of Siberia set forth in the document, two of which key on military-strategic projections:

a. [Increase standard of living].
b. [Improve scientific-technical progress].
c. Strengthening of the economic integration with COMECON countries.
d. Strengthening the defense potential.[10]

The Soviet government's announcement in the spring of 1978 that Brezhnev planned a rather extensive tour of Siberia and the Soviet Far East accompanied by Minister of Defense D. F. Ustinov could leave little doubt in the minds of Soviet readers—or Western analysts, for that matter—that the increasingly enhanced published perceptions of the strategic role of the region had become a practical reality. This fact was underlined by Soviet strategic developments in the region that same year and since, beginning with the military buildup on the Kuril Islands.

In February 1981, V. Koptiug, chairman of the USSR Academy of Sciences' Siberian Division, reported on a large-scale, comprehensive, and long-term scientific program for Siberia. This program, reflecting still another aspect of intensified Soviet strategic interest in the region, amalgamates some 30 special-purpose scientific programs and involves more than 230 separate organizations in its implementation. These programs, the report added, were discussed in detail at an all-union conference held in Novosibirsk in the summer of 1980.[11]

A typical area of concern is the power-engineering sector. Commenting on prospects for the twenty-first century, P. S. Neporozhny, minister of power and electrification, reflected the enthusiasm with which Soviet planners view Siberian developments:

> At present the most important role is played by the existing power-engineering grid in the European part of the USSR which has a voltage of 750 kilovolts. But the "heart" of the Unified Power System will be the Siberian grid with an alternating-current voltage of 1,500kv . . . The Siberian grid will be unified with the power systems of Central Asia and the Far East.[12]

With the advent of the Gorbachev administration and concomitant with the continuing decline in Soviet economic growth, the high hopes that Siberia might prove the answer to the problem began to wane. Figures for Soviet oil production, for example, for the first eight months of 1985 showed a 4 percent decline instead of the 2 percent increase called for in the plan. And there was other disturbing evidence. For good reason, the new Gorbachev policy focused on the need for retrenchment and efficiency and, following still another sobering visit by Gorbachev to Siberia in September 1985, on what can only be termed "damage control."

Gorbachev's keynote speech at the twenty-seventh party congress in February of 1986, as well as the "Basic Guidelines of the Social and Economic Development of the USSR, 1986 to 1990 and in the period up to the year 2000" (put forward at the same Congress), highlighted the critical importance attached to the eastern regions of the nation. "Our plans for the short-term and long-term future," Gorbachev said, "are connected, to a significant degree, with the development of Siberia and the Soviet Far East." N. I. Ryzhkov (chairman of the USSR Council of Ministers) elaborated: "Special attention will be devoted to the comprehensive economic development of Siberia and the Soviet Far East, the development of their natural resources, and the provision of transportation lines to them."[13]

In a major speech at Vladivostok in July 1986 (Tass, July 28, 1986) Gorbachev stressed the critical and growing significance of the Soviet Far East. The general secretary underlined seven urgent developmental and strategic tasks that he termed "orientations": (1) ocean resources, (2) rich natural resources, (3) fuel and power (especially Sakhalin gas), (4) the production infrastructure, especially railways and maritime transport, (5) adaptation of latest technology, (6) further enhancement of export-oriented Far Eastern economy, and (7) more attention to consumer needs, especially improvement of the agricultural and food-industry sectors. There is little new in these re-affirmations.

As to the external thrust of the speech, Gorbachev asserted that, "in accordance with the principles of the Twenty-seventh Party Congress, the Soviet Union would aspire to give more dynamism to its bilateral relations with all countries situated here [in the Pacific/Far East]." Gorbachev then went on to suggest that this "dynamism" might include the withdrawal of a considerable number of troops from Mongolia, cooperation in building a railway linking Xinjiang and Kazakstan, joint Soviet-Chinese ventures in space, various joint economic enterprises with Japan, the creation of an "all-embracing system of international security" including Asian and Pacific areas, and, finally, "the possibility" of discussing with the Chinese a bilateral reduction of forces and other issues.

The foreign policy thrust of this speech thus appears to have been threefold: first, to reduce tensions with Asian neighbors; second, to attract more active Western involvement in the economic development of the Far East; and third, to serve notice that the Far East had come of age, economically and strategically. Gorbachev concluded that "the Far East has traditionally been called the country's outpost on the Pacific Ocean. This is undoubtedly true, but today this view can no longer be regarded as sufficient."

The overall theme of the Vladivostok speech is clear: to downplay the emphasis on Soviet military power in the region and to stress, instead, the Soviet Union's role as a "Pacific partner." At this stage in history, one would expect that the principal parties concerned would have seen enough of past Soviet policy and practice to be able to sort out rather quickly the possible advantages and potential risks in terms of their own long-term national interests.

In evaluating such plans against available (and not always reliable) data, the Western analyst must carefully attempt to avoid the twin dangers of overestimating Soviet capabilities or underestimating Soviet potential.

THE GROWING MILITARY-INDUSTRIAL COMPLEX IN THE EAST

Regional Administration and Control

Responsibility for administration and control of Siberia and the Soviet Far East, as elsewhere in the Soviet Union, is divided among several Soviet ministries, departments, and agencies—the Politburo, Ministry of Defense, Gosplan, and Ministry of State Security (KGB), to name the more powerful—with the Communist Party presumably having the last word on critical issues. Given the Moscow-centered structure, top to bottom throughout the Soviet Union (from

Politburo to regional to district committees), the line-of-command decision-making process and the final authority on most issues would seem clear enough. Observation of the process at work, however, suggests that the picture is not quite so clear. Apart from the built-in shortcomings of the communist political-economic system and the well-known Soviet predilection for bypassing or "beating" the system, two other trends with special relevance to Siberia and the Soviet Far East may be noted.

The first is the trend (suggested by numerous Western analysts, but not easily documented) toward the increasing role of the military in Soviet affairs. This pattern in itself perhaps should not surprise us, since it is only in the military and related intelligence spheres that the Soviet system can justifiably claim any measure of sustained success. In the larger sense it may be said that, along with the Communist Party, the military establishment and intelligence agencies have been responsible for creating and shaping the Soviet state, and that they are what sustain it today. Nor have the interrelationships of these three elements of Soviet control and power historically been without problems, mutual distrust, and decisive crises (the Beria affair being the most celebrated).

On September 1, 1983, the Soviets shot down a South Korean airliner that strayed over Soviet territory, with the loss of 269 passengers and crew. The many complicated and controversial dimensions of the incident need not be examined here. It has still not been established, at least publicly, who gave the orders to shoot down Flight 007. That such a decision may be a local military district commander's option or "standing orders" raises all kinds of potentially dangerous possibilities for the future. Also suggestive is the paramount role played by (or perhaps assigned to) the military in the massive public relations campaign that followed the incident, including an elaborate press conference in Moscow. On that occasion, it may be significant that a Soviet marshal (rather than a Foreign Ministry or party functionary) presided over the press conference, replete with maps and charts designed to "prove" that the Korean flight "was on a spy mission" and had violated Soviet territory. No apology has been offered. Indeed, Foreign Minister Gromyko commented that under similar circumstances the Soviets would do it again.

Worldwide reaction was one of shock and indignation—and worry over the longer-range implications. At a widely reported press conference, President Reagan called the attack a "barbaric act" that "shocks the sensibilities of people everywhere." The usually unflappable Secretary of State Shultz, visibly shaken after giving details of the tragedy, said, "No coverup . . . can absolve the Soviet Union."

The second trend relative to administration and control is the ongoing debate on national versus regional decision-making: should planning for Siberia and the Soviet Far East be conceived, drafted, and determined in Moscow, or in Novosibirsk or Khabarovsk? It is, of course, central to the Soviet system that all the nation's factories, schools, town and country stores, theaters, gas stations, moviehouses, and farms (private plots excepted) be administered through a hierarchy headed by a minister in Moscow. The characteristic result: even a small problem, which may be urgent to an engineer or planner somewhere in Siberia, can take months to be resolved among uninformed or disinterested bureaucrats in Moscow. Moreover, Siberia and the Soviet Far East are dubbed doubly difficult because of their distance from the center and the inadequacy of the communications infrastructure.

A major Institute of Economics and Organization of Industrial Production in Novosibirsk, with A. G. Aganbegian in charge (until mid-1985, when he was transferred to Moscow), proposes to meet these and other economic-development problems by "scientific integration" on a national scale. In Aganbegian's own words:

> One of the most characteristic features of the Institute's Siberian research is that the region is considered as a large open socio-economic system of hierarchic structure, a system whose formation and functioning are inseparably linked with analogous processes taking place in the USSR as a whole and in other regions of the country. *This calls for close coordination with the work on many national and integrated intersectoral and regional problems dealt with in other research establishments* [italics added].[14]

On the military side, the special characteristics and significance of the region were dramatized when in 1979 all military forces were placed under one "strategic directorate" or unified command. This is one of the three unified commands in the USSR that link ground, air, naval, intelligence, and communications forces and installations. The rapid upgrading of Soviet forces and bases in the region, beginning with the Kuril Islands, also dates from this time. The headquarters for the Siberian military district are in Novosibirsk while the headquarters of the somewhat more extensive Far Eastern Military District are in Khabarovsk. A Central Asian Military District, formed during the late 1960s in response to the Sino-Soviet border troubles, has headquarters in Alma Alta. Commanders of military districts are either three- or four-star generals. The relationship between the Soviet military forces and the Communist Party may be seen in the fact that generals and admirals in the military districts—themselves party members—sit on the politburos and central committees in the various cities, regions, and republics where they may be serving.[15] Thus, the party versus the military theme probably should not be overplayed.

The Strategic Implications of the BAM

As the earlier detailed analysis of the BAM and the Trans-Siberian Railway makes clear, a second major rail communication link running from north of Lake

Baikal to the Pacific has immense strategic as well as economic implications for the Soviet Union. The increased capability of military forces in Siberia and the Soviet Far East represents the most obvious impact. BAM's positioning, some 500 miles north of the border with China at its closest point (in contrast to the Trans-Siberian, which comes within 50 miles of the border at one point), further serves to underline the strategic dimension as perceived by Moscow. Finally, apart from enhancing their military utility, linkage with the newly constructed or upgraded Soviet ports on the Pacific, such as Sovetskaya Gavan, Magadan, and Vostochny (Wrangel), dramatize the international commercial aspects of this new formidable transportation link, especially with Japan but potentially with all the nations of the Pacific rim.

The prospects of economic development along the BAM sector (a major theme in the Soviet documentation), while longer range, also suggests the growing strategic potential of the region, pointedly with respect to the exploitation of oil, natural gas, hydroelectric power, coal, iron, and strategic minerals.

"Continued growth of the economic potential of the USSR and its foreign economic ties in the future depends greatly on the development of rich natural resources of the eastern parts of the country, including the zone of the Baikal-Amur Mainline Railway (BAM)." This was the keynote comment of a report on the Third All-Union Scientific-Practice Conference on the Problems of Economic Development of the BAM Zone, held September 22–24, 1981, in Ulan-Ude, the capital of Buryatia, USSR. More than 800 scientists and planners representing 31 academic institutes, 52 sectorial institutes, and 12 ministries and departments participated; 21 reports on economic and strategic topics were presented. Planning projections were made to the year 2000.[16]

The strategic implications of the BAM have long worried the neighboring nations of the Pacific, particularly Japan and China. Speaking to this point at the Second Joint Soviet-Japanese "Peace in Asia" Conference held in Moscow in the spring of 1974, Kiichi Saeki, president of the Nomura Research Institute of Tokyo, said, "If the second trans-Siberian railway (BAM) helps Soviet Far Eastern development, facilitates populating the area and strengthens Soviet military potential, then the Sino-Soviet balance of power will shift further in favor of the Soviet Union."[17]

My own fairly frequent conferences in Tokyo with Japanese Foreign Ministry and Defense Agency officials during the decade since, as well as the conclusions of the official Japan Defense Agency's annual white papers (*Defense of Japan*), have served to underline this theme. Indeed, it has been common, if controversial, in recent years for Japanese officials to term the Soviet Union a "threat" or "potential threat" to Japan.[18]

It may come as no surprise to find that the People's Republic of China also has followed the development of the BAM railway with interest and apprehension. As early as 1977 an editorial in the *Peking Review*, after drawing an analogy with tsarist penetration of the East, asked the question: "Why are the new tsars in a hurry to build the BAM Railway?" Peking's answer: "When the Soviet Union steps up its construction of BAM, its aim is, first to contend with the other super-powers for the hegemony of Northeast Asia . . . and next, to threaten Japan with an eye to other Asian countries as well." [19] As BAM nears full operational status and as other evidence of Soviet military buildup in the east mounts, this theme persists. [20]

Forced Labor

There are several problems endemic in dealing with issues of forced labor in the Soviet Union, especially in so remote a region as Siberia. First, in a one-party, essentially police state, the distinction between labor and forced labor is not as clear as it is in the noncommunist world. Second, the extreme secrecy with which the closed society surrounds all aspects of life makes it more difficult to come by the kinds of data and documentation that are routinely available to journalists and researchers in the nations of the West. Third, it has been fashionable in some Western quarters to dismiss accounts of forced labor in the Soviet Union as partisan, "anticommunist," self-serving, or "fragmentary," even when such accounts are extensive, substantial, and otherwise believable testimony by former camp inmates, eyewitnesses, or respected foreign correspondents. Fourth, Soviet propaganda and disinformation agencies—indeed, the Soviet press as a whole—work diligently and persistently to attempt to combat and to "neutralize" such Western documentation and reporting.

The most elegant and damaging testimony on the subject comes in literary form from Russia's own Nobel prize-winning author, Alexander Solzhenitsyn, in his celebrated *Gulag Archipelago,* published in the 1970s. The slave labor camps along the Trans-Siberian Railway and in factory towns and timber camps elsewhere constitute the archipelago of which he writes so brilliantly. Not surprisingly, the book has had a major impact in the West—and in Moscow. [21]

Over the years Western academicians, journalists, and foreign correspondents have joined the chorus of analysts and critics. Peter Reddaway, a senior lecturer on political science at the London School of Economics, for example, speaking on behalf of the International Committee for the Defense of Human Rights in the USSR in 1973, condemned the West for its indifference to the fate of the estimated one million prisoners in the thousand or so forced labor camps in the Soviet Union. [22] In his 1976 best-selling book, *The Russians,* correspondent Hedrick Smith of the *New York Times* cites a friend from Leningrad: "People know that the real dirty work [in Siberia] is done by convict labor." [23]

A 1982 *Backgrounder* entitled *Slave Labor and the Soviet Pipeline,* published by the Heritage Foundation of Washington, D.C., marshals a good deal of evidence on the subject. Its conclusion: while much of the information must remain fragmentary, the conclusion is inescapable that "slave labor is building the pipeline." This report also cites evidence of the increasing use of Vietnamese labor in these projects.[24]

A report published in 1982 by a U.S. Senate subcommittee investigating possible use of forced labor to build the Yamal pipeline, cites substantial additional evidence from former Vietnamese officials, defectors, "letters from Vietnam," and other sources, of what is termed an emerging "Vietnamese Gulag" in Siberia.[25] The Soviet Union claims that Vietnamese construction workers have gone to the Soviet Union of their own free will under legitimate contract arrangements.

What emerges from available evidence is this: forced labor in the Soviet Union is a documented fact. There are a number of labor camps in Siberia and elsewhere, some of them pinpointed on maps produced by former inmates. These camps contain "political" prisoners as well as those convicted of criminal offenses. An increasing number of Vietnamese, North Koreans, and others have been "hired," conscripted, encouraged, "railroaded," or forced to join the crews building railroads and pipelines in Siberia, and they are now part of the Soviet labor camp system—a system where the distinction between labor and forced labor is sometimes tenuous at best.

Strategic Metals and Minerals

Clearly, one of the important objectives of BAM is to facilitate the exploitation of the vast mineral and metal resources of Siberia and the Soviet Far East. As we have seen, the Soviet Union is the world's leading producer of oil, coal, and natural gas. In strategic terms, its net import reliance is small and its export capability significant. One of the strategic goals of Siberian and Soviet Far Eastern resource development has been to bring the Soviet Union as close as possible to self-sufficiency in the critical mineral and metal area.

The accompanying chart on mineral production (see Table 8.1) reflects world ranking and percentage of world output. The Soviet percentage of world output is impressive, especially in such strategically vital items as asbestos (45 percent), platinum (47 percent), manganese (39 percent), titanium sponge (38 percent), vanadium (30 percent), and chromite (26 percent).

The second chart (Figure 8.1), showing net imports as a share of consumption, contrasts the USSR's near self-sufficiency with the West's almost total dependency. It may be noted with some concern that the Soviets have now reached total self-sufficiency in such critical defense-related items as manganese and chromium (used in airframes, for example) and near self-sufficiency in iron ore and cobalt. The West, by contrast (the United States, Japan, and the European community), is almost totally dependent on imports in these four vital areas (the United States is an exception in the case of iron ore) as well as in other important strategic metals and minerals. All this, of course, is over and above the continu-

TABLE 8.1
Soviet Output and Ratings of Principal Minerals

Mineral	1981 Output (metric tons)	World Ranking	Percentage of Total World Output	Mine (M) or Smelter (S)
Aluminum	2,400,000	2	15.4	
Antimony	6,500	4	11.6	
Asbestos	2,250,000	1	45.1	
Bauxite	6,400,000	4	7.4	M
Bismuth	75	—	2.6	S
Cadmium	2,800	1	16.0	S
Chromite	2,400,000	2	26.3	M
Cobalt	2,250	3	8.4	M
Copper	1,150,000	2	13.7	M
Diamond, industrial	8.6[a]	2	27.7	M
gem	2.4[a]	2	21.1	M
Gold	260	2	21.0	M
Iron ore	241,000,000	1	28.3	M
Lead	570,000	1	16.5	M
Manganese	10,350,000	1	39.4	M
Mercury	2,137	1	32.6	M
Molybdenum	10,200	4	10.0	M
Nickel	145,000	2	20.6	M
Platinum group	101	1	47.9	M
Silver	1,580	2	14.0	M
Tin	16,000	Joint 5	6.8	S
Titanium sponge	37,000	1	38(est.)	M
Tungsten	8,800	2	16.8	M
Vanadium	10,880	2	30.6	S
Zinc	1,010,000	2	16.5	M

SOURCE: D. Hargreaves and S. Fromson, *World Index of Strategic Minerals* (New York: Facts on File, 1982), p. 229.

[a]Million carats.

ing critical Western oil dependence, especially serious in the case of Japan and Western Europe. During the past several years the United States has taken steps to redress this imbalance and to protect vital sources of oil, but the problem is immense and the process will take time.

MILITARY BUILDUP IN THE EAST

The Emergence of the Soviet Pacific Fleet

A critical attribute of great-power status throughout modern history has been the possession of a blue-water navy. Great Britain, the United States, and Japan immediately come to mind as classic examples in our times. The sea-

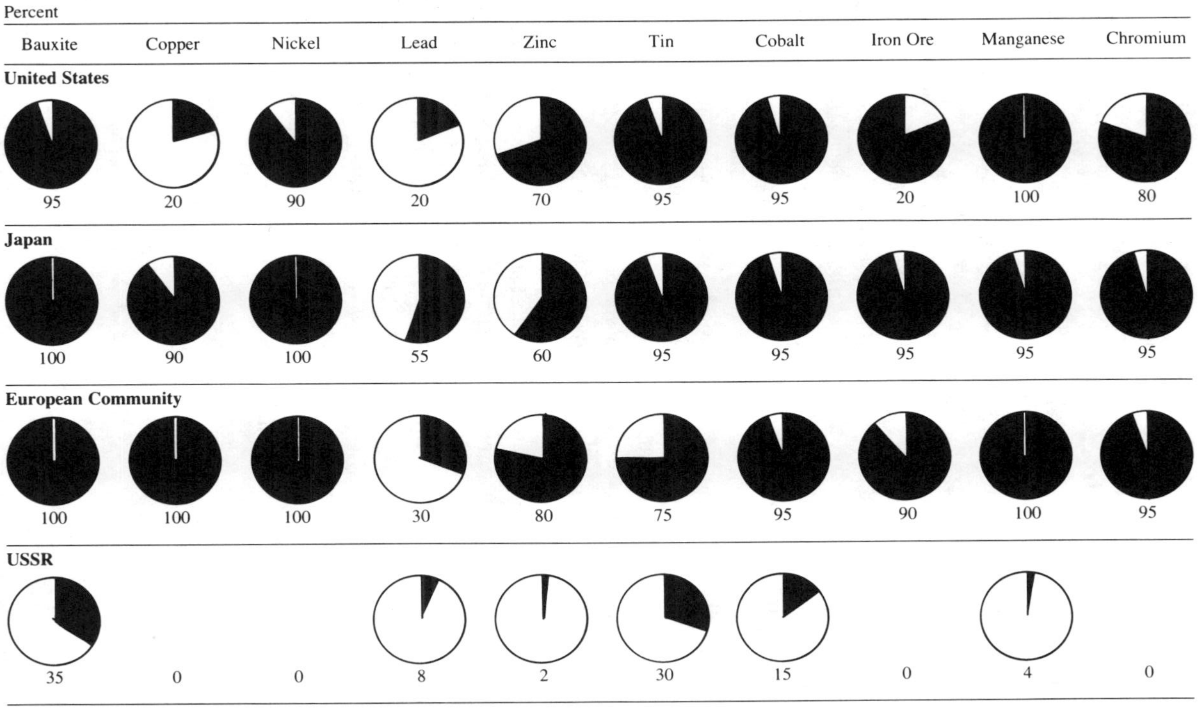

	Bauxite	Copper	Nickel	Lead	Zinc	Tin	Cobalt	Iron Ore	Manganese	Chromium
United States	95	20	90	20	70	95	95	20	100	80
Japan	100	90	100	55	60	95	95	95	95	95
European Community	100	100	100	30	80	75	95	90	100	95
USSR	35	0	0	8	2	30	15	0	4	0

FIGURE 8.1

Minerals and Metals: Net Imports as a Share of Consumption, 1984

SOURCE: U.S. Central Intelligence Agency, Directorate of Intelligence, Handbook on Economic Statistics, 1985.

denial role played by German submarines during World War II may be cited as another case in point. That none of these examples has been lost on the post-Stalin and especially the post-Khrushchev leadership may be judged from Soviet speeches and writings in the field over the past two decades.[26] The point is underlined by the fact that the Soviet Union today challenges the United States and the world in virtually all aspects of sea power.[27]

When the Soviet Union entered the war against Japan in August 1945, its Pacific fleet numbered 2 cruisers, 13 destroyers, 78 submarines, other miscellaneous supporting craft, and about 1,500 aircraft. By the early 1980s, the Pacific fleet counted one-third of the nation's submarine force (30 ballistic and 80 attack submarines), 30–35 percent of its major surface warships (41 vessels), and the largest share of the fleet air forces (over 400 aircraft). The Pacific fleet is also marked by substantial qualitative development, particularly during the past decade as Siberia, the Soviet Far East, and the Pacific have come into their strategic own.

While the official Soviet histories of World War II in the Pacific minimize the role played by the U.S. navy in the ultimate defeat of Japan,[28] still the naval lessons of the war and of the immediate postwar period could hardly have been lost on Soviet strategic planners. Certainly, the issue became excruciatingly clear in the Cuban missile crisis in 1962 when Moscow, without sea power (or nuclear parity), found itself forced to yield to the dictates of the West.

Moreover, with the expansion of the Pacific fleet and enhancement of Pacific rim bases, ports, and harbors, the Soviet active arena of Asian blue-water operations now was expanded to encompass an area ranging from the Sea of Okhotsk throughout the western Pacific to the Indian Ocean. As the Khrushchev decade (1954–1964) gave way to the Brezhnev era, the groundwork was laid for the modern Soviet navy, the adjunct merchant marine, and auxiliary fleets, with Adm. S. G. Gorshkov as principal advocate and prime architect.

In his *Sea Power of the State*, Gorshkov states the rationale for development of Soviet sea power as a critical factor in the "positive" international relations of the Soviet Union.

> The constantly growing sea power of our country ensures the ever wider use of the immense resources of the World Ocean in various branches of the national economy . . . The use of resources of the World Ocean in association with the further development of science in this field is opening up new directions in the economic and political integration of the socialist countries, expanding the sphere of their international cooperation and raising the prestige of the Soviet state in the international arena . . . The growing sea might of our country ensures the successful conduct of its foreign policy, helps constantly to widen trading, merchant, scientific and cultural links with other countries and to strengthen the constructive cooperation of states with different social systems and it places in the hands of our people a most important means for fulfillment

of its historic mission—the constant expansion of economic aid to all countries which have begun independent development.[29]

The fleet that Gorshkov built in the 1960s and 1970s essentially centered on three primary missions:

1. Antisubmarine warfare (ASW) to counter Western strategic missile submarines.
2. Strategic missile submarines (in reality mobile ICBMs) that could form a strategic reserve as well as a strategic fighting force.
3. Conventional surface and air forces, in large part to protect the strategic missile submarines.[30]

The Soviet Pacific fleet, now expanded in scope and mission, is today the largest of the four Soviet fleets. While sources differ in details, the growth of that fleet during the past two decades has been sustained and spectacular (see Table 8.2).

By the early 1970s, the Soviet Pacific fleet is generally thought to have had 56 major surface combat ships (inferior in quality and range to U.S. counterparts) and 160 submarines, of which 80 were nuclear.[31] Along with the upgrading of military facilities in the Kuril Islands (1978) and the Sino-Vietnam war (1979), the Soviets began to give top priority to modernizing the Pacific fleet and Pacific rim ports and bases. The 1979 assignment of the Kiev-class aircraft carrier *Minsk* (and subsequent deployment in February 1984 of the carrier *Novorsiysk*) to the Pacific fleet underlines the qualitative aspects of enhancement that have occurred ever since.

A new Soviet nuclear-powered aircraft carrier (65,000 tons) built at Nikolayev in the Black Sea is undergoing sea trials. It is expected to take some time before the new carrier will be fully operational. This new carrier (the first Soviet carrier comparable to the traditional U.S. large carrier) will give the Soviet navy a power projection capability that it presently lacks. Logic and other evidence suggest that the new carrier will be assigned to the Pacific fleet.[32] A second, similar carrier is also reported to be under construction.

The Soviet Pacific fleet today boasts roughly one-fourth of total Soviet naval strength, that is, some 810 vessels with an aggregate weight of 1.6 million tons. More than 25 ballistic submarines and over 90 attack submarines are augmented by Soviet naval aviation, which has grown by 50 percent since the mid-1960s to a current force of about 440 aircraft.[33] The deployment of some 30 naval long-range Backfire-B aircraft to the Far East since 1980 (in addition to the 40 Soviet strategic air force Backfires, for a total of 70) has significantly increased the potential threat to shipping in the Pacific. Compared with the Northern, Baltic, and Black Sea fleets, the Soviet Pacific fleet now includes some 30 percent of the

TABLE 8.2
Major Soviet Far East Forces

	1968	1973	1978	1981	1984–85
Ground division	25+	40+	43	45+	52
Ships total	660	646	726	720	804
Carriers	0	0	0	1	2
Surface combatants	55	60	67	80	85
Submarine (General Purpose)	95	90	90	99	97
Submarines (SSB-SSBN)	10	20	30	30	31
Amphibious (LPD/LST)	0	4	9	11	19 (LSD/LST/LSM)
Mine War (Ships/Craft)	110	115	110	95	95
Miscellaneous[a]	390	357	420	404	475
Tactical aircraft (Fighter/attack and interceptors)	1,050	1,370	1,405	1,335[b]	1,725[c]
Bombers	215	220	340 (LRA-250) (SNA- 90)	355 (LRA-245) (SNA-110)	355 (SAF-245)[b] (SNA-110)[b]
ASW patrol	65	125	120	130[d]	150
SS-20 IRBM				75	135[e]
Personnel total (thousands)	NA	610	679	701	738[b]
Army	210	380	410	430	500
Navy	105	115	119	121	143
Air Force	NA	115	150[b] (incl. Air Defense Forces)	150[b] (incl. Air Defense Forces)	95 (excludes Air Defense Forces)

SOURCE: Compiled from sources cleared by OASD/PA. Security Review for use in Public Domain, February 25, 1985.

[a] Including patrol combatants, amphibious warfare craft, coastal patrol/river-roadstead craft, underway replenishment ships, material support ships, fleet support ships, and other auxiliaries.

[b] Approximate; update not available at this time.

[c] Excludes Strategic Defense Interceptors.

[d] Includes BEAR F (TU-142), MAY (IL-38), MAIL (BE-12), HORMONE A+B (KA-25), HAZE-A (MI-14).

[e] Additional SS-20 Bases are under construction in the Far East.

USSR's cruisers and destroyers, 30 percent of its submarines, and 33 percent of its attack submarines—one more indication of the increasing priority that Moscow places on that region of the world.

Although calling Vietnam the "Cuba of Southeast Asia" may be too strong a statement, the parallels with the Soviet base in Latin America are nonetheless striking. From 1978 through 1984, the Soviets provided some $5 *billion* in arms aid to Hanoi. More than 2,500 Soviet military advisers in Vietnam support this program and provide political and strategic guidance. In return for this support, the Soviets have transformed Cam Ranh Bay into the largest Soviet naval forward deployment base outside the Warsaw Pact area. Rapidly increasing Soviet air capability in the newly developed base already totals 24 reconnaissance or combat aircraft with 8 Bears and 16 Badgers, including 10 with strike capabilities ranging as far as Asia and the western portion of the Trust Territory of the Pacific Islands. Support facilities have been upgraded with permanently deployed aircraft, including a squadron of MiG-23/Flogger fighters. The Soviets deploy some 30 ships to the South China Sea. If not yet quite a full-fledged Pacific power, the Soviets are clearly moving in that direction.[34]

The Merchant Marine and Commercial Ports

The conventional distinction between a nation's navy and its merchant marine—that is, military and civilian fleets—does not really apply in the case of the Soviet Union, for several specific reasons. First, all vessels flying the flag of the USSR are state-owned and Soviet-operated. Second, the Soviet definition of a warship is essentially any state-owned vessel that flies the naval ensign or the flags of auxiliary vessels, hydrographic vessels, emergency rescue vessels, and so forth. Third, as in the case of military vs. civilian air transport, Soviet passenger vessels are designed to be readily convertible to military use. Although the Soviet navy may operate a single troop transport, it is likely to be identical to a civilian passenger-cargo ship. It also will have ten or more of these "civilian" counterparts. Fourth, how shall we designate those elements of the research and fishing fleets regularly used for intelligence missions? Some of these vessels, operated directly by the navy, are at times painted in civilian colors though they are not otherwise distinguishable from warships. Fifth, Soviet vessels assigned to the KGB frontier forces are not included in the Soviets' own definition of warships though these KGB ships fly a naval ensign and are clearly assigned to security and quasiwartime missions.[35]

Thus, the Soviet distinction between warships and civilian vessels, like the Soviet distinction between war and peace itself (as in "wars of national liberation" or "just" versus "unjust" wars), appears deliberately vague, tenuous, and sometimes confusing. In a larger sense, this may be seen as perfectly logical and in line with the Soviet non-status-quo expansionist ideology, totalitarian organizational structure, and historical practice.

Concomitant with the development of Siberia, the Soviet Far East, and the Pacific fleet, the Soviets have constructed substantial merchant marine, fishing, research, and oceanography fleets.

The impressive Soviet sea power development since World War II is in contrast to the declining number of U.S. vessels in the area:

USSR

| World War II | 433 | | 550% increase |
| Present | 2,449 | | |

United States

| World War II | 4,506 | | Only 13% of its former |
| Present | 604 | | numerical strength |

The Soviet merchant fleet of cargo and passenger ships (some 1,723 vessels) ranks fifth in the world in total number of ships (after Panama, Greece, Liberia, and Japan). By this same measure, the United States ranks tenth, with only about one-third as many ships. The Soviet merchant fleet today plies 70 international trade routes and calls at ports in over 125 countries (though rarely at U.S. ports).

The more important categories of ships in the Soviet merchant fleet include:

1. General cargo ships, particularly well suited by design for carrying military cargo.

2. Container ships. Substantial increase in size and number as Pacific rim Soviet ports have been expanded and upgraded (with Japanese technical assistance) during the past decade.

3. Roll-on-roll-off ships, especially built for military cargo. The USSR has the world's largest fleet of these, more than 50 in service.

4. SEABEE ships, which carry fully loaded barges, and thus have no need for piers or wharves.

5. Ore-bulk-oil ships. The first of this type was built in Poland in 1975, 810 feet long with a capacity of 105,000 dead weight tons (DWT). Twelve or more such vessels, some of them larger and built at Soviet shipyards, are now in service.

6. Tankers, some 465 of these, with capacity of over 7,000,000 DWT.

7. Passenger ships, the world's largest fleet, some 70 such ships.

8. Icebreakers, the world's largest and most powerful fleet.[36]

It is not easy to determine what portion of this impressive Soviet merchant and auxiliary fleet spends substantial time in Pacific waters. Some light may be thrown on the matter by comparing available Soviet statistics on Soviet shipping associations and companies, and the number of ships operated by the Soviet Far Eastern compared to the northwestern and southern merchant fleets. Of a total of sixteen major shipping companies, four are located and operate primarily in the Far East (Vladivostok, Petropavlovsk, Nakhodka, and Kholms). (The others: six each for the northwestern and southern merchant fleets.) The Soviet Far Eastern merchant fleet numbers 362 out of a total of 1,375 ships. Thus, both in terms of shipping companies and relative number of ships, the Soviet Far East makes up roughly 25 percent of the overall Soviet merchant marine basing and operations activity.[37]

Space limitations preclude more than a brief note on the Soviet's extensive Pacific fishing and research fleets, both of which play a larger role in the military and security dimensions of international relations than do their Western counterparts.

The Soviet Union owns more than 4,222 oceangoing fishery vessels and some 70 civilian research and hydrographic vessels—the world's largest fishing fleet. A large portion of these operate in the Pacific and Indian oceans.[38] Norman Polmar puts the strategic issue in a nutshell: "The larger of these ships like Soviet naval and merchant ships, are built under the direction of the Ministry of Shipbuilding and, like the merchant marine, many ships' captains are masters and naval reserve officers." He concludes: "Obviously, the fishing fleet—like the merchant marine—provides intelligence for naval operations."[39] This intelligence activity encompasses observation (both visual and radar), electronic eavesdropping, communications, oceanographic sounding, and supply (logistics), to cite but a few examples. Given the high priority traditionally assigned by Moscow to all types of intelligence gathering, the capabilities of the fishing and civilian research fleets in this critical area are extensive and critical.

With the official completion of a second trans-Siberian railway (BAM) and the parallel development of the Soviet Pacific fleet and adjunct merchant marine and auxiliary fleets, the construction and upgrading of naval bases, ports, harbors, and shipbuilding facilities in Siberia and the Soviet Far East take on an added significance in terms of the East-West strategic balance.

Some of the more significant of these commercial-military ports may be briefly described:

Nakhodka   Port of western entry to Siberia, located 60 miles east of Vladivostok on the Gulf of America (formerly Wrangel Bay). Nakhodka has been Siberia's principal commercial port and is increasingly important to coastal and Pacific fleet trade. The first two docks were completed in 1947; by 1973, the port was handling more than 1,000 containers a day; and in 1977, 30 years from initial dock construction, there were 18 docks covering some 3.5 kilometers.

When I visited Nakhodka that same year, traveling on a Soviet motor ship from Yokohama, we entered a harbor literally jammed with commercial vessels of all types. By that time, Nakhodka had already become one of the five largest ports in the USSR, handling some 2,300 ships a year including 560 foreign ships from 20 nations. There were 20,000 visitors to the city annually (about half of them Japanese), most of them en route to other parts of the Soviet Union via the Trans-Siberian Railway.[40] Since then, the Soviets have further expanded and upgraded the port. The newer Vostochny port, just around the bay, now operates to augment the older, outmoded, and overcrowded Nakhodka.

Vostochny (Wrangel Port)   As noted earlier in this volume, Soviet interest in developing Pacific ports is reflected in a series of agreements with Japan that go back to 1970. That year, the Japan-Soviet Economic Committee, meeting in Moscow, agreed on a joint venture to build a new port on Wrangel Bay of the Sea of Japan, 32 kilometers north of the port of Nakhodka.[41] The Japanese government was to invest some $100 million in equipment, machinery, technological expertise, other production costs, and even consumer goods to sustain the local Russian work force. Originally designed to be completed in 1973, the port was perhaps 75 percent operational by 1975, but not fully completed as originally conceived until about 1977.

This new port on Wrangel Bay, called Vostochny, was designed to become the major commercial port in the Soviet Far East, surpassing Nakhodka (which had 8.0 million tons of cargo in 1975) in bulk, container, and general cargo handling. Ultimately, projecting some 60 large wharves and total berthing length of 12 kilometers, the plan called for a prospective cargo capacity of more than 30 million tons annually.[42]

By 1983, Soviet sources could report that a new dock, the fifth, had been completed at the "highly mechanized Vostochny Port, the largest in the country." The same account notes that the port's handling capacity has thus been increased by 200,000 tons of cargo per year. Construction of a plant for repair of international class, large-tonnage containers is also reported to have been launched as part of the Vostochny complex.[43]

Vladivostok   The original eastern terminus of the Trans-Siberian Railway and a major naval and commercial base, this port city is, from the Soviet point of view, "uncomfortably" located only 10 miles from the Chinese border and less than 100 miles from North Korea. Vladivostok is headquarters of the Soviet Pacific fleet and home port for much of the fleet's surface and submarine forces. Also present in the region are a submarine school, logistic and training centers, shipyards, repair facilities, and extensive radar and other electronics installations.

Vladivostok is mentioned in Soviet sources, along with the other Siberian commercial ports, as one of the complexes undergoing substantial refurbishing and expansion into a "specialized container complex." Off limits to most Soviet citizens, as well as all foreigners, Vladivostok is one of the Soviet Union's most sensitive military regions, so "specialized container complex," in addition to whatever else the term may imply, suggests that only certain categories of Soviet "commercial" vessels may be permitted in the region.[44]

Sovetskaya Gavan   A newly developed port some 400 miles south of the mouth of the Amur River, Sovetskaya Gavan is both a commercial and naval port. Expansion of commercial container facilities has gone hand in hand with the official completion of the BAM railway, which, as noted, terminates on the Pacific at Sovetskaya Gavan. The port appears to be scheduled for additional upgrading, especially as a key commercial link with Kamchatka and eventually with Japan.

Anadyr   This city, to the north, is located at the mouth of the river of the same name, and is an important port of call for arctic shipping. It is also a base for light naval craft, and substantial improvements in facilities have been under way since the late 1970s. Like Magadan on the Sea of Okhotsk and Petropavlovsk on the Kamchatka Peninsula, Anadyr has serious logistic limitations: it is not connected to any of the Siberian rail systems. All three ports are dependent on air and sea transport. As early as 1978, during the four-month arctic navigation season, the Anadyr port was processing more than half a million tons of cargo, including foodstuffs, equipment, building materials, fuel, and timber. Since that time, deepwater moorings and other improvements have been completed. The current five-year plan calls for the installation of ten or twelve large gantry cranes and other substantial upgrading.[45] The plan is thought to be a year or more behind schedule.

Petropavlovsk   This port, on the Kamchatka Peninsula, is both a domestic commercial shipping and fishing center and a major naval base. Two important shipyards are located there; adjacent Talinskaia Bay serves as the principal base for the Soviet Pacific submarine fleet. As noted earlier, the area's major disadvantage is that it must be supplied entirely by sea and air. The Kamchatka Peninsula and the Kuril Islands form a barrier and defensive screen for the Sea of Okhotsk, which has been developed during the past decade into a huge submarine pen from which Soviet strategic missile submarines can strike all areas of Northeast Asia and even parts of the United States. About one-quarter of all Soviet submarines are based at Petropavlovsk. Since 1981, more than sixteen SLBMs (nine SS-N6s, four SS-N-8s, and three SS-N-18s) have been test-fired from the Sea of Okhotsk.[46]

Finally, mention should be made of the Amur River shipbuilding and military-industrial centers of Komsomolsk and Khabarovsk. The latter, with a population of 500,000, is one of the largest cities in Siberia.

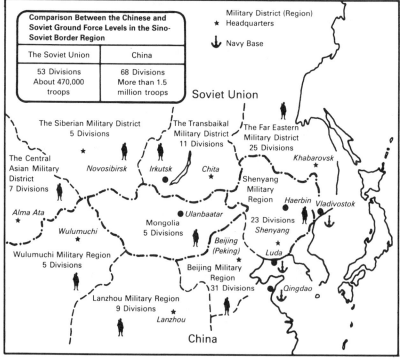

SOURCE: Japan Defense Agency, *Defense of Japan,* 1985, p. 37.

FIGURE 8.2

Deployment and Dispositions of Troops along the Sino-Soviet Border

Ground, Air, and Missile Buildup

The expansion of Soviet sea power in Eastern Asia and the Pacific during the past two decades has been accompanied by a massive increase in Soviet ground, air, and missile forces in the region. This quantitative buildup has been matched by a qualitative improvement that includes introduction of some of the newest Soviet weapons systems, aircraft, and missiles, and a general upgrading of Soviet forces in the region.

The increase in Soviet ground force divisions in the east (including Mongolia) from 20 to the present 52 divisions has been analyzed earlier within the context of the Sino-Soviet mini-war dating from the late 1960s. The accompanying map (Figure 8.2), showing deployment of Soviet and Chinese troops along the border, provides a graphic instant replay of the current situation. Today, Soviet ground forces deployed in the four military districts of the Far East represent about one-quarter of the total 184 Soviet divisions totaling 1.9 million troops—that is, 52 divisions and about 460,000 men.

Soviet ground divisions are mainly deployed along the Chinese border, including fifteen in the maritime provinces, one division in Kamchatka, two in Sakhalin, and nearly a division in the Northern Territories. Qualitative as well as quantitative improvement has been achieved through introduction of the T-72 and T-80 tanks, armored infantry vehicles, the latest surface-to-air-missiles, multi-rocket launchers, other state-of-the-art weapons, and more than 170 SS-20s. Significantly, many of these weapons until recently had been reserved for the "first line of defense," Europe. Further, at least four major Soviet chemical weapons depots are located east of the Urals, two of them in East Siberia.[47]

The Soviet air force numbers a total of some 8,300 combat aircraft, of which 2,100 are deployed in the Far East: 440 bombers, more than 1,500 tactical fighters, and about 150 patrol aircraft. More than 60 percent of Soviet aircraft currently deployed in the Far East are third-generation types such as the Backfire, MiG-23 or MiG-27 Flogger, and SU-24 Fencer.[48]

Finally, a word on Soviet missile deployment in the region. The most celebrated and dramatic development in this area has been the addition of 170 SS-20 launchers (with three warheads per missile) to the Soviet Eastern arsenal—a situation that has become a matter of persistent and public worry to the neighboring nations, especially China and Japan. ICBMs and MRBMs, including the SS-11s and SS-18s, are also deployed all along the Trans-Siberian Railway as far west as Novosibirsk. The rapidly developing Soviet airlift capability makes it likely that within a few years SS-20s could become "swing-system mobile missiles," thereby further blurring the distinction between Soviet deployment west and east.[49] Moreover, some 90–100 launchers for the road-mobile SS-25 (approximately the same size as the U.S. Minuteman ICBM and with a range of 10,500 kilometers) are now operational in the Soviet Union.

INTERNATIONAL RESPONSES TO MILITARY BUILDUP

Reaction of Neighboring Countries

How is the strategic development of Siberia and the Soviet Far East viewed by the neighboring nations most concerned: China, the Republic of Korea, and Japan?

China's ongoing concern with both the Soviet military buildup along its borders since the mid-1960s and the perceived strategic implications of the BAM railway have been discussed earlier in this volume. Recent documentation from Chinese sources further underlines increasing Chinese apprehension over both the economic and strategic development of Siberia and the Soviet Far East and the enhanced Soviet military posture in the region. Not surprisingly, the Chinese see an ominous linkage between the two. An article in early 1981 in *Beijing Review,* entitled "Building up the Siberian Base," makes the point in specific terms: "Obviously, a major goal in the drive to open up Siberia is to strengthen the Soviet Union's military posture in Asia and facilitate its expansions further east and south." [50]

While purporting to project a balanced view of the strategic issues in Asia in such formulations as "the United States and the Soviet Union are intensifying their arms race in the Northwest Pacific" (spring 1983), the Chinese nevertheless speak of "The U.S. strategic response to Soviet intensification of military deployment in the Northwest Pacific" and then go on to elaborate as to why it is the Soviet threat that is particularly worrisome:

> Since last year, the Soviet Union has continued to increase its military strength in the Northwest Pacific. It deployed a division of military strength in the four islands of northern Japan. What causes concern and worry of the United States and Japan was the deployment of the SS-20 in the Far East region, in particular the deployment of the newest "Delta I" strategic nuclear submarines in the Sea of Okhotsk. This submarine carries the SSN-18 long-range guided missile which can reach the U.S. proper. [51]

China calls upon the other noncommunist nations in Asia to "close ranks to counter Soviet military action." The *Bangkok Post* carried a Beijing Xinhua News Agency editorial outlining China's appeal: "Besides its full access to Cam Ranh Bay and Da Nang in Vietnam, the Soviet Union has missiles, including SS-20s, 51 divisions, bomber aircraft [as well as] reconnaissance planes in Vietnam for staging and re-supplying." The same editorial concluded, "All countries have a duty to combat this." [52]

Off-and-on "consultations" and "talks" with Moscow notwithstanding, China continues to take a serious view of Soviet military expansions in the region—in terms of both its own security and that of its neighbors. "It is well known," the Chinese warned again in the fall of 1983, "that a large number of SS-20s have been deployed in the Asian part of the Soviet Union and that they pose a considerable threat to China and other countries of Asia." [53] Some of these "other countries of Asia" have their own long-standing reasons for concern with the Soviet military buildup in the region. Both the Republic of Korea and Japan are classic cases in point.

Contemporary concerns of the Republic of Korea over the Soviet strategic-military buildup in the region are deeply rooted in a postwar history of unfortunate relations with the communist regimes in the Soviet Union, China, and North Korea. Some of the more agonizing events include: (1) the Soviet Union's harsh occupation of North Korea in the immediate postwar era; (2) the North Korean attack in 1950 with Soviet backing, launching the costly Korean War, which destroyed much of Korea; (3) Chinese Communist intervention in the Korean War with one million "volunteers"; (4) the subsequent massive North Korean military buildup (a two-to-one advantage in tanks, aircraft, etc.); (5) the ominous discovery of North Korean tunnels under the demilitarized zone; and (6) North Korean leader Kim Il-sung's ongoing close ties with Moscow and Beijing (including a May 23–26, 1984, visit to Moscow reportedly to discuss further Soviet military aid). These ties have developed considerably since that time.

Anti-Soviet and anticommunist feelings in South Korea continue to run deep. The 1983 Soviet shootdown of Korean Airlines Flight 007, and the death of seventeen South Koreans, including four cabinet ministers, from a 1983 North Korean terrorist bomb are only the most recent provocations. All these events and more constitute the backdrop against which the current massive Soviet and North Korean military buildup in the Far East is viewed from Seoul with increasing apprehension.

Japanese distrust of Moscow is also immense, long-standing, well-documented, and ongoing. Some of the key factors that over the years produced this negative Japanese image of the Soviet Union may be briefly noted: (1) lingering memories of the prewar Soviet Comintern's attempt to subvert Japan; (2) Moscow's violation of the neutrality pact with Japan shortly before the end of World War II; (3) Soviet indoctrination of hundreds of thousands of Japanese prisoners of war in Siberia and the years of delay in returning them to their homes in Japan; (4) Moscow's persistent attempts to influence Japan's domestic politics through the Japanese Communist Party and, later, the Japan Socialist Party; (5) serious difficulties with Moscow over the important fisheries question; and (6) most damaging of all, the Soviet Union's annexation of Japan's Northern Territories, which were incorporated into the RSFSR.

Despite the economic lure of Siberia and the tempting prospects of increased trade with the Soviet Union, these political-strategic questions pervade Japanese public opinion (especially among the older generation) and dominate Japanese political, economic, and security policy toward the great neighbor to the north.

It is against this legacy of distrust and apprehension, then, that the current Soviet strategic-military buildup in Siberia, the Soviet Far East, and the Pacific is viewed from Japan. The aggregate results have been:

1. Japanese public opinion polls that over the years rank the Soviet Union as "a most hated nation."

2. A perception by all the major political parties in Japan (with the exception of the socialist and communist) of the importance of the security treaty with the United States.

3. An increasing inclination on the part of Japanese business, industry, and government to regard China as an asset both economically and strategically.

4. A concerted attempt on the part of the Japanese government to mend fences with the Republic of Korea.

5. An increasing tendency by segments of the Japanese government to evaluate very carefully the strategic dimension of all joint economic projects with and loans to the Soviet Union.

6. Publication by the Japanese Defense Agency of a series of annual White Papers on Defense that, after detailing and documenting the Soviet strategic-military buildup in Siberia and the Soviet Far East, term the Soviet Union "a threat to Japan."

7. The recent emergence in Japan of increasing objective research interest in Soviet affairs (an area, with a few notable exceptions, long dominated by partisan left- and right-wing organizations).

8. Though still modest, systematic and quiet efforts by Japan to improve its relatively limited defense capabilities.

The United States and the Military Balance in Northeast Asia

The past decade has witnessed a complex of international trends and events that have dramatically altered the context in which the United States and the Soviet Union—and their friends and allies—confront one another in Northeast Asia. It may be recalled that only a decade and a half ago, major plans for the economic and strategic development of Siberia and the Soviet Far East (including the crash program for the BAM railway) were just under way; the United States faced a hostile China and was deeply involved in Vietnam; and relations between Japan and China ranged from nonexistent to minimal.

Today's scenario is quite different: economic development plans for the area are well along, with the critical BAM railway partially operational; substantial, upgraded Soviet strategic forces in the region threaten China, Japan, and the Republic of Korea, as well as U.S. interests in the area; Beijing failed to renew its 30-year Treaty of Friendship and Alliance with the Soviet Union (which expired on April 10, 1980) and adopted, instead, a policy stressing defense against the Soviet Union and modernization with Western assistance; and relations between Japan and the People's Republic of China are on a substantial political and economic basis. President Reagan and Secretary of Defense Weinberger's 1983–1984 visits to the People's Republic of China (and Secretary Weinberger's fall 1986 visit to China) as well as Premier Zhao's visit to Washington served to dramatize the new relationship. Moreover, the United States during the past five years has improved and strengthened its own defense capabilities in the region.

The present political-military balance in Northeast Asia, then, reduced to its simplest terms, postures the United States and its friends and allies—China, Japan, the Republic of Korea, and Taiwan—against an increasingly strong and hostile Soviet Union, North Korea, and a communist Vietnam.

The People's Republic of China

One of the celebrated changes in the East-West balance in Asia has been China's shift from a "tilt toward the Soviet Union" to a "tilt toward the West." This metamorphosis is reflected in China's new twin national-policy goals: defense against the Soviet Union, and modernization with Western assistance.

The contribution of the People's Republic of China to the military balance in Northeast Asia over the years has centered on:

1. A massive army and larger number of aircraft that, though primitive by modern standards, nevertheless serve to tie down some 30 percent of all Soviet divisions and 35 percent of all Soviet tactical aircraft, along the long Sino-Soviet border.
2. A modest but increasing nuclear capability, enough to give Moscow pause in any thought of a nuclear exchange with the huge neighbor to the east and south.
3. Intelligence capabilities vis-à-vis the Soviet Union shared, in part, with the United States.

By contemporary standards and in terms of the Soviet challenge and the military balance in Northeast Asia, the current Chinese military establishment leaves much to be desired.

The People's Liberation Army (PLA) actually comprises all three of the Chinese armed services—the army, navy, and air force. It is a massive, aggregate organization, but the impressive figures shown in Figure 8.3 are misleading.

There are an estimated 4.4 million men and women in the PLA, 3.6 million of them in the army but substantial reductions are underway. Weapons and weapons systems are, for the most part, vintage and obsolescent; both the general educational and technological levels of the troops are extremely low by modern standards; training, though rigorous, remains fairly primitive; and the command, control, communications, and logistic infrastructures must be rated cumbersome and inadequate. To be sure, recent trends toward modernization of the armed forces appear under way in China, but the country, the population problems, and the catch-up tasks at hand are all immense.

The Chinese air force, while the third largest in the world (more than 6,000 aircraft) is also the oldest, and with few exceptions can boast no aircraft more formidable than the MiG-21.

The Chinese navy is usually ranked third in the world in terms of number of large ships and manpower totals. Again, numbers are grossly misleading. Western specialists agree that the Chinese navy is aging, obsolete, and no match regionally for its Soviet counterpart. Indeed, cast in conservative terms, some 90 percent of PRC submarines, 30 percent of major surface combatants, 30 percent of patrol craft, all mine-warfare vessels, 95 percent of tactical aircraft, virtually all radar, and all cruise missiles are at the stage of development that the Soviets achieved ten or fifteen years ago; most are copies or adaptations of those craft and weapons.[54]

At the same time, a sustained effort has been under way in recent years to modernize the Chinese navy; some 20 percent of China's annual military budget is allocated to that objective. The result: during the decade of the 1970s, China's conventional submarine force tripled from 35 to 100 vessels; missile craft jumped in numbers from 20 to more than 200; a nuclear-powered submarine was launched; and there are other indications of China's determination to modernize its navy.[55]

China first tested a true ICBM in 1980; a nuclear-powered ballistic missile submarine is in preliminary deployment, but Beijing still relies on roughly 100 medium- and intermediate-range missiles as its strike force. Moreover, these missiles are thought to have relatively poor accuracy, poor reaction time, and poor reliability. Consequently, the Chinese nuclear force remains heavily dependent on about 90 B-6/TU-16 medium bombers, which are totally lacking in modern ECM and penetration aids.[56]

An important part of China's modernization program involves high-technology transfer from the West for purposes of upgrading all weapons systems. Shopping tours in Europe, exchange visits by U.S. and Chinese (and recently Japanese) military officials, procurement of Western high technology (including aircraft engines) are all part of the game, but for reasons suggested earlier this process is likely to take considerable time.

The PRC, then, is currently just strong enough to be unconquerable in a conventional war and just prepared enough strategically to make a nuclear exchange initiated by the Soviet Union—one which Moscow would obviously "win"—an unacceptable, counterproductive risk from the Soviet perspective.

Taiwan's Curious Role

Taiwan occupies a curious role in the region's military balance. It is one of the most economically viable nations in Asia, but its political and military future remains in limbo. Reflecting a kind of quiet two-China policy, the United States has, since recognition of the People's Republic of China, increasingly attempted to help Taiwan remain strong enough to defend itself, not against the USSR but against communist China. Beijing, of course, claims the huge island as its own, citing among other documentation the 1979 treaty of recognition with the United States. Various overtures from Beijing, some enshrined in the latest constitution, promise Taiwan a quasi-independent role as a part of communist China. Such overtures are regularly rejected by Taipei as "propaganda ploys" and the "latest versions of intrigue."

Taiwan presently appears to have sufficient forces to deter a PRC attack, particularly given the other domestic and foreign pressures on Beijing. Moreover, communist China's still relatively mediocre air force and inadequate, though growing, navy and amphibious capabilities would seem to make such an attack across the Taiwan Straits prohibitively costly, even in purely military terms, not to mention the severe damage to Beijing's currently cherished economic relations with the West, particularly the United States and Japan.

The formula presently applied by the United States is a program designed to advance Taiwan's defensive role by walking a delicate tightrope between abandoning a long-time friend and ally and splitting with a new strategic partner of sorts, itself in dire need of U.S. defense-related technology. United States arms sales to Taiwan for fiscal year (FY) 1983 were about $770 million dollars—the highest figure in ten years. Taiwan's budget for FY 1984 (July 1, 1983, to June 30, 1984) earmarks 41.2 percent of total expenditures for what are termed defense and foreign affairs.[58] Moreover, the United States has agreed to permit Taiwan to produce 60 more F-5Es, in addition to the 231 already under coproduction. This plan promises capability sufficient to maintain Taiwan's deterrent through the 1980s without the sale of a new fighter—a decisive distinction in terms of Beijing reaction. With U.S. guidance, Taiwan is also modernizing other defensive weapons systems.

Given the PRC's strategic problems and priorities, including the urgent need for Western technology and trade, the Taiwan issue is likely to remain manageable for the foreseeable future. The longer-term prospects of the curious role of a Taiwan in limbo are, in the final analysis, dependent on future trends in Sino-Soviet relations and the climate of politics and opinion in Washington. The odds on both scores would seem to favor continuity rather than drastic change.

The Military Balance on the Korean Peninsula

Over the years since the end of the Korean War, concern with the threat posed by a heavily armed, hostile North Korea supported by both the Soviet Union and the People's Republic of China has taken a number of dramatic forms:

1. the furor caused when President Carter announced his decision to remove U.S. troops from the Republic of Korea (a decision quickly reversed);

2. the shock accompanying discovery of the North Korean tunnels under the demilitarized zone;

3. the assassination in 1983 by North Korean agents of high-ranking members of the South Korean government while they were in Burma;

4. the 1984 visit by North Korean leader, Kim Il-sung, to Moscow the same year, where the question of additional Soviet military aid to the North may have been discussed.

The dramatic events only serve to highlight the serious, ongoing North-South security problem, a problem that is anything but new.

Here are some of the hard facts on the military balance on the Korean peninsula compiled by U.S. intelligence *a decade ago.*

1. North Korea outguns South Korea in every measurement of ready military power. The disparity is most significant in artillery (2 to 1), armor (2.5 to 1), combat aircraft (2 to 1), and naval combatants (2 to 1), even taking into account the fact that North Korea must maintain two separate navies.

2. All evidence points to continuing North Korean efforts to increase its edge on land and sea and in the air.

3. The combat forces north of the demilitarized zone are so positioned that they can attack with little or no prior movement, and the counter-intelligence screen is so effective that a three-dimensional attack could be launched with no more than a few hours' warning.

4. The combination of interceptors, guns, missiles, and hardening make North Korea the toughest air defense environment outside the Soviet Union. There is no prospect for interdiction of the type implemented by the U.S. air force during the 1950–1953 war.

5. A growing inventory of submarines poses a dangerous threat to a South Korea totally dependent on sea lanes of communication.

6. An indigenous production base and stockpiling give North Korea the capability to sustain an offensive for several months without external support. Kim Il-sung has thus attained the capability to execute a wide variety of military options without concurrence or aid from his allies.[58]

Despite efforts by the Republic of Korea and the United States during the decade since to reduce this disparity, the balance on the Korean peninsula remains critical. Despite a GNP only 20% of that of the South today, the North retains a significant numerical advantage on the ground: two and one-half times as many tanks as the combined resources of the Koreans and the Americans in the South; a two-to-one advantage in armored personnel carriers; a two-to-one advantage in artillery and multiple rocket launchers.

The North Korean air force numbers more than 1,200 aircraft—some 600 jet fighters, including their MiG-21s and a number of recently delivered MiG-23s; it has MiG-19s as well as Korean War–vintage MiG-17s and 15s. Mention should also be made of an increasing number of AN-2s, which fly low and are used to deliver North Korean Ranger-commandoes behind the South Korean lines. The North also has more than 60 transport helicopters. All this adds up to a two-to-one numerical advantage over the combined air forces in the South.

The North Korean navy consists primarily of torpedo boats (the largest torpedo boat force in the world) and the third largest submarine fleet in Asia, consisting of about 20 diesel-powered submarines of Soviet design. Overall, the navy of North Korea has an almost four-to-one numerical advantage over the South. U.S. officials estimate that North Korea could launch and sustain a very large assault without depending on either of the communist superpowers for resupply for a considerable period of time—up to 60 days.[59]

South Korean and U.S. forces postured against the formidable North Korean military establishment are judged to be superior in technology, weapons systems, quality, and training. A second five-year plan for modernization of the South Korean armed forces, which began in 1982, designed to raise the armed forces to a level equivalent to 70 percent of the strength of the North Korean force by the end of 1986 has been largely successful.

U.S. forces in South Korea have been modernized with the introduction during 1983 (part of the modernization of the U.S. Second Division) of M-60 tanks and self-propelled artillery. With the addition of intelligence, communications, and electronics units (some 1,500 strong), total U.S. forces in Korea now exceed 40,000.[60] Moreover, the presence of F-16s as part of the U.S. air defense forces in South Korea dramatically tips the qualitative air balance in favor of the South.

So long as the U.S. overall defense capabilities remain strong and U.S. intentions to defend its allies, including the Republic of Korea, are perceived as absolute, these U.S. "trip-wire" forces in the South, along with South Korea's growing military capabilities, greatly reduce the risk of another Korean War.

Japan

Japan's extreme military weakness in terms of the strategic balance in Northeast Asia is as striking as its celebrated economic miracle. Clearly, Japan holds the near-term key to redressing the military imbalance in the region. Japan's current defense capabilities, however, are inadequate on a number of scores and for four fundamental reasons. First, the constitution as well as Diet debates continue to limit Japanese defense spending to a degree (less than 1 percent of the GNP) incompatible with even a minimum effective defense capability. In terms of the GNP, only a dozen or so nations of the world make less military effort than Japan; they include Iceland, Luxembourg, Sri Lanka, Barbados, Fiji, Jamaica, and Lesotho. For balance, it should be noted that Japan's huge GNP translates this percentage figure into some $18 billion annually, which ranks Japan, on that score, seventh in the world. Second, force structures are small (land, navy, air) and virtually all major military equipment in the inadequate inventory range from 60 to 70 percent obsolete. Moreover, at the current pace of modernization and development, there is only slight hope that Japan will keep up with, let alone gain on, the Soviet quantitative and qualitative lead. Third, while the Japanese government clearly recognizes the threat posed by the Soviet buildup in the eastern regions, the Japanese population as a whole fails to perceive the nature and scope of the problem, even though Japanese public opinion polls reflect generally negative Japanese attitudes toward the Soviet Union. Yuko Kurihara, then director of Japan's defense agency, told Defense Secretary Caspar Weinberger in May 1984, during Weinberger's visit to Tokyo, that while Japanese defense officials understand the threat of the Soviet military buildup in Asia, the Japanese people do not.[61] Fourth, there is the inevitable tendency on the part of the Japanese press, especially the large antigovernment press, to concentrate on the "rising tide of Japanese militarism," when as one extremely well-informed, if outspoken, Western analyst, Anthony H. Cordesman, puts it, "the issue is not Japanese militarism, but modernization of a force structure that is little more than a military joke."[62] Calling it "little more than a military joke" may be exaggerated, extreme, and certainly unkind, but in fact Japan has little current capability to defend itself, even in a hypothetical, highly limited, regional conflict.

A somewhat more low-key Pentagon report (released in June 1984) on the defense contributions of America's allies, notes that "in Japan, both in 1983 and 1984, the rate of growth in defense spending has significantly exceeded that for general government growth including social programs." But, the report continues, "the problems in both equipment and sustainability which prevent Japan from effectively providing for its self-defense (which were pointed out in this report last year), have not been significantly dealt with, nor will the budget planned for 1984 adequately assist in what needs to be accomplished." The report concludes on a note that is only mildly optimistic: "Nevertheless, Japan did make significant progress during the year in clarifying its defense policy, which if carried out, would provide for a realistic defense posture."[63]

This same kind of faintly hopeful optimism is reflected in the 1984 annual report on Asian security published by the authoritative Research Institute for Peace and Security in Tokyo. After stating that "relations between Japan and the United States went very smoothly during the year," the document notes that in October 1983 two defense-related bills were approved by the Diet two years and eight months after they were introduced. The report's qualified conclusion: "If budgetary constraints limit the growth of defense expenditures, this should not stand in the way of qualified and organization changes that could make the operation of Japan's Self-Defense Forces far more effective." [64]

Against this background, a few shining areas of Japanese military progress and promise should also be put on the record. While many of the details must remain classified, the following may be noted:

1. Japan's enhanced radar and antisubmarine capability.
2. Japan's substantial contributions to U.S. intelligence capabilities in the region (the Korean Air Lines incident revealed perhaps too much about progress on that score).
3. Major Japanese advances in sophisticated electronics, computer technology, and ground and air weapons systems.
4. Japan's increased role in protecting the sea lanes up to 1,000 miles from her shores.
5. The high quality and dedication of the Japanese civilian military officials and military officers and the excellent training and dedication of the general military command.
6. The regular, extremely useful, and effective joint Japan-U.S. military exercises. [65]

Japan's security treaty with the United States and the presence of U.S. military strategic bases in Japan, of course, are designed to provide a bottom-line guarantee against aggression from any quarter.

Western critics accuse Japan—not without some basis in fact—of "dragging its feet" and enjoying "a free defense ride" at the expense of the American taxpayers. The Japanese themselves prefer to speak of "constraints in growth of Japanese defense" and argue that "slow progress is better than none at all." [66] While it may be difficult to confront the pure logic of this Japanese position, the "better than none, slow progress" may not be enough to prevent Japan from entering very dangerous strategic waters.

The clear and present danger facing Japan today, then, is not the unlikely prospect of a Soviet nuclear attack, or even an amphibious or airborne invasion, but rather the aggregate potential impact of overwhelming Soviet military pressures, economic enticement, empty promises, or even certain forms of subtle Soviet blackmail. Any combination of these could conceivably (though it is unlikely) produce in some future, weak Japanese government unfortunate compromise, strategically disadvantageous economic arrangements, strategic resignation by the population as a whole, or even, in effect, a general Japanese drift toward neutrality.

Severing Japan's ties with the West and affecting just such a politico-economic about-face has been the main thrust of postwar Soviet policy toward Japan for four decades.[67]

The U.S. Posture in the Pacific

Even though the Soviet invasion of Afghanistan is generally seen as the catalyst in the West's reawakening to the threat of enhanced Soviet capabilities and ominous intentions, the problem had been obvious to many observers much earlier than that. Not surprisingly, communist China, itself having been burned by the contradiction between Soviet words and deeds, had for years regularly warned anyone who would listen against the pitfalls of détente. President Ford even stated that he was not going to use the term détente; "it was too misleading." But in the final analysis, it has been the sheer weight of military evidence— Soviet military spending at 13 percent of GNP; the Soviet intransigent arms control negotiating posture; Moscow's persistent projection of a non-status-quo aggressive ideology and foreign military policy (in Asia, Africa, the Middle East, and Latin America); the Soviet massive missile deployment in Europe and Asia; and the development of extensive Soviet ground, air, and naval forces— that has dictated the dramatic U.S. shift from virtual unilateral disarmament of the early years of the Carter administration to the late Carter then Reagan administration's systematic, stepped-up defense program.

Asia and the Pacific have long been strategic stepchildren. For most of the postwar era, Europe was seen by Washington as the decisive theater and was funded accordingly; when crises occurred in Europe, Africa, or the Middle East, U.S. forces were drawn from the Asian-Pacific Command (the "swing strategy") as required. This policy inevitably stretched U.S. forces in the Pacific area dangerously thin. Those days appear to be largely gone.

After a number of years of systematic upgrading, the nature and scope of present U.S. forces in the Pacific may be judged from the accompanying chart (Table 8.3). While in sheer numbers the Soviet advantage would appear to remain substantial, the picture is balanced by the assignment to the Pacific region of the 6 U.S. aircraft carriers and the 46 U.S. attack submarines (34 of them nuclear-powered); and by basing and security relations with friends and allies in the region (as earlier discussed), which also include U.S. security treaties with the Philippines, and Australia, and important economic and other relations with the Asian nations.

Adm. R. E. Kirksey, chief of plans and operations, CINCPAC (Commander-in-Chief for the Pacific), Hawaii, provides what I consider an authoritative and frank assessment of the Pacific military balance:

> If I were forced to put a bottom line on where we stand at this moment, I believe the momentum is now in the Free World's favor. I am convinced that our current

TABLE 8.3
Major U.S. Pacific Forces

	1958	1963	1968	1973	1978	1980	1981	1982	1983	1984–85
Ground division total	5	5	12	4	4	4	4	4	4[a]	4[a]
Army	3	3	9	2	2	2 (−)	2 (−)	2 (−)	2 (−)	2 (−)
Marine	2	2	3	2	2	2	2	2	2	2
Ships total	347	432	427	277	220	221	217	223	212[b]	206[b]
Carriers	12	13	11	8	6	7	7	6	6	6
Surface combatants	107	142	140	104	85	89	90	92	92	87
Submarines (General Purpose)	43	55	59	47	33	42	48	51	40	41
Submarines (SSBN)	0	0	7	9	10	8	3	1	2	2
Amphibious	82	72	97	41	31	33	31	31	32	32
Mine War	39	42	42	8	0	0	0	0	0	0
Miscellaneous	64	108	78	72	55	42	38	42	40	36
Fighter/attack total	2001	1210	1828	1994	836	838	932	982	990[b,c]	1157[b,c]
Air Force	443	426	846	1386	192	180	192	242	279[d]	285[d]
Navy/Marine	1558	784	982	608	644	658	740	740	711[e]	872[e]
Bombers (SAC-TAC)	132	92	114	56	14	14	18	14	12[f]	16[f]
ASW patrol	253	144	144	108	168	188	190	190	250[g]	237[g]
Personnel total (thousands)	385	445	1042	438	299	315	316	321	351[h]	331[h]
Army	72	101	459	79	51	50	48	47	47	52
Navy	184	203	284	205	148	151	158	159	180	158
Air Force	67	66	171	88	30	42	41	43	45	46
Marine	62	75	128	66	70	72	69	72	79	75

SOURCE: Compiled from sources cleared by OASD/PA. Security Review for use in Public Domain, February 25, 1985.

[a] 25th Infantry Division has two active brigades.
[b] Data obtained from UNITREP DATABASE/ALOC.
[c] Includes NON-OPCON aircraft.
[d] Includes 44 NON-OPCON aircraft.
[e] Includes 158 NON-OPCON aircraft.
[f] NON-OPCON aircraft.
[g] Includes 50 NON-OPCON aircraft.
[h] Data obtained from J13.

emphasis on maintaining a strong political and economic posture is sending the right signal to the Soviets and other potential adversaries . . . A signal that the U.S. will continue to play a leading role in preserving freedom and democratic principles worldwide. At the same time however, it's imperative to recognize that our military strength underwrites these policies and is an indispensable pillar of our freedom. Although our force posture is improving, there is still much to be done. In all candor, should we have a military confrontation with the Soviet Union in the Pacific, I would say that the probable outcome is too close to predict.[68]

Adm. William J. Crowe, Jr., then commander-in-chief of the U.S. Pacific command, appearing before the Senate Armed Services Committee in February 1984, made essentially the same point. Asked to provide an assessment of comparative U.S.-Soviet strength in the Asian-Pacific region, the admiral concluded: "In all candor, the probable outcome of a major U.S.–USSR confrontation in the Pacific today remains too close to call. I submit that this is not good enough for this great nation."[69]

By the summer of 1985—in the wake of perhaps the most serious espionage case in U.S. history and, despite growing U.S. concern over the future of key U.S. military bases in the Philippines, reflecting the ongoing U.S. defense buildup—senior U.S. navy officials sought to reassure Congress, the American public, and, no doubt, friends abroad, that in terms of the U.S.-Soviet military balance in the Pacific, the United States was second to none.[70] Secretary of the Navy John Lehman testified before the House Armed Services Seapower Subcommittee: "We see no developments at this point that endanger the missile-firing subs that form the heart of the U.S. strike force."[71] About the same time, Adm. Sylvester R. Foley, Jr., commander of the U.S. Pacific fleet, told a Naval War College audience that, if required, the forces under his command could destroy the Soviet Pacific fleet.[72]

The relatively improved U.S. military posture in East Asia and the Pacific region and these official reassurances notwithstanding, the United States and its friends can ill afford to remain anything but actively concerned about the major emergence of the Soviet Union from essentially a European to a would-be Asian-Pacific power.

CONCLUSION

The economic and strategic development of Siberia and the Soviet Far East marks the metamorphosis of the Soviet Union from a European to a world power. Like the region itself, the process is fraught with contrasts: substantial progress in transportation, communications, energy, and the military, accompanied by endemic labor shortages, inadequate housing, substandard educational and recreational facilities, few paved roads, virtually no telephones, and the inefficiency, rigidity, secrecy, and lack of political freedom that are the hallmarks of the Soviet, totally planned, closed society.

In all this, the transportation and communications infrastructure provides the key. Here the "official" completion (in 1984) of a second trans-Siberian railway, the BAM, represents a strategic milestone. Other than the legendary Trans-Siberian and the celebrated BAM, plus a few trunklines, the region continues to be almost totally dependent on air and river transport. A west-east intercontinental highway from the Urals to the Pacific is nowhere on the horizon; and paved roads, common even in some of the less populated regions of the United States and Canada, are virtually nonexistent.

Energy development remains the critical, unknown factor in Soviet economic-strategic planning and development. The natural gas program appears to be on target; nuclear power capacity is growing at about half the planned rate; substantial progress has been made in hydroelectric power; the oil and coal sectors are just holding their own. As of 1986, Siberia and the Soviet Far East are thought to supply well over half of Soviet energy output. The future, however, is intrinsically linked to the performance of the Soviet economy as a whole, which in turn remains dependent on such unknowns as the performance of the Soviet oil industry and the demand for natural gas in Western Europe. The general Soviet economy, it should be noted, has been on a downward path for almost two decades.

Unlike the communications, industrial, and energy sectors, where some substantial successes may be reported, Siberian and Soviet Far Eastern agriculture presents more problems than progress. This situation results from lack of incentives, decades of official mismanagement and neglect, aided and abetted by a dogged conspiracy of geomorphology, climate, and sheer distance.

There can be little question that high-technology transfer from the West has played a significant role in the region's economic and strategic development. Without European, Japanese, American, and other Western technology, systematically secured (legally or otherwise) over a period of several decades, the striking rail-communications complex, industrial development, oil and gas pipelines, Pacific seaport construction, and related strategic progress—if possible at all in the near term—would have taken considerably longer to achieve. At the same time, Soviet zeal, ingenuity, and creativity must be given appropriate credit for some of these formidable accomplishments. It may be noted that Moscow displays a continuing sensitivity on this score.

The Siberian–West European connection centers on the controversial natural gas pipeline. At issue have been the possibility of Western energy dependence, resulting increase in Soviet foreign exchange, sensitive technology transfer, and equitable contractual arrangements. Worries over these and other issues produced something of an overreaction by the Reagan administration, including a series of policies, statements, and embargoes that upset the West European allies. Washington's initial, somewhat exaggerated fears have been largely calmed by more sober NATO and U.S. analyses and professional judgment. Some lingering doubt, however, appears to remain within the U.S. military and intelligence communities over the potential long-range implications of this linkage.

Japanese-Siberian relations present a classic dilemma: the evident positive economic value to Japan of trade and development linkage, compared to the negative risk potential of contribution to the growing Soviet military establishment in the east. Moreover, Japanese enthusiasm for joint development projects in Siberia during the 1960s and 1970s has largely subsided, influenced by a lower growth rate and a protracted recession in Japan and by a mounting security concern. Although the Soviet annexation of Japan's Northern Territories continues to upset most articulate Japanese, the population as a whole appears generally complacent regarding the Soviet military buildup in Siberia and the Soviet Far East. This situation prevails, it may be noted, despite a fair amount of Japanese newspaper coverage of Soviet military machinations in the region and the Japan Defense Agency's annual White Paper, which, after detailing the massive Soviet military buildup in the east, has for years termed the Soviet Union "a threat to Japan."

Perhaps most relevant of all is the China connection. Certainly the question is viewed with high-priority concern in Washington, in Moscow, and in Beijing. The issue is set in the context of China's unhappy postwar ideological, political, economic, and military relationship with the Soviet Union and exacerbated by the Soviet Union's extensive and growing ground, air, naval, and missile buildup in the region. Recent talks in Moscow and Beijing have not produced any significant results. It remains to be seen what effect the Gorbachev 1986 Vladivostok speech may have on relations with China. While Taiwan remains a thorny political issue, the increasing strategic interdependence of the United States and China, though still quite limited, is not likely to change (and probably will increase) short of an unlikely major overhaul of Soviet objectives, policy, and practice. With its huge army, large (if old) air force, and increasing (though limited) missile and naval capability, the PRC currently appears just strong enough to be unconquerable in a conventional war and just prepared enough strategically to make a nuclear exchange an unacceptable risk.

After a careful review of the nature and scope of the massive Soviet strategic buildup in Siberia, the Soviet Far East, and the Pacific, and concomitant with U.S. progress toward redressing the military balance, the following conclusions seem warranted:

First, the dramatic improvement of the Soviet communications infrastructure, commercial harbors, and port facilities and military bases in the eastern region have substantially increased Soviet strategic potential in East Asia and the Pacific.

Second, the steady Soviet improvement of military readiness, force levels, and weapons systems, as well as the acquisition of new bases in the region (Vietnam being a case in point) and the massive buildup of other Soviet Pacific fleet and air forces, serve to underline further the Soviet Union's emergence as a would-be Pacific power.

Third, at the same time, in addition to the worsening Soviet economic situation, certain specific shortcomings and severe limitations facing the Soviet Union's emergence as a would-be Pacific power should be underlined. These include: (a) the still relatively small amount of commerce and trade conducted by the Soviet Union throughout the Pacific basin; (b) the natural obstacles represented by the sometimes frozen northern ports and strategic bottlenecks in the form of the several key, narrow straits through which the Soviet Pacific fleet must pass to gain access to the open sea; (c) the still primitive state of communications (roads, trunk rail lines, telephone service) throughout much of East Siberia and the Soviet Far East; (d) the Soviet Pacific fleet's lack of first-rate organic aviation and distant-water sustainability; and (e) the increasing, if still quite limited, defensive capabilities of the People's Republic of China, Japan, and the Republic of Korea (especially in the antisubmarine, radar, and intelligence areas).

Fourth, the U.S. defense buildup in the Pacific during the past five years has achieved some success in overcoming both the traditional "Europe first" mentality and the negative impact of the Vietnam War, but sustained and perhaps increased Western effort will be necessary to meet the growing Soviet challenge.

Fifth, and finally, it is not clear what effect the worsening Soviet economic picture or a possible Soviet return to a policy of détente might have on this situation. In the past a huge Soviet military budget has been sustained with commensurately little apparent linkage to either of the above considerations.

The long-term effect of all this upon the United States and its Pacific rim friends may be that solutions will be sought in terms of short-range accommodation. But until the Soviet Union makes fundamental changes in its assumptions, objectives, policy, and practice, peace-loving nations of the world face an ongoing dilemma and a growing Soviet psychological and military threat.

NOTES

1. Detailed in U.S. Department of Defense, *Entry of the Soviet Union into the War against Japan, 1941–45.* (Washington, D.C., September 1955). Summarized with documentation and quotes in "The Pacific War and Emergence of a Soviet Policy for Postwar Japan," in Rodger Swearingen, *The Soviet Union and Postwar Japan: Escalating Challenge and Response* (Stanford: Hoover Institution Press, 1978), chapter 2.

2. Discussions with Dr. Philip E. Mosely, director of the Russian Institute, Columbia University, New York, Spring 1959.

3. See Rodger Swearingen, "Asian Studies in the Soviet Union" in *Journal of Asian Studies* 17, no. 3 (May 1958): 515–37.

4. See Rodger Swearingen and Paul Langer, *Red Flag in Japan: International Communism in Action, 1919–1952* (Cambridge, Mass.: Harvard University Press, 1952); and Swearingen, *The Soviet Union and Postwar Japan.*

5. On January 23, 1984, the White House (Office of the Press Secretary) released the text of a message to Congress transmitting the President's Report on Soviet Noncompliance with Arms Control agreements as required by the 1984 Arms Control and Disarmament Act. The document specifically addressed the question of the new radar installation in Siberia:

- *Issue:* The study examined the evidence on whether the Soviet deployment of a large phased-array radar near Krasnoyarsk in central Siberia is in violation of the legal obligation to limit the location and orientation of such radars.
- *Finding:* The new radar under construction at Krasnoyarsk almost certainly constitutes a violation of legal obligations under the Anti-Ballistic Missile Treaty of 1972 in that its associated siting, orientation, and capability, are prohibited by this treaty.

6. *Pravda,* February 25, 1956.

7. Report by N. S. Khrushchev at the twenty-second congress of the Communist Party of the Soviet Union, *Pravda* and *Izvestiia,* October 19, 1961.

8. "Directives of the Twenty-third CPSU Congress for the Five-Year Development of the USSR National Economy in 1965–1970," *Pravda,* April 10, 1966.

9. Draft of the CPSU Central Committee directives of the twenty-fourth CPSU congress for the "Five-Year Plan for the Development of the USSR National Economy, 1971–1975," *Pravda* and *Izvestiia,* February 14, 1971.

10. B. P. Orlov, "Objectives of Long-Range Development of the Siberian Economy," *Izvestiia sibirskogo otdeleniia Akademii Nauk SSSR, seriia obshchestvennykh nauk* 1973; *Problems of Economics,* no. 6 (August 1974): 44–45.

11. "Comprehensive Programs: Siberian Dimensions," *Pravda,* February 15, 1981.

12. "A Look into the Future: Energy in the 21st Century; An Interview with P. S. Neporozhny, Minister of Power and Electrification," *Izvestiia,* April 8, 1984.

13. *Pravda,* February 26, 1986; and *Izvestiia,* March 4, 1986. See also Gorbachev's speech to enterprises, specialists, and scientists on "Initiative, Organization and Efficiency" (*Pravda,* April 12, 1985); his call for a modernizing of the economy, "The Acceleration of Scientific and Technical Progress Is a Demand of Life" (*Pravda* and *Izvestiia,* June 12, 1985); and Gorbachev's written reply to six questions that *Time* magazine submitted, particularly: "Since you became General Secretary, you have taken several steps to improve the Soviet economy . . . What, in your opinion, are the main problems of the Soviet economy?" (*Pravda* and *Izvestiia,* September 2, 1985).

14. A. G. Aganbegian, ed., *Regional Studies for Planning and Projecting: The Siberian Experience* (The Hague: Mouton Publishers, 1981), p. 16.

15. For other dimensions and further detail see Harriet Fast Scott and William F. Scott, *The Soviet Control Structure: Capabilities for Wartime Survival* (New York: Crane Russak, 1983).

16. A. Kim, "Comprehensive Development of the BAM Zone," *Moscow obshchestvennye nauki*, no. 3 (April 20, 1982).

17. Kiichi Saeki, "The Second Trans-Siberian Railway," paper presented at the Second Soviet-Japanese "Peace in Asia" Conference, Moscow, spring 1974, p. 4.

18. See Japan Defense Agency, *Defense of Japan 1982, 1983,* and *1984* (Tokyo: Japan Times, cited years).

19. *Peking Review,* July 22, 1977.

20. See, for example, Gui Tong Chang, "Soviet-U.S. Military Confrontation in Asia," *Beijing Review,* March 26, 1984.

21. Alexander Solzhenitsyn, *The Gulag Archipelago* (New York: Harper and Row, 1975).

22. "The Forced Labor Camps in the USSR Today: An Unrecognized Example of Modern Inhumanity (The International Committee for the Defense of Human Rights in the USSR, February 26, 1973).

23. Hedrick Smith, *The Russians* (New York: Quadrangle/The New York Times Book Company, 1976), p. 334.

24. The Heritage Foundation, *Slave Labor and the Soviet Pipeline* (Washington, D.C., September 16, 1982).

25. Hearings, Subcommittee on International Finance and Monitor Policy, Committee on Banking, Housing and Urban Affairs, Ninety-Seventh Congress. *Human Rights Consequences of the Proposed Trans-Siberian Natural Gas Pipeline: Second Session on Possible Use of Forced Labor to Build the Yamal Pipeline in the Soviet Union* (Washington, D.C.: U.S. Congress, June 18, 1982).

26. See, for example, Sergei G. Gorshkov, *Sea Power of the State* (Oxford: Pergamon Press, 1979). This is a translation of the 1976 second revised edition, published in Moscow.

27. For a comprehensive treatment of Soviet sea power see Norman Polmar, *Guide to the Soviet Navy,* 3rd ed. (Annapolis, Md.: Naval Institute Press, 1983).

28. See, for example, A. M. Dubinsky, *The Far East in the Second World War, an outline of international relations and national liberation struggle in East and Southeast Asia* (Moscow: "Nauka" Publishing House, 1972). Dubinsky, one of the Soviets' senior authorities on the subject, manages 457 pages of "history" with virtually no reference to the role of the U.S. army, navy, and marines or to U.S. air power in the defeat of Japan in the Pacific war.

29. Gorshkov, *Sea Power,* pp. 57–58.

30. Polmar, *Guide to the Soviet Navy,* p. 2.

31. This was, for example, the estimate of the International Institute of Strategic Studies (IISS) for that year.

32. U.S. Department of Defense, *Soviet Military Power* (Washington, D.C., April 1985), pp. 99–100.

33. Briefing session, USCINCPAC, Honolulu, Hawaii, April 1984.

34. U.S. Department of Defense, *Soviet Military Power,* pp. 130–31.

35. Detailed and elaborated in Cdr. James John Tritten, "The Soviet Auxiliary Fleet," *Navy International* (April 1984). I am indebted to Commander Tritten, one of my former graduate students, for data and insights in this highly specialized field.

36. Elaborated in Polmar, *Guide to the Soviet Navy.*

37. Sources compiled from Soviet data (incomplete after 1979) in Hana Bohme, "The Organization, Management System, and Marketing Behavior of the Soviet Merchant Marine," *The Challenge of Soviet Shipping* (New York: National Strategy Information Center, 1982), p. 19.

38. For background see Richard T. Ackley, USN (ret.), "The Fishing Fleet and Soviet Strategy," *Naval Institute Proceedings,* July 1975.

39. Polmar, *Guide to the Soviet Navy,* p. 423.

40. A useful, personalized glimpse of Nakhodka at that time is in Stephen Uhalley, Jr., "The Soviet Far East: Growing Participation in the Pacific," *East Asia Service,* vol. 24, no. 1 (September 1977).

41. Details in Chapter 6 of this volume.

42. See Raymond S. Mathieson, *Japan's Role in Soviet Economic Transfer of Technology Since 1965* (New York: Praeger, 1979), pp. 30–39.

43. *Vodnyi Transport* (January 20, 1983): 1.

44. Article by Averchenkov and A. Kolding (chief and deputy chief, respectively, of a department of Dal'morniiproekt [Far Eastern Maritime Scientific Research Institute for Planning]), "The Main Line Route," under the heading "To Increase the Efficiency of the Specialized Fleet," *Vodnyi Transport* (May 19, 1983): 2.

45. Vladivostok Maritime Service in Russian to the Pacific Far East 0700 GMT November 1978.

46. "Soviet Bases in the Far East," *Jane's Defence Weekly,* vol. 1, no. 14 (April 14, 1984): 560.

47. U.S. Department of Defense, *Continuing Development of Chemical Capabilities in the USSR* (Washington, D.C., October 1983), p. 14 (map).

48. Japan Defense Agency, *Defense of Japan 1983* (Tokyo: Japan Times, 1983), pp. 28–32; and Inoki Masamichi, *Asian Security,* ed. Prof. Masataka Kosaka with Brig. Kenneth Hunt (Tokyo, August 1984), p. 66. Figures on SS-20s from USCINCPAC briefings of author in Hawaii, April 1984.

49. The production of the new heavy-lift *Condor* transport (comparable to the U.S. C-5A *Galaxy*), scheduled for deployment in 1987–1988, is thought to be a step in this direction. U.S. Defense Department, *Soviet Military Power* (Washington, D.C., 1984), pp. 83–84.

50. "Building up the Siberian Base," *Beijing Review,* May 11, 1981.

51. Fuzhou, *Fujian Ribao,* April 10, 1983, p. 4.

52. Beijing Xinhua, *Bangkok Post,* September 20, 1983. Italics added.

53. *Beijing Review,* September 26, 1983. Italics added.

54. For background, elaboration, and further useful detail see Donald C. Daniel, "Sino-Soviet Relations in Naval Perspective," in Douglas T. Stuart and William T. Tow, *China, the Soviet Union, and the West* (Boulder, Colo.: Westview Press, 1982), pp. 117–19.

55. See *Chinese Defense Spending,* Research Paper SR 80-10091 (Washington, D.C.: Central Intelligence Agency, 1980); and Bruce Swanson, *Eighth Voyage of the Dragon* (Annapolis, Md.: Naval Institute Press, 1982).

56. For further background and details, see Anthony H. Cordesman, "The Military Balance in Northeast Asia: The Challenge to Japan and Korea (Part II)," *Armed Forces Journal International* (December 1983). It is a sophisticated, hard-hitting article crammed with up-to-date and keen observations.

57. *Asian Security,* p. 103.

58. Richard G. Stilwell, "The Need for U.S. Ground Forces in Korea, *AEI Defense Review,* no. 2 (1977): 19–20.

59. Official USRF Command briefing (current as of April 24, 1984); briefing of author at USFK headquarters, Korea, June 26, 1984.

60. I was impressed by recent plans and progress during my talks with South Korean Defense and Foreign Ministry officials and briefings at the Republic of Korea/U.S. Combined Forces Command Headquarters during a visit to Seoul in June 1984.

61. *Daily Yomiuri,* Tokyo, June 21, 1984.

62. Cordesman, "The Military Balance in Northeast Asia."

63. Caspar Weinberger, *Report on Allied Contributions to the Common Defense: A Report to Congress* (Washington, D.C.: Department of Defense, March 1983), p. 61. Significantly, the report was quoted at length on the front page of Tokyo's *Daily Yomiuri,* under the title "Japan's Defense Contribution Still Inadequate—Pentagon" (June 21, 1984).

64. Inoki, *Asian Security,* pp. 208–9.

65. For these and other details see the Japan Defense Agency, *Defense of Japan, 1984* and *Asian Security 1984,* both cited earlier. Some of these same points were elaborated and detailed, as nonclassified information permitted, during my meetings with Japan Defense Agency and Foreign Ministry officials in Tokyo in June 1984.

66. Masataka Kosaka, "Constraints in the Growth of Japanese Defense—Slow Progress Is Better Than None at All," *Look Japan,* June 10, 1984.

67. For details and documentation (U.S., Soviet, and Japanese) see Rodger Swearingen and Paul Langer, *Red Flag in Japan,* and Swearingen, *The Soviet Union and Postwar Japan.*

68. Adm. R. E. Kirksey, "The USSR as a Pacific Power: Opportunities and Problems." Keynote address, the Fifth Pacific Symposium, National Defense University, Washington, D.C., February 9, 1984.

69. Adm. William J. Crowe, Jr., USN, Commander-in-Chief, U.S. Pacific Command, testimony before the Senate Armed Services Committee, February 29, 1984.

70. In May 1985, John Walker, a Navy veteran, and other members of his family were arrested by the FBI on charges alleging extensive and high-level espionage over a 20-year period, including the theft of some of the United States' most prized naval secrets. For an overview, see "A Family of Spies," *Newsweek,* June 10, 1985.

71. Statement of Hon. John Lehman, Secretary of the Navy, and other testimony, *Hearings on the 600-ship Navy and the Maritime Strategy* before the Seapower and Strategic and Critical Materials Subcommittee of the Armed Services, House of Representatives, Ninety-Ninth Congress. First Session, June 24, 1985. U.S. Government Printing Office, Washington, 1986. Also quoted in *Orange County Register,* June 30, 1985.

72. "Deterrence in the Pacific Basin," June 20, 1985. Naval War College, Newport, Rhode Island (tape furnished); also, quoted in *Los Angeles Times,* June 30, 1985. A detailed, up-to-date analysis of the regional East-West strategic balance is provided in Georges Tan Eng Bok, *The USSR in East Africa* (Paris: The Atlantic Institute of International Affairs, 1986).

Resources for Current Research on Siberia and the Soviet Far East— A Bibliographic Profile

Siberia is the vast land mass that occupies most of the territory of the Soviet Union. Although the boundaries for parts of Siberia fluctuate, the region is divided into three major areas with various political and economic divisions. They are (1) Zapadnaia Sibir' (West Siberia), which includes the oblasts (regions) of Tomsk, Tyumen, Omsk, Novosibirsk, Kemerovo; the Gorno-Altai autonomous oblast; the Altai krai; and two national okrugs, Yamalo-Nenets and Khanty-Mansi; (2) Vostochnaia Sibir' (East Siberia), which includes the Tuva and Buryat ASSRs; Irkutsk and Chita oblasts; the Khakass autonomous oblast; Krasnoyarsk krai; and four national okrugs, Ust-Ordynski Buryat, Taimyr, Agin-Buryat, and Evenski; and (3) Dal'nii Vostok (the Far East), which includes the Yakutsk ASSR; the oblasts of Sakhalin, Magadan, Kamchatka, and Amur; Khabarovsk krai and Primorski krai; the Evrey autonomous oblast; and two national okrugs, Chukot and Koryak.

The Far East in particular is also part of the East Asian continent, and its history is linked with that of China, Mongolia, Korea, and Japan. Other names for this region reflect these ties—Soviet Asia, East Asian Siberia, Northeast Asia, and Asiatic Russia.

The broad themes of this collection of essays are the history, economy, strategic developments, and foreign relations of Siberia and the Far East. The role of the Far East in the developing Pacific regionalism also bears watching. A significant collection of essays has appeared on this theme: *Tikhookeanskii regionalizm; kontseptsii i real'nost'* [Pacific regionalism: Conception and reality], edited by V. I. Ivanov and K. V. Malakhovskii at the Institute of Oriental Studies (Moscow, 1983). This volume examines the nature of international economic ties in the Pacific, particularly the roles of ASEAN, Japan, Australia, New Zealand, Canada, and the United States.

The task of those interested in Siberia will be to keep up with what is being published. This survey will concentrate on Russian publications in recent years.

SOURCES

One begins, of course, with Russian bibliographies (described below); if consulted regularly, they will allow one to be as up to date as possible. Also, remembering that Siberia and the Soviet Far East have both historical and bibliographic ties to Asia, one may find relevant material in bibliographies on China, Korea, and Japan. The *Bibliography of Asian Studies,* for example, has a section on the Soviet Far East in its annual cumulations from 1977 to 1981 (the latest published). A lengthy discussion of Russian history, bibliographies, libraries, and publishing about Asia may be found in my article entitled "The Russians and Soviets in Asia." [1]

Other fields with their own bibliographic sources and literature may also overlap with the narrower Siberia focus. Military literature (journals, primarily) and the daily press should be consulted. Geographic sources will yield materials of interest. The area of foreign relations is not clearly delineated in Soviet bibliographies. Bibliographies and journals dealing with history and general social science are the best places to search for material on politics, international relations, and policy statements. [2]

For retrospective materials the major prerevolutionary bibliography on Siberia is by Vladimir Izmailovich Mezhov, *Sibirskaia bibliografiia* [Siberian bibliography], 3 vols. (St. Petersburg, 1891–1892). The 25,250 items, covering 300 years, are arranged by subject, supplemented at times with a geographic breakdown. It is a monumental contribution. Another important work is Robert J. Kerner's two-volume *Northeastern Asia: A Selected Bibliography* (Berkeley: University of California Press, 1939). Volume 2 contains the section on Siberia and Russia in Asia, and lists over 3,000 items in Russian, Western, and Asian languages. V. V. Tomashevskii's *Materialy k bibliografii Sibiri i Dal' nego Vostoka XV–pervaia polovina XIX veka* [Materials on the bibliography of Siberia and the Far East, fifteenth to first half of the nineteenth centuries] (Vladivostok, 1957) lists over 3,500 items; it is a handy general source. For more specific coverage of the Far East one could also use "Ukazatel' glavneishikh istochnikov i posobii po Aziatskoi Rossii" [Index of the major sources and texts on Asiatic Russia] in *Aziatskaia Rossiia* [Asiatic Russia] (St. Petersburg, 1914, reprinted in 1974; vol. 3, pp. lxxi–cxli). This covers the period 1747–1914 and lists 2,800 items.

There is a 70-year gap from Mezhov to the publication of the bibliographical bulletins of the Gosudarstvennaia publichnaia nauchno-tekhnicheskaia biblioteka (hereafter, GPNTB; translated as State Public Scientific Technical Library). While various bibliographies exist, the systematic recording of the literature is not available. A good effort to remedy this situation is the publication by the GPNTB librarians entitled *Ukazatel' bibliograficheskikh posobii po Sibiri i Dal'nemu Vostoku, XIX v.–1968* [Index of bibliographic guides on Siberia and the Far East, nineteenth century to 1968] (Novosibirsk, 1975). Compiled by A. N. Lebedeva, G. A. Ozerova, and L. S. Pankratova, this work lists 4,556 bibliographies, updated with annual supplements of the same title.

For current awareness, the best source is one or more of the bibliographical bulletins produced by the GPNTB. There are now eleven titles in this series,[3] but those most relevant to this study are: *Nauka, literatura, iskusstvo Sibiri* [Science, literature, art of Siberia]; *Istoriia Sibiri* [History of Siberia]; *Narodnoe khoziaistvo Sibiri i Dal'nego Vostoka* [The economy of Siberia and the Far East]; *Problemy BAM* [Problems of BAM]; and *Kniga, bibliotechnoe delo i bibliografiia Sibiri* [The book, library matters and bibliography of Siberia]. The remaining six titles are in sciences.

In total, the eleven bulletins record an estimated 18,500 items per year: monographs, journal and newspaper articles, dissertations, and reports. They reflect the Russian- and foreign-language materials received at the GPNTB. All the bulletins share some general features: the arrangement is schematic, name and geographic indexes appear in each issue (the name and geographic places from foreign literature are listed in a separate file), some items are annotated, a list of journals consulted appears in the last issue of each year, and a list of abbreviations is beginning to appear in more recent issues. The compilers, contents, coverage, and tirazh (number of copies printed) are constantly changing. There is some duplication of citations among various bulletins. There are no cumulative indexes. If these bulletins are used as received, one will become familiar with names, topics of research, reports at conferences, reports in the regional press, and the latest dissertations awarded.

There are also a series of bibliographies compiled by the regional libraries. They all begin with the title *Literatura o/ob* . . . [Literature about the . . .] and cover these areas:

Western Siberia
Altaiskom krae [Altai krai] 1961–
Omskoi oblasti [Omsk oblast] 1962–
Zapadnoi Sibiri [Western Siberia] 1959–
Tomskoi oblasti [Tomsk oblast] 1963–
Kemerovskoi oblasti [Kemerovo oblast] 1961–
Novosibirskoi oblasti [Novosibirsk oblast] 1958–
Tiumenskoi oblasti [Tyumen oblast] 1965–

Eastern Siberia
Chitinskoi oblasti [Chita oblast] 1962–1964, 1969–
Irkutskoi oblasti [Irkutsk oblast] 1961–
Vostochnoi Sibiri [Eastern Siberia] 1962–1969
Krasnoiarskom krae [Krasnoyarsk krai] 1969–

Far East

Dal'nem Vostoke [The Far East] 1956–1961, 3 vyp.
Kamchatskoi oblasti [Kamchatka oblast] 1976–
Khabarovskom krae [Khabarovsk krai] 1972–
Magadanskoi oblasti [Magadan oblast] 1966–
Amurskoi oblasti [Amur oblast] 1974–
Sakhalinskoi oblasti [Sakhalin oblast] 1972–

Unfortunately, these works are published irregularly and are not available in a complete manner in many Slavic collections in the West. Undoubtedly they are based on new additions to the card catalogs of these regional libraries and are fed into the larger bibliographic compilations being done at Novosibirsk.

There are numerous bibliographies on more specific topics such as agriculture, construction, fishing, forestry, industry, soils, transportation, and so on. Some major bibliographies and sources on themes relevant to the current volume follow.

History

Bibliographies on the Revolution and World War II include: G. A. Dokuchaev, *Sibir' v Velikoi Otechestvennoi voine: bibliogr. ukazatel' rabot, opublikovannykh v 1941–1971 gg.* [Siberia during the Great Patriotic War: A bibliography of works published from 1941 to 1971] (Novosibirsk, 1972, 1,539 items); GPNTB, *Sibir' v gody Velikoi Otechestvennoi voiny (iiun' 1941–sent. 1945 gg.): Bibliogr. ukazatel'* [Siberia during the years of the Great Patriotic War, June 1941–September 1945] (Novosibirsk, 1976, 3,245 items); Irkutsk, Siberia, Oblastnaia biblioteka, *Bor'ba za vlast' sovetov v Vostochnoi Sibir, 1917–1922, bibliogr. ukazatel'* [Struggle for power of the soviets in Eastern Siberia, a bibliography], compiled by N. K. Potapova (Irkutsk, 1962, 2,796 items published 1917–1960); L. K. Kulikova, *Dal'nii Vostok v period Velikoi Oktiabr'skoi sotsialisticheskoi revoliutsii i grazhdanskoi voiny (1917–1922 gg.): Ukazatel' literatury* [The Far East during the period of the Great October Socialist Revolution and the civil war, 1917–1922: Index to the literature] (Khabarovsk, 1968, 2,737 items published 1917–1966).

On the Soviet Far East, two titles will be helpful: *Bibliograficheskii ukazatel' rabot po istorii, arkheologii i etnografii Dal'nego Vostoka* [A bibliography of works on history, archaeology and ethnography of the Far East] (Vladivostok, 1971–   ), published by the Institute of History, Archaeology and Ethnography of the Peoples of the Far East (under the Far Eastern Science Center). Issue no. 1 contains 1,238 items, covering the period 1954–1970; issue no. 3 covers dissertations completed during 1939–1970, about 870 citations. Issue no. 2 has never been reported as published. L. A. Kozhevnikova surveys the literature from the revolution to present in her article, "Bibliograficheskaia informatsiia po istorii i ekonomiki Dal'nego Vostoka" [Bibliographic information on the history and economy of the Far East], in *Sovetskaia bibliografiia* (no. 3 [1977]: 33–43).

These three monographs are quite rich in extensive references: Kurt Spiess, *Periphere Sowjetwirtschaft das Beispiel Russisch-Fernost 1897–1970* (Zurich, 1980); E. L. Besprozvannykh, *Priamur'e v sisteme russko-kitaiskikh otnoshenii XVII–seredina XIX v.* [Primore in the system of Russo-Chinese relations, seventeenth to mid-nineteenth centuries] (Moskva, 1983); and D. A. Shirina, *Letopis' ekspeditsii Akademii nauk na Severo-vostok Azii v dorevoliutsionnyi period* [Chronicles of the Academy of Science's expeditions in Northeast Asia during the prerevolution period] (Novosibirsk, 1983).

Of interest to geographers will be the work by V. V. Vorob'ev, *Geografiia naseleniia Sibiri i Dal'nego Vostoka: Bibliogr. ukazatel'* [The geography of the population of Siberia and the Far East: A bibliography] (Irkutsk, 1968, 2,212 items published 1788–1965).

Economics

These bibliographies provide a useful beginning to a search of the literature: M. I. Kirsanova et al., *Ekonomika, razmeshchenie i organizatsiia promyshlennogo proizvodstva Sibiri i Dal'nego Vostoka: Bibliografiia, 1917–1965* [The economics, distribution, and organization of the industrial production of Siberia and the Far East: A bibliography, 1917–1965], 2 vols. (Novosibirsk, 1968–1969, 2,841 items); *Istoriia dal'Nevostochnoi derevni (1861–1975 gg.): ukazatel' literatury i istochnikov* [The history of the Far Eastern village, 1861–1975: An index to the literature and sources], 2 vols. (Vladivostok, 1979, 4,273 items). Edited by A. I. Krushanov at the Institute of History, Archaeology and Ethnography of the Peoples of the Far East, the second work contains important sections on economic and agricultural developments in the Far East. Excellent lists of sources used are at the end of volume 2.

One of the major research institutes has a bibliography of works produced by its staff: *Bibliografiia rabot sotrudnikov Instituta ekonomiki i organizatsii promyshlennogo proizvodstva (1958–1969 gg.)* [Bibliography of works of the staff of the Institute of Economics and Organization of Industrial Production, 1958–1969] (Novosibirsk, 1970, 1,702 items). There also is an update by T. P. Kolesnikova, "Publikatsii uchenykh Instituta . . . proizvodstva" [Publications of the staff of the Institute . . . Production] in *Ekonomicheskie issledovaniia v Novosibirskom nauchnom tsentre* [Economic research at the Novosibirsk Science Center] (Novosibirsk, 1976; pp. 99–159, 523 items).

The following monographs are particularly useful on Siberian economic development; unfortunately, their availability is often limited by the very small (200–500) tirazh in which they are printed: R. I. Shniper and L. P. Denisova, eds., *Mezhotraslevye sviazi i narodnokhoziaistvennye proportsii Vostochnoi Sibiri i Dal'nego Vostoka* [Cooperative ties and the national economic proportions of East Siberia and the Far East] (Novosibirsk, 1974). V. P. Mozhin, ed., *Ekonomicheskoe razvitie Sibiri i Dal'nego Vostoka (perspektivy razvitiia)* [The economic development of Siberia and the Far East: Perspectives of development] (Moskva, 1980). R. I. Shniper, ed., *Tendentsii ekonomicheskogo razvitiia Sibiri (1961–1975 gg.)* [The tendencies of the economic development of Siberia, 1961– 1975] (Moskva, 1980). M. K. Bandman, ed., *Sibir' v edinom narodnokhoziaist- vennom komplekse* [Siberia in the united national economic complex] (Novosi- birsk, 1980). E. B. Aizenberg and IU. A. Sobolev, *Kompleksnye programmy razvitiia vostochnykh raionov SSSR* [The complex problems of the development of the eastern regions of the USSR] (Moskva, 1982). P. V. Shemetov, *Ekono- micheskie issledovaniia v Sibiri* [Economic research in Siberia] (Moskva, 1983).

Social Sciences/Foreign Relations

The literature on foreign relations, politics, and other social science topics overlaps in many areas of Soviet bibliography. Of general usefulness is *Obsh- chestvennye nauki v SSSR: Referativnyi zhurnal* [Social sciences in the USSR: An abstract journal]. Published since 1973, this bibliography summarizes the major Soviet research in the social sciences. The Institute of Scientific Informa- tion on the Social Sciences in Moscow publishes a series of bibliographies on various countries and topics. Of peripheral use are the following: *Novaia sovetskaia i inostrannaia literatura po obshchestvennym naukam: IUzhnaia i IUgo-Vostochnaia Aziia, Dal'nii Vostok* [New Soviet and foreign literature on the social sciences: South and Southeast Asia, the Far East] (Moskva, 1970–   ; variant titles); and *Novaia sovetskaia literatura po obshchestvennym naukam: Is- toriia, arkheologiia, etnografiia* [New Soviet literature on the social sciences: History, archaeology, ethnography] (Moskva, 1949–   ; variant titles). William S. Heiliger's *Bibliography of the Soviet social sciences, 1965–1975*, 2 vols. (Troy, N.Y.: Whitston Publishing, 1978), is essentially the table of contents for seven journals with the titles of articles translated into English and arranged by subject.

JOURNALS/NEWSPAPERS

Several works on the history and development of journals and newspapers in Siberia are available: A. K. Paikova, *Rukopisnye zhurnaly Sibiri 900-kh godov* [Manuscript journals of Siberia for 900 years] (Ulan-Ude; 1974); L. I. Pan- chenko, "Periodicheskaia pechat' Zapadnoi Sibiri i sotsialisticheskoe sorev- novanie v promyshlennosti v poslevoennoi piatiletke (1946–1950 gg.)" [The periodical press of West Siberia and the socialist competition in industry during the postwar five years, 1946–1950] in *Iz istorii obshchestvenno-politicheskoi zhizni Sibiri* [On the history of the sociopolitical life of Siberia] (Tomsk, 1981; pp. 111–28); S. A. Andronov, *Bol'shevistskaia pechat' v trekh revoliutsiiakh* [The Bolshevik press during three revolutions] (Moskva, 1978), Siberian periodical printing developments from 1907 to 1917 are discussed on pages 114–270; E. T. Tanova, *Periodicheskaia pechat' Tuvy (1924–1944 gg.)* [Periodical press of Tuva, 1924–1944] (Kyzyl, 1979); A. N. Bazanov, *Iz istorii pechati Sakhalinskoi oblasti* [From the history of the press of Sakhalin oblast] (IUzhno-Sakhalinsk, 1970); N. A. Glushchenko, *Bol'shevistskaia pechat' Dal'nego Vostoka v gody pervoi russkoi revoliutsii (1905–1907 gg.)* [The Bolshevik press of the Far East during the years of the first Russian revolution, 1905–1907] (Vladivostok, 1970); and I. G. Striuchenko, *Pechat' Dal'nego Vostoka nakanune i v gody pervoi russkoi revoliutsii (1895–1907)* [The press of the Far East on the eve and during the years of the first Russian revolution, 1895–1907] (Vladivostok, 1982).

The following journals are relevant to the topics covered by this collection of essays. If they are consulted regularly, they would also be good current-awareness sources. Most of these journals are indexed in the GPNTB bulletins; a few are not published regularly, and this is noted.

General
USSR facts and figures annual. Gulf Breeze, Fla., 1977–
Khabarovskii krai. Khabarovsk, 1969–   ; annual
Na severe Dal'nem [In the Far North]. Magadan, 1955–

History
Letopis' Severa [Chronicle of the North]. Moskva, 1949–
Voprosy istorii [Questions of history]. Moskva, 1945–
Voprosy istorii Sibiri [Questions of Siberia's history]. Tomsk, 1964–
Trudy Instituta istorii, arkheologii i etnografii DVNTS [Works of the Institute of History, Archaeology and Ethnography]. Vladivostok
Doklady Instituta geografii Sibiri i Dal'nego Vostoka [Reports of the Institute of Geography of Siberia and the Far East]. Irkutsk, 1962–1976.
Voprosy istorii Dal'nego Vostoka [Questions on the history of the Far East]. Khabarovsk, 1972–   (latest is vyp. 4, 1974)
Problemy Dal'nego Vostoka [Far Eastern affairs]. Moskva, 1972–
Narody Azii i Afriki [Peoples of Asia and Africa]. Moskva, 1959–
Kalendar' znamenatel'nyi i pamiatnykh dat . . . [Calendar of significant and memorable dates] (usually annuals)
   po Dal'nemu Vostoku. Khabarovsk, 1958–

po Buriatiia. Ulan-Ude, 1961–
po IAkutskoi ASSR. Yakutsk, 1963–
po Krasnoiarskomu kraiu. Krasnoyarsk, 1960–
po Tuve. Kyzyl, 1961–
po Kemerovskoi oblasti. Kemerevo, 1966–
po Irkutskoi oblasti. Irkutsk, 1965–
po Chitinskoi oblasti. Chita, 1964 (pub. 1963)–

Literature

Primarily literary journals, but may also contain articles on other topics.
Dal'nii Vostok [The Far East]. Khabarovsk, 1933–
Sibirskie ogni [Siberian lights]. Novosibirsk, 1922–
Sibir'. Irkutsk, 1920–
Baikal. Ulan-Ude, 1955–
Enisei. Krasnoyarsk, 1940–

Economics

Planovoe khoziaistvo [Planned economy]. Moskva, 1923–
Voprosy ekonomiki [Questions of economics]. Moskva, 1948–
Vestnik statistiki [Herald of statistics]. Moskva, 1919–
Ekonomiko-geograficheskie problemy formirovaniia territorial'no-proizvodstvennykh kompleksov SSSR [Economic-geographical problems of the formation of the territorial-production complexes of the USSR]. Novosibirsk, 1969–   (latest is vyp. 5, 1973)
Trudy Dal'nevostochnogo instituta sovetskoi torgovli [Works of the Far Eastern Institute of Soviet Trade]. Vladivostok
Ekonomicheskoe problemy Dal'nego Vostoka [Economic problems of the Far East]. Vladivostok, 1969–   (latest is vyp. 2, 1970)
Voprosy ekonomiki Dal'nego Vostoka [Questions on economics of the Far East]. Blagoveshchensk, 1958–1972, vols. 1–4
Mirovaia ekonomika ia mezhdunarodnye otnosheniia [The world economy and international relations]. Moskva, 1957–
Ekonomika i organizatsiia promyshlennogo proizvodstva [The economy and the organization of industrial production] (often cited as EKO). Novosibirsk, 1970–

Military Affairs

Soviet armed forces review annual. Gulf Breeze, Fla., 1977–
JPRS translations on USSR military affairs
Kommunist Vooruzhennykh sil [Communist armed forces]. Moskva, 1960–
Morskoi flot [The navy]. Moskva, 1941–
Morskoi sbornik [Naval collection]. Leningrad, 1848–
Krasnaia zvezda [Red star]. Moskva, 1918–

Social Sciences/International Affairs
Social sciences. [in English] Moscow, 1970–
Sovrenovanie dvukh sistem [Competition of the two world systems].
Moskva, 1967– (a series of monographs, appearing irregularly)
S.Sh.A.: Ekonomika, politika, ideologiia [USA: Economics, politics, ideology]. Moskva, 1970–
AN SSSR Sibirskoe otdelenie, *Izvestiia obshchestvennykh nauk* [Proceedings of the social sciences]. Novosibirsk, 1963–
[Here also *Mirovaia ekonomika i mezhdunarodnye otnosheniia* applies.]

Regular study of newspapers from Siberian cities would, of course, be desirable; however, they are generally not available in the West. The articles in these papers are indexed in the GPNTB bulletins, so one can at least keep abreast in a secondhand manner. The major newspapers are:

West Siberia
Krasnoe znamia. Tomsk
Zvezda Altaia. Gorno-Altai
Omskaia pravda. Osmk
Tiumenskaia pravda. Tyumen
Altaiskaia pravda. Barnaul
Sovetskaia Sibir'. Novosibirsk

East Siberia
Sotsialisticheskaia IAkutiia. Yakutsk
Zabaikal'skii rabochii. Chita
Krasnoiarskii rabochii. Krasnoyarsk
Vostochno-Sibirskaia pravda. Irkutsk
Tuvinskaia pravda. Kyzyl
Pravda Buriatti. Ulan-Ude
Kuzbass. Kemerovo
Sovetskaia Khakasiia. Abakan

Far East
Tikhookeanskaia zvezda. Khabarovsk
Amurskaia pravda. Blagoveshchensk
Kamchatskaia pravda. Petropavlovsk-Kamchatka
Krasnoe znamia. Vladivostok
Magadanskaia pravda. Magadan
Sovetskii Sakhalin. Yuzhno-Sakhalinsk

These papers, available in U.S. Slavic collections, often contain information on Siberia: *Pravda, Izvestiia,* and *Ekonomicheskaia gazeta.*

INSTITUTES

There are numerous research institutes in Siberia; most deal with the sciences. Listed below are those institutes most closely working with topics of interest in this survey. Blair Ruble's excellent compilation, *Soviet Research Institutes Project: Final Report*[4] provides more details on each of the institutes named here. For a list of works about the various institutes, see *Nauchnyi tsentr v Sibiri: Ukazatel' literatury (1957–1973 gg.)* [The science center in Siberia: Bibliography, 1957–1973] 3d ed. (Novosibirsk, 1974).

General Policy Institutes in Moscow
Moskovskii gosudarstvennyi institut mezhdunarodnykh otnoshenii
Institut mirovoi ekonomiki i mezhdunarodnykh otnoshenii AN SSSR
Institut vostokovedeniia AN SSSR
Institut Dal'nego Vostoka AN SSSR

West Siberia
Institut istorii, filologii i filosofii SO AN SSSR. Novosibirsk. Founded in 1965 as a primary center for study of Siberian peoples.

Institut ekonomiki i organizatsii promyshlennogo proizvodstva SO AN SSSR. Novosibirsk. Founded in 1957 to investigate physical, natural, and economic sciences and resolve the problems connected with the development of the productive forces of Siberia and the Far East.

The history and faculties of the universities in this region usually concentrate on local events. They are: Altaiskii gosudarstvennyi universitet, Novosibirskii gosudarstvennyi universitet, Tomskii gosudarstvennyi universitet, and Tiumenskii gosudarstvennyi universitet.

East Siberia
Institut geografii Sibiri i Dal'nego Vostoka SO AN SSSR. Irkutsk. Established in 1959 to deal with geographical concerns; natural resources, demographic trends.

Otdel ekonomiki i geografii Irkutskogo filiala SO AN SSSR. Irkutsk. Studies resource utilization and regional economic planning.

Otdel ekonomiki Buriatskogo filiala SO AN SSSR. Ulan-Ude. Studies economic planning in Buryatia.

Institut obshchestvennykh nauk Buriatskogo filiala SO AN SSSR. Ulan-Ude. Examines historical development of the culture, language, and artistic skills of the Buryat peoples.

Institut iazyka, literatury i istorii IAkutskogo filiala SO AN SSSR. Yakutsk. Concentrates on the history of the Yakutsk region.

Otdel ekonomiki IAkutskogo filiala SO AN SSSR. Yakutsk. Deals with scientific and industrial planning in the Yakutsk area.

The history faculties of IAkutskii gosudarstvennyi universitet and Irkutskii gosudarstvennyi universitet contribute to studies on their areas.

Far East

Institut istorii, arkheologii i etnografii narodov Dal'nego Vostoka Dal'-nevostochnogo nauchnogo tsentra AN SSSR. Vladivostok. Concentrates on the peoples of the Soviet Far East, Japan, China, and Korea.

Institut ekonomicheskikh issledovanii Dal'nevostochnogo nauchnogo tsentra AN SSSR. Vladivostok and Khabarovsk. Founded in 1970 for study of economic and productive development of the Far East.

Dal'nevostochnyi institut sovetskoi torgovli. Vladivostok. One of the leading trade institutes in the country; founded in the 1930s; library founded in 1964.

Tikhookeanskii institut geografii Dal'nevostochnogo nauchnogo tsentra AN SSSR. Vladivostok. Studies the cultural ties of Asian countries with the Far East and is concerned with population projections; established in 1971.

The history faculty of the Dal'nevostochnyi gosudarstvennyi universitet has produced many studies on local history.

LIBRARIES

Regional cooperation of libraries in Siberia began in the 1950s. They have since been organized into the West Siberian, East Siberian, and Far East zones. Libraries of all varieties—oblast, krai, republic, high school, medical, academic, and others—are structured into the hierarchy. The three principal organizers for the regions are the Novosibirskskaia oblastnaia biblioteka, the Irkutskaia oblastnaia biblioteka, and the Khabarovskaia kraevaia biblioteka. The overall coordinator is the GPNTB.[5]

The GPNTB in Novosibirsk, established in 1918, is the center of a network of libraries that includes all of Siberia. With over eight million volumes, it is the largest on the Asian continent, nearly equal in size to the Lenin Library. It is a deposit library for everything published and maintains a large exchange with foreign libraries. Providing information, one of its primary goals, has been realized with the publication of its numerous bibliographical bulletins. Mechanization and automation are hopes for the future.[6]

In addition to the current bibliographical bulletins, the GPNTB has helped with the publication of numerous retrospective bibliographies on various topics and areas. A high priority is also to produce cumulated indexes for the bulletins. There is an index to the work of the library staff: *Gosudarstvennaia publichnaia nauchno-tekhnicheskaia biblioteka Sibirskogo otdeleniia Akademii nauk SSSR 1958–1977 gg.; Bibliogr. ukazatel' literatury* [The GPNTB of the Siberian Section of the USSR Academy of Sciences, 1958–1977: A bibliography] (Novosibirsk, 1978, 1,102 citations). The staff is also responsible for a journal on library developments in Siberia: GPNTB *Sbornik nauchnykh trudov* [Collection of scientific works]. This title was adopted in 1975 with issue no. 19. Each issue is thematically oriented and has a distinct title. Formerly the journal was called *Nauchnye biblioteki Sibiri i Dal'nego Vostoka* [Scientific libraries of Siberia and the Far East] (vyp. 1–18, 1967–1973). The index by A. N. Lebedeva and L. S. Pankratova is *Ukazatel' soderzhaniia sbornika nauchnykh trudov "Nauchnye . . . Vostoka"* [Index to the contents of the collection of scientific works of "Scientific libraries . . . Far East] (Novosibirsk, 1974).

The library's bulletin, *Kniga, bibliotechnoe delo i bibliografiia Sibiri* [The book, library matters, and bibliography of Siberia] (1976–   ; annual), is an important source for printing, publishing, book studies, periodical press, and the book trade. A relatively new area of research—archeographic studies—is being pioneered by the library; these important efforts are bringing manuscripts and old books to light.

In 1966 the GPNTB inherited the collection of Soviet historian M. N. Tikhomirov—over 10,000 units, including 3,000 manuscripts and old printed books published until the eighteenth century.[7] One of the sources for obtaining new manuscripts and old books are the annual archeographic expeditions, begun in 1965, in which members of the library participate. A series of monographs describing some of the materials collected has appeared: *Arkheografiia i istochnikovedenie Sibiri* [Archeography and source studies of Siberia] (Novosibirsk, 1975); *Istochnikovedenie i arkheografii Sibiri* (Novosibirsk, 1977); *Sibirskaia arkheografiia i istochnikovedenie* (Novosibirsk, 1979); *Sibirskoe istochnikovedenie i arkheografiia* (Novosibirsk, 1980); and *Drevnerusskaia rukopis'naia kniga i ee bytovanie v Sibiri* [The ancient Russian manuscript book and its existence in Siberia] (Novosibirsk, 1982). In English one may read V. N. Alexeyev's "The library and Archeography: Acquisitions from the Field in Siberia" (*Library Review*, 29 (1980): 247–55).

The following major Siberian libraries are the key to the network that has been established, as well as repositories of local history collections.[8]

West Siberia
Barnaul: Altaiskaia kraevaia biblioteka. Founded 1888.
Gorno-Altai: Gorno-Altaiskaia oblastnaia biblioteka. Founded 1920.
Kemerovo: Kemerovskaia oblastnaia biblioteka. Founded 1920.
Novosibirsk: GPNTB. Founded 1918.
   Novosibirskaia oblastnaia nauchnaia biblioteka. Founded 1929.
Omsk: Omskaia oblastnaia biblioteka. Founded 1899.
Tomsk: Tomskaia oblastnaia biblioteka. Founded 1899.
   Biblioteka Tomskogo gosudarstvennogo universiteta. Founded 1888.
Tyumen: Tiumenskaia oblastnaia biblioteka. Founded 1875.

East Siberia
Abakan: Khakasskaia oblastnaia biblioteka.
Irkutsk: Biblioteka Vostochno-Sibirskogo filiala SO AN SSSR. Founded
   1949.
   Irkutskaia oblastnaia biblioteka. Founded 1861.
   Biblioteka Irkutskogo gosudarstvennogo universiteta. Founded
   1918.
Krasnoyarsk: Krasnoiarskaia kraevaia nauchnaia biblioteka. Founded
   1935.
Kyzyl: Tuvinskaia respublikanskaia biblioteka. Founded 1931.
Ulan-Ude: Nauchnaia biblioteka Buriatskogo filiala SO AN SSSR.
   Founded 1922.
   Respublikanskaia biblioteka Buriatskoi ASSR. Founded 1881.
Chita: Chitinskaia oblastnaia biblioteka. Founded 1895.
Yakutsk: IAkutskaia respublikanskaia biblioteka. Founded 1925.
   Nauchnaia biblioteka IAkutskogo filiala SO AN SSSR. Founded
   1937.

Far East
Blagoveshchensk: Amurskaia oblastnaia biblioteka. Founded 1937.
Vladivostok: Primorskaia kraevaia biblioteka. Founded 1887.
   Fundamental'naia biblioteka Dal'nevostochnogo nauchnogo tsentra
   AN SSSR. Founded 1932.
   Biblioteka Dal'nevostochnogo universiteta. Founded 1956.
Magadan: Magadanskaia oblastnaia biblioteka. Founded 1935.
Khabarovsk: Khabarovskaia kraevaia biblioteka. Founded 1894.
Yuzhno-Sakhalinsk: Sakhalinskaia oblastnaia biblioteka. Founded 1946.
Petropavlovsk-Kamchatka: Kamchatskaia oblastnaia biblioteka.
   Founded 1914.

PUBLISHING

A survey of the publishing industry in Siberia can be found in an article by
V. N. Volkova, "Problemy i struktura sovremennogo sibirskogo knigoizdaniia"
[The problems and structure of contemporary Siberian book publishing].[9] Volkova points out that the publishing houses were reorganized in 1963–1964 into
the present arrangement of fourteen major houses with eight otdelenie (branches).
The bulk of the publishing is done by the numerous scientific institutes, as some
of the statistics below demonstrate. Nonscience materials run about 30–40 percent of the total. The publishing "capital" of Siberia is Novosibirsk, with the
Siberian branch of Nauka and the Western Siberian Publishing House located
here. The publishers in the autonomous republics (Yakutsk, Buryat, Tuva) do not
have such a high ratio of scientific books; they concentrate on general political,
children's, and artistic literature, and publications in languages of the nationality
groups.

Although it is possible to obtain the number of monographs published within
a region, there is no definitive way to ascertain the individual titles. Therefore, it
is not feasible to survey the titles published by all Siberian publishers for their
availability in Western Slavic collections. (*Knizhnaia letopis'*, the national bibliography, does not delineate city of publication.) However, in one very brief study
I prepared for the *Libri* article mentioned earlier, using one issue from one bulletin title (*Istoriia Sibiri*, 1976, no. 3), 64 percent of the literature listed was
accessible in the United States.

The major publishing houses[10] in Siberia are as follows:

West Siberia

Zapadno-Sibirskoe knizhnoe izdatel'stvo. Novosibirsk. Founded 1920.
　　　Publishes the journal *Sibirskie ogni*. Branches: Tomskoe otdelenie
　　　and Osmk otdelenie.
Nauka, Sibirskoe otdelenie. Novosibirsk. Founded 1965.
Kemerovskoe kn. izd-vo. Kemerovo. Founded 1947.
Omskoe kn. izd-vo. Osmk. Founded 1978.
Altaiskoe kn. izd-vo. Barnaul. Founded 1947. Branch: Gorno-Altaiskoe
　　　otdelenie.
Tiumenskoe kn. izd-vo. Tyumen.
Izd-vo Tomskogo universiteta. Tomsk. Founded 1955.

East Siberia

Vostochno-Sibirskoe kn. izd-vo. Irkutsk. Founded 1931 as Irkutskoe kn.
　　　izd-vo; in 1963 Irkutskoe and Chitinskoe kn. izd-vo were com-
　　　bined. Today there is a branch in Chita: Chitinskoe otdelenie.

Buriatskoe kn. izd-vo. Ulan-Ude. Founded 1923.
Krasnoiarskoe kn. izd-vo. Krasnoyarsk. Founded 1935.
IAkutskoe kn. izd-vo (or IAkutknigoizdat). Yakutsk. Founded 1926.
Tuvinskoe kn. izd-vo (or Tuvknigoizdat). Kyzyl. Founded 1930.

Far East
Khabarovskoe kn. izd-vo. Khabarovsk. Founded in Chita in 1923, moved
to Khabarovsk in 1963. Publishes the journal *Dal' nii Vostok*. Branch:
Amurskoe otdelenie in Blagoveshchensk.
Dal'nevostochnoe kn. izd-vo. Vladivostok. Founded in 1963. Branches:
IUzhno-Sakhalinskoe otdelenie and Kamchatka-Petropavlovskoe
otdelenie.
Magadanskoe kn. izd-vo. Magadan. Founded in 1954. Publishes the
journal *Na severe Dal' nem*.

Two other significant publishers are the GPNTB in Novosibirsk and the
Academy's Dal'nevostochnyi nauchnyi tsentr in Vladivostok, which was established in 1970.

The publishing statistics from the latest annuals (*Pechat' SSSR v 1980 godu*
[Moskva, 1981]; *Pechat' SSSR v 1981 godu* [Moskva, 1982]) are presented as
an indication of the amount being published. Science publications account for
60 percent of Siberian publications in 1980 and 66 percent in 1981.

1980
Total books and brochures published in the Soviet Union: 80,676
Total published in the RSFSR: 49,563
Total published in the Siberian areas: 2,561

West Siberia		*East Siberia*		*Far East*	
Altai	107	Krasnoyarsk	158	Primorski	147
Kemerovo	88	Irkutsk	192	Khabarovsk	110
Novosibirsk	838	Chita	11	Amur	13
Omsk	147	Buryat	116	Kamchatka	18
Tomsk	172	Tuva	79	Magadan	85
Tyumen	54	Yakutsk	210	Sakhalin	16
Totals:	1,406		766		389
	(55%)		(30%)		(15%)

Total by publishers (as opposed to institutes) in the Soviet Union:
46,555
Total by publishers in the RSFSR: 7,402
Total by publishers in the Siberian areas: 1,004

West Siberia		East Siberia		Far East	
Altai	85	Vostochno-Sibirskoe	66	Khabarovsk	83
Zapadno-Sibirskoe	102	Krasnoyarsk	64	Magadan	38
Kemerovo	54	Buryat	108	Dal'nevostochnoe	55
Tomsk university	130	Tuva	77		
		Yakutsk	142		
Totals:	371		457		176
	(37%)		(46%)		(17%)

1981

Total books and brochures published in the Soviet Union: 83,007
Total published in the RSFSR: 51,963
Total published in the Siberian areas: 2,882

West Siberia		East Siberia		Far East	
Altai	141	Krasnoyarsk	192	Primorski	203
Kemerovo	96	Irkutsk	258	Khabarovsk	101
Novosibirsk	1,014	Chita	9	Amur	13
Omsk	156	Buryat	106	Kamchatka	16
Tomsk	152	Tuva	71	Magadan	70
Tyumen	50	Yakutsk	219	Sakhalin	15
Totals:	1,609		855		418
	(56%)		(30%)		(14%)

Total by publishers in the Soviet Union: 48,022
Total by publishers in the RSFSR: 7,111
Total by publishers in the Siberian areas: 985

West Siberia		East Siberia		Far East	
Altai	93	Vostochno-Sibirskoe	67	Khabarovsk	66
Zapadno-Sibirskoe	93	Krasnoyarsk	62	Magadan	53
Kemerovo	56	Buryat	98	Dal'nevostochnoe	67
Omsk	17	Tuva	57		
Tomsk university	107	Yakutsk	149		
Totals:	366		433		186
	(37%)		(44%)		(19%)

One hopes the future will bring better access to Siberian publications, perhaps through expansion of present exchanges with Siberian libraries. Even being able to identify by title the number of Siberian imprints published each year would be a big step in assessing the holdings of Western Slavic collections. It is fortunate that the bulk of literature being published on Siberia and the Far East is well controlled by the GPNTB bibliographical bulletins.

NOTES

1. *International Library Review* 14 (1982):217–62.

2. A good beginning for geographic sources is Chauncy Harris, *Guide to Geographical Bibliographies and Reference Works in Russian or on the Soviet Union* (Chicago: University of Chicago, Department of Geography, research paper no. 164, 1975). For subjects that fall in the social sciences (economics, government, society, etc.), begin with Paul Horecky, *Basic Russian Publications* (Chicago: University of Chicago Press, 1962); and J. S. G. Simmons, *Russian Bibliography, Libraries and Archives* (Oxford, Engl.: A. Hall, 1973).

3. For further details on the bibliographic history of these bulletins, see P. Polansky, "The Bibliographic Work of the State Public Scientific Technical Library of the Siberian Section of the USSR Academy of Sciences," *Libri* 33, no. 4 (1983):274–88.

4. *Soviet Research Institutes Projects: Final Report,* prepared for the U.S. International Communication Agency by Blair A. Ruble, 3 vols. plus supplement (Washington, D.C., 1980–1981).

5. For a good summary of the Far Eastern network see N. S. Kartashov, "Vzaimodeistvie nauchnykh bibliotek Sibiri i Dal'nego Vostoka v oblasti bibliograficheskoi raboty" [The cooperation of scientific libraries of Siberia and the Far East in the area of bibliographic work], *Sovetskaia bibliografiia,* 1977, no. 3:21–32.

6. N. S. Kartashov, "60 let na sluzhbe nauki" [Sixty years in the service of science], AN SO GPNTB *Sbornik nauchnykh trudov* 42 (1978):5–20.

7. *Sibirskoe sobranie M. N. Tikhomirova i problemy arkheografii* [The Siberian collection of M. N. Tikhomirov and the problems of archeography] (Novosibirsk, 1981).

8. TS. A. Astrakhanskaia, "Svodnye katalogi bibliotck Sibiri i Dal'nego Vostoka i ikh vzaimoispol'zovanie" [Union catalogs of the libraries of Siberia and the Far East and their mutual utilization], AN SO GPNTB *Sbornik nauchnykh trudov* 23 (1975):117–40.

9. AN SSSR SO *Izvestiia: Seriia obshchestvennykh nauk* 3, no. 11 (1979):153–58.

10. *Knigovedenie: Entsiklopedicheskii slovar'*, N. M. Sikorskii, ed. (Moskva, 1981).

Index

298   *Index*